Approaches to
Family
Therapy

Approaches to
Family
Therapy

James C. Hansen
State University of New York'at Buffalo

Luciano L'Abate
Georgia State University

Macmillan Publishing Co., Inc.
New York

Collier Macmillan Publishers
London

Macmillan Publishing Co., Inc.
866 Third Avenue, New York, New York 10022

Collier Macmillan Canada, Inc.

Library of Congress Cataloging in Publication Data

Hansen, James C
  Approaches to family therapy.

  Includes bibliographies and index.
  1. Family psychotherapy. I. L'Abate, Luciano,
1928-   joint author. II. Title.
RC488.5.H34   616.89'156   81-440
ISBN 0-02-350010-7   AACR1

Printing: 2 3 4 5 6 7 8   Year: 5 6 7 8 9

Preface

Family therapy is based on the belief that the family is a social unit, with the therapeutic process involving treatment of the whole family or those individuals and subgroups that interact with the whole family. There are numerous conceptual approaches to family therapy, and a variety of specific techniques can be used in the process.

For some years we have been involved in conducting and teaching family therapy. Frequently questions and discussions in courses and case conferences have focused on various concepts or techniques from the various theoretical approaches. We thought it would be helpful to provide a comparison of the approaches.

A therapist's work to change a family is, in general, determined by theoretical approach. However, family therapy theory is not fully developed, and most prominent writers do not call their approach a theory. Moreover, many approaches in family therapy do not fulfill all requirements for a good theory but are still in the process of development. For a family therapist, the most important aspect of theory involves its serving as a guide in understanding behavior and a guideline for treatment. Therefore, it seems appropriate to title this book *Approaches to Family Therapy*.

This book provides a selection of recognized approaches to family therapy. Each approach is presented as an overview, yet there is sufficient depth to give the reader knowledge and understanding of the approach. We will be pleased if this book helps readers to examine the concepts and techniques in detail and to select one approach to follow or help in developing an eclectic position.

Approaches to Family Therapy does not provide exhaustive coverage of each approach; rather it provides general background to enable a person to examine and formulate his or her own ideas about family therapy. To meet this objective we begin with a chapter on the historical and theoretical antecedents of the field. Chapter 1 shows how most approaches to family therapy derive from and are in continuity with historical predecessors. Chapter 2 reviews efforts to understand and differentiate among degrees of functionality in families. We believe that family therapists profit from a conception of the range of family behaviors across a variety of criteria. Chapters 3 through 15 provide an overview of the approaches to family therapy. We begin with three historical positions: Ackerman's position combines psychodynamic and social psychology concepts, Satir's is a humanistic growth model, and Watzlawick's is a communications approach that is a good background for the system approaches. Several systems approaches—those of Haley, Minuchin, and the Milan group—follow. The social learning position of Patterson and the psychodynamic systems ideas of Bowen are then presented. The next chapters are Bell's family group and Zuk's triadic-based approaches. The last three approaches covered are Laqueur's multiple family position, MacGregor's multiple impact position, and the family network position represented by Speck, Attneave, and Rueveni. The final chapter reviews some of the issues facing family therapy and examines future trends.

Each of the theoretical approach chapters follows a similar format to better permit reader comparison. Each chapter presents the ideas regarding functional and dysfunctional family behaviors, the goals and foci of therapy, the place of history taking and diagnosis, the concepts of the process and stages of therapy, and the role and techniques of the therapist. We have attempted to present each approach as having valuable and important contributions. Therefore, each approach as reviewed presents the theorists' positions as objectively as possible according to their writings. We have reserved the last section of the chapter for our critique and evaluation.

This book is not a creative writing project and does not represent our original concepts and experiences. We have drawn from the work of many writers and acknowledge theirs as the major contribution. Preparation of the book has been a collaborative effort. The outline and materials were formulated through discussions and writing. We edited and critiqued each other's writing with respect in an effort to polish the final presentation. Numerous people have assisted in covering the vast amount of material necessary for this book. We are indebted to the work of Tamee A. Dula, Elaine Levin, Victor Mallenbaum, and Valerie S. Marler on Chapter 1 and to Bruce Freedman who could really be considered a co-author for his work on Chapter 2. Carolyn Hansen assisted with the Ackerman chapter, and W. Douglass Latham, Valerie S. Marler, H. Judith Tully, Sandra Vaughn, and Nancy McKeel worked on the Satir chapter. Valerie S. Marler, Sherry McHenry, Gary Ganahl, Barbara A. Thomason, David Clark, and Jackie Johnson contributed to the chapter on Haley. The Minuchin chapter benefited from the efforts of Jody Frey, Sadell Sloan, and Kay Olsen. The chapter on the Milan Group owes a great deal to the work of Margaret S. Baggett. We are grateful to Thomas S. Bennett and Norma Jenkins who worked on the Patterson chapter and to Gary Ganahl, Jody Frey, Sadell Sloan, and Marcia Weiss who helped with the chapter on Murray Bowen. Barbara Nevergold contributed considerably to the Bell chapter as did Michelle Boyer for the multiple impact chapter. Many other students and colleagues have collaborated with us in thinking about and discussing these approaches. We are also indebted to the publisher's reviewers for their efforts and general comments on the first draft of our manuscript.

James C. Hansen
Luciano L'Abate

Contents

1

Historical and Theoretical Antecedents

This chapter is designed to show how most theories of family therapy derive from, and are in continuity with, historical predecessors that find their roots in three major historical antecedents: humanism, psychoanalysis, and behaviorism. These three main theoretical approaches will be used to illustrate how theories of family therapy are in historical and philosophical continuity along a continuum encompassed by two major approaches to behavior, demonstrative on one hand and dialectical on the other (Rychlack, 1968). The demonstrative view emphasizes the objectively stable, the formally pragmatic, and the realistic empirical versus the dialectical view, which emphasizes the idealistic subjective and informally intuitive.

The demonstrative approach emphasizes logical explanation, reduction to analytic parts, and operational definitions, as seen in the learning theory and experimental psychology. The objective (demonstrative) school of psychiatry essentially emphasizes genetic and hereditary components of behavior and constitutional, bodily, and biological approaches to behavior as seen in "body build" or brain functions.

This is essentially a view that behavior is determined, even if it is multiple determined, that it is usually physically determined, and that many psychological problems can be reduced to real physical causes. The dialectic approach, on the other hand, views reality in terms of relativeness, self-determination, or multi-determination, emphasizes hypothetical concepts that are not considerably visible, and does not bow to science and objectivism as the end-all of all views of behavior. The dialectical view essentially emphasizes that everything that is peculiarly human is dialectical; that is, behavior is the outcome of conflict and contradiction. Change is the major quality of behavior.

These two major views allow us to classify approaches to family therapy as varying along a similar continuum, defined by the polarities of demonstrativeness on one extreme to the dialectical at the other extreme. On the demonstrative side, we have the behaviorists and systems therapists; on the dialectical side, we have the humanists. Psychoanalytics is somewhere in the middle.

A Bit of History

Historically, family therapy finds its roots in the child guidance clinic movement. However, once this movement became institutionalized, it developed frozen and fragmentary techniques of diagnosis and evaluation. Even though lip service was paid to the importance of the family, techniques were still patterned after traditional individual treatment. Only because of the pioneer work of a few individuals, namely, Ackerman (Chapter 3), Bowen (Chapter 9), and D. D. Jackson on the West Coast, did family therapy come of age in the mid-1950s. Because of their efforts, strongholds for family therapy were established in New York, at what is now the Ackerman Institute for Family Therapy; in Washington, D.C., at Georgetown University; and in Philadelphia, at the Philadelphia Child Guidance Clinic. On the West Coast, D. D. Jackson and Virginia Satir (Chapter 4) founded the Palo Alto Mental Health Institute, which Jay Haley (Chapter 6), Paul Watzlawick (Chapter 5), and many others helped to make another mecca for family therapy. Despite their early and arduous beginnings, we must not forget that most of these pioneers had psychiatric and psychoanalytic backgrounds; development was slow but sure, culminating in what amounts now to a mental health movement in its own right.

A Bit of Theory

There is no way in these brief reviews that we can do justice to the wide range of theories and theorists who have furnished the background of recent approaches in family therapy. We apologize for what is going to be necessarily an overview of historical background for us to enter more into present-day approaches. In addition to the three traditional views of behavior, a fourth—systems, with emphasis on the context of a transaction—needs to be added. This school represents some of the major theorists in the field of family therapy. As a result, the historical antecedents of these four approaches to therapy can be found in Table 1-1. From this classification a typology of approaches to family therapy can be derived, as shown in Table 1-2.

Not all the theorists present in Table 1-2 have been included here for review for one major reason, mainly the amount of impact made by one theorist-therapist as judged *subjectively* by us. However, we have attempted to review those whom we feel have contributed the most and have had the largest impact on family therapy in the United States. We hope that someone will disagree with us and add to our review by presenting additional theorists worthy of consideration. We are aware of our exclusions to review important theorists, as well as our inclusions. An all-inclusive review would have taken more time and space than either of us was willing to give.[1]

---

[1] It has been useful for purposes of classification to use an E-R-A-AW model (L'Abate and Frey 1981) in which emotionality is essentially what is emphasized by the humanistic school. Rationality is emphasized by the psychoanalytic school. Activity is emphasized by the behavioral and systems schools. We show in Table 1-1 the major names and historical antecedents of these schools. The important names of the interpersonal approach to psychiatry—Meyer, Sullivan and Ruesch—plus the general systems theorist von Bertanlanffy need to be remembered. For a simple but fairly complete review of these schools, the reader is referred to Havens (1973).

Humanism and Its Trends

Humanism as a philosophical and therapeutic enterprise comprises at least three different trends that need to be clearly demarcated (Table 1-2): phenomenology, existentialism, and experientalism. As far as phenomenology is concerned, we need to go back to the work of Hegel and dialectics (i.e., thesis, antithesis, and synthesis), to Husserl and Heidegger, and to Jaspers and Binswanger. These are the philosophical representatives of phenomenology that find their American representatives in Carl Rogers and, most recently, the work of Klaus Riegel and the dialectical school of psychology (1979). This school essentially emphasizes the importance of subjective perception and intentionality in behavior. This school represents subjectivism and relativism at its best and, in a way, is a denial of the objective realism represented by other schools. The major representative of this trend in family therapy is Levant (1978a, 1978b).

Existentialism finds its roots in the philosophies of S. Kierkegaard, J. P. Sartre, and V. Frankl and here in this country in A. Maslow and R. May. This school represents the importance of "being" over other modalities of either "doing" or "having." In existentialism, the acceptance of life and acceptance of personal feelings and states as being the most important aspect of one's existence are emphasized. The major representatives of this trend in family therapy are Whitaker and Napier (1978).

The third trend will, for lack of a better word, be called experientialism (Schur, 1976). This approach emphasizes the importance of physical and bodily experience, at the cost of intellectual, impulsive, or obsessive actions. The school finds its historical antecedents in the spontaneity and psychodrama approach of J. Moreno, the gestalt therapy school founded by F. Perls, the Esalen encounter movement started by Murphy and W. C. Schutz, the fight training of G. Bach, and the body massage and therapy and the holistic human potentials movement of Ira Rolf and other people. A outline made by Schur (1976) divided this trend further into three subparts: (1) *expressivists,* those who essentially emphasize the importance of letting go and catharsis of one's feelings loudly, verbally and nonverbally; (2) *detachers,* those who emphasize meditation, holding in, and staying with oneself, as represented by the transcendental meditation movement; and (3) *communicators,* those who essentially emphasize the importance of expressing congruent verbal and nonverbal messages in one single message.

Humanism has been generally described as a reaction to the objectivism and realism of the objective schools of philosophy, such as logical positivism, in which the situational and environmental influences tended to make the individual incapable or unable to exercise decisions and responsibilities of his or her own. Thus, the existential school attempted to emphasize the freedom as well as the responsibility of the individual. It tried to put free will inside men and women. This free will, on the other hand, would be taken away from the organic school of psychiatry as well as psychoanalysis, with the individual at the mercy, deterministically, either of unconscious conflicts or of underlying physical and chemical substrata. Kierkegaard is viewed as the originator of the existential school. His effect still appears in the work of most of the existential writers of this century. Our irrational nature

Table 1-1. Historical Antecedents of Family Therapy Approaches: Theorists

Humanistic	Psychoanalytic-Psychodynamic	Behavioral	Systems
Phenomenology	**Historical, Orthodox**	**Historical, Classical**	A. Korzybsky
G. Hegel	S. Freud	E. Kraeplin	J. Dewey and
E. Husserl	A. Adler	P. Janet	M. Bentley
M. Heidegger	C. Jung	J. B. Watson	L. von Bertanlanffy
K. Jaspers	O. Rank	L. Thorndyke	G. Bateson
L. Binswanger	W. Reich	J. R. Kantor	J. Ruesch
D. Syngg and	M. Klein		D. D. Jackson
H. W. Coombs	O. Fenichel	**Drive**	J. Spiegel
C. R. Rogers	A. Freud	C. L. Hull	
K. F. Riegel and		E. Miller and	
dialectics	**Interpersonal-Adaptational**	J. Dollard	
	H. Hartmann	K. W. Spence	
Existentialism	K. Horney	J. Wolpe	
S. Kierkegaard	E. Fromm	T. A. Stampf	
J. P. Sartre	A. Meyer	H. J. Eysenck	
A. H. Maslow	H. S. Sullivan		
V. E. Frankl	S. Rado	**Reinforcement**	
R. D. Laing		B. F. Skinner	
R. May	**Modern-Day Revisionists**	S. W. Bijou	
S. Jourard	E. H. Erikson and stages	T. Ayllon	
	of development	N. H. Azrin	
Experientialism	R. R. Grinker, Sr. and		
J. Moreno and	transactional viewpoint	**Social Learning**	
psychodrama	E. Berne and transactional	A. Bandura	
F. Perls and gestalt	analysis	J. B. Rotter	
school	A. Fairburn and British	F. Kanfer	
G. Murphy and	object relations school	L. P. Ullman	
W. C. Schutz			
G. Bach and			
fight training			

I. Rolf and holistic
  movement
  expressivists, body:
    A. Lowen
  Detachers-meditators:
    A. Watts
  Communicators:
    R. Bandler and J. Grinder

Table 1-2. Schools of Family Therapy Derived from Historical Antecedents (Table 1-1)

Humanistic	Psychoanalytic	Behavioristic	Systems
Phenomenology	N. Ackerman (Chapter 3)	G. Patterson (Chapter 10)	P. Watzlawick and Palo Alto group (Chapter 5)
T. Gordon	M. Bowen (Chapter 9)	R. Stuart	S. Minuchin and structural approach (Chapter 7)
R. F. Levant	I. Boszormenyi-Nagy	J. Alexander	M. Selvini-Palazzoli and Milan group (Chapter 8)
Existentialism	J. Framo	F. J. Thomas	J. Haley and strategic approach (Chapter 6)
C. Whitaker	H. Stierlin	R. C. Weiss	G. Zuk (Chapter 12)
A. Napier		W. S. Jacobson	H. P. Laqueur (Chapter 13)
Experientialism		R. Liberman	R. McGregor (Chapter 14)
V. Satir (Chapter 4)			
R. Duhl and B. Duhl			
L. Constantine			
W. Kempler			

and the importance of irrationality are emphasized against the view of us as rational, thinking-controlled human beings. Irrationality allows us to be free and to be essentially our own wardens rather than to be servants constrained by external forces. In many ways, existentialism exercised a rather antiintellectual and anti-scientific position. There is no bowing and acceptance of science and scientific precepts as the final determinants and deciders of human destiny. This antiintellectual stance allows writers of this school to emphasize the importance of subjective, personal experience as the major component of one's decisions rather than conformity to external circumstances as the major component. In other words, humanism emphasizes an inward rather than an outward outlook on life.

Phenomenology, on the other hand, owes its roots to Edmund Husserl, who conceived his philosophy and was influenced in his approach by Franz Brentano, a psychologist. Brentano's concept of intentionality was used to distinguish psychological from physical phenomena, a concept that was kept by Husserl and is still used by many theorists. The reason for placing phenomenology ahead of existentialism is that, historically, its writers wrote at earlier times than did most existentialists and, clearly, before the experientialists.

Spiegelberg (1972), in a thorough review of phenomenology and existential phenomenology, ends up with Viktor Frankl and his logotherapy as the most important contribution to therapy from this trend. Spiegelberg considered the publication of a book by May, Angel, and Ellenberger (1958) the "most important event in the development of American phenomenological existentialism." He stated (1972),

> Phenomenology as a philosophy has made a significant difference in the fields of psychology and psychiatry. By replacing the destructive methodologies of a narrow positivism and naturalism, it has made room for new phenomena and new interpretations. It has broken the straight-jacket of behaviorism without denying its relative value. It has also contributed to the overcoming atomistic associationism. Concretely, it has helped in reforming the psychology of perception, of the emotions, and of the will, has added to such specialized enterprises as the study of the self and social psychology. In psychiatry, it has made room for a much wider and deeper understanding of pathological phenomena, and has helped to open the way for new therapies. (p. xiii)

The humanistic approach, essentially, sees the individual as possessing free will, choice, and purpose and, in this sense, individual capacity for self-determination and self-actualization within a teleological perspective of human nature. Thus, human nature is a unique system emphasizing individual characteristics that make each of us different from anybody else. Failure and pathology derive when there is a discrepancy between what the individual does and is and what the individual would like to be, that is, when there is a sense of purposelessness and meaninglessness in the self. The self is one important concept that achieves crucial importance in humanistic theory. The purpose of therapy, therefore, would be to foster self-determination, authenticity, and integration of one's human resources by expanding awareness and the ability to express one's feelings and thoughts. The goal is to establish authenticity, especially in expressing one's own immediate experience.

The personal integrity of the therapist is more important than his or her professional expertise, credentials, and authority.

The focus of the phenomenological experience is on the present and the here and now, the conscious experience of the moment. What is important are the subjective perceptions, meanings, and values, as well as the sensorimotor processes of the individual. The emphasis of the humanistic existential therapy is an awareness of the *how* and *what* of experience rather than the *why* of experience. Because experiences are produced by a multiplicity of causes, there is no sense in trying to ferret out what all these causes may be.

In addition to intentionality, there is the importance of the subjective experience of the individual, starting from a vague central pattern to more refined physical reactions. Stress on the subjective experience of the individual, again, is in contrast and in reaction to a science that wants to consider behavior on an objective, quantitative basis. Experience, unadulterated and undistorted from external influences, is the important datum that one needs to grasp.

The next writer to remember is Heidegger (1963), who saw phenomenology as the most promising way in which to discover the nature of human existence. He spoke of the condition of *Dasein.* By *Dasein* is meant the question, "Why am I here and not somewhere else? Since I am here, it is conceivable that I could be nowhere." *Dasein,* which Heidegger almost reified, is not at our disposal, but comes upon us in anxiety. Since we exist, we could also not exist. We could be in a state of *no thing.* We are, therefore, afraid of *no thing,* which means nonexistence. Yet, by existence, Heidegger meant that we are beings who are radically open to being. In our everyday commerce, we become forgetful of our openness to being and meaning, and from this stems our existential dread.

Sartre (1969) continued this line of thinking. He found human nature in a state of "thrownness" in an absurd world. Our project is to try to find some meaning in a meaningless situation. Sartre stated (1962) that "Tó be . . . means to be unified in the world" (pp. 28-29). Although he is considered an atheist, Sartre (1962) made the statement that "human reality is the pure effort to become God" (p. 62). It is of interest that, although Sartre is considered abysmally pessimistic, he does find a project for humans and does see the potentiality of individuals' becoming more than they appear to be on the surface; that is, what they are. Although he viewed the world (as did Camus) as essentially schizoid, he also believed that we can overcome this alienation from both ourselves and the world and, thus, find unity.

The problem of existential dread becomes not easier, but somewhat more manageable, when religious existentialists are considered. Tillich (1952), for instance, saw existential dread coming from four main sources: (1) fear of meaninglessness, (2) fear of alienation, (3) fear of nothingness, and (4) fear of guilt. It is important to note that guilt does not carry fear with it. It is fear of retribution for our acts or thoughts for which we feel guilty that is the source of our anxiety. The extent of this retribution in the extreme is death or nonbeing. Thus, according to Tillich, all existential dread is ultimately a fear of death or nonbeing. But, because, in his philosophy, God is the ground of our being (Tillich, 1948), this anxiety can be reduced. Unlike Heidegger, Tillich does not say that *Dasein* is grounded in nothing; rather, it is grounded in God. Because our existence is grounded in God, then there is something with which we can become unified, and being unified means life.

Buber (1958) also saw the world as absurd unless relationships exist, and to Buber a relationship is of a special type. He spoke of the "I-thou" relationship as opposed to an "I-it" relationship. In the "I-it" relationship, one party is always an object to be manipulated and used. The "I-it" relationship can never be anything better than symbiotic and is probably parasitic. In the "I-thou" relationship, both parties become a "primary person," both of them subjects, both of them merged into one, and both of them retaining their individuality at the same time. For most people, especially those nurtured in the scientific tradition of prediction and control, this is a particularly difficult concept to understand. It is the concept of "community" in the true sense of the word. Probably, a pregnant woman would need no explanation. May (1969) made the same point in his discussion of love as two merging into one and simultaneously each one becoming more oneself. These concepts reappear in the family therapy literature as the paradox of separateness and togetherness.

A common denominator among existentialists appears to be their agreement that the greatest fear of people is their fear of nonbeing. Existentialists find relationships the antidote to existential dread, although some of them would use the term "meaning" instead of relationship. It seems apparent that all would agree that one cannot find "meaning" in anything unless one relates to it personally and individually. The world and all its wonders can exist, progress, and evolve. It would all be meaningless unless the individual related to the process. From a psychological point of view, the relationship of the greatest importance is with another human being, but it is the "I" that must be relating: one self with another self.

This is the beginning of existentialist psychology: the "self" or the "I." Here, it may be important to follow the distinction between "self" and "I" as made by Bugental (1971). He saw the "self" as a conglomerate of past experiences, and, as such, a rather static concept. The "I" is seen as a dynamic entity that chooses, changes, and becomes. Each individual may possess a new "I" from moment to moment, but the "self" remains. The concept of "self," from this point of view, is a limiting entity, restricting freedom because it is fixated in the past. The "I" lives in the present and looks toward the future. It is not the "self" that relates because the "self" is back there. The "I" forms the relationships *now* and plans them for the future (Johnson, 1975; Mahrer, 1978).

Existential psychology focuses as much on the present as on the future, recognizing a usually unconscious fear of nonbeing as the major source of anxiety. It recognizes deep and abiding relationships and a sometimes unconscious desire for them as health engendering (actually life or existence engendering). Its temporal focus is on the present and future. A future orientation is more essential than an orientation toward the present or even the past. This orientation is implied by Frankl (1963) when he says that, if there is a "why" to live, a "how" can be found. Bonner (1965) stated, "the human traits of freedom, responsibility and commitment . . . all imply a tomorrow" (p. 116) and "the present-oriented person is in the paradoxical position of trying to achieve 'happiness' or 'adjustment' in a moment that does not in fact exist" (p. 121). May's (1969) discussion of "intentionality" was to the same point. The existential view, therefore, begins with the "I," with the individual himself or herself. May (1969) presented the dialectical position that for every negative there is a positive. Therefore, the fact that one exists implies that one may not exist. This is the dialectical beginning of existentialism and the beginning of the human being's sojourn through the world. The rest of one's life is an attempt to affirm one's existence and, in that way, dispel the greatest anxiety in existential thought. On a symbolic and perhaps esoteric level, the infant's first cry can be seen as an affirmation of his or her existence juxtaposed to a plea for those around him or her to take note of his or her existence. May (1967) stated that humans affirm existence either in relationship to other beings or in opposition to them.

This is probably a satisfactory model upon which to begin a theory of personality development within the family. From the point of view of existential psychology, this is indeed a very difficult task, because existentialism, by its nature, opposes reductionism. It refuses to accept an engineering, mechanistic model of humans as "nothing but" habits or responses, elements or components, and so on. The individual is a constantly moving, dynamic entity. The "I" is constantly changing (Bugental, 1971). Therefore, when speaking of personality development in the family, one speaks of the development of the personality of every member of the family because each develops in relationship to one another. Bugental's (1965) model could be used as a heuristic aid in establishing a tool to suggest an existentialist model of personality development in the family. Bugental (1965, p. 285) presented this model:

Existential Givens	Existential Anxiety	Existential Need	Authentic Being
Finiteness	Fate and death	Rootedness	Faith
Potential to act	Guilt and condemnation	Identity	Commitment
Choice	Emptiness and meaninglessness	Meaningfulness	Creativity
Separateness	Loneliness and isolation	Relatedness	Love

Finiteness. Somewhere in our unconscious there is knowledge of our end. It is a logical imperative because, if one exists, the opposite must be true that one needs not to exist. Thus, one is faced with the anxiety of fate and death. The desire or the need, then, is for rootedness, and one way in which all societies have found to fulfill this need for rootedness has been some fairly stable form of family. But the family is not a static, motionless institution. It moves. It changes. Partners become older; they change jobs and positions; they become ill; they grow or fail to grow emotionally; children come and go; they grow and mature; members die or leave. Roots are really not deep or firmly implanted in the ground. Therefore, authentic being demands faith that the family will be there, faith that it will not crumble.

Its existence means the individual's existence. The stronger the faith in one's family, the greater one can affirm one's existence.

Potential to Act. Existentialists believe that our actions are us. Our actions are indicative of our intentionality (Bonner, 1965; Mahrer, 1978; May, 1969). However, we can never know all the contingencies involved in our actions. Our actions are in relation to other people who, like us, do not remain static. In the family situation, our actions affect other members. If we cannot predict the consequences of how our actions will affect them, we are faced with guilt and self-condemnation. The fear is that we may aversely affect them. What is needed, then, is a positive sense of identity. If we are given the feeling by other members of the family that we are "good," our sense of identity will be positive. Our identification with the family will be positive. We will be authentically committed to the family. This will give our potential to act a more positive valence. We will not be immobilized. Again, the commitment that begins in the family is generalized to the world outside. If we are open to authentic being, we can become committed to values, ideals, causes, and other people.

Choice. Existentialism does not go beyond freedom and dignity. Indeed, freedom of choice is essential. All our lives are spent in making choices in the present that will have an important bearing on our future. Because we are in a situation of "thrownness" (Sartre, 1969) in an absurd world, our choices have the greatest significance. Indeed, our choices have the power to give some meaning to the absurdity of the world for us. The individual's project is to become God to the extent that one has the task of creating order out of chaos. The anxiety that inheres in this task is that this choice may not bring order out of chaos. Emptiness and meaninglessness may conceivably result from it. This anxiety takes on greater dimensions if significant others in our families also consider our choices meaningless and empty. A family member surrounded by others who consider those choices meaningless is condemned to a life of existential anxiety, for where else can one find meaning? This need is obviously a need for meaningfulness. Indeed, Frankl (1966) stated that the individual is pulled by meaning. This pull always involves decision making for meaning. Furthermore, one must fulfill a meaning in order to actualize oneself. The family has the potentiality to aid or hinder the ability to make choices by perceiving or not perceiving meaningfulness in these decisions. Ideally, reaching authentic being implies making choices with creativity. One will not fear meaninglessness or will be able to accept it on occasions. In the unconsciousness, one will feel that a creative or novel choice may be meaningful. One's family had considered it. This consideration will generalize to choices one must make in the world.

Separateness. This is one of the most salient and frightening points in existential thought. We are born alone and we die alone. Separateness means death. Buber's (1958) entire thesis is a plea to overcome separateness. This, too, is a function that the family can fulfill or fail to fulfill. Indeed, the family is an ideal setting in which one can be made to feel to belong or to be separate. Of course, in reality, we all begin separate. The existential anxiety that goes with this given—that is, separateness—comes out of loneliness and isolation. Buhler (1971) very cogently made this point in her observations of changes in contemporary American youth. Needless to say, the anxiety of facing loneliness and separateness is a very great one, and one that families, communities, and states combat to some degree. A family may do well or poorly in alleviating this existential anxiety. Because the family represents the basic societal unit of our society, its importance cannot be overestimated. The existential need is to feel related. This is a theme that runs throughout the writings of the existentialists. Relationship is of the essence. The one who achieves authentic being achieves relatedness through love. The love that one sees and feels in one's family is a love that one can carry through all his or her life. This love overcomes separateness.

The family is of the utmost importance in helping a person reach maturity or fully develop his or her personality. In the existential model, the fully developed personality is one who has achieved authentic being, which means capability for faith, commitment, creativity, and love with other intimates.

Psychoanalysis and Its Trends

This school could be taken to represent a monolithic, orthodox, and unorthodox movement. Writings can be found in Freud, Jung, Adler, Erikson, and the British Object Relations school. Its most up-to-date popularistic revision can be found in Transactional Analysis and the work of E. Berne. Psychoanalytic writings are, in some ways, considered the most representative of the emphasis on the past, on the historical, with emphasis on rational understanding in contrast to the humanistic approach valuing the seeming irrational, subjectively emotional, aspects of human experience.

In psychoanalysis, importance is given to biological drives, especially to sexually aggressive ones that press for discharge, and to the conflict that this need for discharge finds in restrictions from society. Thus, growth is the development of resolutions of opposing forces through a sequence of psychosexual stages, especially oral, anal, and genital. The ego develops more mature control, and a character structure emerges out of this conflict. Psychopathology is the result of inadequately handled conflicts at early stages of development, when there has not been sufficient or adequate release or fulfillment of gratification for early discharges, especially anxiety, dependency, and aggression. Essentially, dysfunctionality results from inadequate resolutions of these early conflicts. Thus, the general temporal perspective of psychoanalysis is oriented toward uncovering, discovering, and giving some meaning (interpretation) to past conflicts and the attendant repressed feelings that have been essentially put out of consciousness. Most of the material needs to be uncovered because it still controls behavior below the level of consciousness. Emphasis in psychoanalysis is on rational, intellectual understanding (insight), which is much more important than irrational feelings, sudden awarenesses, and inexplicable motivations, which are, instead, much more important in the humanistic–existential approach.

Sigmund Freud's classic theory of personality was developed as the result of years of therapy with clinical patients and an extensive self-analysis of personal processes. Due to these methods of data accumulation, the Freudian theory is strongly individually oriented. In applying Freud's concepts and constructs to a family setting, it must be realized that Freud regarded the family as individuals interacting with each other: in this context, he emphasized the parent–child dyad, particularly the mother–child relationship. Although he did extend his psychological theory to group situations, he distinguished the family group as being characterized by interrelations of a small number of persons, each of whom is enormously important to the other. This special situation results in narcissistic involvement, self and sexual love. Thus, family psychology would fall into the realm of individual psychology. Its laws apply to personality development in the family rather than to those of group or of social psychology (Freud, 1953, 1962, 1963, 1967).

Freud's theory as applied to families rests on two major assumptions. First, to specify the structural aspect of behavior, Freud assigned three levels of functioning to the individual: the id, the ego, and the superego. Behavior is nearly always the product of an interaction among these three systems. On the id level the instinctual drives of the body are given vent. Tension reduction as specified in the *pleasure principle* is the primary aim. Ego operations take place according to the *reality principle*. There is a constant attempt to satisfy id requirements in terms of external reality. The superego consists of moral codes that have been instilled in the individual. It functions to inhibit possibly antisocial id impulses, to persuade the ego to substitute moralistic goals for its realistic ones, and to strive for perfection as defined by the ego-ideal. In family theory all individuals are assumed to have these three levels of behavioral functioning available in varying strengths.

Additionally, there is a secondary topographical arrangement, consisting of conscious, preconscious, and unconscious levels. Freud changed his theory to place primary emphasis on the id–ego–superego structure because, with this topographical system, he found that repression and repressed materials were existing in the same system. However, for the application of his principles to family psychology, it is essential to recognize that in personal interactions all family members will react on both the conscious and unconscious levels. The preconscious consists of a nebulous system of memories and associations that are available to the conscious mind upon demand. These associations can be considered semiconscious or close to awareness.

The second major assumption underlying Freudian theory is a temporal framework consisting of psychosexual stages of development. Each family member can be characterized as to one stage of development—oral, anal, phallic (latency), or genital. Because psychosexual stages are derived from the changing focal points of sexual interest, they are indicative of the type of informational input that is considered most important and is, thus, processed by each individual. The temporal element is imperative for an accurate study of the family because it delineates the types of relationships that can occur in the various dyads. Once again a secondary assumption based on levels of consciousness exists. The unconscious mind is timeless, where the conscious is chronologically arranged and sorted, with regard to past, present, and future (Freud, 1953).

From the basic assumptions presented here, one can derive a postulate of family formation. A family is formed to assist in tension reduction via accommodating the ego's superordinate objective of species reproduction, creating a permanent outlet for the id's sexual needs, and allowing the superego's fulfillment of achieving the two former goals in a socially approved manner. The individuals involved are able to find adequate object cathexes by means of the establishment of a family.

Unresolved Oedipal conflicts are also appeased through the process of mate selection and family formation (Ehrenwald, 1963):

> What factors are responsible for the choice of one's mate—neurotic or other-wise? What drove Heloise into the arms of . . . Abelard? . . . What made Romeo, a Montague, fall in love at first sight with Juliet, a Capulet? . . . The psycho-analytic answer to these questions is virtually built in in Freudian theory. It is implied by the vicissitudes of the Oedipus complex. Every male child's first love, we are told, is his mother, and every little girl carries the torch for her father, even though she may go about it in a circuitous way. In the further course of his development, a young man—unless he be King Oedipus himself—usually relinquishes his incestuous yearning for the forbidden mother figure. Even then, however, he may be drawn to a girl with his mother's bearing, com-plexion, or tone of voice. He may seek a token union with the woman he had given up in order to resolve his Oedipal attachment. The little girl, in turn . . . is apt to go through similar stages in her emotional development. She may search for a man capable of living up to the exalted image of her father, or at least of coming close to her fantasies about him. She may end up marrying a father surrogate.
>
> There is, however, another side to the coin. Both a son and a daughter may recoil from their Oedipal temptations—so much so that they may avoid any and every connection, tie, or hint of a tie even remotely reminiscent of the inces-tuous love object of the past. They will marry outside their clan, religious de-nomination, or nationality. (p. 157)

Speaking from a libidinal point of view, Freud pointed out (1967) that:

> Being in love is based on the simultaneous presence of directly sexual impul-sions and of sexual impulsions that are inhibited in their aims, while the object draws a part of the subject's narcissistic ego-libido to itself. It is a condition in which there is only room for the ego and the object.

A second postulate of family functioning involves the healthy flow of psychic energy to the egos of the family members. The ego acquires psychic energy via the identification process through which ego cathexes are formed. The secondary process supersedes the primary process and, because it is a more adequate tension reducer, the id will divert more psychic energy to the ego's use. Once the ego has obtained a surplus energy, it can be expended on the various psychological processes (perceiving, remembering, judging, discriminating, abstracting, generalizing, and reasoning), on creating new anticathexes with which to control the id, and on formulating new object cathexes to produce derived interests (Hall and Lindzey,

1978). When the various egos are capable of the integration of the three systems, relieving anxiety and using surplus energy for constructive purposes, the family can function effectively.

Family dysfunctioning comes about when one or more of the family members falls victim to intrapsychic conflict (neurosis) and eventually develops excessive dominance by the id, ego, or superego. An imbalance of psychic energy results. It becomes necessary, then, to rely heavily on defense mechanisms for the preservation of internal homeostasis. Such defenses as repression, projection, reaction formation, fixation, and regression falsify and distort reality so that the dysfunctioning family member reacts to inaccurate informational input. Additionally, defense mechanisms operate unconsciously so that the person is not aware that he or she is being misled. The individual makes mistakes in his or interpersonal dealings, and the discrepancy between actual behavior and appropriate behavior is noted by other family members. The dysfunctioning member no longer adequately fulfills his or her role as object cathexis for them. Other family members alter their relationships with the individual and displacement occurs. Failure of one individual's psychological system has thus affected each member of the family. The spread of the dysfunction throughout the family is contingent on the other persons' abilities to effectively create new chaos.

According to Ehrenwald (1963), the concept that neurosis might be provoked and sustained by secondary environmental factors, originating in the individual's family instead of by the Oedipal conflict, or the dynamics of the family in early infancy (primary environmentalism) would require a major shift from the original Freudian position. The individual's neurosis must be caused by unresolved problems drawn from the past of his or her own infancy and is possibly unrelated to existing family interactions insofar as the causative factor is involved.

On the axiomatic level, Freudian theory has one all-important dyad relationship—that of child and parent. The effects of this relationship are felt by the individual, primarily when in the role of the child. Later in life, conjugal and parent–child dyad interactions will be the result of unresolved problems dating from childhood. Within the boundaries of child–parent interactions, it is the child–mother dyad that is of primary importance. Many analytic authors believe that it is wholly the mother's responsibility whether beneficial changes from the infant's state of self-centeredness to an attitude capable of loving occurs. When she fails to welcome the first outflow of feeling and responds inappropriately to it, the mother may destroy the potentiality for love in her child. The father serves as the symbol of the moral code and embodies the incest taboo to the child. The father, therefore, represents socialization. His main influence is found in assembling the superego. Society must defend itself from the possibility that the individual's interests that it requires for the establishment of higher social units might be swallowed up by the family, so it erects an emotional barrier against incest (Freud, 1963).

The Oedipus complex is a crisis imposed upon the individual by the society and is initiated by confrontation with the incest taboo. Briefly, the Oedipal complex consists of a sexual cathexis for the opposite-sex parent that is stymied by the sexual presence of the same-sex parent. A hostile cathexis for the same-sex parent results. The behavior of the three- to five-year-old child is marked to a large extent by the operations of the Oedipus complex. Although it is modified and suffers repression after the age of five, it remains a vital force in the personality throughout life. Attitudes toward the opposite sex and toward people in authority, for instance, are largely conditioned by the Oedipus complex (Hall and Lindzey, 1978).

In a boy the guilt feelings aroused by the Oedipal complex result in castration anxiety—fear that a jealous father will cut off his penis—and the boy represses the Oedipal yearnings. He also represses his hostility toward his father and learns to identify with the male parent. Thus, the boy gains some vicarious satisfaction of his sexual feelings toward the mother through the identification process. In young girls the castration complex in the form of penis envy will precipitate the Oedipal complex. The girl holds her mother responsible for her lack of a penis, and, as the cathexis for the mother is weakened, a cathexis for the father is instituted. Whereas the boy's Oedipus complex is repressed by castration anxiety, the girl's complex persists with some modification due to realistic barriers preventing sexual union with the father. These differences between the Oedipal and castration complexes help to account for many of the psychological differences between sexes (Hall and Lindzey, 1978).

Methods of Study

Traditionally, freudian psychological theory has been oriented clinically, founded on impressionistic observations of neurotics' undergoing psychotherapy. The data come from the verbalizations and behaviors of these patients. No experimental testing of hypotheses was ever done by Freud—all his theoretical development comes from inductive reasoning cross-checked by the criterion of internal consistency over years of psychoanalytic sessions.

In pursuing his career as a psychoanalyst, Freud developed several special techniques for the amassing of data. The most prominent of these are the methods of *free association,* in which the patient follows a stream-of-consciousness verbalization pattern, and *dream analysis,* in which dream material is regarded as unconscious symbolizations expressing the most primitive contents of the mind. The study of specific cases was another technique Freud relied upon for his theory development. It is still the preferred method of obtaining evidence to support the theory today.

A fourth method of study that Freud employed was the extensive self-analysis of his own unconscious through slips of tongue. The material obtained in this manner was used to check out theoretical implications derived from clinical observations. Through reviewing his own childhood fantasies, Freud was able to confirm his hypothesis of infantile sexuality. His own unconscious desires showing up in his dreams allowed him to assume that his dream theory was accurate.

In applying Freudian psychology to the family situation, it is found that, because the classical theory is so heavily individual in nature and was developed specifically for the neurotic, treatment of the family must consist of psychotherapy for the presenting patient. A second reason for confining psychotherapy to one individual is the inordinate expense that would be involved in treating several family members through complete psychoanalysis. Occasionally spouses will both go into psychoanalysis, but in such instances the practice is usually to select different analysts. In that way transference is not inhibited by the knowledge that the same analyst is also learning secrets from one's mate and the lack of confidence that may thereby develop.

It has been found necessary in recent years to develop a means of applying psychoanalysis to children. Basic theory holds that the childhood is the most influential period of life and that the personality is essentially formed by the age of five years. However, Freud himself never chose to examine children. All his experience was with adults recalling the experiences and observations of childhood. (The published case of Little Hans was not a study conducted by Freud—he served as an advisor to the child's father, who conducted the analysis.) Through the use of play techniques, Klein and associates have been able to psychoanalyze children as young as two to three years. In their modifications of Freudian theory for children, Klein and others (1952) have developed the concept of early object relations that are characterized by ambivalence (good versus bad) and therefore produce anxiety and depression in the child.

Additional studies of child analysis have been made by Murphy (1956) through observational research on children in nursery situations, in group play and under free play conditions. She has attempted to integrate the overall picture of a child's way of experiencing and to evaluate the strength and handling of impulses and ego functioning in interpersonal situations. Anna Freud has also devoted a great deal of time to the field of child analysis. Finding that the child, a forced participant in psychotherapy, with the accompanying behavioral aspects of immaturity, was unsuited as a patient, Anna Freud explored the therapeutic potential of play as a partial substitution for verbal therapy. Systematic play observations were combined with limited dream analysis and free association to effect the psychoanalysis of the child.

Empirical Evidence

With regard to the evidence supporting the validity of psychoanalytic theory as related to the family, Sears, in a 1943 review of the scientific status of Freudian concepts, stated that

> Psychoanalysis relied upon techniques that do not admit of the repetition of observation, that have no self-evident or denotative validity, and that are tinctured to an unknown degree with the observer's own suggestions. These difficulties may not seriously interfere with therapy, but when the method is used for uncovering psychological facts that are required to have objective validity it simply fails . . . . The nature of any fact is in part a function of the method by which it is obtained. The findings of psychoanalysis relate to the ideas and verbalizations that accompany various kinds of behavior, for example, sexual development. The data are secured from the free association of adults, usually, and depend upon recall of childhood events. Like any other verbalizations about the experienced world, these communicate to others a picture of the world that cannot accord exactly with anyone's else [sic]; in other words, there are individualized distortions in the picture created by each person's unique language habits. Since the facts of psychoanalysis are derived entirely through

verbal channels, allowance must be made for discrepancies that hinge mainly on the fact that non-analytic investigations frequently represent observations of other kinds of behavior. (pp. 133–134)

Because most practitioners still abide solely by the technique of intensive case description, there is little opportunity to apply the theory of psychoanalysis to controlled situations. The more recent trend toward observation of children, however, seems to have potential for hypothesis testing in laboratory settings. Extensive surveys of most experimental evidence relating to infant care and personality development, including the effects of breast feeding, demand feeding, thumb sucking, and sphincter training, as related to Freudian theory, have concluded that the studies are largely invalid and poorly executed. From the data available, the hypothesis that specific nursing disciplines have specific effects upon the child has been largely rejected. Personality is not the result of instinctual infantile libidinal drives mechanically channeled by parental disciplines. Instead, Horney and Fromm (Hall and Lindzey, 1970) contended that personality is a dynamic product of the interaction of a unique organism undergoing maturation and a unique physical and social environment (Rachman, 1963). Such modifications of the classical theory seem to be more adaptable to the family situation and can explain more fully with scientific support the family development than can a strict application of Freudian principles.

Behaviorism and Its Trends

In behavior therapy, conditioning and learning are the basic avenues on which we become socialized. Behavior is essentially learned through the process of imitation and reinforcement. Symptoms derive from inadequate or faulty learning. Most problems of living are due to learning. Symptoms themselves have no underlying causes, in contrast to the psychoanalytic view, which would essentially interpret any kind of maladaptive behavior as having some kind of unconscious conflict. There is no unconscious in the behavioral perspective. Essentially maladaptive behavior is extinguished by learning new and more adaptive behaviors. The self, self-knowledge, self-understanding, self-awareness, and experience are not the primary focus of this approach. There is little or no concern with the past history or the possible situational determinants of any kind of maladaptive behavior. Emphasis is on the present behavior as it occurs and is measured. There is no need for hypothetical constructs or intervening variables of the type of insight for psychoanalysis or awareness for humanism. What is important is the direct, observable behaviors and actions of the individual. Of course, the behavioral viewpoint is essentially the historical development of the objective descriptive philosophical view, which was also present in organic and descriptive psychiatry (Table 1-1). This particular theory stresses objectification, quantification, classification, and all the various trappings of what makes it scientific. In psychoanalysis, going back to historical factors as well as to the generational development of symptoms is one of the important aspects that need to be considered.

Operant conditioning, according to Skinner (1953), is an application of lawful relationships. Skinner considered operant behavior to be the result of scientific principles. He proposed (1953) a formulation of behavior that resulted from observations of animal performance and bar-pressing activity. Operant conditioning is a procedure for altering the probability of a chosen response. Skinner was opposed to a hypotheticodeductive system. He felt that theories are wasteful and misleading. However, for the purposes of analyzing behavior modification as it applies to family therapy, several assumptions, postulates, axioms, and hypotheses can be derived.

The first assumption affirms that only *overt* behavior is significant. Behavior must be observable or measured in discrete terms of frequency or duration to be of concern to the behaviorist. This is a structural, unilevel assumption and simply means that internal stimuli are not relevant to a behavior modificator.

The second assumption is that the family is a network of consequences. These consequences control behavior. Behavior that is followed by immediate reinforcement is strengthened and will occur more frequently in the future; behavior that is not reinforced is weakened. Retraining can therefore be accomplished by weakening the undesirable behavior while concurrently strengthening a desirable or competing one. There is also a relationship between the number of reinforcements and the kinds of behavior. To maintain a pattern of strength and durability, intermittent reinforcement must replace continuous reinforcement. Behavior will extinguish quickly when reinforcement has been continuous rather than irregular. This weakening is due to satiation.

Derived from these assumptions are three postulates concerning development, functioning, and dysfunctioning. Development of the family members is in terms of imitation and reinforcements. Family formation occurs when two people meet and, in the process of interacting, reinforce each other. Selection of a spouse is accordingly based on similarities of interests. We are attracted to those whose values and attitudes are similar to ours and who, therefore, reinforce and reaffirm our values. Families break up when the reinforcement system fails. An unsuccessful marriage is characterized by a low rate of reciprocally positive reinforcements.

The second postulate concerns reciprocity. It involves positive reinforcers that maintain the behavior of both persons in a dyadic interaction at an equitable rate. In it, there is a systematic giving and receiving. Each partner gets something for something. Perhaps the wife will go on a fishing trip to please her husband after he has entertained a member of her family. A is reinforced when B listens; B is reinforced when A listens.

The third postulate involves coercion or abnormality. It consists of a dyadic interaction in which positive reinforcement maintains the behavior of one person, whereas aversive stimuli control the behavior of the other. This means that the compliant behavior of the "victim" serves as reinforcer to the "aggressor," whereas threatening or punishing stimuli control the "victim's" behavior. Some implications of this postulate of dysfunction are that parents actually teach their children to behave in undesirable ways, just as children can teach their parents to reinforce their undesirable behavior. For instance, the attention the parent gives a child by picking him or her up each time that he or she cries is very reinforcing to the child. Similarly, if children will not respond to mother until she has raised her voice quite loudly, they are actually reinforcing or teaching her to scream. One further implication of this postulate is that siblings provide reinforcing contingencies that lead to coercion. Here again the bully is reinforced by compliant behavior. The role of "victim" and "aggressor" may at some time reverse. However, it is often the larger child in the family who consistently picks on a smaller or younger child. Aggression, therefore, is a learned trait or a social behavior. It results from external stimuli rather than from internal anger or frustration. By changing the stimuli, it is possible to alter the behavior. Behavior patterns are accelerated or decelerated by reactions of the other members of the dyad.

The assumptions and postulates of operant conditioning are both consistent and logical. They account for most of the decisions made by the family that determine how the family will develop. The tasks involved in mate selection, decision of marriage, family interaction, and separation or divorce can all be accounted for by reinforcement principles, according to the behavior modificator. Because operant conditioning conceives of a continuity in the growth curve with no levels or stages along the way, this theory does not include axioms.

The hypotheses of operant conditioning can best be presented as applications of learning principles, as they have been adapted by current therapists. As pointed out earlier, some of these applications involve a departure from pure Skinnerian thought. Stuart (1969), for instance, formulated a token economy in his treatment of couples based directly on the postulate of reciprocity. He suggested that successful marriages differ from unsuccessful marriages by the frequency and range of the reciprocal positive reinforcements exchanged. To improve an unsuccessful marriage, each partner must develop the ability to reinforce or reward the other. Interaction between partners in a marriage represents the best balance that they are able to achieve in terms of costs and mutual rewards. If the husband prefers being with friends to spending an evening with his wife, then the friends are giving him more reinforcement. A poor marriage can be likened to social bankruptcy. Negative means of control have superseded reciprocity.

Stuart developed a treatment within the framework of operant conditioning using a token economy. Because there is usually a lack of trust in a troubled marriage, tokens are an ideal reinforcement. They can be given immediately, and they can be redeemed whenever desirable. In addition, they are a very concrete symbol that is typically associated with positive social interchange. Stuart's program was tested with four couples, ages twenty-four to fifty-two, married three to twenty-three years, with high school to doctorate-level education. In each case, the wife's first desire was more communication and affection. The husband's primary desire was for more physical and sexual contact. Each wife was required to write on a behavior monitoring form her criteria for conversation. Then, with the use of an ordinary kitchen timer, she dispensed tokens to her husband as he met her criteria. If he failed to live up to her specifications, she was required to offer constructive suggestions. In turn, her husband has "a menu of physical affection." The tokens he received from his wife for communicating functioned as a contingency for fulfilling his desires. Each menu was constructed to suit each husband on a sliding scale, beginning with three tokens for kissing, and so on. Tokens earned and spent were recorded on the behavior checklist. In follow-up studies made forty-eight weeks later, all four couples reported that the "game" was helpful to their marriages. It had, in fact, taken them from a consideration of divorce to a higher rate of self-reported satisfaction. Although change was made at the level of behavior, there were definite improvements in self-ratings, such as "How committed are you to stay in this marriage?" and "How much time spent with your spouse do you consider fully satisfying?"

Liberman (1970) similarly described the family as a system of reciprocal behaviors. His hypothesis is that the family can change the nature of their social reinforcement patterns into constructive behavior through the use of the operant conditioning principles. He described the process of continuous reinforcement that is then replaced by the process of intermittent reinforcement to produce more lasting behavior. He reviewed successful treatment of four cases: (1) a woman with a migraine headache, (2) a depressed mother of five children, (3) a twenty-three-year-old man with a low normal IQ, and (4) a couple in which the wife was a sloppy housekeeper and the husband was paranoid. In addition to his use of operant conditioning, however, Liberman used a model similar to Bandura's (1961) to teach the subject what is expected. He suggested structuring a favorable situation for eliciting the desired behavior by providing cues for the appropriate behavior and removing cues for incompatible, inappropriate behavior. Thus, a model was used in addition to rewards and reinforcements for appropriate behavior.

A case study by Coe (1970) is another successful test of the hypothesis that the point system of rewards can be effective in a family with a handicapped child. Dick was neurologically handicapped, a twelve-year-old whose typical behavior involved temper tantrums. He had a very low opinion of himself, which was only reinforced by his negative behavior. His parents had feelings of confusion and guilt and had gone through the gamut of professional help, from psychiatrists and social workers through school counselors. Coe's treatment plan for Dick is typical of behavior modification. Although the family was not particularly willing to try a new therapy, they agreed to cooperate if, as promised, it would give the child the responsibility for determining his own actions. With the therapist's help, three lists of behavior were drawn up. The first included the do's or all the things the family and Dick would like. The second, the don'ts, were all the things he shouldn't do. The third included the things Dick valued the most, the reinforcers (such as staying up after bedtime).

A financial plan of payment in points was drawn up. The family was to serve as its own therapeutic agent under the direction of the "on-call" expert. The members then established a price range or cost and payment scale for each behavior. For instance, going to school would bring the child more points than setting the table. After some trial and error, Dick arrived at the therapist's office claiming he was worth 400 points. Coe, as was mentioned earlier, was particularly interested in changes in Dick's self-image, which went from very negative to fairly positive.

One of the most frequent criticisms of behavior modification is the concept of symptom substitution. Will removal of the symptom without attention to the underlying *causes* of the symptom lead to the formation of a new symptom? Calhoon stated (1971) that behavioristic psychology only deals with overt actions. Therefore, cases involving symptom substitution in which underlying causes are involved must be dismissed as meaningless, except by advocates of nonbehavioristic theories. Calhoon suggested that, if the symptom itself generates the primary cause of anxiety, elimination of the symptom will eliminate most, if not all, of the anxiety and symptomatic reactions to anxiety.

Ullman and Krasner (1965) rejected this critique as irrelevant, even though they agreed that it may be necessary, at times, to extinguish a complete hierarchy of behavior. For instance, they describe a child at a summer camp with a series of maladjustive responses that ranged from self-punishing behavior, tantrums, and public nudity to stealing food. As each symptom was eliminated, another would take place until a complete hierarchy of maladaptive responses had been extinguished. Calhoon concluded that symptom substitution is an empirical, not a theoretical, matter and, therefore, not a just criticism of behavior modification. Some of these critical issues will be considered in greater detail in the chapter reviewing the behaviorist who has contributed most to a therapeutic approach for families, Gerald Patterson (Chapter 10).

Systems Theory and Its Trends

As in the previously reviewed schools, systems theory is no exception. It does have different trends and different theorists. Among the most relevant, we can identify three major ones: (1) communication theory, as found in the work of Reusch and Bateson (1951); (2) transactional theory, as found in the work of Dewey and Bentley (1949); and (3) general systems theory as found in Ludwig von Bertanlanffy (1968).

Communication Theory

Borrowing concepts from cybernetics (Wiener, 1948) and communications engineering (Shannon and Weaver, 1949), Ruesch and Bateson (1951) proposed to view all behavior as communication and human beings as systems and parts of systems. Ruesch saw communication as any process by which one person influenced himself or herself or another in a lawful, interconnected way.

Communicative behavior can occur within four different system levels delineated by magnitude. The first is the intrapsychic or intrapersonal system. The source and destination of messages are both within the person. Thinking and feeling are main communicative functions here. The second system is the interpersonal system, which is composed of two persons. The third level is a group system, which is composed of three or more individuals who occupy certain positions in a matrix of a group. The largest system is the societal, in which individual persons are not considered. The focus of communication is among various groups (Ruesch and Kees, 1956).

Information can be coded for transmission in two basic ways: analogically and digitally. Analogic codification has as its defining characteristic a relationship of similarity between the symbol and its referent. There is a correspondence between proportions and continuous magnitudes of the referent and symbol. Within analogical codification there is no either/or distinction to deal with negatives and error is possible. Both/and are part of this way of thinking. Maps, models, and gestures are illustrations of analogical codification. On the other hand, digital codification has no relationship between the symbol and its referent, only arbitrary either/or correspondence. It is more abstract and more complex, making it more versatile. Digital codification is manipulated according to the logical rules of syntax. Meaning is semantic convention. The alphabet and numbers are examples of digital codification (Ruesch and Kees, 1956; Watzlawick, Beavin, Helmick, and Jackson, 1967).

The satisfactory mediation of information is the purpose of communication. Its functions entail the reception, evaluation, and expression of information (Ruesch and Kees, 1956). Because communication is so broadly defined, it includes much more than the written or spoken language. A great number of messages sent are comments on the communication process itself. Metacommunication, as it is called, concerns itself with making statements about how the message is to be received, what role each participant has, and how the communication will be carried out *in this context*. These metacommunicative messages are evolved and transmitted by the culture in consistent stylized forms. When an exchange of information occurs in any of the four kinds of systems and an agreement is reached by both the sender and receiver, the communication is unsensually validated and successful. If, on the other hand, agreement is not initially reached, the sender then gains more information than the receiver, which allows the sender to clarify or change his or her original message. This process of obtaining new information on how the receiver interpreted the message and making self-corrections is called feedback. Feedback is an important part of communication. Within it learning and the alleviation of misunderstanding is possible (Ruesch and Kees, 1956).

Emphasis here is on the notions of input or reception of information, throughput or processing of information, and mediation between output and input, output or the expression of information, and feedback or knowledge of results that can be possible (maintenance of status quo) or negative (producing change). Other concepts such as *homeostasis* (maintenance of sameness) and *entropy* are part of the overlap of this theory with systems theory.

Transactional Theory

The term "transaction" was originally used by the British mathematician and physicist Cler-Maxwell to describe the interpenetration of processes in a physical field independent of organized or separable entities. Its use in family therapy derives from the work of Spiegel (1971) as taken from Dewey and Bentley (1949). These authors reviewed the history of thought as represented by three distinct stages: action, interaction, and transaction. Action refers to internal states or conditions as explanatory of behavior. These explanations may range from mythical and religious sources (soul, anima, etc.) to clearly intrapsychic concepts (the unconscious, motivation, anxiety, etc.). Interaction refers to unidirectional effects of one individual upon another, supposedly maternal effects on children, without consideration of other facts. Transaction refers to bidirectional and reciprocal effects of individuals within a field; that is, the mother's reaction to her child is not independent from the child's own peculiar behavior and the mother's relationship to her husband as well as the mothering experiences she was subjected to in her childhood (L'Abate, Weeks, and Weeks, 1978).

Systems Theory

The baselines of this theory, as promulgated by its founder, Ludwig von Bertanlanffy (1968), consist of the notion of a system as an aggregate, or set, of interdependent parts or components. These components, in addition to the quality of interrelatedness (overlap among parts), have other qualities pertaining to the relative permeability of the boundaries of one system from other systems, the relative flexibility of component parts to work together effectively or otherwise, and relative importance of each component part in relationship to the other parts, as seen in the size of each subcomponent. These concepts are especially applicable to members of a family in terms of: (1) how separate or enmeshed they are from each other (concepts to be developed further by Bowen, chap. 9 and Minuchin, chap. 7); (2) the overlap of role functions; (3) rigidity or flexibility of role functions; and (4) division of labor and of chores and responsibilities that characterizes or fails to characterize members of a family.

As we shall see, many, many family therapists claim a "systems" orientation. Yet, each major theorist emphasizes different aspects or uses different terms to describe similar functions in a family.

Conclusion

This broad and brief overview of the historical antecedents of family therapy approaches has the function of showing the continuity of these approaches with philosophical and theoretical approaches to individual and to group behavior. Family therapy approaches can be viewed as another evolutionary step in the further differentiation of methods to improve the human condition. From an information processing viewpoint, family therapy approaches can be viewed as emphasizing various rungs of a chain (L'Abate and Frey, 1981). As we shall see, humanistically oriented family therapists, such as Virginia Satir and Carl Whitaker, emphasize the importance of present feelings and intuition over rationality or action. Psychoanalytically oriented family therapists emphasize the importance of the past in determining present behavior, following therapeutic rational processes with cognitive emphasis. Behavioral and systems theorists emphasize the role of activity and problem solving through active interventions, minimizing either feelings or rational explanations as present in the two previous schools (output and feedback) and maximizing homework assignments and paradoxical prescriptions.

References

Bandura, A. 1969. *Principles of behavior modification.* New York: Holt, Rinehart and Winston.

Bertanlanffy, L. von. 1968. *General systems theory: Formulations, development, applications.* New York: George Braziller.

Bonner, H. 1965. *On being mindful of man.* Boston: Houghton Mifflin.

Buber, M. 1958. *I and thou.* New York: Scribner's.

Bugental, J. F. T. 1965. *The search for authenticity.* New York: Holt, Rinehart and Winston.

——. 1971. The self: Process or illusion? In *Existential humanistic psychology,* ed. T. C. Greening, pp. 57–71. Belmont, Calif.: Brooks/Cole.

Buhler, C. 1971. Responses to contemporary challenges. In *Existential humanistic psychology,* ed. T. C. Greening, p. 1542. Belmont, Calif.: Brooks/Cole.

Calhoon, D. D. 1968. Symptom substitution and behavior therapies, a reappraisal. *Psychological Bulletin* 69:149–156.

Coe, C. 1970. Dick and his parents—A case study. Paper presented at the Conference on The Troubled Adolescent and His Family. Mendocino, California, March 1970.

Dewey, J., and Bentley, A. F. 1949. *Knowing and the known.* Boston: Beacon Press.

Ehrenwald, J. 1963. *Neurosis in the family and patterns of psychosocial defense.* New York: Harper & Row.

Frankl, V. E. 1963. *Man's search for meaning.* New York: Washington Square Press.

——. 1966. Self-transcendence as a human phenomenon. *Journal of Humanistic Psychology* 5:97–106.

Freud, A. 1965. *Normality and Pathology in Childhood: Assessment of Development.* New York: International Universities Press.

Freud, S. 1953. Beyond the pleasure principle. In *The standard edition of the complete psychological works,* ed. J. Strachey, pp. 7–64. London: Hogarth Press. (First German edition, 1920.)

——. 1961. *Three essays on the theory of sexuality.* New York: Avon Publishers.

——. 1963. *A general introduction to psychoanalysis.* New York: Pocket Books.

——. 1967. *Group psychology and the analysis of the ego.* New York: Liveright. (First published in English in 1922.)

Hall, C. S., and Lindzey, G. 1978. *Theories of personality.* New York: Wiley.

Havens, L. L. 1973. *Approaches to the mind: Movement of the psychiatric schools from sects toward science.* Boston: Little, Brown.

Heidegger, M. 1962. *Being and time.* New York: Harper & Row.

Johnson, K. E. 1975. *In quest of a new psychology: Toward a redefinition of humanism.* New York: Human Sciences Press.

Klein, M.; Heinmann, P.; and Riviere, J. 1952. *Developments in Psychoanalysis.* London: Hogarth Press.

L'Abate, L., and Frey, J. 1981. The ERA model: The role of emotions in family therapy revisited: Implications for a classification of family therapy theories. *Journal of Marriage and Family Therapy* forthcoming.

——; Weeks, C.; and Weeks, F. 1978. Psychopathology as transaction: A historical note. *International Journal of Family Counseling* 6:60–65.

Levant, R. F. 1978a. Family therapy: A client-centered perspective. *Journal of Marriage & Family Counseling* 4:35–42.

——. 1978b. Client-centered approaches to working with the family: An overview of new developments in therapeutic, educational and preventive methods. *International Journal of Family Counseling 1978,* 6:31–44.

Liberman, R. 1970. Behavioral approaches to family and couple therapy. *American Journal of Orthopsychiatry* 40:106–118.

Mahrer, A. R. 1978. *Experiencing a humanistic theory of psychology and psychiatry.* New York: Brunner/Mazel.

May, R. 1967. *Psychology and the human dilemma.* Princeton, N.J.: Van Nostrand.

——. 1969. *Love and will.* New York: Norton

——. Angel, E.; and Ellenberger, H. F., eds. 1958. *Existence: A new dimension in psychiatry and psychology.* New York: Basic Books.

Murphy, L. 1956. *Personality in young children.* New York: Basic Books.

Rachman, S., ed. 1963. *Critical essays on psychoanalysis.* New York: Macmillan.

Rickman, J., ed. 1957. *A general selection from the works of Sigmund Freud.* Garden City, N.Y.: Doubleday.

Riegel, K. 1979. *Foundations of dialectical psychology.* New York: Academic Press.

Ruesch, J., and Bateson, G. 1951. *Communication: The social matrix of psychiatry.* New York: Norton.

——, and Kees, W. 1956. *Nonverbal communication.* Berkeley and Los Angeles: University of California Press.

Sartre, J. P. 1962. *Existential psychoanalysis,* trans. H. E. Barnes. Chicago: Henry Regnery.

——. 1969. *Being and nothingness,* trans. H. E. Barnes. New York: Washington Square Press.

Sears, R. R., 1943. Survey of objective studies of psychoanalytic concepts. *Social Science Research Council Bulletin,* 51.

Schur, E. M. 1976. *The awareness trap: Self-absorption instead of social change.* New York: Quadrangle.

Shannon, C., and Weaver, W. 1949. *The mathematical theory of communication.* Urbana: University of Illinois Press.

Skinner, B. F. 1953. *Science and human behavior.* New York: Macmillan.

Spiegel, J. 1971. *Transactions: The interplay between individual, family, and society.* New York: Science House.

Spiegelberg, H. 1972. *Phenomenology in psychiatry and psychology: A historical introduction.* Evanston, Ill.: Northwestern University Press.

Stuart R. B. 1969. Operant interpersonal treatment for marital discord. *Journal of Consulting and Clinical Psychology* 33:675–682.

Tillich, P. 1948. *The shaking of the foundations.* New York: Scribner's.

——. 1952. *The courage to be.* New Haven, Conn.: Yale University Press.

Ullman, L. P., and Krasner, I., eds. 1965. *Case studies in behavior modification.* New York: Holt, Rinehart and Winston.

Watzlawick, P.; Beavin, J. H.; and Jackson, D. D. 1967. *Pragmatics of human communication.* New York: Norton.

Whitaker, C., and Napier, A. 1978. *The family crucible.* New York: Harper & Row.

Wiener, N. 1948. *Cybernetics.* New York: Wiley.

2

The Classification of "Normal" Families: Functionality and Dysfunctionality

What is a normal family? What is normality within the family context? Can we ever speak of normality as a statistical or ideal condition when we work with families? These and other questions are those that every beginning family therapist may ask. Up to a decade ago these questions were answered tentatively and mainly intuitively (L'Abate, 1976). More recently, we have been inundated by an avalanche of suggestions that fill the conceptual and empirical vacuum concerning family types and family typologies. To avoid the logical and experiential pitfalls of "normality," many family therapists started looking at families along the dimension defined by the polarities of functionality and dysfunctionality. A perfectly functional family may be so dull or conforming to the extent that its very conformity may become the beginning of a dysfunctional pattern, at least in one member of a family. A possibly dysfunctional family may be quite creative or may, in its nonconformity to acceptable normative standards of life-styles, produce a genius or a very productive individual. Where is the line dividing these two polarities? How can both aspects coexist in the same family; that is, is there some degree of functionality in very dysfunctional families just as there may be some dysfunctional pattern in very functional families? Who needs to be perfect? Functionality does not by any means imply perfection. Nor does dysfunctionality imply "craziness" or destructiveness. Our inability to come up with clear-cut criteria for family classification has rendered this job so much more difficult. The difficulty of the job, however, does not mean that no attempt should be made, if not to solve it, to take a stab at it. It is the purpose of this chapter to review most of the literature on the nature of functionality and dysfunctionality in families and to acquaint the reader with the relevant literature.

Valiant attempts (and failures) have made this one of the most intriguing areas of family therapy, because it is this very area that has raised many questions about traditional definitions of normality based on individual criteria rather than on family-derived criteria. Although the foregoing questions may not be answered satisfactorily, awareness of the definitional difficulties present here may allow the reader to come up with a better (more encompassing and valid) classification than has been possible heretofore.

Of course, classification of clearly dysfunctional families has been an easier task than the classification of functional families. By the same token, classification of dysfunctional families has been hindered by the failure to anchor and link these families to various degrees and types of functionality. Functionality covers as wide a range of families as does dysfunctionality.

Clearly Dysfunctional Families

In these families at least one member ends up in the care of a social or welfare agency, a medical facility, and/or a judicial and/or incarcerary system. Thus far, it would seem that clearly dysfunctional families could be classified along an alloplastic–autoplastic continuum, whereby alloplastic would include acting-out, impulsive, self-gratifying, and/or indulgent behavior, such as seen in (1) abusive, battered and battering, violent families, (2) addiction, (3) criminality, and (4) sexuality (incest, deviance, etc.). Within the autoplastic category we would find (1) psychosomatic, (2) underachieving, underemployed, and learning disabled, and (3) bazarre, psychotic, and autistic families. Alloplasticity would be characterized by distracting, impulsivity, and irrelevance (L'Abate, 1976) as well as by blaming, emotional blackmail, and one-up-manship. Autoplasticity would be characterized by placating, intellectual smugness, and emotional aloofness.

Most classifications of dysfunctional families have been made on the basis of the psychiatric diagnosis of one family member, the I.P. (identified patient), who comes to the attention of mental health and law enforcement agencies for criminal or criminal-like behavior. Most classifications based on the psychiatric diagnosis of one representative signal member usually fail to describe the characteristics of the families of origin and assume (without checking) that the dysfunctionality of one member is representative of the dysfunctionality in his or her total family. These classifications follow standard psychiatric nomenclature (DSM-II, DSM-III).

One of the most ambitious attempts at classification of dysfunctional families is that of Fisher (1977), who has reviewed most of the literature on family classification from the last twenty years and has tried to integrate most of these schemes according to five major criteria: (1) *styles of adaptation* (expressive, repressive, defensive, paranoid, anxious, hysterical); (2) *developmental family stage,* according to the major crises in the life cycle (marriage, child-bearing, school age, empty nest, etc.); (3) *initial problem* or *diagnosis* of the identified patient (using traditional psychiatric nosology); (4) *family theme* or *dimension* (uncontrolled, chaotic, or disintegrated families; rigid versus flexible, or families with versus without rules, etc.); (5) *types of marital relationships* (based on the dynamics of individual spouses, patterns of power and conflict within the marriage, and "normal" marital relationships).

His integration of the literature has yielded six major family clusters: (1) *con-*

stricted (repressive, passive, negative, perfectionistic); (2) *internalized* (isolated, enmeshed, suicidal, etc.); (3) *objective-focus* (child focus, external focus, self focus); (4) *impulsive* (delinquent, aggressive, antisocial); (5) *childlike* (immature, demanding, dependent, inadequate); and (6) *chaotic* (disintegrated, unsocial). The important point to notice about Fisher's scheme is that it deals with dysfunctional, not functional, families.

Adland, Gold, and Goodwin (1979), in a study of manic-depressive illness in multigeneral families, have found the following characteristics (repetitive maladaptive patterns): (1) avoidance of affect; (2) unrealistic standards of conformity; (3) absence of intimate relationship apart from the family; (4) displaced parental low self-esteem; and (5) fears related to illness. All those characteristics maintained the "family pathology."

The systems approach can be used to understand pathological dimensions of family functioning. For example, Justice and Justice (1976) have used this approach to understand the family in which child abuse takes place. Child abuse is seen as occurring within the family system as a whole. Factors leading to abuse are found in the parents, in the child, and in stresses of the life cycle as well as in the operation of the family system and subsystems. The Justices felt that abuse is often related to a parent's competing with a son or daughter for the child position. Usually, the emotional and relationship qualities are marked by much intensity and fusion. These examples show how the systems concept can be used to understand a specific area of dysfunction.

Because the reader can, and will, find many references concerning traditional psychiatric diagnoses, it may be helpful to concentrate on what these readers may not find easily, that is, attempts at definitions of functional families from which one can make inferences about more dysfunctional families.

Attempts at Classification of Functional Families

A first step in understanding types of family functioning is to define some basic concepts. According to Price (1979), "normal" can be defined in several ways in terms of behavior. He has advocated its use to mean the statistical average, the majority, or typical behavior. "Functional" is then defined in terms of several qualities. In looking at a particular behavior, important questions to be answered in attempting to determine the functionality of the behavior are (1) What level of system is functional (i.e., individual, marital, dyad, etc.)? (2) What is the goal of the system? (3) What is the state of the system? (4) Is it desirable for the system to stay the same or change? (5) At what developmental stage, what point in the life cycle, is the system?

The definition of "healthy" depends on several factors, including, of course, the point of view. These factors include (1) the basic assumptions about the nature of humanity, (2) the discipline from which the evaluation is being made, and (3) consideration of whether the evaluation is to be based on a dimension that actually lies within the field of competency of the evaluator.

According to David (1978), who has presented a cross-cultural consideration of family health, effective problem-solving behavior is very important for healthy families. He has proposed a definition of family health as "a family unit (whatever its concept in any given society), effectively coping with cultural–environmental, psychosocial, and socioeconomic stresses throughout the diverse phases of the family life cycle" (p. 329).

He has used rational fertility behavior as an example of healthy family functioning in his review of the World Health Organization Expert Committee on Mental Health, which recommended involving families in mental health treatment. This committee reported that persistent and handicapping mental disorders affect between 5 per cent and 15 per cent of all children between the ages of three and fifteen and that there are 1.3 billion children in the world under the age of fifteen. In addition, because the aged are increasing in the world population, they represent a new area of concern: How the family adapts to its older members is an important aspect of its functioning.

Coping with stresses is another important and general area of family health. Populations worldwide are moving to urban areas. This shift creates stress from the effects of urban living as well as from the transitions themselves. The WHO emphasized community involvement in mental health, which also includes the training of paraprofessional workers.

Healthy family functioning is based on the awareness of times when choices are needed and available, recognition of alternatives at these times, and the degree to which the choices are based on realistic appraisals of costs and consequences. Effective planning and coping skills become important.

Fogarty (1976) has pointed to the simultaneous occurrence of forces of togetherness and individuality in families. Members of a family and role patterns within dyads contain pursuing and distancing activities and attitudes. Fogarty defines "connectedness" as "the ability to stay in the presence of those people who are closest to you, and keep your level of expectation of them at or near zero" (p. 152). This is an unusual dimension, in that it contains complementary roles designed to work with each other.

Cromwell and Keeney (1978) have proposed a general method of diagnosing both marital and family systems and explained this method as a way of training therapists. They emphasize the importance of systems and of considering the context of behavior and problems, advocating the idea of diagnosis of the system as a whole. This goal is accomplished by first looking at the marital subsystem and then looking at the broader family system.

According to Beavers (1979), families can be considered on a continuum of functioning. He has divided families into three general groups: healthy, adequate (midrange functioning), and dysfunctioning. These groups are described and differentiated by Lewis et al. (1976). According to Beavers, looking at the interaction of the family captures the way in which its members handle both space and time. There is an important analogy between biological boundary phenomena and what goes on between family members. Biological boundaries, such as membranes, control what crosses one structure into another and help to define structures. The interactional boundaries in families perform similar functions and are an important place to focus attention and study. Beavers felt that the oppositional–affiliative dimension is a critical dimension in families. In other words, one needs to consider whether the members look at each other as threats, friends, foes, and so on. This seems based on the assumptions that each has about human nature and about the nature of reality as relative or absolute. Healthy families seem able to handle relative, flexible truth and still have somewhat arbitrary, unbreakable rules. The healthy family also operates on ideas of multiple, circular, and relative causation. Healthy and adequate families showed few differences in the children, although there are no real instruments to discriminate between children without symptoms. According to Beavers, chance can play a role in family functioning, with events outside the family's control sometimes benefiting or harming a family's integrity. Beavers indicates that the individual in the healthy family strives to be heard and to be acknowledged. To have successful experiences, the family can promote or discourage these experiences in important ways for its members.

While the problematic family struggles for coherence, the adequate family struggles for control, and the healthy family struggles for intimacy. This creates a hierarchy of family needs; as families improve in their functioning, they are able to move up this hierarchy in how they strive to improve together.

In the dysfunctional family, repetitive interaction is common, and the family members tend to form an undifferentiated cluster, having little vital interaction with the outside world and allowing very little change in their own world. There is often an invasiveness in relationships, high hostility levels are frequent, there may be rather incongruous myths, and the family has much difficulty coping with change, separation, or loss.

The adequate family shows considerable pain, and interactional skills may be limited. There is a lack of spontaneity; there are frequent oppositional orientations and, sometimes, a strained parental coalition. There may be some confusion in communication and a general mistrusting of feelings, and the family finds growth painful, something to be avoided. The family can be energetic and purposeful, having a predictable structure, with the parents taking pride and comfort in trying to raise their family well. There is a continued and predictable effort in doing a good job. They tend to handle separation and loss by clinging to old images and relationships, recreating lost relationships with others. Beavers makes the point that parents in this type of family may have been raised in families that had difficulties, and they are determined to make it better for their children. Their consistent efforts and firm structure seem to provide basic necessities for their children's growth.

The healthy family is affiliative in its attitudes, showing respect for the world views of other family members. Members show openness and directness, and there is a firm parental coalition. Flexibility is demonstrated in the understanding of human motivations and needs. There is spontaneity in interaction, with family members taking initiative and showing unique, impressive, individual qualities. The family uses clear communication without excessive concern for clarity. There are variations in affective intensity without emphasis on extreme emotional expression. Each family member is seen as capable of contributing, and the family enjoys negotiating. The family welcomes new ideas, and the children have less power but are allowed input. There is a general respect for biological drives, and expressions of intimacy, anger, and sexual feelings are allowed. The family shares values that allow separation, loss, and change to be handled.

French (1977) explains the operation of a family in systems terms. Families are to be understood in terms of their functioning as systems, with certain typical properties. He begins with four basic rules for the functioning of family systems: (1) every member of the family is important and must be considered in the operation of the family; (2) tensions that are not resolved will be later expressed, although perhaps in another form; (3) the family as a system has its own wisdom, and any symptom can be understood if the larger pattern that includes it is understood; and (4) families that solve problems only by balancing them with other problems limit their ability to effectively solve problems in the future. French explains the operation of both homeostatic processes, which serve to maintain a steady state of affairs, and transformational processes, which serve to allow change and adaptation. He identifies four important dimensions of family functioning. The first is anxiety, an obvious measure of stress in the system. French explains that the presence of anxiety is not necessarily unhealthy but does indicate the need for some transformation. The second dimension is the capacity for change, the ability of the family to change its reference points or rules and accommodate itself to new situations. The third dimension is the symptom-carrier role. By this, French refers to the identification of a specific person as the problem, and this identification may vary from one family member to another. The fourth dimension is power. This dimension basically consists of a determination of who controls the assignment and operation of the first three dimensions. The person who decides who gets anxious, who must change, and who will be defined as the problem is considered the power in the family. By using these four dimensions, the family's healthy functioning may be assessed. However, this type of assessment is clearly impressionistic and "clinical" as opposed to empirical (objective-data-based) assessment.

Another model of understanding and classifying families is presented by Kantor and Lehr (1975). They, too, utilize a systems approach and base their approach on clinical observations. There are many dimensions in their theory, leading to a classification of families as open, closed, or random types. Like Beavers, these authors emphasize that much of what characterizes a family takes place in the interface between individuals and subsystems within the family and between the family and its environment. According to Kantor and Lehr, as the family members strive for experience, we can understand them better by looking at the physical aspects of this striving, called access dimensions, and the conceptual aspects, called target dimensions. Family members regulate space, time, and energy in their striving for targets of affect, power, and meaning. By understanding what family members and the family as a system aims for and how it attempts to attain these goals, the family can be understood better. Although it is difficult to imagine how some of the three main classificatory concepts presented by these authors (i.e., open, closed, or random) could be operationalized and measured, they are conceptually interesting.

The *random* family type is dispersed in its use of space, irregular in its use of time, and has widely fluctuating energy. It shows unstable structures, always experimenting with new structures. Its aim seems to be free expression and exploration, and it seeks to be original and create inspiration through its experiences. Individual choices are important, and there is complete laterality in decision making. The family's meaning may be metaphoric and highly individual.

The *closed* family uses fixed space, regular time, and steady energy. It aims for stability across various processes and interactions of the family. It tries to care deeply, but staying in control is of great importance to this type of family. Power is organized vertically, with extensive and clearly stated rules Reasoning is important, and discrimination, clarity, and precision in perception and communication are highly valued. This type seems close to the adequate type described by Beavers (1979).

The *open* family of Kantor and Lehr shows an evolving family structure, with movable, variable time, and flexible energy. The family's aim is to create a dynamic system that can adapt to the needs of both the individual members and the family group. The goal is to share, to be open affectively with each other. Power is handled laterally whenever possible, and parents try to persuade rather than coerce. Opposition is seen as a natural part of decision making. Reasoning, relevance, affinity, and tolerance all have high value. This type seems similar to Beavers's description of healthy families.

Barnhill (1979) has tried to identify dimensions of healthy family functioning, which run through various theoretical conceptions of families, by extracting the following eight continua, two continua for each type of dimension:

Dimensions of Identity

1. *Individuation Versus Enmeshment.* This continuum includes autonomy, independence of judgment versus shared feelings, and shared identity. On one extreme of this continuum is a family that allows independence and individuality; the other extreme is that of a family with unclear boundaries, intrusive interaction, and so on.

2. *Mutuality Versus Isolation.* This continuum includes the ideas of joining, intimacy between individuals as opposed to alienation, and lack of contact between members.

Dimensions of How Change Is Handled

3. *Flexibility Versus Rigidity.* Along this continuum, the family is considered in terms of whether the system is adjustable, resilient, and changeable or whether it responds in stereotyped, repetitive ways.

4. *Stability Versus Disorganization.* Is there a consistent structure in family interaction, or is there a general lack of predictability and consistency?

Dimensions of Information Processing

5. *Clear Versus Unclear or Distorted Perception.* Are there clarified, validated perceptions of shared events or confusing, vague, or distorted perceptions?

6. *Clear Versus Unclear or Distorted Communication.* Along this continuum, one extreme consists of effective exchange of information; the other end includes confusion, paradoxical communication, or injunctions against asking about certain areas.

Dimensions Concerning Structuring of Roles

7. *Role Reciprocity Versus Unclear Roles or Role Conflict.* Are there complementary roles that are agreed upon in interaction or are roles poorly defined or constantly disputed?

8. *Clear Versus Diffuse or Breached Generational Boundaries.* At the one end, each generation is involved more with its own members, parents as executives for the children, and alliances within generations; at the other end, there is a lack of clarity about boundaries, cross-generational alliances, coalitions, and so on.

L'Abate (1976) has provided a conceptualization of the family in its healthy state as a necessary basis of understanding for helping families. Basically, there are two assumptions and three postulates across which the individual in the family as a system may be understood. The first assumption is spatial. In terms of activity, the approach and avoidance patterns of the family members are the most important. This assumption can be understood at four levels. The first is the self-presentational level: the visible, outward appearance presented by the family. The second is the phenotypical level: What is the family like, what are enduring and prolonged actions and interactions like? By observing carefully, approach and avoidance patterns can be determined at this level. The third is the genotypical level: this level provides the explanatory basis for observing behaviors and patterns of behavior. The genotypical level includes considerations of striving for mastery, self-esteem, intimacy, or other inferred concepts. The fourth level is the history and development of each member in the family.

The second assumption is temporal, in which control is considered in terms of patterns of discharge or delay. Controls include awareness, planning, learning, ability to postpone rewards, and so on. The first postulate, and perhaps the most important, is that of self-differentiation. This quality is shared by L'Abate as well as by most other family theorists and therapists (French, 1977). It considers how an individual learns to be clear about himself or herself in terms of (1) distinguishing different emotional states, (2) distinguishing one's own ideas and roles from those of others, (3) being able to agree and disagree clearly, (4) taking control of one's life and taking responsibility for oneself, and (5) asserting oneself in a positive way without hurting oneself and others. In terms of relationships, this characteristic would be distributed along a continuum, with the extremes of autism at one end and symbiosis at the other, sameness and oppositeness toward the center, and similarity and differentness in the center. Change becomes more difficult as one goes from the center toward the extremes.[1]

---

[1] Recently, L'Abate (in press) has proposed an interpersonal revision of this "internal" continuum by combining symbiosis and autism into one style: *apathy,* or extreme passivity and violence; *reactivity,* or *rigid repetitiveness* (combining sameness and oppositeness); and *conductivity,* or creative commitment to change (combining similarity and differentness).

The second postulate is one of priorities. It considers how priorities are balanced in a family in terms of roles, values, rules, resources, and so on. In terms of priorities for a family system, they can be importantly categorized in terms of individual, marital subsystem, and family. How does the family as a group or as individuals establish priorities for their commitments in terms of their space, time, and resources?

The third postulate is one of congruence, and here L'Abate utilizes some of the ideas of Satir (Chapter 4). Congruence is functional communication that is consistent across all channels, both verbal and nonverbal. Incongruent communication is based on low self-worth and the fear of rejection. It includes four typical patterns: blaming, placating, computing, and distracting. L'Abate erected nonverbal tests based on pictures to assess families and, at the same time, test the notions of this theory (Gallope, 1978; Golden, 1974).

L'Abate and L'Abate (1977) also provided a basic classification of marriages, in terms of functioning and in terms of possible interventions. The highest level is that of ideal satisfaction, at which no intervention or possible enrichment activities might be provided. The next level is that of average satisfaction, at which enrichment, retreats, or similar activities (encounters) might be prescribed. The third level is the mildly troubled marriage, which might benefit from enrichment, counseling, or both. The fourth level is the moderately troubled marriage, for which counseling or therapy, possibly in conjunction with enrichment or other helpful experiences, would be recommended. Finally, for the seriously troubled marriage, therapy would be recommended, with additional educational and enrichment experiences and changes in the social environment as needed. Obviously, this categorization would apply equally well to families and might serve as a rough guide for planning intervention.

Family Evaluation

As we shall see, family evaluation is often used as a way of classifying families. For instance, Fisher (1976), in his review of the literature on family assessment, groups evaluation strategies into four types: (1) single-concept notions, such as power, conflict, or conflict resolution; (2) theoretical notions, such as Minuchin's (Chapter 7) or Patterson's (Chapter 10); (3) broadly based clinical lists, as used by Epstein and associates in the McMaster approach (1978); and (4) empirical methods, as in the case of Fisher and Sprenkle (1978).

As Fisher has noted,

Because a theory of family behavior is not yet available, assessment strategies based upon family theory have run into two primary problems. First, they have become somewhat abstract and not easily translatable to the clinical setting in a respectable and uniform manner. Second, the utilization of partial theories for the development of assessment criteria has left us with the problem of linking concept to concept to create an integrated series of procedures. (p. 374)

On the basis of overlap among the various dimensions presented by the various sources he has reviewed, Fisher condenses all of them into a fivefold classification of family assessment dimensions: (1) *structural descriptors* (roles, splits, boundaries, patterns of interaction and communication, rules and norms of relating, conflicts and patterns of resolution, views of life, people, and external world); (2) *controls and sanctions* (power and leadership, flexibility, exercise of control, dependency and interdependency, and differentiation and fusion); (3) *emotions and needs* (methods and rules for affective expression, needs satisfaction through giving and taking, relative importance of needs versus instrumental tasks, dominant affective themes); (4) *cultural aspects* (social position, environmental stresses, cultural heritage, social and cultural views); and (5) *developmental aspects* (appropriateness of structural, affective, and cultural aspects to developmental stage). He then divides these dimensions into two levels. Level A contains cultural (4) and developmental (5) aspects, which serve as context for level B dimensions (1, 2, and 3). the interested reader is encouraged to read this paper to notice the minimum amount of overlap between the sources reviewed by Fisher and the sources reviewed in the present chapter.

Gunthner and Veltkamp (1977) have provided an idea for a scale to be used in assessing family functionality and dysfunctionality. While their dimensions are not operationalized, they are based on the concept of personal responsibility for functioning and behavior. They consider how this personal responsibility contributes to family functioning. The dimensions that they proposed to make up their scale are (1) tasks—how they are performed, (2) scapegoating versus shared responsibility, (3) focus—turned inward or toward the outside, (4) crises—how they are handled, (5) language—what members say about their family and its problems and (6) therapeutic intervention—has this become necessary?

Tseng et al. (1976) have proposed a triaxial family classification based on a systems approach and meant to be used for clinical assessment of families. The authors have argued that a classification system should (1) be comprehensive, systematic, and inclusive enough to encompass any pathology present; (2) be well defined and differentiated so that it can discriminate and differentiate between types; and (3) be clinically oriented, meaningful, and practical.

The first axis is one of family development and the dysfunctions at different stages of family development. This is a longitudinal dimension, in that it considers the family over the course of its life cycle. Along this axis, problems could be at specific points in development—child bearing, child rearing, maturing, or contracting (through death or retirement)—or they could be ongoing or chronic. They also could occur at any time: interruptions in family structure, the creation of a single-parent family, the reconstitution of a family, or as the result of a chronically unstable family.

The second axis considers family interaction and disorders divided by subsystem and is a cross-sectional dimension in that it considers difficulties at some point in time. Problems in this dimension could be in the spouse subsystem, such as excessive, rigid, or complementary roles that are dysfunctional, or they could include problems of conflict, dependency, disengagement, or incompatibility. Problems could be in the parent–child subsystem and could be parent or child related, or they could be in dyadic or triangular interaction. They also could be in the sibling subsystem, including destructive rivalry, coalitions against parents, or lack of differentiation among siblings.

The third axis considers the family group as a system and considers dysfunctions of the entire system. Problems in this axis are problems of structure or function and could include many types of difficulties. Among the difficulties could be under-performance, overstructure, pathological integration, emotional detachment, disorganization, social coping problems, socially isolated families, socially deviant families, or special theme families driven toward the maintenance or attainment of some ideal, myth, or secret in ways that cause problems. The triaxial model is oriented toward pathology; however, it utilizes the general scheme of looking at subsystems and how they fit together and considers the family as a unit moving through time.

Epstein, Bishop, and Lewis (1978) have presented the McMaster model, a comprehensive model of understanding family functioning. It is very much oriented toward including healthy functioning and includes skills that are well described in terms of how they can be taught and how they should work. In this model, the family is seen as an open system. It consists of interlocking subsystems, with the children, the marital dyad, the extended family, work, school, and other settings included. The basic principles are the following systems rules: (1) all parts of the family are related, (2) no part can be understood in isolation, (3) the family is greater than the sum of its parts, (4) the structure and organization of the family shapes the behavior of its members, and (5) patterns of transaction also shape the members' behavior.

Families deal with three types of tasks. These include the basic, everyday tasks related to food and shelter, developmental tasks relating to maturational changes, changing roles as members grow, and hazardous tasks, the crises with which every family must deal at times. The model looks at functioning in terms of problem solving, communication, roles, affective responsiveness, affective involvement, and behavior control. Each dimension is broken down clearly, with descriptions of exactly what is meant by healthy functioning in that dimension and component skills when applicable.

Several examples of the breakdown are given here. The first dimension, problem solving, is broken down as follows: (1) identification of the problem, (2) communication of the problem to appropriate resources both within and outside the family, (3) generation of alternative solutions, (4) making a decision on the alternative to be pursued, (5) acting on that decision, (6) monitoring the action, and (7) evaluating the outcome of the action. Another dimension, that of affective involvement, is broken down more according to a continuum. This dimension, similar to that of L'Abate's (1976) differentiation, consists of (1) lack of involvement, (2) involvement devoid of feelings, (3) narcissistic involvement, (4) empathic involvement, (5) overinvolvement, and (6) symbiotic involvement. Another dimension, that of behavior control, is divided among (1) rigid control, (2) flexible control, (3) laissez-faire operation, and (4) chaotic lack of control.

Reiss's (1979) classification scheme is based on two dimensions of how families solve problems together. By using a standard laboratory problem-solving situation,

Reiss has been able to obtain standard measurements on his two dimensions and then shown some ability to predict the outcomes of hospitalization based on these measurements. The two dimensions are coordination and configuration. Coordination is a measure of how much the problem-solving attempts of members are interwoven in the group effort. Configuration is a measure of how effective the combined efforts are, that is, how productive the joint effort is. The two dimensions each have values of low and high, and, because the measures are not correlated, this independence creates four types of families: consensus sensitive, environment sensitive, achievement sensitive, and distance sensitive. The consensus-sensitive family is high on coordination and low on configuration. Its members tend to stick together, although they don't work productively in this way. The environment-sensitive family is high on both configuration and coordination, and its members stick together and gain from their collective efforts. The achievement-sensitive family is high on configuration and low on coordination and seems to do well, although its efforts are basically competitive. Finally, the distance-sensitive family is low on both coordination and configuration, and it keeps its distance. Consequently, its group effort suffers.

Based on classification of families into these four types, Reiss and his co-workers were able to make predictions about their families in terms of the hospitalization of an adolescent member. These predictions held up to a satisfactory degree. As an additional note, Reiss has reported a dramatic connection between interaction in the family and the quality of the family's support systems. In other words, a connected network, one that was somewhat flexible and not overly involved, was helpful to the family in the long run. Reiss has focused on the problem-solving dimension, as did David (1978), first noticing how families changed, distorted, or ignored instructions for tasks. Next, he tried to look at preconceptions that each family had about what the researchers were looking for. Some families thought the researcher wanted to break their family up and would hear instructions as requiring them to stay together. Next, he began to look for styles of interpretative hypotheses that normal families had and found that there were important similarities.

Riskin (1979) has been conducting a longitudinal study of what he terms non-labeled (i.e., "normal") families to see how the families affect the development of their children. He uses monthly visits with a small sample of families. He has found so far that these families, of course, have their problems but that they seem also to have a strong expectation that they can handle them. He agrees with Lewis et al. (1976) that no single quality defines the healthy family. Even a positive working marriage does not seem necessary, depending on how the marital relationship is handled. He points out in addition that it is very difficult for clinically trained professionals to observe and pick out healthy, functional processes in families.

Olson, Sprenkle, and Russell (1979) have presented a circumplex model of family functioning that they hope will reduce the many assessment dimensions of family functioning to a more manageable scheme. The two major dimensions—cohesion and adaptability—are taken as independent, and each is given four values. For cohesion, these four values are disengaged, separated, connected, and enmeshed. Disengaged and enmeshed are the two extremes of this dimension. For adaptability, the four values are rigid, structured, flexible, and chaotic. Rigid and chaotic are the two extremes of this dimension. The two values are set at right angles to each other, with a zero point in the middle, the moderate values on either side of this point, and the extreme values farther out along the axes. The model then generates sixteen theoretical types of families. The four closest to the center are the most moderate in functioning, as in the open-family type of Kantor and Lehr (1975). The four types that are farthest from the center are the most dysfunctional and are similar theoretically to the random family of Kantor and Lehr. The eight types that are midway from the center are midrange in functioning and correspond to the adequate families of Beavers (1979) or the closed type of Kantor and Lehr. The open types are flexibly separated, flexibly connected, structurally separated, and structurally connected. The random types are chaotically disengaged, chaotically enmeshed, rigidly disengaged, and rigidly enmeshed. The closed types are the remaining eight combinations, although the authors assume that these eight types would occur less often, as families extreme on either dimension would tend to also be extreme on the other.

Cohesion consists of the emotional connectedness between members as well as the autonomy or lack of autonomy experienced by individuals within the family. This dimension bears a great deal of resemblance to L'Abate's (1976) differentiation. Adaptability as a dimension tries to capture the systems concepts of negative and positive feedback. It is defined as the ability of the family to adjust flexibly to roles, power relationships, and rules, in response to the stress of situations or natural developments. This dimension bears a great deal of resemblance to L'Abate's (1976) priorities. Cohesion as a dimension considers how the following concepts are handled in the family: independence, family boundaries, coalitions, time, space, friends, decision making, and interests and recreation. The cohesion dimension captures similar concepts by many family theorists and therapists. These include the differentiated self and undifferentiated ego mass of Bowen (Chapter 9), disengagement and enmeshment of Minuchin (Chapter 7), low connectedness and high connectedness of Olson, interpersonal distance-sensitive and consensus-sensitive types of Reiss (1979) centrifugal force and centripetal force of Stierlin (1974), as well as others.

Adaptability includes the concepts of assertiveness, control, discipline, negotiation, roles, rules, and system feedback. This dimension related to the systems concepts of morphogenesis and morphostasis, Haley's (Chapter 6) and D. D. Jackson's (1968) extension of family homeostatic mechanisms, as well as the induced morphogenesis, consensual morphostasis, and forced morphostasis of Wertheim (1973).

Olson et al. (1979) have developed an instrument that allows families to be assessed and assigned to a position in the circumplex model. In addition to the two main dimensions, they are also assessed on two additional "facilitative" dimensions, support and creativity. While functional families are assumed to be in the moderate area of the circumplex model, high values on the dimensions of family support and creativity are also seen as important. They are considered necessary but insufficient in themselves for healthy functioning. The instrument, a self-report inventory called FACES, divides the families into the sixteen types created in the model. It has been empirically developed and tested on a limited basis. From self-report inventories, families or couples accumulate total scores on the two dimensions, and these scores are used to assign families into types. The instrument has no interactional component and creates only a composite of the self-reported observations of family members.

However, an empirical evaluation of the model was performed by Russell (1979), who used a simulated family interaction game (SIMFAM), as well as self-report inventories. He looked at family functioning in terms of how families handled situational and developmental crises. The two main and two facilitative dimensions of the circumplex model were operationally defined. This evaluation was compared with difficulties that the families had experienced in their handling of their adolescent daughters. Difficulties were associated with the more extreme family types, whereas higher functioning was associated with more moderately functioning types of families. The facilitative dimensions were also shown to be linked to higher functioning.

As the reader, no doubt, has observed, most definitions of functional families include ways of defining dysfunctional families. Nonetheless, differentiating functional from nonfunctional or dysfunctional families may still be difficult. Most of the previous classifications were quite abstract, possibly readily visible to an experienced family therapist. The beginning student, however, may have some difficulty pinning down the how, what, and why of this distinction, and additional evidence may be necessary.

Differentiating Functional from Dysfunctional Families

In addition to the previous classifications, which were based on categories using content, it is possible to categorize families according to content-free categories, such as degrees of variability, degrees of apathy, reactivity, or conductivity, and speed of information processing and decision making. Although ideally these categories should be as independent from each other as possible, they are very likely interrelated.

Variability. It is likely that the greater the functionality, the greater the freedom of expression and the range of spontaneous, often creative, options available in a constructing fashion. By the same token, the greater the degree of dysfunctionality, the greater the likelihood of contradictions, role reversals, denials, and doing and undoing present *without awareness* of the destructive implications of such behaviors; that is, rigid patterns may give way to chaotic reactions, and chaotic reactions may become stereotyped and repetitive patterns of behavior. Hall (1976) has differentiated between open (healthy?) families systems, which are less sensitive to aging, and closed family systems, which are more symptomatic as aging takes place: (1) flexible versus rigid relationships, (2) few versus many cutoffs, (3) person-to-person versus distance, (4) high versus low functionality, (5) few versus many crises, (6) effective versus little coping, and (7) speedy versus dubious recoveries.

As Golden (1974) found in her study, variability in task choices was the major discriminating variable between functional and dysfunctional families (the more the dysfunctionality the greater the variability). This finding has been followed up more systematically by Gallope (1979).

Apathetic and Reactive Versus Conductive Styles. The Beels and Ferber (1969) subdivision of therapists into reactors and conductors can be applied to families as well. Most functional families fall within the category of *conductors,* in the sense of taking charge of and responsibility for their lives, planning with a temporal perspective that foresees the possible traumas and stresses that are inevitable in the family life process. Conductive families are actively involved in working and doing something to be *on top* of life's stresses. Apathetic families, on the other hand, on the more dysfunctional side of the continuum, do not seem to possess this quality. They live day by day, chaotically, without plans, preparations, or procedures that would indicate the presence of a temporal perspective. There is very little preparation for meeting possible crises and stresses that are forthcoming. They resist change. Apathetic families seem to be the recipients and the victims of life's "hard luck" without awareness of preventive measures and alternative courses of action. Between these two extremes, there are reactive families, who rigidly repeat rebuttals, recriminations, and revenges against each other, without change (L'Abate, in press).

Speed of Information Processing. Most of the studies on patterns of decision making (Haley, 1976) suggest that most functional families reach decisions faster than do dysfunctional families who are hampered in their decision making by irrelevant interferences, conflictual patterns of decision making, and lapses in leadership, modeling, and agreements. Some of these patterns have been highlighted by Gantman's (1978) research. She has found that families of normal adolescents differ from families of disturbed and drug-abusive teenagers in frequency of scapegoating of the adolescent and ability to reach decisions. Normal families scapegoat less and reach decisions faster than do the disturbed groups of families. In addition, normal families show clear communication, more freedom of expression, more cooperation, and greater sensitivity among members. In other words, her conclusions tend to substantiate the findings of Beavers et al. (1976).

Issues in Classifications of Families

Unfortunately, many of the classifications reviewed here lack empirical and/or clinical verification or consensus from different sources, making them speculative and suggestive at best. One important issue of classification is *measurement,* that is, by which criteria shall *any* dimension be assessed? The answers, of course, would seem to be by as many criteria as are humanly and clinically possible. The issue then becomes one of *efficient, effective,* and *ethical* assessment. But, can classification occur without evaluation? And, if evaluation is to take place, how is it going to take place? Impressionistically? Objectively? Qualitatively? Quantitatively?

Most issues of classification are issues of finding consensual agreement among family therapists concerning the criteria that make for a functional or dysfunctional family. This consensual agreement was the focus of a study by Fisher and Sprenkle

(1978) who, through a questionnaire, asked a representative sample of family therapists (N = 310) to select and rank, in order of importance, the various items that would make for functionality in a family. Essentially, their conclusions paralleled those already reviewed in previous pages. A healthy family is defined by members who feel valued, supported, and safe with other family members. They can express themselves openly without fear of judgment, knowing that their opinions and feelings will be acknowledged. Negotiation is used as a basis for change (communication, cohesion, and adaptability).

Conclusion

This chapter has reviewed efforts to understand and differentiate among degrees of functionality in families. It has summarized the efforts of researchers and theorists who have chosen to concentrate either on functionality or on pathology. It is important to understand what might go right in families, how it is that so many families are able to meet the incredible stresses and problems they are faced with, and how healthy individuals are able to grow up in them.

We agree with Olson et al. (1979) that a dimension with functionality at one hand and dysfunctionality at the other fails to encompass various types and degree of functionality and dysfunctionality (L'Abate, 1976). Consequently, we would like to suggest a continuum wherein dysfunctionality would be found at the extremes and functionality would be found in the middle. As a result, we would have a frequency distribution with optimal or creative families at the top in the middle, healthy adequate families on both sides, and dysfunctional families at the extremes, like this:

Integrated
Optimally Conductive
Conforming Adequate-Adequate Nonconforming
Compliant-Reactive-Oppositional
Symbiotic Dysfunctional-Apathetic-Autistic Dysfunctional

However, once this continuum is presented, one would need to define the dimensions that would make up such a frequency distribution. A continuum of differentiation (L'Abate, 1976), defined by spatial (approach–avoidance) and temporal (discharge–delay) dimensions, may permit a more verifiable classification than has been possible heretofore. Some of these issues will be reconsidered at the end of this book.

References

Barnhill, L. R. 1979. Healthy family systems. *The Family Coordinator* 28:94–100.
Beavers, W. 1977. *Psychotherapy and growth: A family systems perspective.* New York: Brunner/Mazel.

Beels, C. L., and Ferber, A. 1969. Family therapy: A review. *Family Process* 8:280–318.

Cromwell, R. E., and Keeney, B. P. 1979. Diagnosing marital and family systems: A training model. *The Family Coordinator* 28:101–108.

Davenport, Y. B.; Adland, M. L.; Gold, P. W.; and Goodwin, F. K. 1979. Manic-depressive illness: Psychodynamic features of multigenerational families. *American Journal of Orthopsychiatry* 49:24–35.

David, H. P. 1978. Healthy family functioning: A non-cultural appraisal. *Bulletin of the World Health Organization* 56:327–342.

Epstein, N. B.; Bishop, D. S.; and Lewis, J. 1978. The McMaster model of family functioning. *Journal of Marriage and Family Counseling* 4:19–31.

Fisher, B. L., and Sprenkle, D. H. 1978. Therapists' perceptions of healthy family functioning. *International Journal of Family Counseling* 6:9–18.

Fisher, L. 1976. Dimensions of family assessment: A critical review. *Journal of Marriage and Family Counseling* 2:367–382.

——. 1977. On the classification of families: A progress report. *Archives of General Psychiatry* 34:424–433.

Fogarty, T. H. 1976. System concepts and the dimensions of self. In *Family therapy: Theory and practice,* ed. P. J. Guerin, pp. 144–155. New York: Gardner Press.

French, P. 1977. *Disturbed children and their families: Innovations in evaluation and treatment.* New York: Human Sciences Press.

Gallope, R. A. 1979. *Test profile variabilities within families and their relationship to family disturbance.* Ph.D. dissertation, Georgia State University, Atlanta, Georgia.

Gantman, C. A. 1978. Family interaction patterns among families with normal, disturbed and drug-abusive adolescents. *Journal of Youth and Adolescence.* 7:429–440.

Golden, R. P. 1974. *A validation study of the family assessment battery.* Ph.D. dissertation, Georgia State University, Atlanta; Georgia.

Gunthner, R. W., and Veltkamp, L. T. 1977. A scale for assessing family dysfunction-function. *International Journal of Family Counseling* 5:79–85.

Haley, J. 1976. *Problem-solving therapy.* San Francisco: Jossey-Bass.

Hall, C. M. 1976. Aging and family processes. *Journal of Family Counseling* 4:28–42.

Jackson, D. D. 1968. *Communication, family, and marriage.* Palo Alto, Calif.: Science and Behavior Books.

Justice, B., and Justice, R. 1976. *The abusing family.* New York: Human Sciences Press.

Kantor, D., and Lehr, W. 1975. *Inside the family. Toward a theory of family process.* New York: Harper Colophon Books.

L'Abate, L. 1976. *Understanding and helping the individual in the family.* New York: Grune & Stratton.

——. 1980. *Styles in intimate relationships: The A-R-C model,* in press.

——, and L'Abate, B. 1977. *How to avoid divorce: Help for troubled marriages.* Atlanta: John Knox Press.

Lewis, J. M.; Beavers, W. R.; Gossett, J. T.; and Phillips, V. A. 1976. *No single thread: Psychological health in family systems.* New York: Brunner/Mazel.

Olson, D. H.; Sprenkle, D. H.; and Russell, C. S. 1979. Circumplex model of marital and family systems: Cohesion and adaptability dimensions, family types, and clinical applications. *Family Process* 18:3–29.

Price, D. A. 1979. Normal, functional, and unhealthy. *The Family Coordinator* 28:107–114.

Reiss, D. 1959. *Research on normal family process.* A Panel at the 56th Annual Meeting of the American Orthopsychiatric Association, Washington, D.C., 1979.

Riskin, J. 1979. *Research on normal family process.* A Panel at the 56th Annual Meeting of the American Orthopsychiatric Association, Washington, D.C., 1979.

Russell, C. 1979. Circumplex model of family systems: 3. Empiral evaluation with families. *Family Process* 18:29–47.

Stierlin, H. 1974. *Separating parents and adolescents.* New York: Quadrangle.

Tseng, Wen-shing et al. 1976. Family diagnosis and classification. *Journal of the American Academy of Child Psychiatry* 15:15–35.

Wertheim, E. S. 1973. Family unit therapy and the science and typology of family systems. *Family Process* 12:361–376.

3

The Family Therapy of Nathan W. Ackerman

Nathan W. Ackerman is probably the most widely known pioneer of family therapy. He was trained in a traditional program as a psychoanalyst and was a child psychiatrist. Even so, he was strongly influenced by social psychology, believing that one could not treat the patient in a vacuum but must consider both the social environment and the biological heredity from which the client's personality was formed. From a Freudian psychology that saw friends and family of the client as hindrances to psychoanalysis and as contaminating and imbalancing agents to the therapy, Ackerman realized a need for the inclusion of friends and family in treating the broader spectrum of human interactions and relationships.

Ackerman was trained in the old school and respected previous theories, but he realized a need for new ideas and thoughts. He was able to successfully bridge from the old theory to new theories. He avoided becoming a radical by adding to older ideologies. He was able to seek change from the almost exclusively intrapersonal therapy exploration to a therapeutic approach that was more interpsychic in orientation.

Although family therapy did not move toward prominence until after 1950, Ackerman published a paper on the family as a social and emotional unit in 1937. He had an early interest in nonpsychotic disorders in children and the effects of the family environment. He was also interested in the effects of economic hardship on families. Ackerman remained a practicing therapist who also trained others. About 1960 he founded the Family Institute in New York. It provided a place to work and teach as well as a low-cost clinic. After his death it was renamed the Ackerman Family Institute.

In 1962 he and Don Jackson joined to produce *Family Process*, the first journal in the field. Although he was a psychoanalyst and remained influenced by that tradition, Ackerman's individual thoughts were reflected in his approach and influence in family therapy.

Ackerman saw an historical emphasis on family roles in psychoanalysis; therefore, there was an historical need for a type of family therapy, a way of encompassing the phenomena of the relations of personality and social role adaptation. In psychotherapy the family is often considered in the study of a child's behavior problems, but the family is seldom considered in treating an adult. Children's behavior often reflects family homeostasis, but psychoanalyists tend to treat the adult as very separate from family influences. Instead, Ackerman found that the family was a unit in itself and, therefore, a dynamic, ever-changing organism deserving study and treatment. He successfully argued that psychoanalysis is a more specific form of treatment but that there was also a need for an approach to problems in a broader spectrum of human relations and interactions—family therapy.

Often it is found that when an individual enters into personal therapy there is a worsening of family relationships. The individual may be changing his or her behaviors or attitudes but the social group with which the individual must live does not adapt to support those changes. Where individual therapy attempts to work from the inside of the patient to his or her outside world, family therapy attempts to work from the outside world to the inside. Individual psychotherapy seems more limited in scope, too much within the individual, and it therefore often fails to consider the total integration and organization with the society or group. Therefore, individual psychoanalysis is not truly adaptive to all individual needs. Because the primary group into which one's functions of personality are integrated, Ackerman felt that therapy must involve the total family.

Problems within the family are a normal part of the living process. The constant interchange between the individual, the family, and the social world creates the problems and conflicts. Conflicts within the family produce a distorted balance of the role relationships. A family may react to a new situation with rigidity or with fluidity; it may cling to the old or try the new; it may accept a narrow or a wide stance. The healthier family will be able to avoid the extremes of overreaction; it will accept some old role attitudes and will also try some new ones.

Conflict is a necessary process of living, and the epitome of conflict is found in the family. Conflict and how it is handled is the molding force of families. It can be paralytic or catalytic. It can enhance family and individual growth or it can distort growth. It is the functional expression of what the family is or ought to be, how it may or may not serve the members, or how it may and may not fortify their role adaptations within the whole society. Conflict within the family comes at multiple levels. It is circular in that a conflict within one family member affects the other members and ultimately the community. Some of the conflicts are totally within an individual member, some are within the family group or a part of the family, and some are between family members and society.

The concept of treating the family as a unit of mental health and the unit of diagnosis has threatened some analysts and their belief in working in a one-to-one relationship. Family therapy depends upon the therapist's being able to diagnose and treat several people at one time, bringing balance of family role relationships and encouraging the trying of new ways of interacting within the family and society.

Ackerman's theory of family therapy developed new paths for prevention and treatment of individual and group disturbances. It is, as Ackerman projected it, the product of cultural anthropology with group dynamics and communications; it is the link between the social sciences and psychoanalysis, ego psychology and child development. He felt that the family and treatment of the whole unit held implications for future culture change, behavior theory, and the ever-changing ideology of psychoanalysis and psychotherapy.

The Concept of the Family

The family is the oldest and most important human institution. Each person is considered to belong to two families. A person is born into his or her first family and that person establishes the second. A marriage is the beginning of the family cycle, but the first family is never without lasting influence. There is no starting or stopping the family process.

The family exists as the key unit of society. The most basic purpose of the family must be to mate, have children, and survive. In many primitive societies, survival is the only function of the family unit. The purpose of mating is to mold the identities of two people into a family pair that still allows for individual growth as well as for a family group identity. The purpose for the couple is then to create and protect the children, helping them to develop from total dependence to an independent state. The children are educated from being the center of the family to being on the periphery and eventually setting up their own family units. In more progressive societies, where there is time and energy for more complicated behaviors, the family meets the needs of building the humaneness of the people involved. This includes the purposes of economic survival, meeting psychological needs, serving as an exchange medium for affection and material needs, and training for social roles and participation in the community. Many of these purposes of the family are contained totally within the family; some include the family within society; each purpose involves the individual (1958).

The key to Ackerman's theory seems to be the concept of social role, which reflects the influence by Kurt Lewin. Role concepts enabled him to describe a more than two-person system or a plurality of transactions. The concept emphasizes the importance of reciprocal or complementary roles in the family. Unless roles are delineated and understood, interactions among family members will generate conflict. Role complementarity is particularly important for a well-functioning family and society. The family as well as the individual changes when the concept of self has changed. The adapting of one's personality takes place in daily living, and the major source of role influence comes from the immediate environment and the heredity of the family. One's social roles becomes one's social self. Ackerman differentiated three parts to a person's psychiatric illness: interactions within the person, those between the person and his or her family group, and those between the family group and the larger society.

There are two central concepts that Ackerman used to operationally define the dynamics of family life. The first concept is one of psychological identity, which includes the family's strivings, expectations and values. It is the "Who are we?" that each family must ask itself. Psychiatric identity helps the family explain itself. Ackerman saw each family member's identity as being interwoven with that of the family unit. Although the therapist can treat both the individual and the family, diagnostically the therapist must diagnose them together as a unit. Ackerman wrote, "The image of self and image of family are reciprocally interdependent. At each stage of development, personal identity is linked to and differentiated from the identity of parents and family in a special way" (1958, p. 85).

The second concept central to family therapy is the stability of behavior. It cannot be totally removed from psychological identity but must be studied as interrelated. Ackerman claimed that the family will try to keep to expected behaviors during a conflict, but the family must also look for new solutions to conflict situations and new ways of growing.

To have family stability there is an essential need for flexibility and adaptability in role relations. Role relations must allow for change and growth and form a sense of a shared family identity. If allowance is not made for change and growth in roles or if there is basic disagreement over roles within the family, there will be conflicts. Ackerman's philosophy of the interrelations between the individual family member and his family is presented in Figure 3-1.

The boundaries of the family are in constant change. In today's complex society, who to include as a family member and who not to include depends on the intent and the needs of the family therapy. When treating a family, Ackerman believed that one must have a rubber fence around the family. If the parents and children give the necessary, precise data, then that family group is the unit of treatment. Sometimes grandparents, divorced parents, and live-in parents are also involved in a

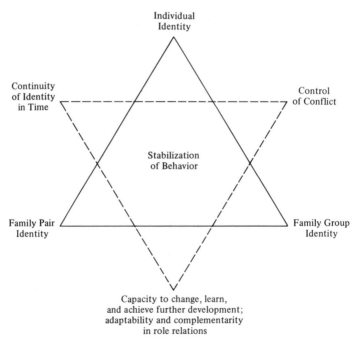

Figure 3-1. Interrelations Between Individual Family Member and His Family. (*Source:* Nathan W. Ackerman, *The Psychodynamics of Family Life.* New York: Basic Books, p. 87.)

family conflict, and the therapist must determine where to draw the relevant boundary for therapeutic purposes. Creating a new role complementarity to solve a conflict must involve the active participation of all those involved.

Ackerman believed in the need for family balance or homeostasis. If a conflict disrupts the equilibrium of the family, it is the purpose of the family, or when necessary, the therapist, to restore the balance. While homeostasis generally refers to the quality of equilibrium or staying the same, Ackerman chose to note the need for change within the family dynamics. His preference was that the family not return to the status quo but seek a new level of balance or complementarity of roles. This concept of homeostasis acts as a principle that allows for change; it is dynamic rather than static. He conceived an interaction within the social unit of the family that had the capacity for creative adaptability to change, which at the same time had enough coordinated control to prevent the individual or the family from being overwhelmed. Therefore, each change in an individual would modify the role complementarity within the family and push them to establish a new balance or homeostasis. Failure to establish new satisfactory role complementarity would lead to family problems.

Family Problems

The major conflicts in the family are characterized by a unique life cycle. From the beginning a family grows together from two separate families. As the couple matures it forms changes that at first are slow and then are more rapid. Eventually the family begins a sequence of crises. How the family grows from the changes in roles is critical to the family's health. For a family to maintain equilibrium, it must weather each crisis and regain its composure, but it must move forward with a potential for change or lose its vibrancy.

How does the family change? The members must shift the balance of roles. They do this by learning to relate to each other in new ways. They can also change by examining their value system and by deciding to make necessary changes. Change itself can be a decline or a growth process and does not necessarily involve conflict. How the family and individuals deal with change and the shifting balance within the family determines the amount of conflict that will be manifest. Some family conflicts are temporary and can enrich and mature the family. If there is severe, prolonged conflict, the tendency is toward alienation within the family and progressive damage to the family unit (1966).

Ackerman believed there is no such clear clinical distinction between a mentally healthy and a sick family. He viewed the family as a carrier of elements that include mental health and mental illness. Ackerman considered sick families as those that progressively failed to carry out their essential family functions. He graded the amount of failure within a family according to the following levels at which the family deals with its problems.

1. The family confronts, accurately defines, and achieves a realistic solution of its problems.
2. Though unable to achieve a realistic solution, the family can nevertheless

contain the problem and control the potentially anxious effects, while giving itself a longer period within which to find a solution.

3. Unable to find an effective solution or to contain the destructive effects of conflict, the family responds to the tension of failure with an "acting out" pattern of impulsive, ill-judged, self-defeating, harmful behavior. Sometimes the family as a group seeks a scapegoat, either within the family or outside. In this condition the family as family cannot long maintain its defenses.

4. With persistent failure at the preceding three levels, the family shows increasing signs of emotional disintegration, which in some circumstances may culminate in disorganization of family ties. (1958, pp. 99–100)

Ackerman perceived the manifestations of family illness or breakdown as (1) showing indications of emotional alientation or isolation of the family members from each other, (2) building up of critical barriers of communication, (3) emerging of family factions and splits, (4) demoralizing of the family, and (5) failing of the family to fulfill minimum functions.

The family values and identity are in constant change. This structural involvement is influenced by extended and immediate family members as well as by present and past generations. The family identity is also influenced by the needs of the individual members and the needs of the total community. In addition, the family values and identity are molded by society's changing goals. Role complementarity expresses in action the implicit identity and value orientation of each family. When there is a family breakdown, there is a failure in the complementarity of individual members.

Ackerman supported Spiegel's (1957) five causes of failure of complementarity in the family: (1) cognitive discrepancy—not knowing what is required, (2) goal discrepancy—having different goals, (3) allocative discrepancy—being the victim because of age or sex, (4) instrumental discrepancy—not having what is needed such as money, and (5) value orientation discrepancy—having different values. When the family has a problem it will fall in one of these categories. Conflicts in some areas are more difficult to work with than others, but when the family settles on a point of complementarity it can function in a healthier climate. Ackerman claimed that the growth of a family is determined by its control of conflict. If controls fail the family will cling to old ways and become very rigid in its behavior. One can judge a family's coping and adapting by looking at its fulfillment of aims and goals, its regulation of necessary tasks, and its resulting mental and physical health.

When a conflict within a family becomes overwhelming and therapeutic help is wanted, the problem within the family may appear localized. The family has often identified a specific failure in one member's role or the family may not even be aware of a specific problem. The weakest member of the family often is used as a scout for therapeutic assistance. Ackerman referred to this person, the first family member to seek help, as a symptom of disturbed family homeostasis. He found that there was seldom a case of an isolated psychiatric illness in family life because usually more than one member of the family is sick. The sick behaviors reinforce each other, and the family becomes a carrier of emotional disturbance. If one member of the family is emotionally ill, the other members of the family will have the same illness, have a complementary illness, or have a severe clash with the ill member.

No one person can totally and accurately perceive problems within a family and implement effective controls. That is the role of a family interaction. The whole family with the therapist must work together to seek conflict solutions. Evaluating what happens within and without the family as well as between individuals and within the individuals is a major task for all involved in the family therapy. Often a family comes to therapy seeking help for a specific problem. As therapy unleashes defenses, the roots of the problems begin to appear. The family is, was, and always will be a vibrant, open system; therefore, the family's problems and conflicts will be very complex to diagnose. There is an interdependence between the individual defenses and the family's patterns of control and stabilization. The problems will continue to create imbalance within the family; but with creative family therapy the family can be given tools for gaining its own equilibrium through the understanding of complementarity of roles.

Therapeutic Goals

The purpose of family therapy, according to Ackerman, is to evaluate and treat a system of interacting personalities. Family therapy must strive to correlate the inner workings of the individual and the family with the outside community. The therapist must attempt to compare and integrate all elements of cause for specific behaviors and conflicts. The family therapist must diagnose the cause for family upheaval and then conceptualize a therapeutic approach to join the individual, the family, and the environment.

Ackerman listed six specific aims of family therapy with respect to treating family conflict (1961). The first goal is to help the family achieve a clearer and sharper definition of the real content of conflict. This is accomplished by dissolving the disguises of conflict and resulting confusions in family relationships. This should provide a greater accuracy of perception of family conflict. Often a family will seek therapy really not knowing the source of conflict. The family is in a state of unbalance and needs first to define the problem before seeking solutions. The therapist must take the dynamics used in the family and build on them to gain information and increase communication about the problem.

A second goal listed by Ackerman is to energize dormant interpersonal conflicts, bringing them overtly into the live processes of family interaction, thereby making them accessible to solution. Sometimes the conflict has been hidden for so long that the source of the problem is totally buried. Family members may have failed to communicate their feelings until it is necessary for the situation to explode. If the family unconsciously or consciously has not reached a point of complementarity, the unit will be unable to seek solutions to problems within the family.

Ackerman's third goal is to lift concealed intrapsychic conflict to the level of interpersonal relations, where it may be coped with more effectively. It is known from individual therapy that the family member who seeks an individual therapy often finds that other members in the family change. If one person enters therapy, often other members of the family will become involved in the experience. In other words, there is a reciprocity of behavior in therapy; if one family member is treated, it will affect the rest of the family group. For this reason Ackerman felt that it is of central importance to remove the source of conflict from one member to the family unit. This removes the conflict from being the sole responsibility of the individual to being a shared issue within the family.

Ackerman's fourth and fifth goals are somewhat related. The fourth goal is to counteract inappropriate displacements of conflict; the fifth is to neutralize the irrational prejudices and scapegoating that are involved in the displacement of conflict. The goal is to put the conflict back where it came from in family relations, to reattach it to its original source, and to attempt to work it out there. This will also counteract the trend toward prejudicial assault and disparagement of any one member. This should relieve the excessive burden of conflict on one victimized part of the family and ease the load on the family member who fulfills the role of family healer. Ackerman seems to have felt that conflict displacement and scapegoating were the most common methods used in families when there was not adequate conflict resolution. A weaker member of the family might be scapegoated so that other family members could hide the real problem or source of the problem. Until the family realizes that it is using this method to avoid the real source of conflict, there can be no real resolution.

Ackerman's first five goals for family therapy deal with dissolving family conflicts and fears by getting them out in the open. Family members must be free to express honest emotions and must be able to understand others' feelings and attitudes. Ackerman's final goal deals with promoting the family and therapist's forces and abilities toward positive emotional health and to activate an improved level of complementarity in family role relations.

The therapist must work hard to make the outcome of family therapy the responsibility of the family, not the therapist. The therapist must encourage honest emotions and the flexibility of roles. Family members must not be too rigid and unchanging, and they must not be too fluid and run over by others. The therapist must help the family to create a new way of living where there is improved communication but also a change in family and individual members' attitudes. It is not enough to rid the family of a particular conflict, but the therapy must help the family face future conflicts by adjusting personality and behaviors. Family members come to therapy wanting to dissolve a particular family conflict or fear, but therapy must use the positive forces of the family to work toward a better level of emotional health.

History Taking

Family intervention must start with a meeting of the therapist and the family to give the therapist the pertinent information surrounding the problem or conflict. The history-taking process offers a unique challenge to the therapist. The therapist must gather accurate information, put members in a position of not being threatened too much, and give the family hope for resolution of the problem. By necessity the whole family must be included in this session. Often a family will bring only the child it has identified as having the problem. It is also important to determine the boundaries of the family for problem solving. Ackerman stated that all members who live at the same address must certainly be included, but it may be necessary for significant others such as grandparents, close friends or neighbors, or former family members to be included as well.

Although there has generally been a previous meeting between the therapist and at least one member of the family, it is best to begin the family intervention process with fresh information. Some facts may have been gathered in the previous meeting, but all relevant historical data should be elicited from the group. Often the group will present the information more accurately. Family members can validate information and disclosures from each other. What one person leaves out of his or her data another person can reveal. Often parents will hide certain details and the children will expose those details. What one member twists or distorts can be corrected by another. Young children's additions or responses are important ways of reality testing the parents' descriptions.

If the family comes to therapy in pain, it is often unable to explain exactly what is wrong. Members are confused and baffled, and they cannot put their finger on the problem let alone resolve the conflict. When the family anxiety exceeds the critical threshold, there is a silent pact against disclosure of any conflict related material. Eventually and with patience on the part of the therapist, collective denials emerge. The closely guarded privacy of the family will eventually accept the addition of the therapist. Of course, there is the extreme of unhealthy privacy, but in general most necessary information for a complete family history can be gathered through an initial interview. The therapist must help to determine what should be kept private and what should come into the open. Ackerman thought that the clinician must be the catalyst and coax out important data. He or she must prod for more information. The history of the family is the basis for diagnosing the family and later treating the family.

The therapist must help the family to determine or understand what is wrong within that group and help to select possible solutions for correcting it. The clinician must relate to all members of the family, not just to the parents or to the one brought in as the "sick" member. Adult responses, both verbal and nonverbal, are often strained and filled with double meaning. Ackerman was particularly keen on nonverbal clues. It is up to the therapist to determine the realistic history of the family by utilizing comments and cues from all members.

The development of the history-taking session will set the tone for future work sessions. The information gathered at this session will answer many questions and help the therapist to fill in an elaborate outline necessary for diagnosis. Often during this session parents have more real fears than the children. They know that there is something wrong and they are the ones who have arranged the therapy while the children are generally just brought. The therapist must support the parents as much as possible during the history taking, but the therapist must not ignore the children and must make them feel that their additions are important to the family history.

Diagnosis

Diagnosis is a complex process that must include diagnosing both the individual members and the family as a group, with attention given to roles and interrelationships. Ackerman believed that to diagnose is to "distinguish by knowing" (Ackerman and Behrens, 1974, p. 37). The therapist must acquire a "knowing" by exploring interviews with the family and seeing into and feeling with the family.

The diagnosis is not a constant but changes as pieces of theory are tested, amended, and verified. Ackerman subscribed to a stage-by-stage, not static, development of diagnosis. He believed that diagnosis and therapy are parallel functions but interdependent.

Ackerman perceived diagnosis as a guide for action or a strategy for therapeutic intervention. The therapist's major task is to establish a dynamic relation between the balancing forces. This is done by observing, conceptualizing, and interpreting for the family. Ackerman was disenchanted with the medical model of diagnosis. He felt that the medical model was passé, useless in family therapy and even harmful to the family. He felt a bias against labeling people and families with illnesses. Instead, he sought an ecological perspective that included changing behavior theory, changing therapeutic processes, and changing beliefs about mental illness and its causes.

Ackerman incorporated into his "manner of inquiry" the needs for better methods of clinically oriented family diagnosis that would explore the contagion and spread of family problems. He felt a need for wider interpretation of disorder or illness in the family that would expose clusters of disturbances that are interdependent, interacting, and emerging in a series across time. Ackerman believed that even in individual therapy the diagnosis of an individual will be assisted by placing the individual problems within the matrix of the family as a behavior system.

In brief, Ackerman believed that family diagnosis begins with a clinical hunch, an intuitive fragment of theory. Gradually the therapist must move to a more formal, explicit, systematic diagnostic judgment, a shift by progressive stages from a subjective toward a more objective formulation. The use of more than one observer or therapist facilitates this process (Ackerman and Behrens, 1974).

In family therapy, the therapist makes instant observations of appearance, mood, and the behavior of members and their integration into family roles. The therapist observes the manner of entry into a room, seating arrangements, who speaks, openness of members to change, general attitudes, and who wants to actively participate or retreat. Once the therapist has developed a rapport with the family and has given them hope for something better, he or she works at catalyzing interchange of conflict-loaded materials. The therapist supports the family in exposing its secrets and conflicts. The therapist must then formulate a "hunch" and zero in on the most destructive level of conflict that is that relationship that generates the most extreme anxiety.

The therapist's "tickling" of the defenses will involve individuals' sharing, supporting, slashing, and destroying former beliefs about individuals, the family, the society, and even the therapist. The quest for relevant facts should move from the whole family toward differing subgroups, to the cluster of conflicts, and eventually to the labeled primary patient. In this process, the therapist must be quick to judge the relative severity of the disturbance and the family's ability to cope and change.

From the initial family interviews, the diagnosis will identify or classify family types according to potentials of health and growth and take into account the ability of the family group and the individuals to change. Ackerman's criteria for family diagnosis includes (1) the most destructive foci of conflict, (2) the typical family role relationships and patterns of complementarity, (3) fulfillment, harmonization, and balancing of family functions, (4) identity, stability, value, and growth, and (5) evaluation of the family's capacity for change and growth: discrepancy between actual performance of family and a theoretical model of a healthy family (Ackerman and Behrens, 1974).

The Most Destructive Foci of Conflict

Ackerman claimed the most destructive foci of conflict are the contagious anxiety, the alignment and splits within the family, and the coping patterns of individuals and the family. The first task in diagnosis is to determine the most destructive levels of conflict. It is the major purpose of the therapist to help the family control conflict, first, between the family and the community, second, between members of the family, and, third, within the individual members of the family.

Ackerman believed that there are levels of controlling conflict within the family. First, the family must perceive the conflict and seek an early resolution. Second, the family must see the conflict and attempt to solve the problem. Third, the family may misperceive the conflict. Fourth, the conflict is not controlled and there is disruption of the family complementarity. For a family to effectively control a conflict, it must first perceive the problem.

Ackerman characterized several types of family conflict as being appropriate or inappropriate, rational or irrational, within or peripheral to the family, dormant or overt, conscious or unconscious, diffused or circumscribed, benign or malignant, reversible or irreversible, and displaced or substituted. The corresponding methods for coping or controlling the stress lead to compromise. The family selection of a method of coping, for example, denial or projection or displacement, relates to the dominant role of the family complementarity. Some methods are injurious to the family group and will foster prejudice and scapegoating, setting one subgroup against another and resulting in someone's being a victim.

If blame for the conflict is given to one person, the conflict cannot be solved. It will become entrenched and isolated and will lead to the distortion of the original problem and even to new conflicts. The longer the conflict is absorbed by one member, the less likelihood there is of reversing the situation. If the conflict is within one person, it will affect the relationships within the family that affect family's relationships to individuals—it becomes cyclical. When this happens, the original problem or conflict may be totally structured, masked, and lost.

Conflict with the family can be characterized as revolving around issues of security, need satisfaction, love expectation, struggle for control, or support of a needed self-image (Ackerman and Behrens, 1974). The purpose of the family's coping mechanism is to protect the integrity, continuity, and growth of the family unit. An important part of diagnosis involves the therapist's awareness of the family's level of coping. Ackerman identified the levels of coping as follows:

1. A shared search for specific and suitable solutions to conflict, leading to a changed configuration of family relationships.
2. A strengthening of family unity, integrity, and functional competence through an enhancement of the bonds of love and loyalty, and with this a consolidation of sound family values.
3. "Repeopling" of the family, that is, removing a person from or adding a person to the functioning family unit.
4. Mobilization of external support for family integrity through social service, psychotherapy, religious guidance, and so on.
5. A spiritual rebirth, an enhancement of family closeness and health, after recovery from a family crisis such as the death of a family member.
6. Reintegration of family role relationships through: (a) a tightening of the family organization, rigidification of authority, sharper division of labor, constriction and compartmentalization of roles; (b) a loosening of the family organization, dilution of the family bond, distancing, alienation, role segregation, thinning of the boundary between family and community, and displacement of family functions from inside to outside; and (c) reorganization of the complementarity of the family roles by a reversal of parent–child roles.
7. Reduction of conflict and danger through avoidance, denial, and isolation.
8. Reduction of conflict and danger through compromise, compensation, and escape, that is, sexual escapades, delinquency, alcohol, drugs, and the like.
9. Realignment of family relationships through splitting of the group, scapegoating, and compensatory healing. (p. 43)

Ackerman also noted that coping techniques may vary according to the family's social status and cultural position. The poor, for example, have the primary pressure of money.

The Typical Family Role Relationships and Patterns of Complementarity

For the second criterion for diagnosis, Ackerman identified the typical family role relationships and complementary patterns. He examined complementarity in terms of five items: (1) self-esteem, (2) need satisfaction, (3) a shared search for solutions to conflict, (4) buttressing of needed defenses against anxiety, and (5) support of growth and creative development. He attempted to determine at what point a family will preserve or sacrifice complementarity.

Ackerman classified role complementarity in three broad categories: lacking, partial, and complete. The lack of complementarity exists when there is a critical reduction at all levels. Partial complementarity exists when it appears on some but not all levels. Partial complementarity is characterized by Ackerman as a form of negative complementarity. Complete complementarity occurs when there is reciprocal emotional satisfaction on all five items.

The diagnosis of the family must include exposing the marital relationship.

Ackerman emphasized two special features of marital complementarity as (1) the use of the marital partnership to compensate anxiety and support one or both partners against the threat of breakdown and (2) the quality of integration of each partner into the marital role and the fit of marital and parental roles. From this evaluation of the marital pair, the patterns of complementarity of the parental pair can also be judged. Ackerman and Behrens (1974) suggested that parental performance be judged according to the complementarity of parental roles, the mutuality of adaptation, adaptation to external change and adaptation for growth; the levels of conflict, benign or destructive; the integration of each partner into the parental role; and the effects of parental behavior on the child and the effects of the child's behavior on the parents.

Fulfillment, Harmonization, and Balancing of Family Functions

Ackerman judged the family's ability to fulfill, harmonize, and balance its many duties according to: (1) survival and security, (2) affection, (3) the balance between dependency and autonomous development, (4) social and sexual training, and (5) growth and creative development. The therapist should look at the importance the family gives to these items. The therapist should attempt to learn how they are integrated and balanced and which are safeguarded or neglected or distorted. The priorities the family uses to protect certain functions is important information for the therapist.

Identity, Stability, Value, Striving, and Growth

What the family stands for is family identity. It includes shared goals, values, and strivings. Family identity is never static but, rather, is fluid and ever changing. It is changed as individuals change, as pairs change, and as the family group changes. Family identity involves who its members are as a family at a given time and place and in a defined life situation.

Family stability must be considered with family identity. Stability describes the family's ability to continue to pursue its identity under the demands of society. Stability must also allow for the flexibility to adapt to new experiences and to learn and grow from the new experiences. The effective adaptation of homeodynamic equilibrium demands a balance between the constance of old behaviors and the accommodation to change. It needs the preservation of old behaviors coupled with the new.

Evaluation of the Family's Capacity for Change and Growth: Discrepancy Between Actual Performance of Family and a Theoretical Model of a Healthy Family

Ackerman's concern in evaluating the family's capacity for change and growth was to determine where the family gets stuck on the growth curve (from simple biological survival to creativity) or where the family fails to meet its own perceptions of itself. The therapist must then attempt to conceptualize the family relationships, alignments, and splits and the effect on the emotional development and health of individual members. This is the manner that Ackerman chose to use in diagnosing the forces that cause family breakdown and illness or protect health and growth. The attempts to classify family types according to their mental health potentials may lead one to look for parallel disturbances in the family and individual members. The therapist may also find correlations in family disturbances and psychiatric illness in members. The common features for disturbed families are schizoneurosis and character disorder.

Ackerman assessed the performance of a family according to the following criteria:

1. Fulfillment of strivings and values.
2. The stability, maturity, and realism of the family.
3. The presence or absence of regressive and disintegrative trends.
4. The quality and degree of successful adaptation.

Family life acts as a conveyor belt for pathogenic conflict. The family becomes a source of sick, emotional contagion. If there are destructive effects, they may shift erratically. One member may achieve immunity by victimizing others. Often family therapists will see families where illness of one particular member is caused by the needs of other family members; for example, one part of the family holds itself together at the expense of another part or individual. Sometimes the core of the conflict is passed down from generation to generation. Sometimes it crosses generations, and sometimes the same conflict is expressed differently. Ackerman found that unhealthy families usually have several problems and that they rarely have only one disabled member.

"Clinical diagnosis is perforce only partial unless all these elements—individual, role, family group, and their interrelationships—are taken fully into account" (Ackerman, 1958, p. 109). In Ackerman's view, family diagnosis and family therapy are interdependent processes. Diagnosis involves observing, conceptualizing, and interpreting revelant emotional events that are inherent in the interview. The step-by-step testing of clinical hunches against realities leads the therapist to hypotheses concerning the relations of family interactions and adaptations.

Therapeutic Foci

The therapeutic foci in Ackerman's approach are closely aligned with the goals and the process. He believed that the therapist should be concerned with becoming involved with the family and getting them to talk, observing the family, understanding their conflicts, and concentrating on the individuals and whole family as the therapeutic process proceeds.

Ackerman thought that the therapist should focus on moving himself or herself into the family interaction. According to Ackerman, the therapist should gain a rapport with the family, gain a feeling of trust, empathy, and hope for the better. Family counseling is an individual art that utilizes existing knowledge of family and individual behaviors, and no one therapist is able to work with every family. Each combination of therapist and family has its own peculiar qualities that determine possible therapy and diagnosis. The therapist must be able to accept openness and be able to join the family where it is. The therapist must focus on the idiosyncrasies of each family's mood and language, who and what they talk about, and what they don't talk about. The therapist must be a catalyst to openness and conflict materials. When the family denies a problem or confrontation, the therapist must penetrate the wall of silence. He or she helps to determine and judge reality for the family. The family therapeutic sessions should be free-wheeling, open-ended interviews with the limits made only by each family member and each therapist.

The therapeutic sessions are face-to-face confrontations between the therapist and family. The therapist focuses on instant observations of the family's appearance, order of appearance, manner of communicating, mood, behaviors, and the integration of family roles. The therapist should note the amount of eagerness or hesitation, the individual member's conduct and seating arrangements, who supports whom, who joins whom, and who sides against whom. It is also easy to observe who talks to whom, who is quiet or loud, who is open to new ideas, who is sad or happy, who is a risk taker or retreater. The therapist will be noting how members reflect joy, hurt, anger, confusion, mistrust, hostility, apathy, or happiness. The therapist will note which members are receptive to each other and to the therapist.

During this face-to-face appraisal, the therapist must focus on the most destructive levels of conflict and determine the relationships that create the most anxiety within the family. Tension mounts during family interviews, and the strain will be felt by all members. It is important in the earlier sessions especially to steer a middle path between avoidance of issues and explosive closeness. The therapist must act as a calming influence but "tickle the defenses" to stir movement and change within the family.

A central focus for Ackerman was the connection between the interpersonal conflict in family relations and the intrapersonal conflict within the mind of one member. The therapist must not lose sight of the individual within the group just as he or she must not overlook the group when working with an individual. The therapist's focus will shift as conflict is moved from one member to the whole or parts of the whole family. When conflict becomes sharply pointed, the therapist uses all his or her knowledge of interpersonal and intrapsychic conflict and treatment to keep the family working toward conflict resolution. The therapist's first responsibility is to give hope to the family and its individual members, to enhance the quality of interchange between members and between the family and society. The therapist must keep a constant watch for dyads, shifts in grouping, and joining and leaving the therapist. Active involvement in the therapeutic process by all family members will cause realignments within the family. As the specific conflicts are better defined by the family, they will be shifted from the back of one individual member to the shoulders of the family unit. As the family assumes the responsibility for the conflicts, the therapist should have a plan of action for helping work through the problems. There must be priorities; certain conflicts must be resolved before the family is ready or prepared to handle larger, more encompassing dilemmas.

When a therapist is called into family conflict, it is necessary to give immediate assistance to the family. It is important to provide a matrix for resolution of the conflict and to provide an outlet for living out the conflict while satisfying valid emotional needs. The role of the therapist is to interject part of himself or herself into the family and help to neutralize the imbalance. The therapist must become a catalyst and seek to understand the family within its own environment and within the larger community environment.

When the family seeks therapy, the therapist initiates a process to help create new ways of acting and relating within the family. Ackerman saw the therapist as a conductor helping the family perform its own behaviors and guide the individual members to the point of relating differently toward each other. It is imperative that the therapist not determine the goals and objectives for change, although it may sometimes be necessary for him or her to specifically tell the family how to handle a situation. The therapist must at points take a stand with some members and in opposition to others. In other words, Ackerman believed that the purpose of family therapy is to change family complementarity (1966).

Ackerman believed that the therapist's entry into the family crisis should be carefully timed and programmed. The most appropriate entry would be a home visit by the therapist. It is the therapist's task to carefully observe the family in action on its own turf. This gives many insights that may or may not compare with information gained before the therapy began—information from referrals, telephone conversations, and office visits by the family members. This home visit helps the therapist to develop a more comprehensive family diagnosis. The therapist must interpret data from his or her observations and determine the need and timing of active intervention.

When the crisis is very serious, it may even be necessary for the therapist or a member of the therapist's team to "live in" if there is severe disorganization and the family seems unable to restore balance to continue functioning. The therapist in this extreme situation must be a calming force. It is especially important to protect vulnerable members such as children at this point. Living in is an extreme measure and not often necessary.

After the therapist has observed the family in its environment with all members present, Ackerman advocated that a series of office interviews be scheduled. The membership of the family session varies according to the needs and problems. Sometimes the whole family will attend the sessions, whereas some sessions will include part of the family and some sessions may be with one individual. The purpose of the interviews is to clarify family interrelations, afflictions, and conflicts. The therapist must aim to identify the specific conflicts, disturbances, and connections between individual and family balance. The result of this process is to determine patterns of interaction that are potential solutions for conflict resolution as well as directions for change.

Ackerman stressed the importance of the interview by stating that "The basis of family treatment is the therapeutic interview with a living unit, the functional family group, all those who live together as a family under a single roof and any additional relatives who fulfill a significant family role" (1961, p. 37). The therapist's prime function is to foster the family's use of his or her own emotional participation in the direction of achieving a favorable shift in the homeostasis of family relationships.

During the interviewing process the primary patient—the person identified by the family as having the problem—becomes the fulcrum to family balance. The identified family member is often the most in distress and serves as the prime example of symptomatic family pathology. This person is often scapegoated, silenced, or rejected by the family; therefore this primary patient is very likely to be the entering wedge for the therapist. The primary patient is often most eager for help and will seek the therapist's attention and support.

The therapist must move from working with the total family group to specific alignments and subgroups to individual problems. The therapist must assess the severity of the problems and conflicts to the family and to the individual members. This is another stage-by-stage process in which change that comes will result from the family's testing new ways of thinking, feeling, and doing. This is considered good change for the family and may not be the ultimate change but an intermediate step.

The therapist must work to utilize each generation in the family, especially children. Often there is a special feeling between every other generation, and this must be taken into account and used to advantage. When the therapist is working with a family with young children, it is important to keep to specifics, not abstractions. For example, a child cannot easily understand what "help" might mean. The therapist must convey the need for the child's participation at the sessions. The therapist must stress that the child's feelings carry weight. This sort of encouragement will help the child in family therapy because that child is encouraged to speak out with honest feelings. At times, at crisis points, it may be necessary to constrain a child, either by passive or physical restraints. This should not be made an issue. The therapist can make alliances with the adults and children, control children's behavior when necessary, and attempt to ease individual and group fright regarding therapy. Face-to-face family group therapy elicits special empathy and special challenges to the therapist (1970).

Stages of Therapy

Ackerman's plan of action begins with an evaluation of the family. This is done by initial interviews with the family group or with individual members. Ackerman found that a slow progression from individual family member to a group of family members to finally interviewing the whole family makes for more reception of therapy and a better family climate for therapy. The purpose of the initial evaluation is to determine the problem as viewed by the family.

The second stage requires the therapist to apply appropriate support and guidance to the family or to individual members of the family. The therapist must provide acceptance, affirmation of worth, understanding, and support. The therapist must validate expressions of emotion, needs, and anger. At times the therapist may have to stand with the weaker members against the stronger; at times the therapist may have to reiterate the feelings of the stronger family members with regard to the weaker members. The therapist must recognize thwarted personal needs, fears of punishment, and innate abilities and help to open new avenues of satisfaction and reality testing. It is extremely necessary that the therapist help to break up the anxiety of sharing problems.

The third step in Ackerman's approach to family therapy involves therapeutic help to family members in restoring homeostasis and ridding the family of conflict. The therapist must work to facilitate acceptance of sameness and difference between individuals within the family and between the family and community. The therapist must awaken respect for differences and activate the need to examine family needs, goals, and values. At this point the therapist must spur recognition of the potential within the family for growth and change.

Ackerman's fourth stage in family therapy is to offer individual psychotherapy to particular members or subgroups within the family for whom it would be appropriate in helping restore family balance. He viewed individual therapy as being auxiliary to the total family therapeutic program. Not all family therapy will involve this fourth aspect, but it is sometimes a necessary approach having preventive as well as therapeutic values.

Role of the Therapist

There are many facets in the role of the therapist in changing the family's complementarity. One particularly basic role according to Ackerman is to become a medium through which change can take place within the family. He believed that the therapist must become a part of the family in treatment to get in touch with the feeling level of the family—in a way to touch the hurt the family is experiencing. He believed that the therapist must actually repeople the family and become a part of the family but that the therapist must reserve a freedom of action that allows him or her to also remove himself or herself and become an observer. The therapist must be aware of the risk of being a part of the family system and of losing his or her ability to be flexible and autonomous and an intervener. Functioning as a member of the family, the therapist consciously works to develop priorities and set an agenda for interventions that involves careful timing. The rapport with the family is much like assuming the role of an elder relative endowed with special powers of wisdom and a keen interest in this particular family. The family must be willing to accept the advice of the therapist, and the therapist must be knowledgeable regarding the family. The family will respond with both real emotion and with transference projection toward the therapist. As the therapist interacts within the family groups, he or she must work to mobilize meaningful interactions with members. The therapist's purpose is to stir closeness, empathy, and intercommunication among family members. The therapist can use his or her own behaviors within the family as examples for other family members to model. As the therapist "touches" them, other family members will be better able to get in touch with one another (1970).

The therapist's active participation within the family will shake up alignments and conflicts within the family. The therapist must challenge the barriers of fear, distrust, and hatred between members of the family. The therapist within the family will challenge existing patterns of behavior such as alienation or fragmentation. The therapist must energize emotional release, mobilize action and reaction, and activate awareness of sharing, intimacy, levels of identification and realignments of relationships. In brief, the therapist must develop a rapport with the family so that it will accept him or her as a leader and member.

Ackerman liked to describe a method for getting important information from a family by what he called "tickling the defenses" of the family. He believed that the therapist could confront contradictions within the family by catching them by surprise. When discrepancies are exposed in verbal expressions or in verbal statements versus nonverbal gestures, the therapist can challenge the statements, the empty words, and the pat formulas. This teasing for information will invite more candid disclosures from family members and can assist in getting more meaningful interchange between family members. In this way the therapist can zero in on the destructive levels of the family's interactions.

The therapist must be a careful observer of the family and determine the family's patterns for facing conflict. Over a period of many years the family has developed its own personal ways of dealing with crisis situations, of managing individual members special needs, and of meeting their own goals. The therapist must become keenly aware of these patterns and must keep them in mind when trying to change family behavior patterns.

The family's initial reaction to intervention may be an attempt to avoid change on the part of some individual members. The therapist moves the family from blaming one member to blaming the whole family for the conflict and leads the family group toward mutual support and family strengthening. Breaking the cycle of blame may require the therapist's taking sides in the issues facing the family. If the therapist does not take sides, it is unlikely that the family will accept him or her as being totally honest with them.

As the therapist moves the family from blaming one particular member to assuming the blame, the therapist must attempt to change some family forces and therefore the balances within the family. As the therapist interjects himself or herself into the family, he or she provides new emotions, perceptions, relations between family members, solutions, reality testing, and, it is hoped, growth. Active intervention must cut through the cycle of blame and help to create new ways of coping.

The therapist works as the fulcrum for the family interactions. What one member suppresses, another must be encouraged to reveal. What one member twists and distorts, another member must straighten. The therapist must constantly work to test his or her ongoing hypotheses. The therapist must work to test clinical hunches step by step along the way of therapeutic process. He or she must compare and contrast family types, and the general pattern must be to remain flexible according to the needs of the particular family. The family must progress from one stage to the next as the balance of reciprocity shifts.

The family therapist works within the family and at the same time becomes the target of projection. From the beginning of therapy to the final session, the therapist will have a dual role in family therapy—that of participant and of observer. In addition the therapist's role must include the tasks of conceptualizing and interpreting what he or she observes. Family therapy, according to Ackerman, offers a unique challenge to the clinician. It is different from individual therapy because the therapist must treat the whole family, not simply the family member identified by the family as "sick." Some therapists will have a wide variety of people—different sexes, different ages, different backgrounds, different goals (1966).

Techniques

The techniques that a family therapist uses in working with a family lie somewhere between the extremes of individual psychoanalysis and group therapy, the two primary psychoanalytic methods. Individual therapy usually highlights parent–child relationships and focuses on the reliving of the relationships to remove the destructive elements. Ackerman saw the rationale for group therapy in the fact that the child is influenced not only by the parent–child interaction but also by the membership in the family. Ackerman saw the need for family therapy "to formulate a theoretical frame within which can be integrated two hitherto separate bodies of knowledge—that which bears on the intrapsychic life of the individual and that which bears on the psychological processes of the group . . ." (1958, p. 278). The exact methods or techniques that may be used are any that will alleviate the family distress. The therapist must be flexible in adapting any method that might benefit the family.

Ackerman (1958) saw the therapist's contributions to therapy as having several important facets:

1. Constant effort to understand the genuine emotion being experienced, not simply listening to the words spoken by family members.
2. Attention to nonverbal patterns of behavior such as facial expression, body posturing, quick shifts in motor behavior as patient's react to family interaction process or even subject change or avoidance.
3. Spirit in reaching out for genuine emotional communication that is contagious and affects attitudes of family members.
4. Accelerated push for more honest self-revelation.
5. Arousal of members' curiosity by interpreting obvious attitudes or behaviors.

The therapist's skill in entering the family dynamics is of critical importance. The timing, the level, and the preparation are issues that will determine the positive outcome of intervention. Another major technique involves observation. All family therapy sessions must provide sharp, carefully recorded observations. The therapist must observe looks first, noting the physical appearance of members, clothes, neatness, physical health, and any other significant obvious observations. The therapist also notes the family's group appearance, which includes seating arrangements, where children are placed, who takes responsibility for young children, and other group appearances. It will be important to determine a social class for the family that will affect expected outcomes.

Finally, the therapist must try to determine the family's diagnosed problem for the conflict. This self-evaluation may not be correct, but it will lead the therapist to the underriding source of conflict. If at all possible, the therapist should videotape at least some of the interviews for his or her own help in diagnosing problems and determining future avenues for treatment. It is easier to see some of the interactions from outside the family group, and often the therapist is quickly drawn into the family and is less able to see the conflict and its manifestations. If necessary the therapist should use selected psychological examinations, psychological tests, and follow-up home visits.

The interviews should be evaluated by the use of psychodynamics by the therapist. During or at the conclusion of family interviews, family members should be given the opportunity for spontaneous evaluation. The therapist may choose the Bales method of interaction analysis or may consciously evaluate the family identity and values and awareness of these aspects. Special study should be made of the agreements, disagreements, and coalitions within the family. The family should be able to achieve some level of fluidity in subgrouping. Finally, the therapist must evaluate the amount and level of prejudice and scapegoating (1966).

Ackerman's primary technique was the use of the therapist's personality. He described the therapist as an activator, challenger, supporter, confronter, interpreter, and reintegrator (1966). He worked more with his personality to "tickle the defenses" of the family and help in shifting the balance within the family so they can relate to each other in a different way.

Critique and Evaluation

Everyone pays homage to Ackerman as a pioneer. A primary contribution of his position was to integrate the biological intrapsychic orientation with social psychology concepts. His interest in the interaction between the individual, family, and society gave breadth to the field. His approach served as an early model, and many therapists have used his ideas as springboards to further their ideas or to differentiate their concepts.

His approach is logical and well developed. The basic concepts are still useful; however, he cannot be copied. His writing about his approach to therapy was conceptual, and he did not, or maybe could not, describe the specificity of style. He wrote about the therapist as a catalyst but did not describe how vividly he offered himself, that is, to hold a child, comfort a crying mother, or give a cigarette to a woman whose husband wouldn't let her smoke. Through such personal behaviors he could illustrate the conflict to the family and open interpersonal balances that could continue between members.

Ferber et al. (1972) classified him as a conductor and charismatic leader. He talked a lot during family sessions, and, although he promoted family interaction, he remained the central figure. He mobilized family interactions, watched nonverbal clues, and "tickled the defenses." He had a confident manner that permitted his cutting through denial, hypocracy, and projection to force members to be open with him and with each other. His manner also permitted the family a relationship with him. Any reader of this approach will have to use his or her personality with Ackerman's concepts.

Ackerman's participation in moving the mental health field toward family therapy, originating ideas of working with families, establishing a family institute, and producing a leading journal attests to his significant role in this field.

References

Ackerman, N. 1958a. *The psychodynamics of family life.* New York: Basic Books.
——. 1958b. Toward an integrative therapy of the family. *American Journal of Psychiatry* 14:727–737.
——. 1961. A synamic frame for the clinical approach to family conflict. In *Exploring the base for family therapy,* pp. 35–52 New York: Family Service Association of America.
——. 1964 Family psychotherapy and psychoanalysis: The implications of difference. *Family Process* 1:30–43.
——. 1966. *Treating the troubled family.* New York: Basic Books.
——. 1970a. Child participation in family therapy. *Family Process* 9:403–410.
——, ed. 1970b. *Family therapy in transition.* Boston: Little, Brown.
——, and Behrens, M. 1974. Family diagnosis and the clinical process. In *American handbook of psychiatry,* ed. G. Caplan. 2nd ed., pp. 352–369 New York: Basic Books.
Ferber, A.; Mendelsohn, M.; and Napier, A. 1972. *The Book of family therapy.* Boston: Houghton Mifflin.
Spiegel, J. 1957. The resolution of role conflict with the family. *Psychiatry* 20:1–16.

4

Experience and Its Derivatives of Virginia Satir

Virginia Satir is a family therapist whose background and original formal training were in the area of psychiatric social work. She has had extensive experience as a therapist, consultant, and teacher in a variety of clinical settings and private practice. She found the Freudian model limited in its effectiveness and progressively moved toward the communication model. During the time in which she worked with Jackson and Haley at the Mental Research Institute in Palo Alto, California, the theories and treatment approach of conjoint family therapy evolved. In studying Gregory Bateson's work with schizophrenic families, they realized that the identified patient was expressing the illness of his or her family (Satir, 1969). With a higher probability than could be attributed to chance alone, another family member would begin to display the same symptoms as soon as the formerly "identified patient" began getting "better."

Whereas the psychoanalytic theory (medical model) sees the illness in the person (identified patient), the growth model (transactional communications) sees the illness in the family expressed by a person who is then labeled the patient (Satir, 1967). In reality, the family is the patient. Any individual's behavior is a response to the complex set of regular and predictable rules (overt or covert) governing his or her family group. The family is viewed as a system that influences the behavior of its individual members. Within the schizophrenic families, no messages (communication) were straight and congruent, that is, in the the words matching how the person looked and sounded. Instead, there were double-level messages (Satir, 1969): "It is therefore believed that illness goes away when the individual is removed from the maladaptive system or the system is changed to permit healthy responses and communication" (Satir, 1967, p. 182).

The growth model, then, is based on a communication theory that focuses not on sickness but rather, on the interactional and transactional relationships between people—relationships that are not conducive to personal and familial growth and development (Satir, 1972). Communication theories have been constructed by many individuals and by a variety of groups of individuals. These theories differ in content, structure, and applicability to family formation and functioning.

Satir (1967a) has acknowledged the influence upon her work of several persons. Among those listed are M. Bowen (Chapter 9), S. Minuchin (Chapter 7), E. Berne, D. D. Jackson, G. Bateson, J. Haley (Chapter 6), J. Riskin, and J. Weakland. To this list, one could add Fritz Perls, Sigmund Freud, and Carl Rogers. The influence of some of these persons is less obvious than others; however, a flavor of each is found in Satir's work.

An understanding of Satir's historical antecedents is best derived from an overview of her personal history. In 1936 she received her B.A. from Wisconsin State University, followed in 1948 by an M.S.W. from the School of Social Service Administration, University of Chicago. Her specialization was in psychiatric social work. This was during a time when the dynamic concept of the individual and psychoanalytic treatment had arrived at a place of power and prestige in the therapeutic community. Anyone who was of standing in the therapeutic community practiced psychoanalysis or at least gave psychoanalytically oriented treatment (Haley, 1971, pp. 2-3). It is safe to assume that Satir's formal training was in the psychoanalytic medical model.

In discussing the history of family therapy, Haley has stated (1971, p. 2) that for many reasons groups of therapists began on their own to treat whole families. This was in the 1950s, and, according to Haley, this was the beginning of the family therapy movement. At this time, Satir had just finished graduate school and was beginning to practice.

Satir began her professional career by teaching handicapped and gifted children. While engaged in this effort, she looked to her clients' families for further information about pathological manifestations (1978, p. 118). This beginning is consistent with reports from other pioneer family therapists regarding the genesis of their work with family units (Haley, 1971, p. 2).

From 1955 to 1958, Satir was an instructor in family dynamics at the Illinois State Psychiatric Institute, Chicago. Her first book (1967) is composed of her initial training outlines.

Around this period, Satir reports that she came under the influence of those persons interested in systems, family homeostasis, and communications:

> I worked on a systems approach long before I understood anything about it and before I had ever heard a name for it. Then in 1957 I read Don Jackson's article "Toward a Theory of Schizophrenia," and I began to know what was going on. (Satir, Stachowiak, and Taschman, 1975, p. 165)

In 1959 Satir joined the systems group (Bateson, Jackson, Haley, Riskin, Weakland) to become a part of the initial staff of what was called the Mental Research Institute, located in Palo Alto, California. The impetus of the work at the institute was to do research in the relationship of family interaction and its relationship to health and illness of its members. After being there for a year, Satir began a training program in family therapy. This institute makes claim to being the first training program in family therapy in this country (Satir, 1972, p. ix).

At this point in her life, Satir began to make a shift in her therapeutic focus. Although maintaining her basic theories of homeostasis, systems, and communications, she began to add the theories of gestalt, growth, and awareness. In 1961 she spent three days in suicidal ideation, deciding whether she would live or die (Satir, 1971a, tape 2). Satir has dated this time as a turning point in her life (Satir et al., 1975): "Until about 1964 I was unaware of how to utilize the senses directly in the service of helping people to grow" (p. 165). Sometime after this personal life crisis, in the mid- or late 1960s, Satir went to work at the Esalen Institute in Big Sur, California. She became the director of the residential program. The orientation at Esalen was toward growth, feelings, and awareness. Fritz Perls was still there, not leaving for British Columbia until 1969. Spitzer commented (Satir, 1972, p. xi) that, shortly before Perl's death, he described Satir as the most nurturing person he had known.

Satir did not incorporate into her work all the tenets of gestalt therapy. What she did draw from those therapists of an experiential orientation was a belief in the necessity of experiencing concepts. Thus, her work was characterized by experiential exercises: a focus upon awareness and an integration of all the senses, a differentiation between content and process (process in a systems context, not individual, however), a belief in the importance of differentness and differentiation, and an emphasis upon feelings with a focus upon the here and now.

The influence of Rogers is manifest in Satir's discussions of genuineness and empathy (Satir et al., 1975, p. 200). The influence of Berne and transactional analysis can be found in (1) her discussions of early learning experiences and their survival functions (Satir et al., 1975, p. 39); (2) her emphasis upon rules (which coincided with the concept of scripts) (Satir, 1971, p. 128); and (3) her belief in the importance and impact of family transactions (Satir, 1972).

Satir's citation of Bowen (1967) as influential in her work may be surprising at first blush. However, careful analysis of her discussions reveals the influence. For example, Satir stresses the importance of not being drawn into the family's defensive system (Satir et al., 1975, p. 162), as Bowen does. Satir (1967a) gives specific instructions for the handling of "loaded material." She specifically instructs the therapist to switch to a less loaded topic "when things get hot" (p. 170). One interviewer (Satir, 1967b) asked Satir about a sudden change in her tone of voice. The change is from nurturing to "matter of fact." She made this shift because she detected the presence of tears (p. 148). It is important to note that the latest reference cited is 1975. With Satir's increasing emphasis upon feelings and process, one would be surprised if she still makes a point of deescalating emotional display and avoiding emotionally charged subjects. Unfortunately, one cannot find a more recent source to either support or dispute this point.

In conclusion, influencing the tenets of Satir's theory and practice are the postulates of psychoanalytic theory, systems theory, communication theory, transactional analysis, Rogerian therapy, Bowenian therapy, and Gestalt therapy. To view her historical antecedents, one would say that she has been influenced by persons of all persuasions, with the heaviest influences being the emotive, the affective, and the present (here and now).

Concepts of Family Functionality

The words that Satir uses to describe the families that she sees are indicative of her humanistic approach. She calls these families: troubled/untroubled (1972, p. 3), nurturing/unnurturing (p. 4), and functional/dysfunctional (1971b, p. 128). Each of these descriptions better relates to survival and/or pain than to illness or pathology.

Satir views the family as an interactional, transactional system that supports and produces the behavior of its individual members (1967). Behavior does not occur in a vacuum but takes place within and because of the structure of the family. It is the family system that allows for and maintains those behaviors necessary to the maintenance of family homeostasis (1967).

The basis of Satir's beliefs about family functionality lies in the concept of homeostasis. Jackson and Weakland (1971) provide a clear definition of this concept as Satir seemed to use it:

> These observations, in connection with existing ideas about homeostatic systems generally, suggested that a family forms such a dynamic, steady-state system: the characters of the members and the nature of their interaction—including any identified patient and his sick behavior—are such as to maintain a status quo typical of the family; and to react toward the restoration of this status quo in the event of any change, such as is proposed by the treatment of any member. (p. 16)

Given that the family is a system that is homeostatic Satir differentiates families as either open systems (functional) or closed systems (dysfunctional). These concepts will be discussed more fully. Satir (1967) has expanded the definitions of open and closed systems to include her concepts of communication and differentiation. Accordingly, the differences between the two types of systems lie in the area of communication and change.

Communication exerts effects on our interpersonal and intrafamilial relationships. "Once a human being has arrived on this earth, communication is the largest single factor determining what kinds of relationships he makes with others and what happens to him in the world about him" (Satir, 1972, p. 30). The ability to communicate is also one of the most complex skills humans have to learn in their lifetimes. All communication is learned. The place where it is first and most extensively learned is within the family system.

Satir (1967) has identified three basic levels of communication. The first and most easily understood and interpreted level is the denotative level. The denotative level consists of verbal communications: words and the literal content of those words.

The second level, more complex and therefore less easily understood and interpreted, is the connotative level. The connotative level has two basic aspects. First is body and sound communication, which deals with externally visible signs, such as facial expression, body position, muscle tonus, and voice tone. Second is metacommunication, which Satir describes as a message about a message. Metacommunication is an internal aspect of communication. It concerns itself with attitudes, namely the sender's attitude toward the message, the sender's attitude toward himself or herself, and the sender's attitude, feelings, and intentions toward the receiver. Satir states, "Metacommunication is a comment on the literal content as well as on the nature of the relationship between the persons involved" (1967, p. 76).

The last level—context—concerns itself with the time and/or place in which communication occurs. The role of context can be understood by this example. It would be quite different for a person to appear on a tennis court wearing tennis shorts and tennis shoes than for the same person in the same attire to attend a funeral. The person, his or her attire, and even his or her words can remain the same, but the situation, the context, has been changed. Likewise, the family system develops and changes over time. There are stresses that occur and have their effects on the family as a unit. Children mature, parents change, and the family system functions differently at various points in time (Satir, 1967, 1972). All these influences result in changes in context.

In addition to these three levels of communication, there are also two basic patterns of communication. The first pattern is referred to as incongruent. This consists of double-level communication (Satir, 1967). Double-level responses appear in various forms. One type is that in which the words do not match the body actions and/or inner feelings. For example, if you are feeling pain, wearing a smile, with tears rolling down your face, and you say, "I feel fine," you have made a double-level response. Another type can be seen as a combination of words and/or body actions that are incongruent with the context. For example, a man pulling his wife close to him, saying, "Let's make love," while they are at a neighbor's house and he has a fearful look on his face is sending an incongruent message.

The second pattern is referred to as congruent. This is also known as unilevel or leveling communication (Satir, 1967, 1972). Leveling responses have only one form. Leveling occurs when the person's words match his or her inner feelings, facial expressions and bodily actions, and the context or situation in which the response occurs.

Within these two basic patterns of communication, Satir believes that there are five different and specific ways that individuals communicate or conduct themselves. She further believes that she can tell how a person stands in relationship to others, or their basic method of communicating, by the observation of only three interchanges.

The first style is the *placating* stance. The individual agrees no matter what. The metacommunication is that "I am no good, and you are better." In the complex of self, other, and context, self is disregarded while context and other are considered important. The placator is the "good one" and is probably dependent, weak, and clutching. He or she passively allows, permits, and condones all sorts of irresponsible excesses. In his or her considerations, he or she never counts.

The second stance is that of *blaming*. To survive, the individual must demonstrate power by disagreeing, blaming, and criticizing. Others and context are disregarded and only the self remains as an important consideration. The blamer usually disagrees. He or she may be violent, hostile, tyrannical, nagging, bad, or paranoid. He or she spends a great deal of time self-righteously finding faults and criticizing all the shortcomings of society and other people. Anything that occurs is someone else's fault, never his or her fault. He or she is always pretty certain that he or she is right. Both the placating and blaming positions indicate that the basis of the self's survival lies in the other person.

The third communicative style is called *super reasonable*. The individual communicating in this mode acknowledges no feelings. Self and other are disregarded and only the context is considered. This style, also referred to as the computer or intellectualizer, is very reasonable, yet nonmoving. He or she is generally rigid, principled, objective, obsessive, and compulsive. The computer talks about empiricism, magnifying it to the nth degree as the only view worthy of consideration. Yet his or her logically clear discussions of empiricism in no way deal with the hard facts of empiricism. This intellectualizer has not done any research or may not have actually experienced that on which he or she is such a professed authority. This type of communicator feels that survival is outside any individual's control and is instead controlled by things and events.

The fourth communication style is termed *irrelevant*. In this mode, communication appears unrelated to anything. This highly distracting individual is continually moving in an erratic, inappropriate, purposeless, and/or psychotic fashion. He or she does not consider self, others, or the context in communicating or decision making. The self has no predictable basis for survival.

The fifth style of communication is termed *congruent*. The words relate appropriately to other and context, and the emotional effect is congruent with the verbal message. There are no double-level messages (discrepancies between the words and the effect or between the words and the context) or double binds (double-level messages with a rule that one cannot comment on any discrepancies). With the congruent response, self, other, and context are all present, relevant, and considered. Functional families with open systems engage in this fifth style of communication, whereas dysfunctional families engage in combinations of the four incongruent communication styles.

Satir et al. (1975) later adds the concepts of awareness, integration of the entire self in a gestalt sense, and self-esteem to the assessment of family functionality.

> Somehow there must be restored in the human being the use of all of his resources out of which he can create his own wholeness. This is where "illness" comes from, I think—the person's inability to use all his parts. (p. 83)

> Another belief basic to my work through the years has been that people function according to their feelings of self-worth or value, and if a person does not value himself, he cannot make it. (p. 166)

Satir (1972, p. 4) notes the following common elements in the families she treated: Self-worth was low; communication was indirect, vague, and not really honest; rules were rigid, inhuman, nonnegotiable, and everlasting; and the link to society was fearful, placating, and blaming.

Dysfunctional families operate at a survival level. Self-worth of the individuals is low. Because of this low self-worth, these families are really devastated by stress. This type of family cannot roll with the punches; it lacks inner strength, which self-esteem would furnish. Communication tends to be incongruent and double level. It stands as an obstacle to growth. Because communication is vague at best, rules are covert and role expectations are unclear. Furthermore, the known rules tend to be rigid and nonnegotiable. They are not changed to fit the individual or the situation. For example, if a family rule is that everyone drinks a glass of Florida orange juice every day, even if allergic to it, one is expected to drink it. This type of family disregards or is unaware of personal privacy. Rules in a dysfunctional family will tend to be inhuman (Satir, 1972). The family handles changes by attempting to maintain the status quo and by denying or distorting the change. The rules dictate that the present be seen in terms of the past. The dysfunctional family that attempts to meet present changes with old rules and methods will produce pathology. The overall outcome is a family that is painful to be with and to be a part of.

Dysfunctional families constitute a "closed system": closed systems are those in which every participating member must be very cautious about what he or she says. The principal rule seems to be that everyone is supposed to have the same feelings, opinions, and desires, whether or not this is true. In closed systems, honest self-expression is impossible, and if it does occur, the expression is viewed as deviant, or "sick" or "crazy" by the . . . family. Differences are treated as dangerous, a situation that results in one or more member having to figuratively "be dead to themselves" if they are to remain in the system. The limitations placed on individual growth and health in such a group are obvious, and I have found that emotional or behavioral disturbance is a certain sign that the disturbed person is a member of a closed family system. (Satir, 1967a, p. 185)

In vital and functional families, individual and familial self-esteem is high, and the family is nurturant of these feelings in individual members. Communication patterns are congruent, leveling, and growth producing (Satir, 1972). Such communication patterns allow for overt rules and clearly understood role expectations. Furthermore, the rules are flexible and kept up to date, allowing the family to meet changes openly and appropriately. The rules are appropriate to the situations and are formulated with consideration of each individual's needs as well as the family's needs. There is respect for personal privacy (Satir, 1972). The individual is allowed to move in and out of the system as the individual matures. The link to society, ways in which people relate to other people and institutions outside the family, is open and hopeful. The outcome is a family that is nice to be with and to be a part of.

The functional family is an open system. An open system permits honest self-expression for the participating members. In such a group or family, differences are viewed as natural, and open negotiations occur to resolve such differences by "compromise," "agreement to disagree," "taking turns," etc. In open systems, the individual can say what he feels and thinks and can negotiate for reality and personal growth without destroying himself or the others in the system. (Satir, 1967a, p. 185)

In summary, Satir's concept of family functionality incorporates individual and system components. Individual factors involve awareness and integration of the total self and issues of self-worth. These factors fit into the family system, which is open or closed as manifested by communication styles and response to stress or change.

History Taking

Satir's use of a history-taking tool, which she has called the family life chronology (1967a), further manifests the influence of those persons of a cognitive–rational therapeutic orientation on her work. Satir's discussions of the methodology involved in taking the family life chronology are extensive and detailed. Only a few of its more salient features will be highlighted here.

Satir believes that family dysfunctionality is really a manifestation of problems in the marital relationship. The chronology helps to put the focus back on the marriage and off the identified patient. Satir states that the tool is used to demonstrate the therapist's power and control. Its process is used to give the family a sense of structure and order. It indicates a beginning and an end, ultimately implying hope and resolution.

The chronology is used for information gathering. It exposes what she has called the "cast of characters." It allows her to see which old homeostatic systems are operating in the present family, to expose what she calls the "witches" and the skeletons in the closet, to verbalize facts and realities, and, most important, to observe the rules and the communication patterns present in the family.

Satir also uses the chronology for instructive purposes. She states that dysfunctional families have no sense of the difference between present and past and that this tool helps them to differentiate the difference. The process of taking the chronology involves each member's expressing ideas, feelings, and memories, thus aiding family members in experiencing their differentness from one another. The phasing of the chronology assists the family in viewing their problems from a systems viewpoint, in thinking in terms of family, in viewing problems in terms of pain, and in taking the focus off the identified patient and viewing things from a group perspective.

Briefly, the order of the chronology begins with the meeting of the mates, moves to their families of origin, returns to the planning of the children, finally focuses on the routine facts of a typical day. Each family member is involved in the process. Facts, as well as feelings, hopes, and disappointments, are discussed.

Satir states that the taking of the chronology, which can take as long as several days, is usually begun after the therapist hears the presenting problem as the family sees it. However, Satir (1967b, p. 143) indicates that she is not consistent about when the chronology is taken. She has stated that the point at which she engages in the chronology differs from family to family and that it is more of a strategic maneuver. She sometimes uses it to deescalate emotionally charged situations. Additionally, she has stated that she uses it to give family members a sense of power by reminding them of their exercising of choices.

In conclusion, Satir (1967b) has indicated that she always regrets a failure to obtain a complete family life chronology. She has likened evaluating a family without this information to a physician's diagnosing an illness without appropriate diagnostic tests.

Diagnostic Framework

For the purposes of a working tool, Satir has created her own diagnostic classification system. She stresses the use of her tools, believing them to be an integral part of her therapy (1967a, p. 103). Some examples of her diagnostic system are the analysis of the family's handling the presence of differentness (p. 103); the role function analysis (p. 103); the model analysis (p. 105); the communication analysis (1971, p. 130); and the rule analysis (1967b, p. 144).

Satir accepts the use of traditional diagnostic categories as valuable tools, inasmuch as such nomenclature provides clinicians with common terminology with which to describe behavior. Her problems with such usage are in the assumptions made about the individual's personhood by the use of such labels. In practice it appears that she accepts the psychiatric diagnosis as an indication of the behavior manifested by the presenting problem but then proceeds to categorize the family or individual within her own diagnostic classification system.

In specifically addressing the issues of diagnostic labels, Satir (1967a) has stated that labels, such as sociopath or schizophrenic, are used by clinicians to describe behavior that is deviant from the individual's character, from the context, and from other's expectations. She further states that this labeling system is a method of shorthand for describing behavior, which is the net product of years of clinical observation. These labels presume a duplication of behavior across persons and each carries implications of description, prognosis, and treatment. Satir warns that the dangers in using such a system lie in the possibility of the clinician's dealing with the client in terms of his or her own opinions of the label rather than as a human being possessing many other labels. Her recommendation is that the therapist say, in effect, to the patient that:

> You are behaving now with behavior which I as a clinician, label "schizophrenia." But this label only applies *at this time, in this place,* and *in this context.* Future times, places, and contexts may show something quite different. (1967a, p. 103)

One further comment on her feelings about symptoms in general is necessary before closing this section. Satir views the symptom, regardless of the label ascribed to it, as a signal. She sees the identified patient as signaling the presence of dysfunction:

> The symptom of the Identified Patient is a comment on a dysfunctional family system. The Identified Patient is signaling distortion, denial, and/or frustration of growth and the presence of pain, discomfort, or trouble in survival

figures–those who have provided nurture, economic support, and directing functions. (1971b, p. 128)

She believes that symptoms manifested by either parent indicate dysfunction in the marital relationship and in parenting functions and that symptoms in a child indicate problems in the marriage.

Therapeutic Focus and Goals

Satir was quite clear about the focus of her therapy. It is not problem solving (action); it is not the gestalting or cathecting of feelings (emotional); it is the identification and habilitation of "process" (rational). Satir believes that the problem is only the ticket for admission to therapy. She leaves it at the door and goes to work on process.

Satir has delineated some of her ideas about process (1967a). Process implies movement. Process is more a matter of "how" than of "what." She believes that the basic process that occurs in any relationship is the encounter between two persons at a particular place and time (p. 178).

It is often difficult for the therapist to refrain from commenting on content, but Satir emphasizes that focus on process is far more important (1967b). She relates the concept of process to her meanings of gestalt and systems, believing that focusing on fragments of content results in the family's feeling lost and failing to perceive the overall gestalt. Her goal is the perception of the gestalt.

Emerging from Satir's focus on process is her "growth model." The basis of this model is her belief that behavior changes through process, which is represented by transactions with others. Illness is considered a type of communication that is an appropriate response to a dysfunctional system or context. Illness disappears when the individual is removed from the system or when the system is altered in such a way as to permit healthy responses and communication (1967a). It is important to remember that included with the concept of process are self-esteem, integration of the senses, awareness, and communication. All these components are subsumed within the complex of process, the primary focus of Satir's intervention.

Satir's discussions of therapeutic goals involve rational–cognitive and experiential–growth–emotional aspects to the exclusion of any attention to specific problem solving. Such lofty aspirations and broad concepts are not readily amenable to contracting or concrete negotiation. When she does discuss goals with the family, it is in such terms as "returning to a time when everyone in this family was happy," or "changing things in this family so that no one hurts," or "getting to know ourselves and others better."

Throughout Satir's writings can be found numerous references to the goals or tasks of therapy. Satir's goals are ambitious. She does not want merely to repair the family but is also concerned about prevention and expansion of possibilities for each individual (1967b).

She has defined (1967a) the task of therapy as working out ways in which everyone can get more pleasure from family life (p. 117). When speaking of the criterion for termination, she sums up the goals of therapy as the time when each person can use "I" messages with an active verb and a direct object (1967a).

Satir (1971b, p. 130) has given a more specific explanation of her therapeutic goals. They are (1) that each member be able to report congruently, completely, and obviously on what he or she sees and hears, feels, and thinks about self and others in the presence of others; (2) that each person is addressed in terms of uniqueness, so that decisions are made in terms of exploration and negotiation rather than in terms of power; and (3) that differences be openly acknowledged and used for growth.

Satir's most recent thoughts on the goals of therapy are summed up in the following quote:

> The main points are that to help a human being change and grow, the reconstruction of that person takes place (1) in the area of communication, (2) in the area of belief about being able to grow, and (3) in the area of restoring the use of the senses. (Satir et al., 1975, p. 83).

It is obvious from this discussion that Satir's identified therapeutic goals are consistent within a growth orientation. She aspires to stimulate growth through awareness, increased self-esteem, and congruent communication within the singular individual (I/I, awareness), within the individual as a member of the group (me/you, communication), and within the family as a system (me/them, rules).

Role of the Therapist

Satir presents a contradiction between theory and practice in her position on the role of the therapist. When presenting a theoretical discussion on the therapeutic role, she uses such descriptions as a leader (1975, p. 38) or a resource person and model (1967a, p. 97). In practice the therapist is described as a very active, manipulative clinician, who possesses a whole array of skills and techniques (1967b, pp. 97-173).

In her later writings, she is quite adamant about placing method in a secondary position and, instead, emphasizing the therapist's awareness and personhood. She maintains that she cannot teach anyone techniques or how to do family therapy. She teaches ways in which therapists can use themselves under certain circumstances. She also teaches by helping people to become more personally aware and familiar with the kinds of interaction phenomena between people (1975).

Satir places responsibility on the therapist in seeing therapeutic failure as a function of a deficit in the therapist's skill and personal awareness; yet she states that she does not place the burden of responsibility for change on the clinician.

> Now that puts—not exactly a burden—but a big chunk of responsibility on the therapist. . . . the chief reason any therapeutic endeavor fails is that the therapist does not know how to have the kind of communication that makes it possible for people to get "connected with their guts." (1975, p. 37)

The seed you plant has to have a place to grow and has to be nourished; but I consider the therapist the leader of the treatment situation, just as I consider parents the leaders of developing human beings. That does not mean they are totally responsible and do it all by themselves, for what evolves also depends upon the nature of the context that is used. (1975, p. 30)

Satir's opinions on the roles of the therapist involve that person's being a very special human being. This individual needs to possess competency in numerous intervention techniques, such as interviewing, confronting, supporting, acknowledging, and so on. In addition, that person needs to be actualized, congruent, and in touch with his or her own process.

The role of the therapist within the Satirian model is active, involved, and circular. To even attempt to delineate a linear, step-by-step ordering of the therapist's responsibility or methodology would be futile. The therapist's degree of awareness or process is not a linear concept.

Before this section closes, one further point needs to be made. The Bowenian influence can be seen as manifested once again in Satir's beliefs about the role of the therapist. Satir (1967a, p. 97) makes a point of describing the therapist as one who stays out of the family struggle or system and who is, instead, in the role of an official observer.

Intervention Strategies

In Satir's early work, she used the family chronology to ascertain important information about families of origin, mating patterns, marital expectations, parenting patterns, and perceptions of the children about the family architects. In later work she focused more on the communications techniques of the here and now of family interaction. In her manual on family therapy, Satir suggests the importance of awareness that the identified patient is but a reflection of well-entrenched patterns of family interaction.

Satir asserts that any family with an identified patient is dysfunctional and must be treated carefully, for the identified patient is often the basis for the family's fragile homeostasis. Using Haley's model of communication (Chapter 6), the essence of good family therapy is helping the members of the family to achieve congruence in their communications with one another. Hoping to avoid the pressures of the double bind, Satir has attempted to be a model of balanced communication for the family, attending to the importance of the sender, the message, the receiver, and the context of the interaction. Asserting that sex is not the basic drive of human personality but that self-esteem is, Satir has categorized the four patterns of poor communication described earlier that hinder self-esteem: blamer, placator, irrelevant distractor, and super-reasonable computer.

As a therapist, Satir has tried to create a climate in which people could be clearly objective about themselves. In nonjudgmental mirroring of the client, Satir hopes to build self-esteem. By decreasing emotionality, she hopes to decrease threats and to reduce the reign-of-terror atmosphere that often dominates the dysfunctional family. In setting the limits for therapy, Satir tries to reeducate the members of the family for healthy adult functioning and accountability. Interested in explaining critical aspects of the past as they impact on the present, Satir tries to sculpt her families into more functional patterns of interaction, delineating family roles and functions, concentrating on interpretations of nonverbal communications, and insisting on congruent verbal communications. For Satir, the effective therapist is a resource person, an experienced observer outside the family system, an impartial official, and a model of congruent communication. Therapy's success is indicated when all family members can objectively and congruently criticize, evaluate, acknowledge observations, find fault, report annoyance, and identify being puzzled. Therapy can be terminated when everyone in the therapy group can use the first person "I" followed by an active verb and end the statement with a direct object. The emphasis on clear communication is central to this apparently emotion-oriented therapist.

Satir's basic assumptions about human nature are that humans are geared to survival and tend to grow toward maximum functionality, that sick behavior is a cry for help, and that humans can be limited only by the extent of their knowledge and can use reason to free self. Such assumptions could well have come out of a time machine directly from eighteenth-century Enlightenment. Such a focus on the power of reason is remarkable in a therapist who is noted for her fantasy and awareness trips, focusing on the realm of human emotionality. Satir's interview techniques (1975) seem to focus exclusively on feelings. Satir appears, on the surface, to be clearly emphatic on feelings. On closer inspection, this conclusion may be incorrect. Under all of Satir's emphasis on feeling is a faith in the power of reason to heal by creating congruent communicators in the dysfunctional family. What looks like emotion in Satir's therapy may be, in fact, a fundamental faith in the rationality of human behavior.

The strategies that Satir describes are verbal and nonverbal, circular and linear. They fluctuate between passive and active. She discusses the use of such techniques as prescribing the symptom explicitly, implicitly, literally, or in reverse. She states that she gives homework assignments, calling them prescriptions. The technique of making "ego-enhancing" statements and asking "ego-enhancing" questions is discussed. She engages in statement reframing and rephrasing within a positive, family, and systems complex. Satir discusses the strategy of "paving the way for" and making "discrepancy comments" and of redistributing possessive pronouns. This list of strategies is by no means exhaustive.

In addition to verbal techniques, she proposes the use of experiential, growth-oriented exercises. She makes extensive use of the techniques of role playing and sculpting. In addition, she has devised numerous games, each designed to focus on a specific area of awareness. Some examples of these games are the rescue game, the lethal game, and the communication game (1967a). The goal of such exercises is to enable clients to experience the message of the exercise: to have cognitive understanding but also to have awareness throughout all of their senses and, additionally, to be in touch with their feelings.

In her intervention strategies and treatment techniques, Satir neatly combines her rational and emotive historical roots. Left out are problem-targeted, action-oriented maneuvers. Her cognitive–rational techniques are verbal and circular and fluctuate being being active and passive. Satir's experiential techniques are non-verbal, linear, and active.

Important Derivatives

Satir's analysis of the causes for the institutional crisis of the family focuses on external social forces. Although Satir's primary focus is on the internal dynamics of family communication, she does acknowledge the following external causal factors in family conflict: the Industrial Revolution's separation of work from the home, devaluation of the woman as an unpaid houseworker in a cash-based society, pervasive alienation of the male in meaningless work in the office or on the assembly line, impersonality of the urban environment, mass mobility of the automobile society, confusion of male and female roles engendered by women's liberation, unclear guidelines for raising children, suburban neurosis for the woman who decides that the wash 'n wear life-style offers no meaning for existence, increased numbers of day care centers, freeing parents of real responsibility for their children, birth control techniques and changing sexual mores, changed attitudes toward divorce, and disillusionment of a couple with traditional roles and decision to live together for the child.

With such a morass of social crises impacting on the family, Satir sees the primary task of a family as the overcoming of alienation and aloneness in the creation of a community of persons who know and care for each other. Unfortunately, low self-esteem often retards this process of communication. Because each partner in the marriage never really separated from the family of origin and may have much unfinished business still to conclude, moving from strangers to intimate partners may be difficult. In a family in trouble, the family architects felt as if they had nothing to give and so married to get. The appearances of differences after the honeymoon indicate the primary dysfunction in the partners' assumption that, if loved, the other would do what was wanted without asking what that was.

Stachowiak (Satir et al., 1975) reported that his research has validated Satir's ideas. In a ten-year investigation, children and their families were observed in various stages of the children's developmental cycles. Differences between families fell into four categories: family productivity or efficiency, leadership patterns, expression of conflict, and clarity of communication.

Maladaptive families overemphasized task-oriented activities while neglecting to attend to members' emotional needs or their attention to emotional needs resulted in inability to complete tasks; in adaptive families there was a balance of attention between these foci. In maladaptive families, there was no clear leadership; in adaptive families leadership was clear in given situations and could shift as indicated by the context. Maladaptive families had either too much or too little conflict; adaptive families could express differences and had the resources to deal with and resolve these differences. In maladaptive families, there were a greater number of speeches with no intended recipient but also fewer speeches than in adaptive families (Satir et al., 1975).

In another study, Stachowiak (Satir et al., 1975) discovered that clinicians continue to adhere to myths concerning the family, such as one-parent families are bad for children, democratic family structure is associated with successful functioning, and expressions of overt conflict are bad and pathological. In differentiating types of adaptive and maladaptive families, clinicians identified maladaptive families as adaptive, using the preceding criteria as evidence of good functioning.

Stachowiak (Satir et al., 1975), who has been heavily influenced by Satir, suggested that there are progressive stages in the process of therapy. These are rituals, passing time, games, and, finally, intimacy. These occur not only through the overall process of therapy but also within individual sessions. The names and descriptions of these stages are consistent with Eric Berne's terminology and descriptions. Stachowiak states that the biggest errors he has made in therapy were related to failure to recognize where family members are in this progression and consequently pushing them too fast or holding them back.

Stachowiak (Satir et al., 1975) also emphasized that intervention is unique for each family. It may occur in traditional family sessions. It may consist of on-the-spot intervention in the family home. Finally, it may require an intersystem approach, involving, for example, the school system. Thus, he expresses an awareness that there is no established pattern for family therapy. This seems to represent an expansion of Satir's ideas.

Bandler and Grinder (1975, 1976) have followed Satir's rational stance in regarding communication and the structure of language as essential to good therapy. There is clearly a mutual admiration society between Satir and both followers with expressions of love and affection in dedications and prefaces. Grinder and Bandler began their search for magic's structure by observing that certain gurus, such as Fritz Perls, Jay Haley, and Virginia Satir, seem to have great powers of healing in their psychotherapies. If this power is personal, then little can be done toward the goal of establishing a method for effective family therapy because only a few people would ever possess such personal magnetism. After analyzing the different approaches to therapy, Bandler and Grinder conclude that all therapeutic wizards have one characteristic in common; that is, they introduce changes in their clients' models that allow for greater options in behavior.

The analysis begins with the structure of choice and the statement that all people create models or maps of reality upon which they base their behavior. Repeating Korzybski's famous dictum that "the map is not the territory," the authors reinforce Korzybski's basic insight that it is impossible for the map to be a total representation of the territory but that maps are important tools for helping people to find their way about the world more easily. Bandler and Grinder then discussed the neurological, social, and personal limitations in human perceptions of reality.

Critique and Evaluation

Satir's theoretical assumptions are sound, and they constitute critical components of the human experience. The status of one's self-worth does have an effect on functionality and one's ability to relate. Persons today do not utilize all their senses and have largely deadened the awareness of their feelings. The ability to communicate in a straight, congruent manner is not a skill that most persons have. The family is a homeostatic system in which the sum is more than the total of its parts. Satir's concept of open versus closed systems is somewhat in error: There cannot be any such thing as a closed system. No system is totally impervious to incoming stimuli. Inasmuch as a closed system is representative of resistance to change and adherence to nonfunctional, old rules, the term fits dysfunctional families.

There is no doubt that Satir is a warm, loving, nurturing woman who is an extremely skilled clinician. One doubts, however, whether the clinical skills that she possesses and the intervention techniques that she utilizes can be inductively derived from her theoretical assumptions. It is unfortunate that she has not put as much energy into developing a clear methodology as she has in writing about her thoughts on the nature of human experience and on the nature of pain, illness, and dysfunction.

The ambitious goals that she holds for therapy are not such as to be readily amenable to measurement of effectiveness. Satir has clearly stated that she is a *growth-oriented therapist,* the presenting problems are left at the door, and from there she goes on to work on process. Her work may be very effective. Family members begin talking, crying, and touching each other. They make real movement toward one another. What her work reminds one of is long-term psychotherapy within a family context. This process may not be appropriate for all families, especially those in acute crisis. Because of the long-term nature of Satir's therapy and the ambitious goals she sets, this is certainly not a cost-efficient treatment modality.

Satir's work is similar in approach to that of persons of a systems, rational, and gestalt orientation. With her interest in feelings and her experiential work, she deviates from the rational–cognitive, the systems, and the psychoanalytic therapists. Her work deviates from the gestalt approach inasmuch as she does not incorporate the concepts of defense mechanisms (introjection, retroflection, regression, and projection), she does not do body work to cathect blocked emotions, she is somewhat interested in history, and she does not place emphasis on anger. Satir's work is not at all similar to that of therapists of an action–problem–solving orientation to be reviewed later. She does not address the presenting problem or its literal nature; instead, she sees it as a signal of a dysfunctional system.

Satir is an experiential family therapist who works from a systems framework but whose orientation appears to be of a more emotional nature. Although she places a heavy emphasis upon experience, awareness, and feelings, her major therapeutic focus is on process and communications. There is no doubt that Satir is an excellent clinician who has contributed greatly to the family therapy field. Her major drawbacks of vague, ambitious, growth-oriented goals and a lack of concise methodology make duplication of her style and technique impossible. It would require an impossible feat: a duplication of Virginia Satir herself.

References

Bandler, R., and Grinder, J. 1975. *The structure of magic.* vol. 1. Palo Alto, Calif.: Science and Behavior Books.

——, and Grinder, J. 1976. *The structure of magic.* vol. 2. Palo Alto, Calif.: Science and Behavior Books.

Haley, J. A. 1971. Review of the family therapy field. In *Changing families, a family therapy reader,* pp. 1–12. New York: Grune & Stratton.

Jackson, D. D., and Weakland, J. H. 1971. Conjoint family therapy: Some considerations on therapy, technique, and results. In *Changing families, a family therapy reader,* ed. J. Haley, pp. 13–35. New York: Grune & Stratton.

Satir, V. 1967a. *Conjoint family therapy.* 2nd ed. Palo Alto, Calif.: Science and Behavior Books.

——. 1967b. A family of angels. In *Techniques of family therapy,* eds. J. Haley and L. Huffman, pp. 99–113. New York: Basic Books.

——. 1971a. *Conjoint family therapy: Didactic sessions.* San Rafael, Calif.: Big Sur Recordings (tape).

——. 1971b. The family as a treatment unit. In *Changing Families, a family therapy reader,* ed. J. Haley, pp. 127–133. New York: Grune & Stratton.

——. 1972. *Peoplemaking.* Palo Alto, Calif.: Science and Behavior Books.

——. 1978. *Your many faces.* Millbrae, Calif.: Celestial Arts.

——; Stachowiak, J.; and Taschman, H. A. 1975. *Helping families to change.* New York: Jason Aronson.

5

The Communications Theory of Paul Watzlawick

Watzlawick was trained in languages, communication, and literature (Ph.D., University of Venice, Italy) in addition to his numerous years as a psychotherapist (Watzlawick, 1974). Certainly, his unusual background and training prior to becoming a psychotherapist have contributed much to his particular approach to psychotherapy as well as to his continued attempts to systematize and articulate a theoretical grounding.

For the past three decades, he has been a clinical psychotherapist, and, for the last two of those decades, he has worked as a research associate and investigator at the Mental Research Institute in Palo Alto. He has also taught and consulted on a clinical appointment in the Department of Psychiatry at Stanford University (Watzlawick, 1976). The more acknowledged and visible influences on his theoretical approach are paradox—G. Bateson and D. Jackson, systems—von Bertalanffy, language and reality—B. Russell, L. Wittgenstein, and M.Erickson, and mathematical logic—K. Godel.

Watzlawick's training in psychotherapy was orthodox. He reports that it was his frustration with the uncertainty of the methods, length of treatment, and paucity of results, coupled with many unexpected and unexplainable successes of occasional "gimmicky" interventions, that prompted him and his colleagues to leave the orthodox fold. In 1966, at the suggestion of Robert Fisch, the Brief Therapy Center of the Mental Research Institute was established. Here, Watzlawick and his colleagues began to investigate the phenomena of human change and, to date, the group continues to study interpersonal communication and its disturbances in family and larger social contexts.

Watzlawick now practices interactional psychotherapy as it has been developed by what is known as the Palo Alto group under Gregory Bateson's theoretical and D. D. Jackson's clinical leadership. Watzlawick also acknowledges the profound influence of Milton Erickson, with whom he came in contact through his training and experience in hypnosis.

Theoretical Background: The Family as a System

Watzlawick's theory of human communication developed directly out of general systems theory and information theory (Chapter 1). His first premise is that a phenomenon remains unexplainable as long as the range of observation is not wide enough to include the *context* in which the phenomenon occurs. It is the relationship among parts of the larger system that is of interest. Relationships, rather than isolated behaviors, are the focus of study, and relationships are manifested in communication.

Communication can be subdivided into three areas: syntax (information transmission), semantics (meaning), and pragmatics (behavioral effects of communication). Watzlawick is primarily concerned with the latter. Several properties of communication have fundamental interpersonal implications. The first property of communication is that one *cannot not* communicate. Activity or inactivity, words or silence *all* convey something; they influence others, and these others cannot not respond to these communications (Watzlawick and Beavin, 1967).

The second property is that "every communication has a content and a relationship aspect such that the latter classifies the former and is therefore a metacommunication" (Watzlawick, Beavin, and Jackson, 1967, p. 54). The report aspect of a message conveys information, but the relationship aspect conveys how the information is to be taken in. Watzlawick clearly explains that this aspect of the communication is rarely deliberate or conveyed with full awareness.

The relation among these aspects of a communication is the crux of many interactional problems. When *relationship* and *content* levels become confused, that is, when communicants attempt to resolve a relationship problem on the content level or when one is coerced into denying his or her own correct perception to maintain a relationship, several problems arise. For instance, one partner could say "I love you" and still look away from the one receiving the message. The relationship aspect and content aspect are, therefore, contradictory. Which of these messages should be believed?

A third property of communication that lies at the root of many relationship struggles is that of *punctuation*. Communication can be observed as an uninterrupted sequence of interchanges. Punctuation serves to organize this sequence of behavioral events by giving it a beginning and an end point. Punctuation is spurious (consequently, differential interpretation may take place). Discrepancies in the punctuation of jointly experienced events are at the root of many conflicts—the blindness for the other's punctuation, coupled with the naïve conviction that reality is the way one sees (punctuates) these events, almost inevitably leads to conflict. The resulting vicious circle can go on indefinitely. For instance, the message "I am ready if you are" could be interpreted in at least two ways: "I am ready now" or "I am ready whenever you are ready." In one possibility, the speaker indicates being ready regardless of the other's behavior. In another interpretation, the speaker's behavior is made contingent on the other's behavior; that is, "I am only ready if and when *you* are ready." Hence, in unclear or contradictory communication, punctuation is important to indicate emphasis, meaning, and interpretation.

Two basic modes of communication are digital and analogic. Digital language is objective, logical, and analytic. It is the language of reason and is the mode through which humans share information about objects in a discrete, either-or, true-false, black-white, right-wrong dichotomous fashion. Analogic language is the language of relationships, the language of imagery, metaphor, synthesis, and totality. It is undirected, illogical thinking based on continuity both/and shades of grey. For instance, the light switch is a digital mechanism. It either gives light or it does not. The amount of light in the room is analogic to the extent that an almost infinite number of lamps could be lit, varying in watts from a few to thousands. These differences are important, first, because they are analogous to the content-relationship dichotomy of messages and, second, because translation from one mode to another—from content to relationship, or vice versa, or from digital to analogic, or vice versa—results in a huge loss of information. To talk about relationships is extremely difficult.

The final principle is that all communication interchanges are either symmetrical (based on equality) or complementary (based on oppositeness). Both have potential pathologies—escalation in symmetry, rigidity in complementarity. Both symmetry and complementarity, plus previous properties of communication, bring about contradictory or incongruous communication. In fact, the degree of contradiction or incongruity in human relationships can reach extreme paradoxical results.

Watzlawick's concern with the role of paradox in communication is best conveyed in this quote:

> There is something in the nature of paradox that is of immediate pragmatic and even existential import for all of us; paradox not only can invade interaction and affect our behavior and sanity, but also it challenges our belief in consistency and, therefore, the ultimate soundness of our universe. (1967, p. 187)

Watzlawick defines paradox as a "contradiction that follows correct deduction from consistent premises" (p. 188) and divided it into three types: logicomathematical paradox, semantic paradox, and pragmatic paradox. Again, he is interested in the third type. Pragmatic paradox is further subdivided into two types—paradoxical injunction and paradoxical prediction. The former is the core element in the double-bind theory of schizophrenia, one of the most important contributions made by Bateson and his group (Bateson, Jackson, Haley, and Weakland, 1956). The ingredients of the double bind are (1) two or more people involved in an intense relationship; (2) a message so structured that it asserts something, that it asserts something about its own assertion, the two assertions being mutually exclusive; and (3) the recipient's being prevented from getting outside the frame set by this message. If such a message is an injunction, it must be disobeyed to be obeyed, and, if it is used as a definition of self or the other, "the person thereby defined is this kind of person only if he is not and is not only if he is" (p. 212). The importance of paradox in Watzlawick's theoretical scheme cannot be overemphasized. He saw paradox as a contradiction that is a correct and logical deduction from its premises (1967a) and often results in creating an impasse, for example, "Be spontaneous" (1974). Paradoxes arise out of the self-reflectiveness of a statement and out of a confusion of member and class, a confusion of logical types (1974). Watzlawick (1967) sees the paradoxical injunction as one that "bankrupts" choice, because nothing is possible when an injunction self-reflexively contradicts itself (Watzlawick, 1967). He has also treated the double bind as a special case of paradox (1963).

The last element in Watzlawick's theory is derived from general systems theory. The family is conceptualized as a system. This model for family interaction was proposed by Jackson when he introduced the concept of family homeostasis (Watzlawick et al., 1967). Jackson observed that the families of psychiatric patients often reacted drastically when the patient improved. He postulated that these behaviors, and perhaps the patient's illness as well, were "homeostatic mechanisms," operating to maintain the disturbed system at its delicate balance, that is, the same as it was. Watzlawick adopts this idea and describes human interaction as a communication system characterized by the properties of general systems.

The properties included are (1) *wholeness,* that is, the behavior of every individual within the family is related to and dependent upon the behavior of all others; (2) *nonsummativity,* that is, the characteristics of the system transcend the characteristics of the individual members; (3) *feedback and homeostasis,* that is, the input is acted upon and modified by the system (consequently the nature of the system and its feedback mechanisms must be considered as well as the nature of the input); and (4) *calibration and step functions,* that is, there are continuous adjustments to internal and external changes.

These theses have several implications for the notion of abnormality. Once it is accepted that, from a communications point of view, a piece of behavior can only be studied in the context in which it occurs, the notion of "abnormality" becomes questionable. The patient's condition is not static but varies with the interpersonal situation as well as with the bias of the observer. Psychiatric symptoms are viewed as behaviors appropriate to an ongoing interaction. Schizophrenia is viewed as the only possible reaction to an absurd or untenable communicational context. When this model is adopted, one particular behavior can be said to cause the others; each is both the cause and effect. The behavior of each participant in an interaction is predicted on that of the other participant(s).

Watzlawick (1967) has also commented on human interaction and its organization as a system in time. What he sees as vital is the relationship or command aspect of communication between persons rather than its content. He sees families and any ongoing relationships as *open* rather than closed systems in that they are influenceable *by external sources.* Systems, in general, are characterized by (1) wholeness (change in one part results in a change in all parts and in the total system); concomitantly (2) nonsummativity (a system can*not* be taken as the sum of its parts, which would fail to account for its emergent qualities); and (3) no unilateral connections (interactions are circular and operate according to feedback and circularity; i.e., results are from the process of the system or its organizational parameters rather than from its origin or genesis). Relationships can be seen as rigid systems when certain variables remain within certain limits. In such systems, every communication sequence can be seen as narrowing and limiting the next moves possible. Such systems also have relationship rules that help to stabilize them; these rules are visible in the redundancies of the relationship. Watzlawick sees these characteristics and aspects of systems as applicable to the family.

Mathematical Analogies. Other important aspects of this theoretical framework are the links that Watzlawick makes to mathematical logic (1974) through the theory of groups and the theory of logical types. These provide an analogy for him in looking at both persistence and change. For instance, group theory, as he presents it, defines the group's properties in the following ways: (1) a group has members that have one common characteristic; (2) its members can be combined in any sequence, without changing the outcome of the combination; (3) the group has an identity member whose combination with another member maintains the other member's identity; and (4) every member has an opposite, and combination with such always produces the identity member. Watzlawick sees in this theory a useful way of thinking about the interdependence between change and persistence. But it is in his use of logical types that he finds a theoretical analogy for his understanding of second-order change (change that transcends a system) and other higher-order change. Its most basic premise is that the group, or class, has members, and whatever involves all the members must not itself be a member of the class. Also, logical levels must be kept separate to prevent confusion and paradox. To go from members to class entails a shift out of the system (second-order change), whereas change can also occur within a system (first-order change).

Reality and Language. Watzlawick (1978) also discusses the importance of a person's perception of reality, for it is in such a relationship to the world, or because of one's world image, that a person suffers. The unresolved contradiction between the way things appear and how they should be is painful. Consequently, therapeutic change focuses on changing a person's image to resolve his or her suffering over the contradiction.

To sum up, Watzlawick (1967) has articulated five axioms of human communication that, even though formulated early in his career, still contain the assumptions of much of his understanding about families. As we have already discussed them, these axioms are that (1) it is impossible to not communicate; (2) communication both imposes behavior as well as conveys information (i.e., it has command and information aspects); (3) the nature of a relationship is contingent on the punctuation of sequences within communication; (4) there is both digital and analogic communication, the analogic being that with the appropriate vocabulary for thought without the needed qualifiers to describe a relationship; and (5) communication is based on equality or difference and is thus either symmetrical or complementary.

Attempts to *not* communicate are often visible in a schizophrenic or in any context in which the individual is attempting to avoid the commitment inherent in communication and are seen through disqualifications, rejections, or symptoms (Watzlawick, 1967a, 1967b). In any communication with a context (e.g., marriage), both content and relationship aspects exist in such a way that these aspects may be confused or in conflict. In the relationship aspect of a communication, a confirmation, a rejection, or a disconfirmation of self may occur. Furthermore, in a relationship, unresolved discrepancies in communication sequences can lead to impasses in the interaction; such discrepancies usually occur when one member does not have the same amount of information as the other. Because analogic messages are open to multiple interpretations, difficulties often arise in translation between the digital and the analogic. Both symmetry and complementarity are needed in communication, in differing realms of a relationship. Both kinds of relationships are vulnerable to breakdown; finally, both concepts focus on the importance of the communication pattern and the lesser importance of the content.

Because Watzlawick set his task in the framework of communication, his comments on families are usually incidental or serve as examples for the fleshing out of his notions. Accordingly, his understanding of family functioning is based on the understanding of a system, with its own homeostasis, circularity, and feedback methods. Watzlawick (1967a) thus finds the whole concept of "abnormality" highly questionable, in that a person's condition is dependent on the context and the observer rather than being fixed in and of itself. For Watzlawick, psychiatric conditions are reactions to a situation or context that the person finds intolerable, and the symptom itself is a nonverbal message concerning perception. Instead, Watzlawick focuses on the redundancies in the communication interactions within a family and talks of scanning families for patterns in their process of communicating.

History Taking and Interview Methods

Given that information needed for family therapy is often outside the family's awareness, Watzlawick (1966) does not see direct questioning as useful in eliciting the needed information. Rather, he finds prolonged interviewing, in which the specific process of the family's communication can be observed, to be more revealing. With these concerns, Watzlawick (1966) has arrived at a structured format for initial interviewing of families that consists of five main areas: "main problems," "plan something together," "how did you meet?," "proverb," and "blame." "Main problems" is first and consists of asking each family member what he or she sees as the main problem in the family. This is done alone with each member, and each is told that the answer will not be disclosed to the others. When this is completed, all members are brought together and told that there are discrepancies in their views and that they are now to discuss the problem together. The interviewer leaves the room at this point and also tells them they will be observed through the one-way mirror, that they do not have to disclose what they had stated individually, and that their task is to reach a conclusion as a family. As this is the first task of the interview, it serves, among other things, to redefine the presenting problem and, additionally, assumes a variety of problems. It also serves to focus on the family as a unit.

Following this task, the interviewer asks the family to take five minutes to plan something together that they could do as a family ("plan something together"). The interviewer then leaves and asks to be informed upon return of what they have planned. Again, the process involved in this task is most illuminating, as is whether or not the family reaches a decision.

For the next portion of the interview ("how did you meet?"), the children and parents are separated, and the interviewer meets with the parents and asks how the two of them got together. Here, what is most useful are the revealed patterns of marital interaction that occur as the two interact in this situation.

While the children are still separated, the parents are given a card with a proverb on it ("A rolling stone gathers no moss"), told that they have five minutes to discuss its meaning, after which they are to call the children in and teach the meaning of the proverb to them. Because proverbs have possibilities for both literal and metaphorical interpretations, and its logical value requires that opposite values be assigned, the potential for disagreement is high. Again, the process of the interaction is most important—do they admit their disagreement or attempt to cover it by disqualification?

In the final task ("blame"), the family is seated in a specific order—father to left of interviewer, mother to left of father, then children in order of age—and each is given an index card and told to write on it the main fault of the person sitting on his or her left. The family is told to hand their cards to the interviewer; no one's identity as author will be revealed. The interviewer adds two statements, "too good" and "too weak," and starts reading the cards aloud by reading his or hers first. The others are shuffled and read aloud by the interviewer in a random order. As each is read, each family member, in turn, beginning with the father, is asked to whom the card applies. What is revealed here are the blaming and scapegoating patterns of the family.

Although primarily organized as an intake interview to detect the family's patterns of interacting, Watzlawick (1966) has also found it to have therapeutic value in spontaneous insights that develop in the family members as well as an appreciation and recognition of the family's own total involvement. In Watzlawick's use of this interview format, the interview is not conducted by the therapist, although the therapist often observes all the interaction through the one-way mirror.

A more recent article details a more general interview technique (Weakland et al., 1974). The approach is four pronged. First, the therapist extracts a clear definition of the problem in concrete terms. In that way problems are separated from "pseudoproblems," and those problems that cannot be dealt with (e.g., the death of a loved one, fear of earthquakes) are sorted out.

Second, the therapist investigates the solutions attempted thus far. This highlights the kind of change that must *not* be attempted and shows what kinds of things maintain the situation that is to be changed.

The third step is to obtain a clear definition of the concrete change to be achieved. By doing this, utopian goals can be sized down at the beginning of therapy, sometimes by "utoping." The goal needs to be reachable, because it is believed that, once the patient has experienced a small but definite change, the experience leads to further, self-induced changes.

The last step is the formulation and implementation of a plan to produce the desired change. Methods of intervention will be discussed later at some length. Here, just a few more points about interviewing will be mentioned. The interactional therapist is not interested in past history except to the extent that it reveals how patterns of behavior have been maintained. Genograms are not drawn because the Palo Alto group feels that insight and understanding are, at best, unrelated to change. As I mentioned earlier, diagnoses in the form of categorizing individuals are not made. Psychiatric classifications are viewed as having outlived their initial usefulness. Problems are systems related; consequently, intervention is at the systems level, and individual classification has no relation to this approach.

Diagnostic Framework

Watzlawick (1978) rarely addresses the issue of diagnostics explicitly. Through his writings, he does not appear hesitant to draw from examples of the schizophrenic, hysteric, or juvenile delinquent and their families. However, his view of therapy is not grounded in traditional diagnostic understanding. Rather, he views deviancy as that which exceeds certain normative boundaries (1974) and finds it important to look at the system or context of the deviancy. He sees traditional diagnostic terms, in focusing on individual pathology, as missing the interdependent nature of the pathology, which resides within the relationship rather than within the individual personality structure (1965).

Therapeutic Foci and Goals

As is usual in looking at someone's thinking over time, one can find in Watzlawick various statements about what is to be changed. Overall, he sees the task of psychotherapy as having to do with second-order change, as in a marriage, in which he sees the implicit and tacit contract as that which must be changed. Often it is the attempted solution itself that is the problem (Watzlawick et al., 1974); hence, it is the solution that needs to be changed. The solution as problem may occur when action is taken at the wrong level (first rather than second order), when action is taken when it should not be, or when action is needed and not taken.

Watzlawick et al. (1974) also has a clear view regarding what has been termed the "utopia syndrome," namely, those psychotherapies that set out to deliver happiness and self-actualization to the world. Here, the premise is what needs to be changed, the premise or assumption of the goal of the therapy (second-order change). For Watzlawick et al. (1974), the focus of therapy is to relieve suffering and symptoms rather than to guarantee happiness or to look for the eternal "why."

At the Brief Therapy Center in Palo Alto, the goal of psychotherapy is problem resolution. Thus, the approach is fundamentally pragmatic. Interventions are based on direct observations in the treatment situation of *what* is going on in systems of interaction, *how* they continue to function in such ways, and *how* they may be altered most effectively.

The focus of change is the system. Watzlawick and the Palo Alto group view the problems that people bring to psychotherapy as situational difficulties between people, as problems of interaction. They are symptom oriented and are not interested in patient insight or understanding. They believe that accepting a family for treatment involves a responsibility for relieving the complaint. But they also feel that the symptomatic behavior itself is disruptive of system functioning and, there-fore, alleviation of the symptom immediately leads to progress. They contend that "the presenting problem offers, in one package, what the patient is ready to work on, a concentrated manifestation of whatever is wrong and a concrete index of any progress made" (Weakland et al, 1974, p. 148). This is an antihistoric, anticausal orientation in which problems are seen as existing in the here and now and have their own lawfulness and to perpetuate themselves by their own momentum (Fisch et al., 1972). Therapy works to change the rigid rules of problematic behavioral patterns. Relationships and the systems formed of such relationships are the focus of change.

Therapeutic goals of the family are clearly and concretely negotiated at the very beginning of treatment. Watzlawick insists on setting reasonable, reachable goals. He contends that change can be effected most easily and rapidly if the goal of treat-ment is small and clearly stated at the beginning of therapy. The patient's experience of small change seems to provide the impetus for future self-motivated, self-induced change. Symptom removal, the goal of the family, is also the goal of the therapist. Beyond symptom removal, the interactional therapist is working to change the system. This, however, is a natural consequence of removing the symptom.

Finally, in a more global sense, Watzlawick (1978) sees the task of psycho-therapy as altering one's reality or perception of the world by changing one's lan-guage. Language is the *what* that is to be changed to affect a person's world image. Psychotherapy is the *how* by which such change occurs.

Watzlawick discusses just that, the language that is most conducive to change. Once the *what* of change is identified, one can proceed with the *how*. The lan-guage of change, the analogic mode, is in the right hemisphere. It is the "royal road to therapeutic change" (1978, p. 47). In this book Watzlawick subsumes his tech-niques under three general approaches: utilization of right hemisphere language patterns, blocking the left hemisphere, and specific behavioral prescription. Certain linguistic patterns speak to the right hemisphere, and Watzlawick finds these par-ticularly conducive to therapeutic communication. The structure of the language is primitive. It lacks negation; consequently, injunctions are more effective when given in positive language. These are two of the many characteristics of the language of the right hemisphere.

Another method of gaining access to the right hemisphere is by blocking or circumventing the left hemisphere. Utilization of homonyms, synonyms, ambi-guities, and puns are methods of blocking the logical. Other techniques in this category are symptom prescription, illusions of alternative, reframing, and asking for worst fantasies.

Behavior prescriptions offer a third access to the right hemisphere. They range from very simple direct commands to highly complex combinations of therapeutic double binds, reframings, and illusions of alternatives. Watzlawick (1974) details many intervention techniques. They include "making the covert overt," that is, exposing the game so that it becomes impossible to go on playing it blindly, and "advertising instead of concealing," as in the case of announcing shyness. Here, the solution *is* the problem. "Utilizing resistance" includes techniques such as telling the client not to change, that his or her situation is hopeless. Techniques for study problems include telling the student with a "writer's block" to *try* to write a "C" paper instead of an "A" paper; telling the procrastinating student that come 9 P.M. he or she *must* stop studying. In this case, the reward becomes the punishment. A technique called "benevolent sabotage" is one suggested for parents of potential juvenile delinquents. They are instructed to "accidentally" lock the child out of the house if the child is not home by 11:00 P.M. or to drop (many) crumbs in his or her bed if it has been left unmade. Many more of these paradoxical techniques are described in the references already cited.

In summary, the intervention techniques used in interactional therapy are verbal and active. Interventions are always framed positively and are directed toward breaking through the vicious, circular patterns inherent in rigid systems. Change is always second order.

Intervention Strategies

Because Watzlawick (1978) is primarily concerned with altering a person's perceptions of the world and language is that which embodies one's perceptions, many of his interventions are centered on the verbal level and are both active and largely circular. Primarily, Watzlawick (1974) focuses on a metalevel, that of higher-order change, and his methods center on changing the rules in a system. He has a four-step procedure for approaching a problem: (1) getting a clear definition of the problem in concrete terms, (2) investigating previously attempted solutions, (3) getting a clear definition of the change that is aimed for in concrete terms, and (4) formulating and implementing a plan for such change (Watzlawick et al., 1974).

If a child masturbates, how often does he or she do it and under what circumstances? What has the family done in the past to deal with this problem (spanked, "shamed," etc.)? What would the family like to see done about this problem (stopped, used selectively rather than compulsively, finding another problem, etc.)? On the basis of this information, Watzlawick would formulate a plan of action based on (1) reframing the symptom positively (i.e., as long as the child masturbates, no one in the family needs to change; hence, the symptom protects the family from changing); (2) prescribing the symptom under idealistic conditions ("could you increase its frequency to twice a day instead of once?"); and (3) limiting it to the system by making other members of the family responsible for it ("Dad, from now on, it's up to you to remind him each day that he needs to masturbate at least twice"). Some of these techniques will be discussed in greater detail in Chapter 8 on the Milan Group.

Watzlawick's (1978) "techniques" of directing the therapist's language and linguistic patterns to the patient's nondominant or analogic hemisphere are important. Both confusion techniques à la Erickson and self-reflective paradoxes are examples of left hemisphere blocking. Behavioral prescriptions may be solely linguistic, such as the "worst fantasy" technique, reframing, or creating an illusion of alternatives, or they may focus more directly on behavior (e.g., symptom displacement).

Reframing (changing the emotional or conceptual setting in which a situation is experienced) is an intervention on a *meta*level, as are other suggested methods, such as making the covert overt, advertising rather than concealing, utilizing the resistance, and inattention. All these techniques involve changing the rules of the game or altering the context of the symptoms (Watzlawick, 1974). The kinds of interventions that Watzlawick proposes are those that occur from outside the system, second-order change.

Watzlawick also speaks often of paradox and characterizes many of his interventions as paradoxical. Particularly in his earlier work (1967), the focus was on prescribing symptoms and other double-binding techniques for symptom removal. Watzlawick (1978) has also written of the importance of preempting (e.g., "I know this sounds silly, but . . .") and of therapeutic rituals. Finally, he (1978) emphasizes the tremendous importance of the therapist's coming to know and speak the client's language.

Role of the Therapist

Watzlawick (1978) is very clear that the therapist cannot *not* influence and that, more important, given that influence occurs, the therapist must assume some responsibility for deciding how the laws of human communication are obeyed in the most "humane, ethical and effective manner." In his conception, the therapist is *active* and is simultaneously responsible for the moral and ethical judgments that he or she makes.

The therapist is also *circular* in approach. Watzlawick (1978) sees the task of the therapist as learning the language of the right hemisphere (analogic, figurative, metaphoric) and utilizing this as the road to therapeutic change. It is in the right hemisphere that Watzlawick conceptualizes that one's world image is conceived and expressed. In altering this image, one can alleviate a person's sufferings in relationship with the world. He metaphorizes the therapist as a chameleon, whose task is to adapt to the world images of clients and to learn their languages, to understand and change the premises or world views that determine their relationships.

Similarly, Watzlawick (1967a) sees the psychotherapist as using the power of paradox and imposing new rules in a system for therapeutic purposes. The therapist as an outsider is capable of supplying what the system itself cannot: a change in its own rules or premises.

The role of the therapist is to treat human relationships. He or she is concerned with concrete results and thus works to specify goals of therapy and formulate strategies and tactics involving a variety of manipulation to achieve these goals. The therapist is actively involved in working toward change. He or she is willing to issue authoritative directions. Because directions are more effective when carefully framed and made indirect, the indirect approach is usually taken. A change is suggested cryptically rather than ordered. If the patient is reluctant, the therapist backs off. When particular actions are requested, the therapist may assign them to be carried out between sessions. Homework assignments of various kinds are regularly employed by the interactional therapist. Paradoxical instructions are frequently used. Usually, they are in the form of case-specific "symptom prescriptions," the encouragement of symptomatic behavior to lessen it or bring it under control.

Paradoxical instructions are also used at a more general level. Although there is a ten-session limit at the Brief Therapy Center, the therapist routinely stresses "going slow" at the outset of treatment and greets reports of improvement with comments such as "I think things are moving a bit too fast."

Interactional therapists usually have observers watching from the next room. The therapist and the observers also constitute a system of relationships frequently used to facilitate treatment. All these techniques are means toward maximizing the range and power of the therapist's influence.

At the end of treatment, which is ten sessions or sooner, the therapist usually reviews briefly the course of treatment with the family, pointing out the gains— giving the family maximum credit for things achieved and noting unresolved matters. The therapist tells the patients that treatment was not intended to achieve final solutions but, rather, to make an initial breakthrough on which they themselves can build further. Of course the type of termination, as the type of treatment, is case specific. In sum, the therapist is active and directive and commonly intervenes in a nonlinear or circular fashion.

Watzlawick contends that, to effect change, second-order change techniques are necessary. Staying within the system simply perpetuates it. Consequently, one must go outside the system to alter it. Watzlawick suggests some basic principles of effective intervention. First, the target of change is the attempted solution. Second, the tactic chosen has to be translated into the person's own "language." A third principle of interactional intervention is that paradox plays as important a role in problem resolution as it does in problem formulation. Paradoxically, he has found that symptom prescription (second-order change) is the most powerful and most elegant form of problem resolution.

Reframing is also second-order change. Reframing is changing "the conceptual and/or emotional setting or viewpoint in relation to which a situation is experienced and to place it in another frame that fits the "'facts' of the same concrete situation" (Watzlawick et al., 1974, p. 95). With reframing, the situation is not changed, but the *meaning* attributed to the situation is changed for positives. This shift moves the problem out of the "symptom" frame and into another frame that does not carry implications of unchangeability.

Critique and Evaluation

As stated earlier in the chapter, Watzlawick's theory of the pragmatics of human communication is based on general systems theory and the theory of logical types. In biology, it would be unthinkable to study any organism in isolation from its environment. General systems theory postulates that organisms are open systems that maintain their steady state and even evolve toward states of higher complexity by means of a constant exchange of energy and information with the environment. "In order to survive, the organism must obtain not only the substances necessary for its metabolism, but adequate information about the world about it" (Watzlawick and Beavin, 1967). Communication and existence are inseparable concepts.

Watzlawick examines the kinds of knowledge necessary for survival. There are two kinds of knowledge: knowledge *of* things and knowledge *about* things. The former is that which is picked up by our senses; it is first-order knowledge. The latter is knowledge about first-order knowledge; it is second order. Third-order knowledge evolves from the sum of the meanings that one has deduced from contacts with numerous objects. From this, a unified view of the world is developed. Theoretically, the levels arise infinitely. For change to occur, Watzlawick posits that it must take place outside the system and on a higher level of abstraction than the level in which the change is sought. The system must be reclassified.

From the premises already described, Watzlawick derives his assumptions from the pragmatics of communication. Clearly, his theory is directly related to the intervention strategies he uses in therapy. The use of paradox to expedite second-order change is an example of the direct relation between the theory of logical types and practices. Systems theory is utilized in the way in which Watzlawick visualizes the problem as well as the way in which he attempts to institute change in the family system.

Nature of Theoretical Assumptions. Watzlawick bases his theorizing in the notion of humanity in the interpersonal realm, with communication central. From these premises, he moves to the centrality of language for the interpersonal and the individual reality: language is our view of the world, both the digital (left brain) and the analogic (right brain). Watzlawick also grounds himself in the existential approach (1967) and sees communication and existence as inseparable, for communication is grounded in the nexus of meaning that each of us has about living, which are third and fourth levels of existence.

Watzlawick brings together an unusual set of assumptions in his theoretical framework. In his thinking, he thoroughly articulates a position from an internal perspective, in all its logical and interrelated aspects, and then he steps back to understand and ruminate on his theorizing from a larger perspective, from a bigger context or nexus of meanings. He brings together communications theory, systematic concerns, and an existential grounding in his theoretical assumptions. In his thinking, he does what he sees as essential for change; he steps beyond his initial system to contemplate the bigger picture. His thinking is grounded in principles of change, the creation of new meanings and of new premises.

Relationship of Theory to Practice. As a pragmatic theorist, Watzlawick's theory derives, first and foremost, from the behavioral realm. Although his theory has bases in philosophy, it is also intimately connected with the practice and the pragmatics of communication. Watzlawick sees all theories or views of reality as representing a particular perspective and believes that an adherence to one's own reality as the only reality is dangerous (1976). Once again, one can see that his commitment to change within his own theory is based on this view. Hence, although his practice is clearly and forthrightly related to his theory, he works hard to maintain interaction with other theories and views of reality. More specifically, he understands *context* as important and thus works primarily with families. He sees *language* as one's view of reality, and most of his techniques are *verbal* and *lin-*

guistic. For Watzlawick (1976), psychotherapy is basically a process of changing a person's view of *reality.*

Demonstration of Effectiveness. Watzlawick does not focus heavily on any empirical notion of reality. Instead, his writings are full of tales and examples of the effectiveness and efficacy of his work and of selected techniques. Consequently, any demonstration of effectiveness is largely "impressionist clinical."

The Palo Alto group has undertaken the task of comparing what they proposed to do with observable results (Weakland et al., 1974). They had an interviewer who did not participate in treatment call the family several months after the termination of therapy. He asked them (1) if the specified treatment goals had been met; (2) what the current status of the main complaint was; (3) if any further therapy had been sought since termination; (4) if there were improvements in areas not specifically dealt with in treatment; and (5) if any new problems had developed. The results of 97 cases averaging 7.0 sessions were as follows:

Success,	39 cases	40%
Significant improvement,	31 cases	32%
Failure,	27 cases	28%

The first category represented complete relief of presenting complaint. The second group included clear and considerable, but not complete, resolution of the problem. The third group included those who experienced little or no improvement.

The results of this study are comparable with the evaluation results reported for other, longer-term therapy. Although the criteria for success may vary among therapies, the success of this approach does suggest the potential for more investigation. If, in fact, it is successful, the approach is extremely cost efficient. There is a clear reduction in the usual length of treatment; correspondingly, an increasing number of patients can be treated, apparently without sacrificing effectiveness, as it has been measured thus far. Their claim that the approach is so clear and simple that it could be taught to lay therapists remains to be seen. One can take issue with this point because it seems that effective intervention would require complete familiarity with systems theory, an understanding of human communication, exposure to grasp of the patient's milieu, and an understanding of pathology. However, overall, the cost effectiveness of interactional intervention is apparent.

Demonstration of Cost Efficiency. As mentioned, Watzlawick does not base his views in an empirical approach in which the demonstrative, in the empirical sense, is of much concern. Rather, his own early training was in philosophy and languages, and he seems to prefer these dialectic modalities in any evaluation of his methods.

Still, he is quite concerned, with and committed to, brief, short-term interventions. He sees, as a major responsibility of psychotherapists, that they should be *most* effective in their influence because influence is an inherent aspect of psychotherapy. He does not "demonstrate" cost efficiency in any empirical sense of the word, but he is committed to efficient and effective short-term service.

Relationship to Other Approaches. Partly because of his background, Watzlawick succeeds as well as any theorist in grounding his thinking and interventions in the realm of normality. Clearly, he has blended his own work with that of others and explicitly acknowledges the work of Selvini-Palazzoli et al. (Chapter 8) on rituals, Haley (Chapter 6) with the double bind, and Erickson in his communication with the right hemisphere as significant contributions in his therapeutic armamentarium.

The work of the Palo Alto group is Haley's work (Chapter 6) in that its members approach intervention from a rational, problem-solving perspective. As Haley does, they plan strategies of change and frequently employ paradoxical directives. The primary difference is that the Palo Alto group does not try to alter the whole system. They aim at a small aspect of it with the rationale that just one change perpetuates others. This approach is very different from the humanistic approach of Satir (Chapter 4). Emotions are never the focus of the therapy. In addition, techniques such as role playing and structuring are never used. However, as described in the structured family interview, techniques for amplifying typical family interactional behaviors are employed. Although Bowen's approach (Chapter 9) to therapy is also rational, his, too, is very different from Watzlawick's approach. Watzlawick has no interest in the past or in what caused the behavior. He is only interested in what maintains it. His is an anticausal, antihistorical approach that focuses only on the here and now.

In conclusion, Watzlawick has indicated a lessening interest in the field of psychotherapy and an increasing investment in theoretical developments. His last work on family therapy was in 1967. Since that time he has continued in the development and synthesis of his theory of communication. Originally, his training was in philosophy and, in coming back to it, he has contributed toward a fuller understanding of our environment. In addition, many of his formulations (e.g., the location of the unconscious in the right hemisphere) are intriguing. His continuing work in this area should prove increasingly interesting and perhaps provide additional approaches to systematic change.

Watzlawick has brought to family therapy the unmatchable contribution that can be made only by someone who is first trained in a different discipline; that is, Watzlawick was free of many of the biases toward pathology in which the psychiatrist and psychologist are often bogged down. Instead, he began afresh, and so his biases are different from those of psychological thinking. Thus, his theorizing is analogous to interventions made outside a system. As he put it, true change occurs only when the rules or premises of systems are changed. It usually takes someone outside the system to attain this goal. Similarly, Watzlawick has also served this function for the helping professions. As an outsider, he has been able to see the rules and premises of our thinking about interventions, free from the confines of the system itself. Hence, he has, as other family theorists have, been in a unique position to question the very premises of helping.

References

Bateson, G.; Jackson, D. D.; Haley, J.; and Weakland, J. H. 1956. Toward a theory of schizophrenia. *Behavioral Science* 1:251–264.

Fisch, R.; Watzlawick, P.; Weakland, J.; and Bodin, A. On unbecoming family therapists. In *The book of family therapy,* eds. A. Ferber, M. Mendelson, and A. Napier, pp. 597–617, New York: Science, 1972.

Watzlawick, P. 1963. A review of the double-bind theory. *Family Process* 2:132–153.

——. 1965. Paradoxical predictions. *Psychiatry* 28:368–374.

——. 1966. A structured family interview. *Family Process* 5:256–271.

——. 1976. *How real is real? Confusion, disinformation, communication: An anecdotal introduction to communication theory.* New York: Vintage Books.

——. 1978. *The language of change: Elements of therapeutic communication.* New York: Basic Books.

——, and Beavin, J. 1967. Some formal aspects of communication. *American Behavioral Scientist* 10:4–8.

——; Beavin, J. H.; and Jackson, D. D. 1967. *Pragmatics of human communication: A study of interactional patterns, pathologies, and paradoxes.* New York: Norton.

——; Weakland, J.; and Fisch, R. 1974. *Change: Principles of problem formation and problem resolution.* New York: Norton.

Weakland, J.; Fisch, R.; Watzlawick, P.; and Bodin, A. 1974. Brief therapy: Focused problem resolution. *Family Process* 13:141–168.

6

The Strategic Therapy of Jay Haley

Jay Haley was born in 1923 and received his B.A. degree from U.C.L.A. in 1948. He has done research on animal behavior, hypnosis, schizophrenia, therapy, families, and family therapy. He has been a member of the Mental Health Research Institute in Palo Alto, from which came the theory of the double bind. He is past editor of *Family Process* and past director of research at the Philadelphia Child Guidance Clinic. His therapeutic practice has, in the main, involved brief therapy, primarily in the areas of marriage and family therapy.

Haley is not a psychoanalyst, a psychiatrist, or a clinical psychologist. He is a "communications analyst." He has had years of experience in psychotherapy in various capacities. He was a researcher and has held research positions with the V.A. hospital in Palo Alto, the Department of Anthropology at Stanford University, and the Palo Alto Medical Research Foundation. His research has mainly been in the areas of psychotherapy with schizophrenics and with families. More particularly, he was associated with his co-workers, Bateson and Jackson (Chapter 1), in their joint investigation of communication therapy with special regard to the concept of double bind and its role in the etiology of schizophrenia.

On the level of theory, Haley's main contribution to psychotherapy has been the discovery of common factors in essentially all methods of therapy, along with the development of a descriptive system capable of including people who are involved in a pathological system. Whereas traditional psychiatric terminology deals with intrapsychic events and focuses on pathology as an individual problem, Haley's approach uses a language that is much less inferential in that it deals rather directly with more readily observable events. His approach is a contextual one, which sees pathology as related meaningfully to a system or nexus of interpersonal relationships.

Haley has used insights to discover common factors in various methods of psychotherapy as well as devising effective psychotherapeutic interventions. His approach stresses the relationship between two or more people versus a focusing on the intraindividual; thus, the emphasis is on communicative behavior. Moreover, his approach can be called interpersonal, as he looks at how a therapist induces a patient to change in the context of the psychotherapeutic relationship. More broadly, he is concerned with the need for an efficient and economical approach to emotional problems and a descriptive system that accounts for changing persons involved in a pathological system.

Haley evolved from primarily a communications analyst to what can now be called a strategic brief systems therapist. His theory and approach currently consist of a combination of a communication systems approach, paradox, and the techniques of Milton Erickson. Treatment is focused directly on the presenting symptoms and the reality of the problem defined as narrowly as possible. Strategies of intervention are planned with the premise that strategic interventions will bring about an alteration of and redefinition of reality in the form of a more functional solution (Guerin, 1976). This approach may be considered a specific problem-oriented one as well as a narrowly defined approach as it has evolved from Haley's experience since the early 1950s.

Historical Antecedents and Theoretical Developments

In 1952, Gregory Bateson received a federal grant to study the communication patterns of families with schizophrenic members in the Palo Alto V.A. hospital. Bateson was an ethnologist, primarily interested in communication. He hired several individuals with communications backgrounds as members of the project staff. Among these were Don D. Jackson, John Weakland, and Jay Haley, who, at the time, had a master's degree in communication. The result of this project was the now classic paper, "Toward a Theory of Schizophrenia," which proposed the double-bind theory of schizophrenia (Bateson et al., 1956). The double-bind theory proposed "a complex interactional network which was schizophrenogenic. The child is repeatedly given a series of mutually contradictory injunctions which are primarily negative but which carry secondary injunctions at a more abstract level denying the primary command" (Watzlawick, 1963). Haley's contribution to the double-bind theory, as described by Bateson (1978), was the idea that symptoms of schizophrenia are suggestive of an inability to recognize logical types.

The influence on Haley, regarding his contributions to the idea of schizophrenia as a communication disorder characterized as a disorder of logical types, included Bertrand Russell's idea of logical types (i.e., whatever involves all of a collection must not be a member of that collection), cybernetic theories of the 1940s, Bateson's idea of paradox, Ruesch and Bateson's work regarding the role of feedback and information theory in communication (Chapter 1), and Sullivan's interpersonal theory (Guerin, 1976).

Haley's major interest, evolving from this project, became the study of schizophrenia as a form of adaptive behavior (Haley, 1959a and b). When the Bateson project formally ended in 1962, Haley joined Don D. Jackson at the Mental Research Institute (MRI) in Palo Alto, California and also became the first editor of *Family Process* (Ackerman, 1970). At MRI, Haley was influenced by Jackson's communication and role theory (Haley, 1978) and became interested in the experimental study of covert coalitions (Haley, 1962). The idea of a covert coalition was that an identified patient was always a product of two individuals in a coalition against a third individual, the identified patient. Haley added to his idea of schizophrenia as a disorder of levels of communication the idea of relationships as constant power struggles between people. As Haley further developed his symptoms approach to the study of the family, he became interested in the power tactics of families, that is, "those maneuvers they use to give themselves influence and control over their social world and make it more predictable" (Haley, 1969).

During the early 1960s, Haley was classified with Don D. Jackson and Virginia Satir as a communications theorist primarily due to his further study of communication among family members. Haley's contributions during this period consisted of his further delineation of relationships defined by communication patterns. Haley's central idea consisted of defining a relationship as the way in which two or more people interrelate, with the relationship's taking place through communication, which takes place at different levels of meaning. This basic definition of relationships was similar to Jackson's theory but stressed more the role of power in relationships. Haley added that any relationship is a power struggle, with the people involved constantly struggling to define or redefine the relationship.

To Haley, the central issue is *control*. In any relationship, the parties are posed two mutual problems: what kinds of behavior (messages) are to take place in the relationship and who is to control what takes place and thereby control the definition of the relationship (Haley, 1963). The first problem may be restated as "What are the rules of this relationship?" and the second as "Who sets those rules?" Just as it is impossible not to communicate (Jackson, 1968), it is also impossible not to engage in this struggle for control over the definition of the relationship. Every time that a person speaks (or fails to speak), that person is inevitably indicating what kind of relationship he or she is in, either by directly defining it or by counteracting the other's definition. Any message is simultaneously a report and a command. Even the "helpless" person in reporting his or her helplessness is at the same time commanding the other to take charge.

On the basis of the types of behavior exchanged, relationships may be defined as *symmetrical, complementary,* or *metacomplementary* (Haley, 1963). The symmetrical relationship is one in which the parties exchange similar types of behavior. It may be termed a peer relationship in which power and status are usually roughly equal. In the complementary relationship, the parties exchange different types of behavior. A prototypical example is the teacher–student relationship. One person is "superior" and the other is "subordinate." In the symmetrical relationship the rules are set by both parties equally. In the metacomplementary relationship, the "subordinate" explicitly *allows* the "superior" to take control, thereby defining the relationship as one in which the seemingly less powerful party is actually in control.

All relationships, whether simple dyads or complex family relationships, include in them a homeostatic function that serves to maintain continuity and stability. Haley (1962) likens this homeostatic function to the familiar thermostat: When something occurs that moves the relationship outside the range of behaviors agreed upon, some member(s) acts to return the system within the agreed limits. This is the "governing" function. The thermostat, however, must first be placed on some temperature setting; this is the "metagoverning" function. In addition to the error-activated governing function triggered when someone exceeds the limits (rules), parties in a relationship also attempt to be the ones who set those limits. There is, however, an additional level of complexity: Humans not only communicate, they communicate about their communication (metacommunication). Metacommunicative messages are said to *qualify* communications. Ways in which humans qualify messages include the context in which a message is given, other verbal messages, vocal and linguistic patterns, and bodily movement ("body language").

It is impossible not to qualify messages. A message may be qualified either *congruently* or *incongruently.* Congruent qualification affirms a message, whereas incongruent qualification negates. If congruent, the qualifiers (tone of voice, body language, etc.) will be in agreement with the primary message and communication will be clear. Clear communication leads to clearly defined relationships. When messages are qualified incongruently (e.g., "I love you" spoken between clenched teeth), incongruent statements are being made about the relationship, and the relationship cannot be clearly defined.

Haley further analyzed communication into four basic elements: (1) I, (2) am saying something, (3) to you, (4) in this situation (1963). That is, all communication is an attempt to define the relationship and, in a relationship, one cannot not communicate. Haley stated that, if one attempts to avoid a relationship, one denies one of the four elements of communication (1969).

Levels of communication were divided into a first level, or content level, and a second level, or metacommunication level. Metacommunication was defined as a message about the content message, which is not always verbal. Haley added that one cannot understand what is being said until one understands both levels of communication. In the double bind, the two levels are not congruent. In 1963, Haley stated that his communication–power approach was a new way of looking at people with "the ultimate description of relationships being in terms of patterns of communication in a theory of circular systems."

In the mid-1960s, Haley left MRI to further develop his ideas about the family as a system and joined Salvador Minuchin at the Philadelphia Child Guidance Clinic where he was influenced by Minuchin's theory of structural family therapy (Chapter 7), Braulio Montalvo's emphasis on the nature of change, and, particularly, Milton Erickson's techniques of therapy.

Haley began consultation with Milton Erickson regarding his hypnotic techniques in 1967 and was primarily influenced by Erickson's use of paradoxical interventions (Haley, 1973a, 1976). Concurrently with his association with Erickson, Haley's reputation as a family theorist and family therapist began to grow (Guerin, 1976). During the late 1960s, Haley began to focus more on change and less on communication. His growing criticisms of the failure of traditional insight therapies to produce change led to his being known as an antigrowth therapist due to his emphasis on the negative connotations of growth-oriented approaches. Haley further collaborated with Minuchin on the development of structural family treatment, which eventually evolved, for Haley, into strategic therapy. Again, he was most influenced by the techniques of Milton Erickson.

Guerin (1976) recently described Haley as a systems purist reactor because his current ideas consist of critical observations, making heavy use of paradox to manipulate the power structure of the family. Haley (1978) describes himself currently as a strategic therapist.

Regarding Haley's growth since the 1950s, Haley has both added and discarded various ideas and stances concerning the theory of family functionality and the treatment of family dysfunctionality. Haley's major changes in theory and practice are as follows:

1. He has rejected the original idea of double bind because the theory forces one to focus on a "victim" and take sides; the theory is one of stability rather than change; the theory takes away individual responsibility; and the theory falsely focuses on each family member equally (1978).
2. He has discarded the biological or genetic theory of schizophrenia and claims that the causes of all forms of schizophrenia are psychological.
3. He focuses more on therapeutic methods instead of theory or technique (see Chapter 16 for differentiating methods from techniques).
4. He has quit using the label schizophrenia due to its negative connotations for the practitioner and for the family.
5. He focuses more on change than on stability.
6. He focuses on Bateson's idea of paradox instead of the idea of double bind.
7. He claims that he has attempted to simplify the field through emphasis on problem-solving methods rather than verbosity.
8. He has a multigenerational view of family functioning.
9. He focuses more on dyads than on triads.
10. He focuses more on training practitioners.
11. He focuses more on the results of crossing natural family hierarchies (1978).

Haley (1978) has also added that theorists should focus on developing therapies that "succeed." Numerous times during the past decade, he has stated that the research problem consists of the question of how to conceptualize the repeating responsive behavior in the ongoing social network in such a way that statements about regularities in the interchange will hold true over time (1973). Although Haley is not currently engaged in research, he repeatedly states the need for research regarding which relevant facts one should gather in studying families (1978).

Concepts of Family Functionality and Dysfunctionality

Haley stresses that the family is a system wherein the actions and reactions of one member influence the actions and reactions of other members. The social context of human problems is emphasized as is the multigenerational viewpoint of family functioning.The multigenerational viewpoint states that patterns of relating are passed down through many generations but must be continually reinforced if they are to continue. At a minimum, two people, each of a different generation, must cooperate to perpetuate the pattern. Included in the multigenerational viewpoint is the idea that there are natural hierarchies in families that, if crossed, will result in symptomatic behavior of one or more family members. The basic hierarchy is the generational hierarchy, that is, parents and children. When this hierarchy is crossed, there is always symptomatic behavior in the child who is aligned with one parent in a coalition against another parent (Haley, 1976). This idea incorporates Haley's earlier ideas regarding coalitions as well as his early idea of "perverse triangles," namely, two members in a coalition *against* a third member, with the coalition usually violating the generational hierarchy (Foley, 1974).

The family is defined as a system that involves power relations and a governing process. There is no single governing process in the family; each member governs so that the family has a metagovernor. The heart of the power relationships in a family consists of the power struggle related to what kinds of behavior are to take place and who will control them (Foley, 1974). It should be noted that Haley's definition of family functioning goes beyond the homeostasis model of relationships and adds a more active and adaptive factor to family functioning.

It is assumed that families progress through stages of development. Families go through a series of stages or crises that are normal and developmental (e.g., a child's leaving home), and families create circular patterns of communicating and relating, with rules governing the patterns. Haley equates family functionality with flexibility. He states that "normalcy is synonymous with flexibility while the more rigid the system, the more pathological the system" (1978).

In the healthy family, the child starts out being quite dependent, gains increasing autonomy, competence, and personal identity with age, becomes elevated to a more equal status vis-à-vis the parents, and finally leaves to form his or her own family. In the healthy family the child learns how to operate in both complementary and symmetrical relationships, learns how to communicate clearly (with congruent qualification of messages and clear definitions of relationships), and attains a facility in maneuvering and shifting into new patterns of relationships as appropriate. The family of origin is a training ground for clear and productive communication.

Regarding family dysfunctionality, as families progress through stages of development and crisis, disturbance may occur through the clustering of several different factors at a particular time. When the family has difficulty developing a shifting point along with two or three external difficulties (such as change in job, death, etc.), the family system, rather than specific individuals, becomes pathological. Therefore, the solution to problems in families must be an alteration and redefining of reality in the form of a more functional solution. Because reality is defined as one chooses to define it, change is oriented toward redefining reality. Haley rejects the concepts of normal and abnormal and describes families primarily in terms of functional, pathological, and nonfunctional.

Incongruent qualification of messages is typical of dysfunctional families. Incongruent communication leads to two types of problems: unclear relationships and devious methods of control. According to Haley, it is not pathological to attempt to control someone, but "a relationship becomes psychopathological when one of the two people will maneuver to circumscribe the other's behavior while indicating he is not" (1963, p. 17). Haley offers as an example a wife who has frequent anxiety attacks and cannot be left at home alone. Her symptom effectively controls the husband, but there are some negative results, too. For example, since the husband is responding to her anxiety rather than to *her,* he cannot take credit for being loving and caring. Therefore, the wife, unsure of his affection to begin with, still cannot be sure of his love and may wonder whether he would stay home if he did not have to. Finally, the wife must adopt a helpless posture and cannot take credit for being powerful. The incongruence occurs because the wife denies that *she* is requiring him to be home—it is her *anxiety,* over which she has no control.

Haley has a rather unusual view of psychological symptoms. To Haley, a symptom is highly influential on other people, and responsibility for the symptom is denied by the person displaying it. A symptom, then, is a special case of the "devious methods of control" discussed previously. To Haley (1963, p. 19), "the primary gain of symptomatic behavior in a relationship could be said to be the advantage of setting rules for that relationship. The defeat produced by symptomatic behavior is that one cannot take either the credit or the blame for being the one who sets those rules."

One of the reasons that relationships in which symptoms are used to control others are pathological is that the symptom tends to become entrenched—it tends to perpetuate itself. Consider Haley's discussion of the marriage in which the wife suffers from anxiety attacks:

> The husband who must remain home every night with an anxious wife will qualify his staying home with an indication that *he* is not doing this in response to *her,* or out of choice, her anxiety is requiring this involuntary behavior from him. The wife cannot win an acknowledgment that he wants to be home with her or that he does not. She also cannot be sure that *she* has control over the relationship in this area. She wins only the response she offers; an action qualified by a denial that the person has voluntarily chosen to make that action. Consequently, as long as she behaves in a symptomatic way, she cannot receive reassurance that he wants to be with her and would choose voluntarily to stay at home. She therefore cannot be reassured and so take responsibility for asking him to stay at home for her sake, but continues to ask him to stay home for the anxiety's sake, and the perpetuation of the symptom is assured. (1963, p. 18)

The model of a simple homeostatic system, such as a household thermostat, is not adequate to describe a family. In such a system the elements respond in error-activated ways to changes in range, but the setting of the range is made by a meta-governor, that is, by someone outside the system. In the family no outsider sets the limits of family behavior, although the culture might be said to function partially in that way. Instead, the limits of the family system are set by the members of the family as they influence each other. Therefore, in describing a family, Haley emphasizes that two levels of governing process must be included: the error-activated response by a member if any member exceeds a certain range of behavior and the attempt by family members to be the metagovernor (i.e., the one who sets the limits of that range). It is at this metagoverning level that the control problem enters the picture, because the governing process at this level will manifest itself as a struggle by each family member to be the one who determines the limits of the behavior of the others. Furthermore, an additional complexity is the existence of subsystems within the family that govern one another; the in-law subsystem has its influence on the nuclear family, the sibling subsystem has its influence upon the parental relationship, and so on. Thus, the addition of a family therapist is not a mere metagovernor of a single system but of the interlocking subsystems, each of which has a reciprocal influence with the therapist (Haley, 1970).

To Haley, the ultimate in pathology is schizophrenia, which he elevates to an art form, calling the schizophrenic a master of devious communication (1969). The schizophrenic must come from "the right sort of family," one in which certain types of communication take place. The double bind has been described by Bateson, Jackson, Haley, and Weakland (1956), and it is suggested that the double-bind situation is characteristic of families that produce schizophrenics.

There are several necessary ingredients for a double bind:

1. *Two or more persons.* One of these is the "victim." The bind may be inflicted by either or both parents, by siblings, or by any combination of these. If all members do not participate, it is necessary that no member effectively intervene.
2. *Repeated experience.* To produce schizophrenia, the double bind must be a recurring event, to the point at which it becomes a habitual expectation.
3. *A primary negative injunction.* The learning context is one of punishment rather than reward seeking; the child learns to avoid.
4. *A secondary injunction conflicting with the first at a more abstract level.* Like the first, this is enforced by punishments or the threat of them, again supporting avoidance behavior. This injunction is usually communicated nonverbally: posture, gesture, tone of voice, implications of the verbal content, and so on. Usually, this injunction communicates qualifications, such as "do not see this as punishment"; "do not see me as the punishing agent"; or "don't think or comment." These conflictual injunctions become much more numerous when two or more people are inflicting the double binds, as, for example, when one parent negates the other parent's commands at a more abstract level, the first parent then negating the other's negation, and so on and so on.
5. *A tertiary negative injunction prohibiting the victim from either metacommunicating or leaving the field.* The child gets labeled as bad or ungrateful if he or she tries to comment or get help somewhere else. Or the child may be seen as vaguely disloyal or disobedient or may simply become unrecognized (encounter a deaf ear) and so encounter the threat of ceasing to exist as a person.

Once the person has learned to perceive the interpersonal world in double-bind patterns, any part of the sequence may be enough to precipitate rage or panic. Eventually, the pattern of conflicting injunctions may become taken over by hallucinatory voices. A child growing up in such a family develops something akin to disorientation—he or she develops an inability to know what people mean when they say things, an inability to accurately interpret the qualifying messages of others or of the self. The child in such a family finds himself or herself involved in an intense relationship in which he or she feels it vitally important to discriminate the messages being communicated to him or her. He or she is caught in a situation in which it is impossible to respond appropriately or congruently without moving to a more abstract level. However, the child is prevented by punishment from any movement toward a more abstract (metacommunicative) level, so that he or she remains unable to correct his or her discrimination of what order of message to which he or she is really being asked to respond.

Being placed in such a situation gives one the feeling of "being on the spot"; that is, a normal person in such a situation will react defensively and become at least somewhat aware that his or her own behavior in response to the demands is a bit "funny." The schizophrenic feels on the spot all the time but seems unable to attribute it to the situation. The situation has become so habitual that he or she has only dim awareness of it. The person who has always lived in a double bind suffers from a breakdown of the metacommunicative system. That person is unable to judge accurately from voice tone, gesture, verbal message, and so on what another person means and is excessively concerned with what is meant, with no skills for checking it out.

A person with this set of circumstances might decide that behind every statement there lies a concealed (and discrepant) meaning, seeing hidden meaning in almost every message and even in chance occurrences. The person who goes this route is labeled paranoid and is characteristically defiant and suspicious. Or a person with a long history of double-bind situations might come to take every statement from others with extreme literality and to laugh off any nonverbal components of the message. Such a person comes to treat all messages as unimportant, or to be laughed at, and gets labeled hebephrenic. Still another pattern of response is to ignore all messages, to see and hear less and less of what goes on in one's environment and to avoid provoking any responses from this world. This person typically looks severely withdrawn and is often mute and gets labeled catatonic.

The only option that can save the schizophrenic is checking out the messages of others, discussing and exploring what others really mean so as to correct any distortions. This self-correcting system is what the schizophrenic conspicuously lacks. Without built-in self-corrective skills (which can only be developed with considerable support from someone else), the schizophrenic's communicative system spirals into distortion piled upon distortion.

Haley offers the following as characteristic of the family situation that ultimately leads to schizophrenia:

1. A child whose mother becomes anxious and withdrawn if the child responds to her lovingly—the mother experiences intimacy with this child as dangerous.
2. A mother for whom feelings of anxiety and hostility are unacceptable. She denies these feelings by overtly expressing "loving" behavior and insists that the child respond to her as a loving mother, withdrawing if the child does not. The "loving" behavior may not carry any real affection but may focus on doing the proper things, being "good," polite, considerate, and so on.
3. There is no one in the family, such as a strong father, who intervenes between the mother and the child so as to mitigate or clarify the mother's contradictory messages.

This, then, has the mother conveying at least two orders of messages, each negating or denying the other: hostile or withdrawing behavior when the child approaches her with affection and simulated loving that in some way labels the child's response to her withdrawing or hostility as inappropriate and that denies that she is withdrawing or hostile. The child is also constrained from accurately discriminating between these two orders of message. The child would be punished for discriminating accurately by perceiving himself or herself as hurting mother terribly, by risking the loss of the most important relationship in his or her life, by having to face the fact that his or her mother does not really love him or her, by encountering her wrathful accusations, and so on. Beyond all this, such a mother typically is very willing to label her child's own experience, for example, by saying "Go to bed. You're very tired and I want you to get your sleep," when she means, "Get the hell out of my sight, I'm sick of looking at you." So the child comes to distort both what mother means as well as his or her own internal states.

Consistently, then, in this type of family, the individual members manifest an incongruence between what they say and how they qualify what they say. Many people do this under certain circumstances, but, when the family of the schizophrenic interacts, its members confine themselves almost entirely to disqualifying their own statements.

The only congruent response that can be made to a double bind is either to leave the situation or to comment metacommunicatively on the impossibility of the situation. Neither of these responses is possible for the schizophrenic, who is too dependent and too invested in his or her family to leave it. No one in the family will tolerate any metacommunicative statements, as those messages will painfully reveal the contradictions inherent in the family situation. The schizophrenic may expect punishment no matter what he or she does; any response will fail to satisfy one or more of the parental injunctions, resulting in punishment, and any metacommunicative statement will also be punished.

The only alternative is to respond incongruently. By denying that a message is being sent or that any message was sent, or by denying that the message was intended for the receiver, the schizophrenic may avoid punishment. The schizophrenic, however, not only qualifies his or her messages by denying them but also *denies his or her denials.* This is the true "art of schizophrenia"—the schizophrenic may deny sending a message, but the denial may consist of the fantastic claim to be, not himself or herself, but Napoleon or Jesus. By making the denial ludicrous, the schizophrenic effectively denies it, too. The denial is so absurd that it is only partially effective, and, therefore, the message "gets through" after all, but the schizophrenic still has an "alibi" for avoiding responsibility and thereby avoiding punishment.

Haley has argued that psychotic behavior is triggered when the schizophrenic violates an implicit family prohibition. The person must act in such a way that he or she either returns within the limits of the family rules or somehow indicates that he or she is not actually infringing them. Psychotic behavior, with its piling of denial upon denial, allows the schizophrenic to violate old rules and set new ones by denying that *he* or *she* is violating the rules.

The family of the schizophrenic would seem to be not only establishing and following a system of rules, as other families do, but also following a prohibition on any acknowledgment that a family member is setting rules. . . . Since whatever one communicates inevitably governs the behavior of others, the family members must each constantly disqualify the communications of one another. . . . Schizophrenic behavior can be seen as both a product and a parody of this kind of family system. By labeling everything he communicates as not communicated by him to this person in this place, the schizophrenic indicates that he is not governing anyone's behavior because he is not in a relationship with anyone. (1959a, p. 373)

The nucleus of schizophrenic behavior is the avoidance of defining relationships. The schizophrenic wishes to do this because he or she cannot meet the impossible demands imposed by others' definitions of relationships and cannot make the necessary metacommunicative statements to maneuver to change the definition of the relationship. Because it is impossible not to communicate and because it is then impossible not to define relationships through communication, then, one needs to consider all contextual signs of any interaction including verbal, non-verbal and atmospheric factors.

According to Haley, then, the central nucleus of schizophrenia is a determined and consistent avoidance of defining relationships with other people. For anyone determined to avoid any definition of relationship, the other path available is to behave in ways that constitute the symptoms of schizophrenia. In traditional psychiatric systems, schizophrenia is talked about in terms of ego weakness, primitive logic, dissociated thinking, hallucinations, and so on. Such systems offer little for determining how the patient became the way that he or she is or for determining strategies of therapeutic intervention. When the patient is described in terms of the ways in which he or she observably interacts with others, it becomes possible to infer the kinds of learning situations that would foster such behaviors. It also becomes possible to infer the kinds of interventions that would effectively counter such behaviors so as to offer new learning situations more consonant with healthy interpersonal behavior.

Beyond theorizing about the kinds of family communication patterns that produce schizophrenia, Haley has found quite good support for his hypotheses in his observations of schizophrenics and their families. His observations suggest that the schizophrenic's way of incongruently qualifying statements is a habitual response to incongruent messages from the parents. The parents and the schizophrenic have become locked into a pattern of incongruent communication (Haley, 1973b).

In summary, the term "double bind" refers to communicational paradoxes, presented to the schizophrenic in his or her family, and to the schizophrenic's techniques—generalized out of the family setting—for avoiding defining relationships with others. The double bind serves two main functions for the schizophrenic's parents: it allows these parents to avoid defining their relationship to the child, and it makes it impossible for the child to define his or her relationship with the parents. When presented with a double bind, the child can only respond with incongruent messages. The congruent options of leaving the field (ending the relationship) and of metacommunicating are typically not open to the child of so-called schizophrenogenic parents. Such parents simply will not permit congruent metacommunicative statements (one mother was observed to cut off her son's beginning attempt to comment on her messages with, "Go ahead and criticize me if you want to, dear. I don't mind being hurt if it will help you"). As to the option of escaping from the field, the very young child obviously cannot end parental relationships even if faced with loss of survival. At older ages, the parents usually manage to keep the child locked into perceiving the relationship with them as all important by such devices as discounting the validity of any relationships the child may have formed outside the family, by capricious promises of love, and so on. Furthermore, by this time in life the child is objectively deficient in the ability to form meaningful relationships outside the family—just a little effort from the devoted parents can maintain almost total dependency on them. In effect, the options have come to staying with a crazy primary relationship or dying.

Diagnostic Framework

Haley has rejected the traditional medical model of diagnosis, but the therapist must become part of the diagnosis because he or she is a part of the problem (i.e., the social dilemma of the family). There are still no adequate diagnostic terms to describe family interaction. The therapist's focus should be on change only. However, Haley does diagnose the problem in descriptive terms. According to Haley, in a family in which someone has broken down, there is a hierarchy of confusion (1978). He stresses that, as the identified patient in a family improves, others suffer distress and symptomatic behavior. Therefore, the identified patient is usually holding the family together (1963, 1967, 1978).

Haley's diagnostic framework includes looking at power and coalitions, control, circular communication, and metacommunication. He describes the cause of distress and unresolvable conflict. A pathological system is further described as one that will lead to a dissolution of itself, violence among the elements, or inappropriate behavior. There is usually continual conflict with one or more symptomatic members, and there are perverse (cross-generational) triangles that are against one member (Haley, 1978). Haley has rejected labeling. In treatment, he focuses primarily on the problem that is defined as the repeating sequences of behavior. His basic paradigm defines the problem as a system problem that dictates that the therapist change the problem and the system (Foley, 1974).

Because the family is a communication system, there should emerge reliable patterns of interaction. Haley (1968, 1969), Ferreira (1964), and Ferreira and Winter (1968a) found that there were consistent stable interaction patterns among families on such variables as spontaneous agreement (SA), decision time (DT), and choice fulfillment (CF). Spontaneous agreement refers to family members' having chosen the same items prior to coming together for a family decision. Decision time refers to the amount of time taken to reach a family decision. Choice fulfillment refers to agreement of an individual's choices with the family's final choices. Second, if communicative dysfunctioning is truly a family phenomenon and not just an individual one, all dyads within dysfunctional families should be equally affected. Variables such as SA and CF should significantly differ from those of normals. It was shown that decreases in SA evenly affect all dyads (Ferreira and Winter, 1968a). Also, Friedman and Friedman (1970) found that distortions in communication occurred even when the identified patient was absent. This finding also supports the notion of the family as the pathological unit and suggests that dysfunctional families take longer to reach a decision.

The concept of the double bind has not only been broadened with changing characteristics, but it has also been posited as a universal pathologic situation. It has been applied to hysterical, phobic, and obsessive–compulsive personalities by Sluzki and Veron (1971). The hysteric individual sees himself or herself as bad and others as good. He or she has been punished for activity and rewarded for passivity. The binding message for the hysteric person is "Take the initiative, but remember, it is forbidden to take the initiative."

The phobic individual's problem is to distinguish dangerous from safe situations. He or she is enjoined to be independent but is also told that the world is a dangerous place. He or she is punished for risking and rewarded for avoiding. He or she can be independent only when it is safe. So the binding message becomes "Be independent by being dependent on me."

The obsessive–compulsive person uses some neutral acts to avoid dangerous ones. He or she has been punished for doing the wrong thing and has only avoided punishment when he or she has done the correct thing. Because demands have been made on him or her beyond his or her maturational capabilities, the individual fails and is labeled intrinsically bad. The individual is thus always in danger of committing bad acts. The binding message is "Be independent, although, of course, you are incapable of it."

Families of delinquents show inconsistent messages sent in terms of nonverbal permissions (Haley, 1969) or encouragements. The delinquent child, through acting out, may be carrying out parental impulses (Stierlin, 1977). Inconsistent communication leading to delinquent behavior cannot only occur from one individual but between individuals. Here, prohibition comes from one parent while permission comes from the other. Ferreira (1964) has referred to this process as the split double bind, which has no injunction against leaving the field (Watzlawick et al., 1967), in a case in which the father was militaristic, authoritarian, and demanding, whereas the mother encouraged her son to flaunt authority. From this notion, delinquent children would then logically perceive their parent(s) as sanctioning their behavior. Parents are perceived as sanctioning their children's behavior more than are the delinquent boys themselves.

As a unit, delinquent families demonstrate failures and lack of clarity in communication (Stabenau et al., 1965). They take longer to reach decisions and have more silences than do normals. They have low SA and CF (Ferreira and Winter, 1965; Ferreira, Winter, and Poindexter, 1969). When delinquent parents are placed in a double-binding situation, in which the diagnostic task is to discuss proverb meanings, they show a number of significant differences from schizophrenic and normal parents. They demonstrate a greater frequency of switching the level of meaning of the metaphor and a greater number of tangential and evasive statements. Delinquent parents disaffirm that a message is addressed to themselves or another. This disaffirmation is most frequent after at least five simultaneous or successive disagreements have occurred. Concurrent with disaffirmation is a high frequency of indications that the speaker is talking to himself or herself and that the other person is talking to himself or herself. Finally, more remarks about the interviewer and more negative comments about the proverb occur.

Within normal families, individuals are able to communicate their wants and desires. They make more self-disclosure statements. Over time, each family member should be able to accurately know and perceive others. Ferreira (1964) found that within families there exists a relationship between how many items are rejected and how many items are expected to be rejected among family members. There is a greater discrepancy between these two measures (number rejected and expected to be rejected) for abnormal families. This result shows that they have less accurate information and less open communication. Going along with the same line of reasoning concerning accurate knowledge, the SA index can be viewed as a measure of how well families communicate. As the members interact with one another, they tend to become more alike. This would then increase SA. Normal families do have the highest SA scores (Ferreira and Winter, 1968b). Using the same reasoning, as children grow and communicate more, they should show increases in their SA scores with parents. There is a positive correlation between the age of the child and SA score with parents (Ferreira, 1964; Ferreira and Winter, 1965, 1968b). This relationship exists for normals and for some maladjusted families but not for schizophrenic or delinquent ones. A greater SA was also found with like-sexed parents for children in normal families but not for abnormal ones.

Combining the ability to communicate preferences and increased amount of SA between like-sexed parent and child, coalitions should be capable of forming. In normal families there were significant coalitions between same-sexed members, father–son, mother–daughter. This factor was not true for abnormal families (Ferreira, 1964). Furthermore, dysfunctional families, such as those of schizophrenics, should have difficulty in forming and maintaining coalitions. Schizophrenic families spent significantly less time in coalitions, their coalitions were of shorter duration, and they were less consistent in responding to coalition signals (Haley, 1962).

Functional families with adequate and open communication should meet the needs and wants of each family member. Choice fulfillment is an index of individual choices that become family choices. Normal families consistently show the highest CF. Significantly lower are other dysfunctional groups, with schizophrenic families the lowest of all (Ferreira and Winter, 1965, 1968b). Furthermore, healthy families, being flexible, should be able to make room for children as they come along. This adjustment would show up in the lack of significant differences between older and younger children on amount of CF. No such difference exists in normal families, yet there are significant differences in the pathological families (Ferreira and Winter, 1968b).

Finally, Jackson and his associates (Watzlawick et al., 1967) stated that the relationship aspects of communication in normal families stays in the background. The definition of the relationship is done out of real awareness and, as such, is not specifically attended to. Conversely, this aspect gets more attention in pathological families. Loeff (1966) found that, although both adolescent groups could distinguish between conflictual and nonconflictual messages, pathological adolescents attend a great deal more to the metacommunicative level.

Presently (Haley, 1976), there seems to be a deemphasis on diagnostic categories and formal diagnostic labels. The interview is the main tool for gathering information about the family, especially in *present* rather than in past contexts.

In keeping with this focus on the system, Haley has included himself (the therapist) as part of the overall family diagnosis. This represents a marked departure from others who practice family therapy. Whereas the latter tend to describe the family as a set of problems independent of each other, Haley includes himself in the description of the family. This former practice (of excluding therapist from the family) is also seen in the writings of Ackerman (Chapter 3), Satir (Chapter 4), and Bowen (Chapter 9). As Haley has stated, "Evaluation of a family is how the family responds to your therapeutic interventions." An important aspect of this contextual view is the realization that Haley not only takes the family into account, including the extended kin who influence a family, but also other helping professionals who may be involved (i.e., social workers, school counselors, medical doctors, pastors, etc.). One may then draw from this information that there are not different diagnostic categories of families but rather, different families in different treatment contexts.

In addressing the "problem," Haley focuses on referral issues. His most common procedure is to inquire why the family is there, or what the problem is. Usually, the family members say that one person is the problem, which Haley nonverbally reframes in terms of more than one person (a systems approach). Therefore, he will be thinking about the problem in a different way from the way in which family members think about it, but he does not attempt to persuade them to think about it his way. In brief, he takes the problem as presented (e.g., a problem child) and then silently restructures this in terms of what is happening in the total situation of the child that is causing him to behave as he does.

1. *Past history.* Little or no emphasis, as Haley sees the present situation as the major causal factor and the process that must be changed.
2. *Interpretation of feelings and attitudes.* Haley is very parsimonious with interpretations except when using them tactically to persuade family members to behave differently. In particular, he does not feel it helpful to confront family members with how much they dislike one another. Instead, he tends to interpret destructive behavior in some positive way, for example, as a protective act.
3. *Emphasis upon outcome.* Success is measured in terms of what therapeutic re-

sults are happening in terms of quite specific goals. If the family is not changing, he shifts his approach.

Therapeutic Foci and Goals

The basic premise of strategic therapy is that reality is defined as one chooses to define it. As people define their reality, their attempted solutions to problems often become the problem. It is hoped that strategic interventions will bring about an alteration and redefinition of reality in the form of a more functional solution (Haley, 1976).

Haley does not focus much on diagnosis or history but attempts to intervene as soon as possible with an emphasis on the participation of everyone. He stresses that the role of the therapist is that of one who is in charge, neutral, and involved, with an initial focus on the digital communication of the family and the presenting problem (1976). The therapist is directive and is considered effective to the extent that he or she enforces a dominant position and controls the relationship.

The essence of therapy is the "technique of interviewing" (Haley, 1976). Change is the focus and is brought about by a system of interaction rather than by insight and interpretation. Change is considered the only valid outcome, with the kind and degree of change determined by the family and the focus of change to realign alliances. In the initial stage of treatment, the therapist relabels the behavior and the problem with an emphasis on positives. The therapist narrowly redefines the presenting problem and gets family members to talk with each other about the problem. The therapist encourages the usual behavior and gives paradoxical directives that force the family to take the initiative (Haley, 1976).

A paradox (Chapter 1) is defined as describing a message containing a relationship directive that qualifies another directive in a conflicting way, either simultaneously or at a different moment in time. The receiver cannot obey or disobey because of the conflicting nature of the paradox. The person posing the paradox will "win" in controlling the relationship and the familiar becomes redefined (Minuchin, 1974). The therapy becomes strategic because the clinician is in charge and determines how therapy will proceed (Haley, 1973a).

Haley has stressed that, if one changes behavior, one changes feelings; therefore, feelings are not an essential focus of the therapy. The family changes by being forced to act in different ways, and the therapist moves the family to the new ways of operating. However, Haley contradicts himself by stressing that the degree of change should be determined by the family. In therapy, the family is faced with a relationship containing multiple paradoxes that force them to abandon old behavior, as the family can only deal with the relationship or escape from it amiably by undergoing change (1969).

Therapy also consists of the therapist as model (Haley, 1963), the therapist as metagovernor of the system, and the therapist's determining how therapy will proceed (Haley, 1973b). While the therapeutic paradox forces the family to take the initiative, the behavior is determined by the therapist (Haley, 1976). Finally, creative change is the outcome of the struggle for control between the therapist and the family members. The therapist is the agent who produces family change by directions that are ambiguous, emphasizing the positive, relabeling, and encouraging the usual behavior. Therapy is effective when the therapist wins the power struggle with the family, is in control of the therapy, and produces change in behavior (Haley, 1978).

Faced with troublesome behavior in a family, the therapist paradoxically encourages the family to continue. The therapist gains some control in doing this because what happens is now defined as occurring under his or her direction. The therapist may further increase control by directing the family to *increase* the problem behavior. Then, and only then, can the therapist shift direction to bring about therapeutic change, a reduction in the problem behavior. To Haley, any attempt to produce therapeutic change that is made before the establishment of the therapist's control of the relationship is a waste of time and doomed to failure. The therapist cannot deal straightforwardly with conflicts about who is to set the rules because, if the therapist has become important enough to the family members to influence them, he or she, too, has become involved in the same struggle. If the therapist has not become important, he or she will not be caught up in this struggle, but the family will ignore the therapist and the therapist will be rendered ineffective.

"The first obligation of a therapist is to change the presenting problem offered. If that is not accomplished, the therapy is a failure" (Haley, 1976). However, as is usually the case, if a person with symptoms is offered as a problem, Haley would probably take the view that changes must take place in that family "system" before that person can change. In this vein, Haley would not attempt to persuade the family that the real problem lies in the family and not in the person. "The goal is not to teach the family about their malfunctioning system, but to change the family sequences so that the presenting problems are resolved" (1976).

Haley is a strong proponent of an implied therapeutic contract with the family members that provides the baseline for the goals of therapy. This contract is considered sine qua non if the therapist is to enjoy full cooperation from the family members; the clearer the contract, the more organized the therapy. Haley would settle on the problem that the family wants to change and the problem must be put in a solvable form. The negotiation that takes place involves how to make the problem operational. When using a directive approach, Haley has pointed out that "it is essential that a clearly defined presenting problem be negotiated and that the therapist use the presenting problem as leverage for inducing change."

Haley has presented family therapy as a task of strategic problem solving in which the therapist assumes the responsibility for maneuvering families outside their awareness to change. Integral to acquiring the skills to do therapy is knowing how to take a presenting problem and reframe it so that it becomes a solvable problem. Consequently, the therapist will have a yardstick by which to measure change and whether or not the therapeutic goal was achieved. Thus, the first premise of problem solving—correct preparation in stating the problem—is utilized in Haley's approach. Expressed another way, Haley simply but eloquently operates on the assumption that the therapist has the answer for showing covertly that the clients have the answer if the "right" question or problem is asked. This reminds one of Gertrude Stein's parting words to Alice B. Toklas. Gertrude asked, "What's the question?" She did not hear Alice's answer and went on to say, "If there is no question, there can be no answer." Supposedly, Gertrude died thereafter.

Haley implicitly claims to demystify therapy by removing it from an esoteric art to a teachable skill with the goal of producing practitioners instead of theoreticians. Part of the demystification process comes from Haley's assumption that therapy is for people who have problems. Further, the problems do not reside within the individual but arise within a system or context composed of at least a "triad." Thus, change occurs when the context or system is changed. It is commonly accepted that most people enter therapy with problems to be solved. Haley reminds the therapeutic community of how this fact is ignored. For example, he, more than once, attacks insight schools of therapy for their modi operandi that circumvent presenting problems to work on the real problems via well-timed direct interpretations to the client. Haley radically differs in his approach in that he avows that insight via direct therapeutic interpretation is unnecessary and disrespectful of the client who already knows. Instead, the presenting problem is taken as the point of departure. All therapeutic interventions are related back to it without using any direct interpretations.

Because Haley's basic operating principle is that the context of the client must be changed, his approach is consistent with systems theory. Accordingly, one of his basic assumptions is that concerning the structure of a given system. Haley states that "all creatures capable of learning are compelled to organize." Being organized means following "patterned, redundant ways of behaving and to exist in a hierarchy" (1976, p. 101). Furthermore, members of a hierarchy are differentiated by function and status, which means that each person in a given hierarchy is unequal in status and power. This description is the closest that Haley came to describing health or functionality—a system that is organized with clear rules and differentiated by function and power. The most basic hierarchy is that organized according to generational lines.

Conversely, his description of pathology or dysfunctionality, as discussed earlier, is disorganization—violation of the organization of a given hierarchy that typically results from coalitions, especially secret, across generations or levels of hierarchies. Pathology also results when the sequences (repeating patterns of events) became narrow and rigid. Sequence, in Haley's approach, is best assessed by the communication cycle in which the same behaviors—actions or verbal and nonverbal communication—take on a self-regulating function to maintain the malfunctioning system. For example, a single-female-parent family who has coaligned herself with a parentified child and excluded herself from parenting functions with other children in the family would most likely manifest detectable, rigid sequences of behavior. Haley made an important point regarding the detecting of rigid sequences in a family; that is, the therapist has to be trained to assess multiple sequences before intervening within a system. Thus, the goal is to create new situations for the clients whereby this sequencing could be changed.

Haley has defined therapeutic change "as a change in the repeating acts of a self-regulating system" (1976, p. 105). Important in his concept of change is its accomplishment in steps. That is, a malfunctioning system does not go directly from an abnormal to a normal state. Instead, the typical pattern is to go from one abnormal to a different abnormal state. The enactment of stress through creating a new problem in the family is part of the design for change.

Haley proffers the idea that the best procedure for accomplishing change is to create new situations in which the family members can experience new patterns of behavior. His operating principle here is not unusual. However, his procedure for intervention is unusual and reflects his training in hypnosis, his work with Gregory Bateson on the "double-bind" hypothesis, and his study of Milton Erickson (Haley, 1973a). For example, Haley is adamant about the therapist's manipulating the family to change without using direct verbal interpretations or insight. He advocates training in hypnosis for therapists who use his approach because hypnosis will enable them to learn the skill of covertly moving clients into new situations and behaviors. Part of his rationale here comes from his description of the therapist who is the "gatekeeper" and, thus, controller of information within a given system while remaining distant enough to be outside the system. The therapist redirects the flow of information according to planned strategies and assumes total responsibility for changing the family because the therapist is the expert and has the skills. The armory of the therapist consists of connecting with the family through understanding its metaphorical language, issuing directives, enacting tasks within a session, and, when appropriate, joining in coalitions with different family members. If the family is resistant to change or is too stabilized, then Haley conjures up relevant paradoxes in the Erickson mode to force the family into a winning situation and thereby produce the desired change. In many ways, Haley seems to be cataloging and defining many of Erickson's techniques as presented in *Uncommon Therapy* (1973a).

Haley's approach could be considered narrow and not useful for all clients or systems. Instead, the best strategy seems to be when to use which approach with whom, and this idea brings one to the importance of doing therapy within a theoretical framework. Haley argues pursuasively that the best training of therapists occurs through learning by doing and that "theory grows out of action, not action out of theory" (1976, p. 183). He argues against exposing trainees to different theories and teachers in other settings, because this will confuse and distract them. Furthermore, he proposes that teaching theory is a waste of time until much later in the training program, when the student-therapist has gained some experience. His philosophy on theory is consistent with his action-oriented approach to therapy, whereas his philosophy is not consistent with other schools of therapy. It is easy to infer that Haley takes this position because he does not have a theory to teach in the strictest sense, and, until he does, he refuses to teach any other theory. Here, one is reminded of Kant's axiom: "Experience without theory is blind, and theory without experience is mere intellectual play." Kant's axiom fits personal experience and the preferred mode of learning about how to do therapy. Bright therapy trainees cannot do therapy without the guidance of some theoretical framework: loosely, the philosophical notions that anyone has about life, value systems, and so on. So, why not study approaches and theories of those far more experienced and educated rather than entering therapy with only one's own notions about it (i.e., reading theory, trying out theoretical ideas in practice, and building one's data bank about whether the clinical data support the theory)? Furthermore, what one may adopt in terms of theory may be congruent with one's own personality and therapy style.

In addition to the description and evaluation of Haley's problem-solving approach, further comments are necessary. Haley is a provocative, stimulating thinker and writer, although it may be difficult at times to reconcile some of his ideas to one's preferred therapy style. He offers family therapists one valuable and important approach, particularly in the areas of communication and paradox. However, one could consider him an extremist at times, based upon his polarization of concepts. Paradoxically, this quality in his style of thinking challenges the reader to think about what he is saying and challenges one to synthesize his or her views with those of others. Perhaps this was one of his goals in writing *Problem-Solving Therapy*—to create a new situation for the reader to change the reader's metaphors.

Intervention Strategies

Haley has deployed the use of directives, which may take the form of paradoxical intent or of telling people what to do when the therapist wants them to do it. In keeping with his "systems" approach, "no one should be left out of the action designed to take place in the home." In this way, emphasis is keyed to the family aggregate.

Inherent in the directions is the issue of assigning tasks, which often takes the form of directing someone metaphorically. The logic behind this approach lies in the fact that people will sometimes be more willing to follow a directive if they do not know consciously that they have received one. It is also a method that allows one to show something in action that resembles something else that the individual wants to occur. The issue of assigning tasks may also manifest itself in terms that require members of a family to role play, either paradoxically or nonparadoxically.

Haley devotes an entire chapter (1976) to the idea of "Communication as Bits and Metaphor." Here, he addresses both digital and analogic ways of communications. It is quite clear from his therapeutic bent that he attempts change at both levels, depending on the situation. However, he is quite adamant that the change in behavior of the family occurs as an aspect of the analogic changes in the relationship with the therapist. In one example (1976, p. 91), Haley talks of a hypothetical situation in which a man enters therapy because he is afraid he is going to die of a heart attack. Haley "would assume that the patient's statement about his heart is analogic to his current situation, and would construct a theory that the man's communication about his heart is a way of stabilizing his marriage."

One approach to this situation might be paradoxical intervention, whereby he would take literally the person's metaphor about dying. After first establishing a trusting relationship with the individual and assuring him that there is nothing wrong with his heart, he then would advise the person that he not only is going to die with a heart attack, but he should drop dead right now. The person's communication is not received as an analogy about something else but as a digital statement about his heart. As Haley has stated, "when the therapist is successful, the patient abandons his analogy about his heart."

A different twist to the preceding, which takes the family into account, was developed by a mentor of Haley, Milton Erickson. In such a situation, the wife usually believes the doctors who say that her husband's heart is normal, but she also responds to her husband's behavior by taking the metaphor literally. When the therapeutic relationship is set, the wife encourages the husband to die of his heart attack. Each time the husband expresses his fear of dying of a heart attack, the wife is encouraged to react in certain ways, such as calling an ambulance, visiting funeral parlors, collecting and distributing funeral literature throughout the house. This method allows the wife to form a basis for communication that heretofore had been blocked by the husband's metaphoric pattern. A symptom is changed by changing its context of relationships.

A further approach involves the intervention or blocking of a circular sequence. Because the sequence is one of a repeating cycle, there is a series of steps, each leading to the next and so back to the beginning again. The therapeutic task is to change the sequence by intervening in such a way that it cannot continue. A point is made that, when a triad is involved, changing any one of the steps or the behavior of any one of the three people is usually not sufficient to bring about change in the sequence. At least two behaviors must be changed.

Role(s) of the Therapist

It is quite evident from the foregoing that Haley is very much action oriented. He keeps himself neutral in terms of choosing sides in a family, save in those instances in which choosing sides is for the purpose of therapeutic manipulation. At times, he appears to use both linear and circular maneuvers, but, for the most part, he is circular. An excellent example of the circular strategy is the discussion of the hypothetical situation involving the heart attack analogy in which paradoxical intervention was employed.

Haley describes family therapy as the "art of coalitions" (1978). His therapy is directive, active, and problem oriented. Insight is not valued, and the only focus of treatment is change in behavior.

Haley argues that symptoms are devious methods of control and that the patient will attempt to control the therapist with his or her symptoms in the same way that he or she controls everyone else. If the therapist tells the patient to reduce the symptomatic behavior, the therapist will have lost control and therapy will not go well. The patient will "attempt" to change, but his or her resistance will inevitably cause him or her to "fail," thus defeating the therapist's attempt to control the patient. If the therapist, however, tells the patient to continue or even increase the problem behavior, the problem of resistance is circumvented. The only way in which the patient can resist is to improve! Actually, it is impossible to resist, because the therapist has posed a paradox and is simultaneously asking for change and no change.

As in any other relationship, the issue of control is important in the therapeutic relationship. It is important that the therapist gain control of the relationship if change is to take place.

It is of crucial importance that the therapist deal successfully with the question whether he or the patient is to control what kind of relationship they will have. No form of therapy can avoid this problem; it is central, and in its resolution is the source of therapeutic change. If the patient gains control in psychotherapy, he will perpetuate his difficulties since he will continue to govern by symptomatic methods. (Haley, 1963, p. 19)

To gain control, the therapist poses a paradox for the patient. In a setting whose purpose is defined as change, the therapist asks for no change. The rationale for this particular strategy is found in Haley's theory of how relationships operate:

Granting that people in ongoing relationships function as "governors" in relation to one another, and granting that it is the function of a governor to diminish change, then the first law of relationships follows: *When one person indicates a change in relation to another, the other will act upon the first so as to diminish and modify that change.* Granting the functioning of this law, the therapist must *avoid* making direct requests for change. (1963, p. 189)

Haley compares the therapeutic relationship with the relationship between hypnotist and subject and the relationship between Zen master and pupil. In all three, one party imposes a paradox upon the other, and the other undergoes a "spontaneous" change. The therapy patient improves, the hypnotic subject enters a trance, and the Zen pupil attains *satori.* In both hypnosis and therapy the hypnotist-therapist asks the subject-patient to do some thing and, at the same time, tells him or her not to do it. When the subject-patient responds by doing it but denies that he or she is responding to the hypnotist-therapist, then a trance has been induced or therapeutic change occurs.

Aside from telling everyone, from hypnotists to psychoanalyst, to behaviorists, and to nondirective therapists, that they are not really doing what they think they are doing, but are really all doing the same thing (imposing paradoxes), Haley's major contributions to therapy have been in the field of marital and family therapy. According to Haley (1963), conflict in families may be of three types: (1) disagreements about the rules for living together, (2) disagreements about who is to set the rules, and (3) attempts to enforce rules that are incompatible with each other. The family therapist, like the individual therapist, serves two main functions, those of providing an educational factor to help them behave differently and using therapeutic paradoxes to force them to do so (1963).

The major difference between family and marital therapy is not the approach of the therapist but the issue of shifting the emphasis from focus on an identified patient (usually a child) to focus on the family as a whole. Once this is accomplished (by "binding" the symptom to the family), the therapist's tactics are similar in both cases. Those tactics are threefold: (1) "directing" the family by the use of injunctions, which are so ambiguous that they cannot be resisted, (2) redefining and reframing behaviors in positive terms, and (3) imposing paradoxes by "prescribing the symptom."

In dealing with conflicts about what the rules in a relationship are, the therapist can be straightforward and need not bring out the "big guns" of paradox. The therapist's main function here is to clarify the rules (which are usually vague, unspoken, and often secret), since "when they are explicit, they are more difficult to follow" (Haley, 1963, p. 140). The therapist begins the process by such ambiguous directives as, "Now let's get at the real feelings behind this situation so we can understand it." Any comment that follows this statement may be labeled a cooperative effort as the directive is so vague. As the family talks with each other, the therapist constantly relabels behavior in positive terms. In general, "the therapist defines the couple [family] as attempting to bring about an amiable closeness but going about it wrongly, being misunderstood, or being driven by forces beyond their control" (Haley, 1963, p. 139).

Relabeling behavior is therapeutic because "by subtly focusing on the opposite, or a different, aspect of a relationship, the therapist undermines the couple's [family's] typical ways of labeling the relationship and they must define it in a different way and so undergo change" (Haley, 1963, p. 140). Although the therapist's approach here is contradictory, it is not paradoxical. In Haley's view, conflicts about what the rules are can be dealt with by the therapist's encouraging the family to talk together and by relabeling behavior positively. Conflicts about who is to set the rules, however, require more active direction by the therapist, primarily in the form of therapeutic paradoxes. Change in this area is much more difficult to obtain.

Because the family is a homeostatic system, the therapist must expect continuing resistance to his or her efforts to change it. To overcome and circumvent this resistance, the therapist must resort to paradox. Haley described the nature of this resistance as follows:

> There are two major factors which inhibit family change: the complications which develop in a self-corrective system when one element behaves differently, and the fact that when a therapist becomes included in the family system he will be dealt with at the level on which family members are struggling with each other—the level of who is going to govern the behavior of whom. (1963, p. 162)

Critique and Evaluation

Concerning the nature of Haley's approach to other systems of family therapy, one may describe Haley as an action-oriented therapist representing one of the major approaches to problem-oriented behavior change. Compared with the humanistic theorists, such as Satir (Chapter 4), Haley does not focus on insight and awareness or give the major responsibility for change in therapy to the family. Compared with Bowenian theory (Chapter 9), one may say that Bowen's approach is much more similar to its psychoanalytic origins in the sense that it focuses more on logic and understanding, whereas Haley focuses solely on change with the family's intellectual understanding of the process of therapy having no importance.

Comparing Haley's approach to behavioral approaches to family therapy (Patterson, Chapter 10), one may say that, although behaviorists, as Haley does, emphasize change, their interventions, unlike Haley's, are devoted to first-order system change, whereas Haley promotes second-order system change, as described by Watzlawick (Chapter 5). Haley, unlike most major family theorists, does not promote or advocate a focus on changes in self-worth, awareness, feelings, or positive aspects of personality. The problem is always a behavioral one.

Regarding the nature of Haley's theoretical assumptions, Bateson (1978) has criticized Haley for ignoring the components of learning in the family system. Although Haley offers valuable descriptions of family systems, the causes of certain behavioral problems are still unknown. As Bateson (1978) has stated, there is still no specific knowledge regarding the etiology of schizophrenia. Haley has also focused primarily on the aspects of communication and power to the exclusion of other factors. His main assumption is that the therapist must control people for change to take place. Haley's assertion that behavioral change is the only valid outcome of therapy not only requires the therapist to decide what the outcome of therapy should be for the family but also ignores the validity of the goal of "feeling better." For example, the alleviation of depression or anxiety in many cases is a problem of feeling better. It is a moot point to argue with Haley's assumption that changing behavior causes a change in feelings. However, it should be added that changing feelings sometimes causes a change in behavior. It is interesting to note that Haley is aware of the circular nature of cause and effect but ignores this circularity in defining what will cause change.

One could question the authoritarian stance of deciding what kind of change should take place in a family and subsequently "forcing" the family to change according to the therapist's goal. This stance not only ignores the possibility that some families will cooperate in their therapy but also leads to the possibility of the family's needing to rely on the therapist for each new crisis that may appear. Although Haley has at times declared that his model is partly educative, it does not require or encourage the family's understanding of its own problems.

It cannot be denied that Haley's theoretical assumptions and treatment model have validity and make "sense." However, the beginning reader of Haley's work should be aware that it is deceptively simple. The nature of paradox and analogic thinking requires a major shift in logic. This shift in logic is not only difficult to make but it also may be impossible for some to make. Paradoxical interventions not only require a shift in thinking for the therapist but also require timing and a thorough understanding of the problem. Paradoxical directives are an art, and like an art cannot always be taught.

Ultimately, one must question the use of paradoxical directives in relationship to the assumption that paradoxical interventions are effective because the family cannot consciously understand the double bind. As literature on the nature of paradox becomes an integral part of the field of psychotherapy, the sophisticated client may "resist" the therapist in other ways. Milton Erickson's use of paradox was an intervention designed to combat resistance in the patient (Haley, 1973). The patient in many ways was "tricked" into cooperating. When the resistive patient in the future understands the "trick," paradoxical interventions may lose their effectiveness. One could hypothesize a situation similar to that of the child who understands parent effectiveness training and tells his or her mother, "I know what you're trying to get me to do."

Haley's approach offers a certain security to a fledgling therapist who wants a "how-to-do-it" handbook. However, his approach is deceptively simple and much more than a how-to-do-it handbook. For example, he clearly delineates the major steps of a first interview, discusses how to look at sequences, and explains reasonably well the rationale behind tasks and pitfalls of paradoxes. Among other stimulating tidbits, he justifies the ethics behind his directive approach and offers his conceptualization of digital and analogic communication. Also, his book (1976) and approach include information for supervisors, training procedures, and training centers that one may find invaluable. However, his approach and style of presentation are at times authoritarian and not without weaknesses.

For example, he more than once has conveyed the impression that his approach to family therapy is brief, effective, and applicable to all families. In fact, Haley exalts his own brand of therapy largely by polarizing his concepts and by discounting what insight and interpretative approaches have to offer. This is demonstrated classically through his polarization of the therapeutic community into either A or Z therapists. The A therapists are distinguished on one end of the continuum by being insight oriented, interpretive, and more "touchy-feely" and, among other things, viewing changes as beginning within the self. Thus, the A therapist is exonerated from any responsibility for the change process. Conversely, Z therapists, who are on the other end of the continuum, are directive, problem oriented, cognitive, and clear that the change process is the therapist's total responsibility. In the A approach, therapy seems to be more of an art and intuition. In the Z approach, therapy is a skill that can be taught, and theory has no place in the beginning training of a therapist. Theory comes later, after the therapist has learned by doing, ideally through watching videotapes of other kindred therapists and through being supervised on the spot by an experienced supervisor behind a one-way mirror.

Haley has some interesting ideas for training and makes compelling arguments for his approach up to a point. His polarization and dogmatic tone mark the point at which one may begin to be turned off by his approach. One would like Haley more as a writer and therapist if he would differentiate his concepts or at least qualify them as follows: "There are general types of therapists that can be inferred to fall on a continuum ranging from 'A' to the 'Z' ends. My approach is *predominantly* 'Z' because . . .". It is difficult to buy the idea that there can be a purely Z therapist and, for sure, no one has ever met a purely A therapist. Furthermore, no data support the superiority of Haley's approach over other therapeutic approaches. Which approach is most effective will be determined by such variables as the therapist's personal style, the population of clients, and where the clients are at a given point in therapy. At best, Haley's approach may be effective for him because of his usual client population—generally lower class, black, and practically oriented. It seems reasonable to infer that many clients, ranging from middle to upper class, educated, and sophisticated, would profit from insight therapy as well. However, until technology is found for demonstrating which approach works with whom, the issue of which approach to use remains a controversial one. (This point will be discussed further in Chapter 16.)

Another possible criticism of Haley's approach lies in his use of a directive but covert style of engineering families into change. The therapist does not take credit for any of the change, which is acceptable up to a point, but the therapist keeps his or her skills from the clients. The Haley family members do not learn to problem solve for themselves if new problems arise upon termination. Problem solving per se could be a teachable skill that can be taught to clients.

The case of "A Modern Little Hans" illustrates some of the preceding criticisms. In this case, Haley claims that the mother, without any direct interpretation from the therapist, saw that she and her husband used the children for dealing with their marriage conflict. In addition, her insight here revealed that she already knew her situation and that, when change occurred (in the dog phobia of her son), she could then concede what she knew. Two years later, in a follow-up interview, the mother voluntarily attributed the family's changed situation to her husband's bonus, which enabled the family to take a long-needed vacation.

Here, Haley's belief in the maintenance of change has to be accepted on faith. That is, he conveys the impression that changing two situations—the boy's dog phobia and marital conflict of the parents—would somehow cure this family. However, the mother's comment to the therapist about the bonus raises the possibility that she really did not learn anything about problem solving or how to develop coping strategies if new problems should arise. Thus, it will be interesting to see if Haley's approach will come to share a similar criticism leveled against the behaviorist's approach—symptom substitution.

The Hans case serves to demonstrate another criticism of Haley: his dictum that direction interpretations are not used by the therapist. Haley does not interpret verbally, but he interprets in such a way that the client would have to be blind not to receive the message. For example, the therapist restricted session 8 to the parents. Prior to this session, he had made attempts to open up the marital conflict between them. The therapist's questions around the marriage and his asking the couple to come alone are selective forms of communication and are interpretable by the clients. How the clients interpret what the therapist does is relevant to the context. His approach to therapy may still be interpretative *but indirectly so*. It seems logical to paraphrase Haley's dictum that "one cannot not communicate" into "the therapist cannot not interpret." Again, it appears that Haley may have contradicted his claim of not using interpretations.

Another thorny issue in Haley's approach, which he uses to support his nonuse of insight and interpretation, is his concept of "courtesy" therapy. Haley assumes that clients know their problem but not its solution. Thus, it is discourteous and antitherapeutic to confront the client on what is already known. His rationale for this assumption seems to be based upon the importance of conducting therapy outside the client's awareness and that the therapist either engages in self-disclosure or does not. Haley has polarized his thinking on self-disclosure and left no room for a middle-ground position. He demonstrates his logic behind courtesy therapy through the case of the couple who enter therapy to deal with the wife's anxiety. Accordingly, it is courteous to assume that the couple knows the real problem behind the wife's anxiety, which is a marital conflict. Thus, the goal is to make change as easy as possible. The couple's awareness or knowledge of the real problem behind the anxiety is an assumption and nothing more. How can Haley know that others know their real problems when research has shown time and time again that even highly trained professionals often cannot agree on what the clients' real problems are?

If Haley were to differentiate different levels of awareness, one could possibly see using his courtesy tactic. For example, consider the distinction between knowing and knowing that you know, which is being conscious, and knowing, but not knowing that you know, which is being somewhere below consciousness. This information may or may not surface into awareness; not knowing and not knowing that you do not know can go on ad infinitum. If Haley can validate that the client is on the first knowing level, perhaps the courtesy approach is appropriate. However, some therapists subscribe to the view that the client really wants to be seen by the therapist and part of this means confronting and calling the client's cons or showing the client that the therapist knows what he or she knows. If this assumption is correct, the Haley approach would be ineffective with such clients.

More valuable contributions of Haley are his ideas on communication. He discusses the importance of conceptualizing two types of communication—digital, a message with discrete referents such as "yes" or "no," and analogic, a message with multiple referents (Chapter 1). Analogic communication is relationship language and central to therapeutic procedures because the therapist must understand the metaphors of the clients. Haley seems to say that the most basic goal of any therapy is to change the metaphors of the clients. He assumes that communication cannot be changed directly by working on the client's communication. That is, communication change occurs through making organizational changes in the situation to which "the clients are adapting" (Haley, 1976, p. 90). Specifically, Haley postulates that organizational changes occur through the process of the therapist's being "gatekeeper" and controlling the flow of information that passes across boundaries among the different subsystems (1976, p. 217). Thus, Haley explains his rationale for treating families or systems in lieu of the individual. His commitment to the dictum "change the situation to change the behavior (communication)" is one sided. He offers no data to support this contention as the most effective way of doing therapy. One can agree with the systems orientation to therapy, and it seems logical, based on systems thinking, that a change anywhere within a system will affect the whole system. Thus, working directly on the client's communication to effect change in the situation seems to be a viable alternative that has not been disproven.

Despite criticisms of Haley's philosophy, one must still acknowledge his numerous contributions to the field of family therapy. Haley has added an understanding to the nature of communication in a system as well as pioneering in the systems viewpoint of psychological disturbance. He has made clear the nature of power struggles, triangulation, and the cause of some symptomatic acting-out behaviors in adolescent family members. Finally, he has created strategic interventions designed to alleviate rapidly the symptomatic behavior in families. Although one may question Haley's problem-oriented symptom–relief model as one that may fall short of family health, behavioral symptom alleviation is an appropriate goal.

Haley's approach does offer many attractive features. Significant among these is the problem-oriented, molar approach. By taking this direction, much time is saved by the avoidance of intellectualizing and insight production, which, indeed, may have little utility. There is a refreshing air behind the idea of being able to go to a therapist with a problem and having him or her focus directly on it. Moreover, this approach does provide a vehicle for measuring success, albeit imperfect.

Haley's method can be analogous to going to a medical doctor with a broken leg. His emphasis is on restoring the broken leg to normal (the problem one brings in). The doctor is in charge of the process, and implicit within it is the notion that the broken leg is what is to be fixed (therapeutic contract).

Haley would like to give the impression that theory is not used in his practice. One almost gets the idea that he feels that theory can get in the way of a therapist in that it can hinder flexibility. However, it is quite clear that materials presented are representative of his foundation, call it theory or a rose by any other name. He does not appear to be rigid and stereotyped in his approach, but flexible and spontaneous. Evidence of the latter is found in his belief that, if one's course of therapy is not working, a therapist should then be prepared to try something else. There are limitations to this flexibility, of course, such as in the fact that he is adamantly against the use of co-therapists.

In conclusion, Haley, is a brilliant synthesizer and eloquently presents his case. His collaboration with Bateson, Jackson, and the others of the Palo Alto group stands as a landmark in the progression of psychological theory from an individual to a relational conceptual base. The double-bind theory of schizophrenia is thought by some to be a possible candidate for the Nobel Prize. Haley's description of how symptoms can be used to control others is a major contribution both to theory and practice. His analysis of the "active ingredients" common to all forms of therapy is brilliant, insightful, and integrative. In many of his articles, he gleefully satirizes us all, reminding us that we are human and do not really know much about what we are doing.

Haley's approach to therapy is designed to get results and to get them quickly. This is at once its greatest asset and its greatest liability. For the individual, couple, or family with a clearly defined problem and a clear goal, it seems ideal. By Haley's own admission, however, it is a limited approach. It is a "goal-oriented" therapy rather than a "growth-oriented" one. Some people come to us not out of deficits and problems but out of a desire to expand their capabilities and explore potential. It is uncertain how (or even if) Haley would deal with them. In spite of his emphasis in therapy on positives, Haley still frames therapy itself in negative terms—you have to have a "problem" for the therapist to deal with.

References

Ackerman, N., ed. 1970. *Family process.* New York: Basic Books.
Bateson, G. 1978. The birth of a matrix or double bind and epistemology. In *Beyond the double bind,* ed. M. M. Berger, pp. 41–64. New York: Brunner/Mazel.
——; Jackson, D.; Haley, J.; and Weakland, J. 1956. Toward a theory of schizophrenia. *Behavioral Science* 1:251–264.

Bowen, M. 1978. *Family therapy in clinical practice.* New York: Jason Aronson.

Ferreira, A. J. 1964. Interpersonal perceptivity among family members. *American Journal of Orthopsychiatry* 34:64-70.

——, and Winter, W. D. 1965. Family interaction and decision making. *Archives of General Psychiatry* 13:214-223.

——, and Winter, W. D. 1968a. Decision making in normal and abnormal two-child families. *Family Process* 7:17-36.

——, and Winter, W. D. 1968b. Information exchange and silence in normal and abnormal families. *Family Process* 7:251-276.

——; Winter, W. D.; and Poindexter, E. J. 1969. Some interactional variables in normal and abnormal families. In *Research in family interaction,* eds. A. Ferreira and W. Winter, pp. 222-231. Palo Alto, Calif.: Science and Behavior Books.

Foley, V. 1974. *An introduction to family therapy.* New York: Grune & Stratton.

Friedman, C. J., and Friedman, A. S. 1970. Characteristics of schizogenic families during a joint family story-telling task. *Family Process* 9:333-352.

Guerin, P. 1976. Family therapy: The first twenty-five years. In *Family therapy: Theory and practice* ed. P. Guerin, pp. 2-22. New York: Gardner Press.

Haley, J. 1959a. The family of the schizophrenic: A model system. *Journal of Nervous and Mental Disease* 129:357-374.

——. 1959b. An interactional description of schizophrenia. *Psychiatry* 22:321-332.

——. 1962. Family experiments: A new type of experimentation. *Family Process* 1:265-293.

——. 1963. *Strategies of psychotherapy.* New York: Grune & Stratton.

——. 1968. Testing parental instructions to schizophrenic and normal children: A pilot study. *Journal of Abnormal Psychology* 73:559-565.

——. 1969. *The power tactics of Jesus Christ.* New York: Grossman.

——. 1970. Family therapy. *International Journal of Psychiatry* 9:233-242.

——. 1973a. *Uncommon therapy.* New York: Ballantine Books.

——. 1973b. Toward a theory of pathological systems. In *Family therapy and disturbed families,* eds. G. Zuk and I. Boszormenyi-Nagy, pp. 11-27. Palo Alto, Calif.: Science and Behavior Books.

——. 1976. *Problem-solving therapy.* San Francisco: Jossey-Bass.

——. 1978. Ideas which handicap the therapist. In *Beyond the double bind,* ed. M. Berger, pp. 67-82. New York: Brunner/Mazel.

——, and Hoffman, L. 1967. *Techniques of family therapy.* New York: Basic Books.

Jackson, D., ed. 1968. *Communication, family, and marriage.* Palo Alto, Calif.: Science and Behavior Books.

Loeff, R. G. 1966. Differential discrimination of conflicting emotional messages by normal, delinquent, and schizophrenic adolescents. *Dissertation Abstracts* 26:6850-6851.

Minuchin, S. 1974. *Families and family therapy.* Cambridge, Mass.: Harvard University Press.

Napier, A. Y., and Whitaker, C. A. 1978. *The family crucible.* New York: Harper & Row.

Sluzki, C. E., and Veron, E. 1971. The double-bind as a universal pathogenic situation. *Family Process* 10:397-410.

Sorrells, J., and Ford, F. 1969. Towards an integrated theory of families and family therapy. *Psychotherapy: Research and Practice* 6:150-160.

Stabenau, J.; Tupin, J.; Werner, M.; and Pollen, W. 1965. A comparative study of families of schizophrenics, delinquents, and normals. *Psychiatry* 28:45–59.

Stierlin, H. 1977. *Psychoanalysis and family therapy: Selected papers.* New York: Jason Aronson.

Watzlawick, P. A. 1963. A review of the double-bind theory. *Family Process* 2:132.

——; Beavin, J. and Jackson, D. 1967. *Pragmatics of human communication.* New York: Norton.

7

The Structural Theory of Salvador Minuchin

Minuchin's structural theory of family interaction was established through continual contact with the families of disturbed patients, combined with a keen eye for causational occurrences. Minuchin was trained at the University of Cordoba in Argentina, South America, where he received his M.D. degree in 1947. From there, his experience included service in the Israeli army as a physician during 1948 and 1949 and postgraduate work in child psychiatry at Bellevue Hospital in New York City in 1951. He went on to become psychiatric director for the Youth Aliyah, Department for Disturbed Children, in Israel, from 1952 to 1954. He became a candidate for a certificate in psychoanalysis at the William Alonson White Institute in New York from 1954 to 1959. Currently, Minuchin has a private practice in psychoanalysis, is professor of clinical child psychiatry at the University of Pennsylvania School of Medicine, and was director of the Philadelphia Child Guidance Clinic.

Minuchin's metatheory, intially in intent and now more and more in practice, is of the demonstrative school of thought. Minuchin began as a psychiatrist and psychoanalyst; he first developed techniques and then theories that broke away from the analytical dialectical processing of his training. In its place came observable processes, such as family subsystems, communication forms, and so on, that were founded initially only on theoretical concepts but gradually came to be substantiated by empirical evidence, which Minuchin and collaborators carried out (Minuchin et al., 1964, 1967, 1974, 1975, and 1978).

Family Concepts

Minuchin felt that the theory of family therapy is predicated on the fact that individuals do not live in isolation. One is an acting and reacting member of social groups. What one experiences as real depends on both internal and external components (Minuchin, 1974a). Thus, Minuchin approaches the individual in his or her context. Therapy based on this framework is directed toward changing the organization of the family. When the *structure* of the family group is transformed, the positions of members in that group are altered accordingly.

One initial assumption that Minuchin implies throughout his writings, although without any substantive evidence, is the concept of the individual as an inherently social animal. Although this position could be criticized, it is not particularly relevant in Minuchin's theory because he effectively deals with this proposition only as a function of here-and-now behavior; that is, the social nature of the individual is relevant only insofar as it affects the family grouping and interaction. Minuchin's structural approach to family therapy is based on the concept that a family is more than the individual biopsychodynamics of its members.

Minuchin has written that "a family is transformed over time, adapting and restructuring itself" (1974a, p. 65). The *adaptation* process occurs (as a construct of family functioning) when a family is subject to inner pressure, coming from developmental changes in its own members and subsystems, and to outer pressure, coming from demands to accommodate to the significant social institutions (Minuchin, 1974a). Minuchin has defined family *structure* as an invisible set of functional demands that organizes the ways in which family members interact, that "the family has a structure which can be seen only in movement" (1974a, p. 65). Certain patterns are preferred, which suffice in response to ordinary demands. Minuchin views a family as a system that operates through transactional patterns. Repeated transactions establish patterns of how, when, and to whom to relate, and these patterns underpin the system. Repeated operations in these terms constitute a transactional pattern (Minuchin, 1974a). These transactional patterns regulate family members' behavior. They are maintained by two systems of constraint. The first is *generic,* involving the universal rules governing family organization. An example Minuchin presents of the generic rule is that of the necessity for a power hierarchy in the family, in which parents and children have different levels of authority and in which there must be a complementarity of functions, with the husband and wife accepting interdependency and operating as a team. The second system of constraint is *idiosyncratic,* involving the mutual expectations of individual family members. The origin of these expectations is based on years of explicit and implicit negotiations among family members (Minuchin, 1974a).

Human experience of identity has two elements: a sense of belonging and a sense of being separate. The family, then, is the matrix of identity. The family system differentiates and carries out its functions through subsystems. Individuals are subsystems within a family; subsystems can be found by generation, by sex, by interest, or by function. Minuchin sees at least three subsystems within the context of the family. The first formed is the *spouse subsystem.* This is generated, naturally, when adults of the opposite sex join with the express purpose of forming a family. The main skills required for the implementation of its tasks are complementarity and mutual accommodation. The second subsystem formed is that of the *parental subsystem.* In this, the spouse subsystem must differentiate to perform the tasks of socializing a child without losing the mutual support that characterizes the spouse subsystem.

The final structural subsystem to be formed is the *sibling subsystem.* This comprises the first social laboratory in which children can experiment with peer relations. The boundaries of this subsystem should protect the children from adult interference, so that they can exercise their right to privacy, have their own areas of interest, and be free to make mistakes (Minuchin, 1974a). The family system, as composed of these subsystems, maintains itself, offers resistance to change beyond a certain range, and maintains preferred patterns as long as possible. Any deviation that goes beyond the system's threshold of tolerance elicits mechanisms that re-establish the accustomed range. Because the family must respond to internal and external changes, it must be able to transform itself in ways that meet new circumstances without losing the continuity that provides a frame of reference for its members (Minuchin, 1974a).

To ensure proper family functioning, the boundaries of its subsystems must be clear. A boundary of a subsystem is described as the rules that define who participates and how. The function of boundaries is to protect the differentiation of the system. All in all, the composition of subsystems organized around family functions is not nearly as significant, according to Minuchin (1974a), as the clarity of subsystem boundaries.

The concept of subsystem boundaries is probably the best developed and indeed the most basic component of Minuchin's theory. He writes that the clarity of boundaries within a family is an extremely useful parameter for the evaluation of family functioning. All families can be conceived of as operating along a continuum, the poles of which are the two extremes of diffuse boundaries and overly rigid boundaries. Minuchin feels that some families turn in on themselves to develop their own microcosm, which results in a consequent increase of communication and concern among family members. However, this introprojection also results in a decrease of distance between family members and blurred boundaries. The differentiation of the family system diffuses in what Minuchin terms *enmeshment.* On the other hand, some families develop overly rigid boundaries in which communication across subsystems becomes difficult and the interdependent, protective functions of the family are handicapped. Minuchin labels this phenomenon *disengagement.* It must be emphasized here that, according to Minuchin, the terms "enmeshment" and "disengagement" refer to a transactional style, or preference for a type of interaction, and not to a qualitative difference between functional and dysfunctional behavior. Minuchin is adamant on this point: Normal family functioning includes *all* the patterns of interaction, and pathology is indicated only when family operations are continually at either end of the extreme.

Minuchin buttresses his concept of functional families through the two family interviews (1974a). He conveys the important message that, in his approach, the therapist needs to have a conception of how normal families function. It is the conceptualization of what constitutes an effectively functioning family that guides the therapist in the important first interview with a family. Also, part of a therapist's idea of what a normal family is depends upon paying attention to where the family is developmentally. Although Minuchin does not delineate a life-cycle model of developmental stages, he does differentiate how tasks and functions differ in a family of formation vis-à-vis a newly married couple. Here, Minuchin includes a broader conceptualization—developmental life-cycle stages and relevant family tasks—as a necessary parameter in conflict resolution with families. Furthermore, he advocates that many families who are seen as pathological are in reality trying to develop coping mechanisms for transitional problems in which they are trying to accommodate to new developmental stages (e.g., birth of children, adolescence, retirement, etc.).

It would be difficult to discuss further the processes of family functioning as Minuchin sees them without first looking at Minuchin's models for family interactions (see Figure 7-1). In these models, he presents not a picture of how families *do* operate but gives pictorial tools that are used to depict how a family *is* operating at that specific time. The tools are eight representations of subsystem boundary permeability and individual behavior. The composite of these representations, when used to describe a particular family, constitutes a transactional pattern.

The strength of the family system depends on its ability to mobilize alternative transactional patterns when internal or external conditions of the family demand its restructuring. This demand for restructuring can come, as cited earlier, either from developmental changes in its own members or from pressure to accommodate to significant social institutions: "A family adapts to stress in a way that maintains family continuity while making restructuring possible" (1974a, p. 48). This process

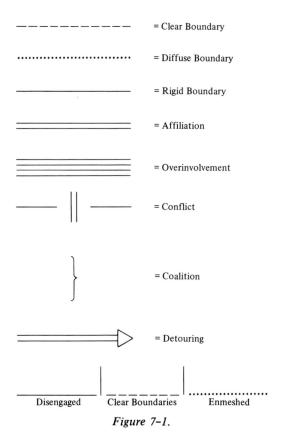

Figure 7-1.

of adaptation is the necessary basis for family growth. If a family responds to stress with rigidity, dysfunctional patterns occur. These transactional patterns of adaptation to new situations, which carry the lack of differentiation and the anxiety that characterize all new processes, may be mislabeled as pathological (Minuchin, 1974a): "Since a normal family cannot be distinguished from an abnormal family by the absence of problems, a therapist must have a conceptual schema of family functioning" (p. 35). This schema, based on viewing the family as a system operating within specific social contexts, has three components: (1) the structure of the family is that of an open sociocultural system in transformation, (2) the family undergoes development, moving through a number of stages that require restructuring, and (3) the family adapts to changed circumstances so as to maintain continuity and enhance the psychosocial growth of each member. It is when the family fails to restructure and fails to adapt that family dysfunction occurs.

It is evident that only the "clear boundary" form of communication, if used to an extreme, will not result in dysfunctional family behavior—all other boundary types, used excessively, will. The process of socialization is inherently conflictual. In dealing with these conflicts, then, a family, of necessity, runs the gamut of the interactional processes, both functional and dysfunctional. It is only through the development of these dysfunctional interactions into dysfunctional *sets* that families begin demonstrating pathological behavior (Minuchin, 1974a). A set, in this instance, is defined as a patterned sequence of interaction among family members.

The main components of Minuchin's process of family dysfunction would come under the general heading of *stress*. This concept Minuchin divides into four categories. The first is stress of one family member with extrafamilial forces. This precipitator occurs when one member is stressed and the other family members feel the need to accommodate to his or her changed circumstances. This accommodation may be contained within a subsystem, or it may permeate the whole family. If the family responds to these changes with rigidity, dysfunctional transactional patterns will occur. The second precipitator of stress is conflict of the whole family with extrafamilial forces. The processes and outcomes of this stress situation are seen as the same as in the stress of an individual member (see Figure 7-1). The third stress category occurs at transitional points in family development.

There are many phases in a family's own natural evolution that require the negotiation of new family rules. Conflicts inevitably arise and, ideally, they will be resolved by negotiations of transition and the family will adapt successfully. These conflicts offer an opportunity for growth, but, if such conflicts are not resolved, the transitional problems will give rise to dysfunctional family behavior. The fourth and final stress category relates to idiosyncratic problems. Many types of individual problems, such as retardation, physical handicaps, sickness, and so on, may overload coping mechanisms and create dysfunctional transactional patterns (Minuchin, 1974b). Thus, Minuchin reserves the label "pathology" for families who, in the face of stress, increase the rigidity of their transactional patterns and boundaries, avoiding or resisting any exploration of alternatives.

Developmentally, inherent in the human condition is the fact that the individual survives in groups and that, because the family is the first and most important group to which an individual belongs, the family becomes the matrix of the individual's identity. Families mold and program the child's behavior and sense of identity. The sense of belonging comes with the child's accommodation to family groups and with his or her assumption of transactional patterns in the family structure that are consistent throughout different life events (Minuchin, 1974a). The sense of separateness and individuation that a person develops occurs through participation in different family subsystems in different family contexts as well as through participation in extrafamilial groups. The subsystem organization of a family in this sense provides valuable training in the process of maintaining the differentiated "I am" while exercising interpersonal skills at different levels (Minuchin, 1974a).

Marriage and partner choice is a direct result of the consequences of the development of the family subsystem interactions in which an individual is reared. A marriage must replace certain social arrangements that have been give up for the formation of the new unit. Creation of the new social system means the creation or strengthening of a boundary around the couple. When partners join, each expects the transactions of the spouse unit to take the form with which he or she is familiar. Each spouse will try to organize the spouse unit along lines that are familiar or preferred and will press the other to accommodate (Minuchin, 1974a). Thus, the task of establishing a family can indeed take a long time, depending primarily on which social situations in which the couple were embedded that might handicap the formation of a viable spouse unit.

The interaction processes that a couple undergoes in making its decisions and in adjusting its accommodations are in effect the very same procedures about which Minuchin writes as occurring in a total family unit.

As an overall view of the processes hypothesized in his theory of family development, Minuchin offers this conceptual scheme of a normal family (1974a, pp. 65–66):

1. A family is transformed over time, adapting and restructuring itself so as to continue functioning.
2. The family has a structure that can be seen only in movement. Certain patterns are preferred, which suffice in response to ordinary demands. The strength of the system depends on its ability to mobilize alternative transactional patterns when internal or external conditions of the family demand its restructuring. The boundaries of the subsystems must be firm, yet flexible enough to allow realignment when circumstances change.
3. A family adapts to stress in a way that maintains family continuity while making restructuring possible. If a family responds to stress with rigidity, dysfunctional patterns occur.

In summary, Minuchin's definition of the family unit encompasses it as (1) a natural social system that has evolved ways of organizing and transacting economical and effective methods that work for that system; (2) a socializing, education, and separative unit that works as a self-perpetuating system; and (3) a family system made up of subsystems, dyads, individuals.

Diagnosis

Unlike the traditional psychiatric model of diagnosis, Minuchin sees diagnosis and intervention as inseparable and labels his diagnosis as interactional. Interactional diagnosis changes as the therapist accommodates to the family and continues to change as interventions are rejected or assimilated into the family structure (Minuchin, 1974a, p. 131).

In making a diagnosis, the family therapist is aware of family structure and of transactional patterns used within that family. The therapist examines the flexibility of the system and its sensitivity to individual members. He or she evaluates the sources of both stress and support within the system; he or she makes note of the developmental stages of the family members and the degree of success in meeting the demands of those stages; he or she also considers the identified patient's symptoms and the functions they serve within the family. The therapist evaluates and explores the family system while forming the therapeutic system. The therapeutic system consists of the therapist and all family members present (Minuchin, 1974a, p. 130).

A meaningful diagnosis includes (1) noting behavior that is stressful for the family; (2) determining the source of stress, which may be internal or external or both; (3) developing an evolving, broader analysis and description of relevant sequences rather than a label describing a "contextless intrapsychic entity"; (4) delineating implications for therapeutic interventions; and (5) developing understanding achieved through therapeutic strategy. Minuchin describes joining as an ongoing process when he discusses diagnosis. Accordingly, "diagnosis is a working hypothesis that the therapist evolves from his experiences and observations upon joining a family" (1974a, p. 129).

Therapeutic Foci and Goals

Minuchin's approach to helping dysfunctional families is very much a part of his theory of dysfunctional family development. He suggests that in dysfunctional families the implicit messages defining the ways in which "me and you" are connected are really central to the problem but are obscured by the background noise of content messages, which are merely carriers. By examining the explicit content as carriers of relationship messages and paying attention to the basic ways of me-you relatedness, Minuchin feels that the therapist can then come to the exploration of a limited number of rather global themes. These are central, dynamic, and idiosyncratic for each family; they exert a compelling demand for response on the part of each family member (1969). Minuchin sees this behavior as rooted in the phenomenon known as generalizations. He defines generalizations within the family system as the developing of shortcuts in the organizing of experience and the allowing of such a cataloging of experiences so that one need not always repeat the total process of perceiving and apprehending what has already been experienced. Although these generalizations may lead to distortions of individual situations, they compensate for such distortions by increasing one's speed in organizing responses to new situations. Clearly, this process blunts the familiar: people lose their ability to perceive not only nuances in unknown situations but also new elements embedded in familiar experience (Minuchin, 1965).

Minuchin views therapy with the dysfunctional family as a transitional process, which he schematized (1974a) as (family) + (therapist) = (family + therapist) = (family + therapist's ghost) − (therapist). The process entailed by this scheme involves primarily restructuring. Because experience, especially within the dysfunctional family, tends to be cognitively undifferentiated and emotionally blunted, a therapeutic method is needed through which learning anew from familiar experience can be fostered. Minuchin justifies a theoretical rationale for this type of therapy by stating that, to become aware of one's manner of functioning, one must observe one's own actions. Acting as a participant observer, in effect, involves a paradox: to become an observer, one must stop participating; yet, while one is participating, one cannot observe his or her participation because of the process of commitment (Minuchin, 1965).

This focus on the structure of family functioning results in a family therapy based on altering the immediate context (i.e., the transactional patterns) of family members in such a way that their positions change vis-à-vis one another: "By changing the relationship between a person and the familiar context in which he functions, one changes his subjective experience" (Minuchin, 1974a, p. 13). Thus, the therapist's primary concern and goal is to change the family organization. The secondary goal, which results or follows from the primary goal of structural change, is that the subsystems (i.e., family members) will experience a change in subjective experience. Because structural family therapy is focused on changes of transactional patterns in the system, interventions are designed to change the process of feedback between circumstances and the persons involved. In other words, the focus is on "the changes imposed by a person on his circumstances and the way in which feedback to these changes affects his next move" (Minuchin, 1974a, p. 13). Minuchin's structural therapy is conceived of as an experiment. The therapist joins with the family, emphasizing those aspects of himself or herself that are syntonic with the family's style. The therapist then probes the family for possible areas of flexibility and change and activates the structural alternatives that have been submerged.

Therapy proceeds in stages, beginning with hypotheses about which patterns the therapist has pinpointed as functional and dysfunctional. From his or her own experience with the family and from observations of such matters as the degree of congruence between verbal communication and actual behavior in the family, the therapist derives a family map or organizational scheme that assists in determining the therapeutic goals. Once this is done, the therapist begins to introduce tasks aimed at changing the behavioral sequences among family members. Structural family therapy is thus action oriented within the therapy sessions themselves. The therapist must maneuver the family members into new transactional patterns. Minuchin is very clear that, although "the family is the matrix of the healing and growth of its members, the responsibility for reaching this state, or failing to do so, belongs to the therapist" (1974a, p. 111). Minuchin's therapeutic goals, then, are

(1) to alleviate stress and symptoms, (2) to achieve a more adequate family organization in which the spouse dyad can function without triangulating the child and in which each family member can achieve the maximum growth potential, and (3) to restore a functional equilibrium and a realignment of family members and of the rules.

Role of the Therapist

The family therapist, according to Minuchin, finds himself or herself in a natural social group, a family, whose interacting members follow rules established over years of mutual accommodation. The therapist, in meeting with the family, sees himself or herself as forming a new social system in which he or she is a controlling participant. Communications, both verbal and nonverbal, are multiple. They tend, for the most part, to move along established pathways. Although past experiences may often activate the material, the content of the session is almost always the here and now, and its actuality almost guarantees a wide range of affective components that can be very intense (Minuchin, et al., 1967). The therapist finds his or her freedom of intervention curtailed by the patterns available: To maximize his or her therapeutic effectiveness and be able to make use of the total range of human experience and behavior, the therapist must become a clearly defined member of the system. Consequently, the roles of the therapist consist of being *extremely active* (e.g., joining the family in eating to observe what goes on in cases of anorexia nervosa) (Minuchin et al., 1978); *confrontive* and yet supportive; and *involved* without being engulfed by the family. The therapist needs to emphasize process rather than content and stress the present rather than the past. The therapist joins the family first and then tries to change it.

Intervention Strategies

Minuchin describes two general categories of intervention strategies: coupling and change production; Minuchin calls these same concepts accommodation and restructuring, respectively. He defines coupling as "everything the therapist does to enhance his therapeutic leverage within the therapeutic unit" (1974a, p. 183). Change production he describes as "the strategems directed toward changing dysfunctional sets" (1974a, p. 183).

Accommodation is a key concept in Minuchin's approach, and his discussion of accommodation or joining is a valuable contribution to any therapy. Minuchin states clearly that accommodation is necessary before any restructuring operations and transformation of a family can occur. Accommodation is "the glue that unites the family and therapist throughout therapy" and is a necessary part of therapy that "many family therapists prefer not to analyze" (1974a, p. 124). He systematizes three accommodation techniques: *maintenance* (supporting the family where it is and reinforcing its members' strengths), *tracking* (showing interest by posing relevant questions, listening, and obtaining clarity), and *mimesis* (stressing similarities and modeling the family's pace, such as mood, tone, speed of speech, and so on). Through accommodation or joining, the therapist and family form a therapeutic system whereby the therapist adopts the family, akin to a distant relative, and becomes the leader of it to induce change. In joining, Minuchin dares to discuss what some schools of therapy term "presence." Further, Minuchin adds that joining will not occur if the therapist does not feel or hear the pain of a family, is insensitive to the family's style, and does not know how to express his or her humanness as it reflects the humanness of the family.

Minuchin delineates seven categories of restructuring. This list is not exhaustive, as the personalities of both therapists and families create variations of these categories: (1) *Actualizing family transactional patterns* to avoid the therapist's becoming overcentralized in the conversational patterns during therapy is one strategy. The therapist has the family enact typical transactions as he or she observes them; the therapist helps them to recreate typical transactions, observing the patterns rather than the content of the conversation; and the therapist manipulates space by positioning family members into more constructive dyads (e.g., placing the spouse dyad together, apart from the sibling subset). (2) *Marking boundaries* is another strategy. In an enmeshed family the boundaries must be strengthened to create individuation of members, whereas, in a disengaged family, the therapist would work to decrease the rigidity of the boundaries. The therapist helps the family to recognize individual boundaries and subsystem boundaries. (3) *Escalating stress* can be accomplished by blocking typical transactional patterns, by emphasizing differences among family members, by developing implicit conflict, or by joining in alliance with one family member or subset against other family members. (4) *Assigning tasks,* to be done during the session or as homework, can be another effective strategy. (5) *Making use of the symptoms* by focusing on those symptoms, deemphasizing them, or exaggerating them might involve the therapist's relabeling the symptom, moving to a new symptom, or changing the symptom's effect. (6) *Manipulating the mood* of the family is another strategy. (7) *Nurturance, education, and guidance* are also seen as restructuring strategies by Minuchin.

Minuchin stresses the need for maintenance of change upon termination. Still, he does not give this issue enough attention and does not discuss whether the approach returns families to the status quo of society and, thus, homeostasis, or returns families as open systems and, thus, "morphogenesis" (Speer, 1970).

In brief, Minuchin's strategies are to actualize family transactional patterns through enacting transactional patterns, recreating communication channels, and manipulating span. Marking boundaries among subsystems is achieved through delineating individual boundaries and clarifying subsystem boundaries. Escalating stress is achieved through blocking transactional patterns, emphasizing differences, developing implicit conflict, and joining in alliance or coalition. Assigning tasks to be done within session and outside the office through homework assignments is very important. The symptoms are used by focusing on symptom, exaggerating the symptom, deemphasizing the symptom, moving to new symptoms, and changing the symptom's effect by manipulation of the family's affective mood about the system, with additional support, education, and guidance.

Minuchin et al. (1978) wanted to verify their structural model of family functioning in anorexia nervosa as characterized by enmeshment, overprotectiveness, rigidity, and lack of conflict resolution through four different sources of data: structured family tasks, physiological data from diabetic and anorexic children, weight changes related to the family lunch sessions, and long-term outcome data for the total anorexic sample. No direct data were given to support the first source. The second source failed to demonstrate significant differences in physiological measures between experimental and control groups. The third source was tested on eight families out of a total sample of fifty-three families. Consequently, whatever statistical significance was found, it was based on too limited a sample to generalize outside it. The fourth source of data (long-range outcome) indicated an 86 per cent recovery rate within a seven-year follow-up period. This outcome would be remarkable if the only treatment strategy had been family therapy. Unfortunately (for theory testing, but fortunately for the patients), treatment was based on a variety of behavioral, structural, and pediatric management techniques (but no methods) in the hands of a wide range of professionals from various disciplines. Hence, one cannot claim that one specific treatment modality (i.e., structural family therapy) was the major independent variable to produce the dependent variable of successful long-term outcome. To use treatment as the acid test of any theory (be it psychoanalytic, nondirective, behavioral, or what-have-you), one must demonstrate that the treatment is specifically derived from theoretical assumptions; that the treatment and only *that* treatment is responsible for the outcome; and that the treatment effects are not due to the charismatic influence of the leader but indeed to the therapeutic strategies used in treatment, as Haley (Chapter 6) would like us to believe. Under these conditions, treatment, instead of being a *technique,* with maximal reliance on the personal style of the therapist, must become a *method,* with minimal reliance on the therapist's own style, as Haley also insists and as will be discussed in the final chapter.

Critique and Evaluation

Guerin (1976) reports that Minuchin is a "conductor," as he is directive and impacts the family with his own personality. Minuchin's approach is soundly established, adaptable to a number of different personality styles, and it is developed along theoretical lines. For these reasons and others presented in this chapter, Minuchin's approach explains a broad area of the universe of family therapy and has more utility.

Currently, Minuchin and his theory appear to be in a unique and exemplary position. He is a psychiatrist involved in movement away from a psychiatrist's traditional background of dynamic individual behavior and toward a position of social, qualitative interaction. His is a theory of succinct, easily represented criteria. What remains to be done is to substantiate empirically his hypotheses. His current research seems more directed at global success–failure criteria than it does toward emphasizing the existence and interactions of his theory constructs. The key here would be to evaluate not only how successful his theory is but why it is successful, evidenced by what makes this particular technique result in a "happier" or "better adjusted" individual and family. He has the components, and he has the results; now we need to know if what we believe he says is happening, *is* indeed happening!

Minuchin's theory reads like a sociology textbook on structural functionalism. Even before he presents his theory, he talks about the social context of the individual. This gives his theory a whole different approach from Bowen's—whose theory approaches the family from the individual. Minuchin is concerned with family as an interlocking set of small groups arranged hierarchically. The task of the therapist is to restructure these small groups (subsystems) so that the whole (family system) can function adequately (i.e., adapt to the demands placed on it by internal and external forces).

Minuchin describes effectively the variety of techniques he makes available to the family therapist to reposition the family's subsystems so that they can respond adequately. His techniques are highly manipulative and are likely to make the specters of deceased humanists shudder. Minuchin's philosophy is hard-core Americana: If it works, use it. First, change a person's position in the family; then, that person's subjective experience will follow suit. There is no choice presented to the individual about restructuring. However, families become dysfunctional when they no longer perceive options—they have no choices. Minuchin's "manipulative" techniques free the family from being stuck and provide the members with new experiences of reality. This may not be humanism, but it is human.

Minuchin's theory is relatively simple and clear and lends itself to specific intervention strategies that are designed to change the family system. The theory's relative simplicity may be its downfall, because family functioning may be a little more complex than the theory makes it. In this regard, it may be better to conceive of it as a "theorette" rather than as a theory. Minuchin's attempts at demonstrative evaluation of outcome effects from treatment should be considered noteworthy, despite the criticism leveled against its possible methodological shortcomings.

References

Carter, E., and Orfanidis, M. Mc. 1976. Family therapy with one person and the family therapist's own family. In *Family therapy: Theory and practice,* ed. P. J. Guerin, pp. 193–219. New York: Gardner Press.

Grinker, R. S. 1968. Conceptual progress in psychoanalysis. In *Modern psychoanalysis,* ed. J. Marmor, pp. 19–43. New York: Basic Books.

Guerin, P. J., Jr., ed. 1976. *Family therapy: Theory and practice.* New York: Gardner Press.

Liebman, R.; Minuchin, S.; Baker, L.; and Rosman, B. L. 1976. The role of the family in the treatment of chronic asthma. In *Family therapy: Theory and practice,* ed. P. Guerin, pp. 312–319. New York: Gardner Press.

Minuchin, S. 1965. Conflict resolution family therapy. *Psychiatry* 28:278–286.

——. 1969. Family therapy: Theory or technique? In *Science and psychoanalysis*, ed. J. Masserman. vol. 14, pp. 401–409. New York: Grune & Stratton.

——. 1974a. *Families and family therapy.* Cambridge, Mass.: Harvard University Press.

——. 1974b. Structural family therapy. In *American handbook of psychiatry*, ed. G. Caplan, pp. 178–192. vol. 2. New York: Basic Books.

——; Auerswald, E.; King, C.; and Rabinowitz, C. 1964. The study and treatment of families that produce multiple acting-out boys. *American Journal of Orthopsychiatry* 34:125–134.

——, and Montalvo, B. 1967. Techniques for working with disorganized low socioeconomic families. *American Journal of Orthopsychiatry* 37:880–887.

——; Montalvo, B.; Guerney, B.; Rosman, L.; and Shumer, F. 1967. *Families of the slums.* New York: Basic Books.

——; Liebman, R.; and Baker, L. 1974. The use of structural family therapy in the treatment of intractable asthma. *American Journal of Psychiatry* 131: 535–539.

——; Baker, L.; Rosman, B.; Liebman, R.; Milman, L.; and Todd, T. 1975. A conceptual model of psychosomatic illness in children. *Archives of General Psychiatry* 32:1031–1038.

——; Rosman, B.; and Baker, L. 1978. *Psychosomatic families: Anorexia nervosa in context.* Cambridge, Mass.: Harvard University Press.

Speer, D. C. 1970. Family system: Morphostasis and morphogenesis, or is homeostasis enough? *Family Process* 9:259–278.

8

The Paradox and Counterparadox Model of the Milan Group

The Milan (Italy) Family Therapy Group consists of four physicians who were originally trained in psychoanalysis: Mara Selvini-Palazzoli, Gianfranco Cecchin, Givliana Prata, and Luigi Boscolo (1978b). This group practices at the Milan Center for Family Studies and has been hailed as innovators of "the revolutionary thrust of the new paradigm of family therapy" (Stierlin, 1978, p. vii). Indeed, these four family therapists have tackled two psychiatric conditions particularly difficult to treat—anorexia nervosa and schizophrenia—from a systems point of view, including the whole family system as their patient.

This chapter follows a discussion of the origin of this group and its methods, as well as a description of its present practices.

Background of Group Members

Perhaps the presentation of a timetable might be more elucidating than a narrative for describing the evolution of the Milan group. The focus will be on one member in particular—Mara Selvini-Palazzoli, as it was her work with anorectic patients that laid the foundation for the development of the family-oriented framework and research (1978b). She also founded the Milan Center for Family Studies and organized the present research team. The following outline is a brief overview of the development of the Milan Group, with an emphasis on Mara Selvini-Palazzoli.

1951-1967 Selvini-Palazzoli relied chiefly on psychoanalytic methods in which she was trained. She studied medicine in Milan and began to treat anorectic patients as a house physician at the University Medical Center of Milan. Selvini-Palazzoli trained as a psychotherapist under G. Benedetti (Basel).

1963 Original appearance of *Self-starvation,* in Italian, without the chapters on family therapy.

1965	Selvini-Palazzoli, frustrated by the tremendous amount of effort she invested in anorectics whose cure rate was discouraging, began studying family psychotherapy literature.
1967	Selvini-Palazzoli founded the Milan Center of Family Studies.
1968-1969	Selvini-Palazzoli initiated pilot inquiries directed toward parents of anorectics (and toward a couple, one of whom was anorectic). Lacking the courage, however, to involve the whole family in treatment, she continued using her psychoanalytic approach and saw the subsystems of the family separately.
1970	Selvini-Palazzoli published the research on the parents of anorectics, which appeared in English years later (1978). Still, she focused on the existence of intrapsychic dynamics.
1971	The present family therapy group was formed, and the research plan was devised for the Milan Center for Family Studies.
1972	Research planned a year before was begun.
1974	The second edition of *Self-starvation,* in English, was published in London. This time, there was an additional section describing family therapy with anorectic patients (1978).
1975	The Italian edition of *Paradox and Counterparadox* was published. It concerned research with families of psychotics and schizophrenics, using family therapy.
1978	The American editions of both *Self-starvation* and *Paradox and Counterparadox* (English translations) were published.
Present	Mara Selvini-Palazzoli teaches at the Psychological Institute of the Catholic University in Milan. She is chairman and research director of the Milan Center for Family Studies.

Recently, due to the overwhelmingly positive responses to their research and publications, the Milan group has begun to train psychotherapists from all over Italy as well as elsewhere. Because of the pragmatic realities of most therapeutic operations, it is difficult to use a team of four therapists, as the Milan group has done. Therefore, they are training single psychotherapists in their novel approach (Boscolo, 1979).

Theoretical Underpinnings

In general, the Milan group pledges its allegiance to three broad areas: general systems theory, the pragmatics of human communication, and cybernetics. However, heavily emphasized throughout its publications is its members' loyalty to the methods and theories of the Palo Alto group (Haley and Bateson, in particular) and to the revolutionary thinking of Watzlawick and his colleagues (Selvini-Palazzoli et al., 1974).

In addition to his research method and formulation of the schizophrenic family's description as an interactional system, Haley (Chapter 6) is credited with enhancing other extensions of the Milan group's thinking (i.e., each family necessitates the creation of a novel intervention). The Milan group also uses "coalition" in the same sense as Haley does, that of two or more persons joining in an alliance (sometimes secretly) against another, or third member, of the family. Also, according to Montalvo and Haley's suggestion concerning the avoidance of directing accusation to parents of dysfunctional children (1973), the Milan group employs the method of positive connotation or reframing. Otherwise, the parents become indignant, angry, negative, or render the therapists impotent with "depressive maneuvers of the 'we-have-completely-failed' type" (Selvini-Palazzoli et al., 1974).[1]

Along the same lines as Haley (Chapter 6) and Watzlawick (Chapter 5), the Milan group has focused on context (family, etc.) rather than on the individual as a self-contained entity. Basically, the Milan group has adopted three axioms on communication, which it has elaborated.

Axiom 1. It is impossible not to communicate, because all behavior is communication. The Milan group capitalized on this when it regarded the family's failure to follow a directive, such as presenting the group with as much information as possible, as being as important as if the family had followed it (Selvini-Palazzoli et al., 1978b).

Axiom 2. Every behavior takes place on two levels: a content level (usually verbal) and a nonverbal level. The Milan group considers also digital and analogic levels (Selvini-Palazzoli et al., 1978a; Selvini-Palazzoli et al., 1978b). The message interpretation (messages have four parts: sender, message, receiver, and context) depends upon the reception of *both* levels of behavior. A message may be responded to by the recipient in three ways: (1) confirmation (I received your message and I agree with you), or (2) rejection (I received your message and I disagree with you). Healthy communication is an alternation between these two responses to coherent messages. Rejection becomes dysfunctional when it is a systematic or predominant response, as in the example of rigidly symmetrical relationships; (3) disconfirmation (you do not exist). This response pattern is invariably pathological.

Axiom 3. All communication interchange is either symmetrical or complementary. These principles, as elaborated, are some of the basic tenets that have contributed to the thinking of the Milan group in its approach to family therapy and research (Selvini-Palazzoli et al. 1978b).

Family Concepts

The overall general systems view contributed to the following broad principles leading to the formulation of family concepts developed by the Milan group and overlapping with Chapter 1, Chapter 5 (Watzlawick), and Chapter 6 (Haley):

1. A system suggests "wholeness," a unit that is more than the sum of its parts—a gestalt that is also independent of its parts.

[1] Unless indicated otherwise, all page references refer to Selvini-Palazzoli et al., 1978b.

2. Self-regulatory (cybernetic) processes characterize a system. "A family is a rule-governed system, which tends to constancy within a defined range (homeostasis). "This resistance to change is organized into *rules* that are often neither conscious nor explicit. . . . The 'rule of rules' is . . . that it is forbidden to make comments, or to metacommunicate, about the rules" (Selvini-Palazzoli et al., 1978, p. 196).
3. Transformations can take place in a system. Here, the effectiveness of therapy enters the scene. If we can change the rules, we can change the system's functioning. The modal point of the system (P_s) is the point at which the maximum number of functions converge. Consequently, if an intervention is directed to this point (it requires careful observation and clear understanding of family dynamics to discover this area), it can effect the most impact to the system with the least expenditure of energy. Likewise, there is a particular time span (T_s) inherent in family systems. This time span refers to the time that a system requires to complete an action–reaction process, which is sequential and which is necessary for describing a present operating state, as well as a change when something new has been introduced into the system (Selvini-Palazzoli et al., 1978a, 1978b, 1980a, 1980b).

In addition to these main theorists—Haley and Watzlawick—who are mentioned repeatedly, other theorists are also mentioned. Bateson, additionally, has been credited with conceptualizing the concept of "epistemological error," which concerns the mistaken notion that the self is capable of being part of a system of relationships of which it consists to gain control of it (Selvini-Palazzoli, 1978b, p. 232). Bowen (Chapter 9) is cited as noting that three generations are required to create schizophrenia, an observation with which the Milan group agrees (Selvini-Palazzoli et al., 1978b).

Boszormenyi-Nagy and Sparks (1973) are credited with the concept of "parentification." Because the concept of parentification will not be reviewed elsewhere in this book, it may be helpful to inform the reader about it because of its relevance not only to the Milan group but to the whole field of family therapy. It is part of a dialectical theory based on concepts of "loyalty" and "justice," which derive from the transgenerational accounting of a ledger of obligations and merits accumulated throughout life. Conflict arises when this ledger is used to produce guilt and to face the individual with contrasting loyalties to the family system and to himself or herself. Thus, conflict brings about an imbalance in relationships that is redressed through maneuvers that will reestablish the original balance. These maneuvers can be constructive or destructive. Because pathology (i.e., "imbalanced ledger of obligations") is intergenerational, it is important to include grandparents in the therapy whenever possible (Boszormenyi-Nagy and Sparks, 1973):

> Parentification implies the subjective distortion of a relationship as if one's partner or even children were his parents. Such distortion can be done in a wishful fantasy or, more dramatically, through dependent behavior. (p. 151)

Of course, Minuchin (Chapter 7) is mentioned in reference to characteristics of and interventions with families of anorectic patients (Selvini-Palazzoli, 1978). Incidentally, Minuchin, with well-controlled studies and excellent follow-up dimensions, reports an 86 per cent cure rate with anorexia nervosa; Selvini-Palazzoli (1978, p. 241), with tentative follow-up results, reports a 75 per cent cure rate with her patients; however, her sample was less than a third the size of Minuchin's. Sufficient time has not passed to determine adequate conclusions from follow-up data. Ferreira (1963) has been credited with the delineation of the process by which family myths developed, from first to third generation (Selvini-Palazzoli et al., 1977). Thus, it appears that the Milan group has based its innovations on a structure extracted from existing theories of family development, functioning, and intervention as reviewed in other chapters of this book.

Concepts of Family Functionality

Many of the assumptions about the family, as based on general systems theory, cybernetics, and the pragmatics of human communication were mentioned in the preceding section. In this section, some specific aspects of normal families, families with anorectic members, and families with schizophrenic members are elaborated.

Again, as mentioned earlier, normal communication patterns are based on a combination of the sending of a congruent message with the confirmation or rejection of the message by the receiver. If the predominant response mode is rejection, the family then becomes rigidly symmetrical, as in the case of families of anorectics. If the primary mode of response is disconfirmation, the family develops a pathological communication system, even more rigidly locked in and resistant to change, as in the case of the family in schizophrenic transaction. The Milan group asserts, according to Haley's transpersonal view of the family, that "all forms of mental illness must be considered logical adaptations to a deviant and illogical transpersonal system" (Selvini-Palazzoli, 1978, p. 193). Thus, anorexia nervosa, as well as schizophrenia, and, for that matter, other forms of dysfunctionality, have come to be considered by the Milan group as "the only possible adaptation by a *given* subject to a *given* type of family functioning" (Selvini-Palazzoli, et al., 1978, p. 193). In other words, a dysfunctional symptom is an adaptation by an individual to his or her family's particular functioning mode, to its members' rules of communication.

> I am absolutely convinced that mental "symptoms" arise in rigid homeostatic systems, and that they are the more intense the more secret is the cold war waged by the subsystem (parent–child coalitions). We know that such pathological systems are governed by secret rules that shun the light of day and bind the family together with pathological ties.
>
> In other words psychiatric "symptoms" tend to develop in family systems threatened with collapse; in such systems they play the same part as submission rites play in the animal kingdom: they help to ward off aggression from one's own kind. There is just this tragic difference: the specific human rite, called "illness," acquires its *normative* function from the very malfunction it is trying to eliminate. (Selvini-Palazzoli et al., 1978b, p. 239).

Consequently, the Milan group finds that problems manifested by a young child are nearly always the expression of marital problems stemming from the child's parents

(Selvini-Palazzoli et al., 1974). "Decisional paralysis" results when one parent interferes negatively with another, leading to subsequent homeostatic rigidity.

> If in such homeostatically rigid family systems a child begins to show "symptoms," the type of his symptomatic behavior will be related not only to the mutual interference of the adults but also to the totality of the organizational parameters, rules and communicational styles.
>
> Stating it more simply, when the leadership is taken up by a psychopathic or a schizophrenic subject, it will depend in the first case on the prevalence of the communicational modalities known as rejection and *disqualification,* in the second case on the prevalence of those communicational modalities called *denial, double-bind,* and/or *disconfirmation.* (Selvini-Palazzoli et al., 1978b, pp. 4–5)

Logically, it follows that, the more dysfunctional a family is, the more rigid it is, and the more incongruous the two levels (analogic versus digital) of rules are with each other.

From general descriptions of functionality and dysfunctionality, the focus moves to specific descriptions. First, unlike families with schizophrenic members, the family with an anorectic member can communicate, focus its attention, conclude an argument, and send coherent messages; it does not display the schizophrenic sense of discouragement, futility, meaninglessness, chaos, or "drawing room attitude." Anorectic families exhibit

1. a clear display of drama and suffering.
2. a frequent rejection of messages transmitted by others, especially concerning definitions of self in relationships. (Schizophrenic families are more likely to disqualify messages sent to them. In addition, psychotic communication often confuses past and present.)
3. a reluctance to assume personal leadership, so that members blame their decisions on others.
4. a coalition between the patient and the parents. In Selvini-Palazzoli's opinion, this is the most serious aspect of the dysfunctionality of these families. She terms this coalition "three-way matrimony" (p. 211). The mother is married both to the patient and to her husband; the father is married both to the patient and his wife; and the patient is married to each of the parents and tries to "make up for" the shortcomings of each.
5. an isolation between the patient and his or her siblings.
6. an inability of the patient to develop the independence required in adolescence since the patient is married to the parents.
7. a rejection of open two-person alliances inside or outside the family as a betrayal of the others.
8. a façade of respectability and marital unity beneath which the parents are deeply disillusioned with each other. They are symmetrical but do not acquire allies because they must maintain their façade of respectability.
9. a competition between the parents for the support of the patient. Neither,

however, really wants the patient's support, since uppermost in this game is the maintenance of one-down-manship, which the support of a third person would destroy.

10. a rejection of food by the patient, which is congruent with a family interactional style of communication rejection. Suffering is the best move in the game of who is the most downtrodden, and this anorexic affliction also provides its victim with the mistaken perception of his or her own power (Selvini-Palazzoli, et al., 1978).

In contrast to the rejecting communication style of the family with an anorectic member, the family in schizophrenic transaction uses disconfirmation as its supreme maneuver in the "game," the term the Milan group employs to describe the intricate communication patterns devised to maintain homeostasis. Whereas the family with an anorectic member is rigid, the psychotic system is even more rigid, engaging in exceedingly complex and impressive transactional patterns. The Milan group maintains that "the family in schizophrenic transaction sustains its game through an intricacy of paradoxes which can only be undone by counterparadoxes in the context of therapy" (Selvini-Palazzoli et al., 1978b, p. 8).

The Milan group presents two hypotheses with reference to the schizophrenic game:

Hypothesis 1: . . . the family in schizophrenic transaction is a natural group internally regulated by a symmetry which is exasperated to the point that each member perceives its open declaration as extremely dangerous. Therefore, everyone cooperates in keeping it hidden. (Selvini-Palazzoli et al., 1978b, p. 21)

To avoid the prevalence of the risk of failure in the relationship, this family avoids defining its relationships. In fact, "each must disqualify his own definition of the relationship before the other has the chance to do it" (pp. 24–25). Thus, the rules of the game are formed.

Communication between the two becomes more and more cryptic in their mutual attempt to avoid exposure. They learn how to skillfully avoid any *patent* contradiction and become expert in the use of the paradox, taking advantage of that possibility, specific to man, to communicate simultaneously on the verbal and the nonverbal level, jumping from one logical class to a member of that class, as if they were the same things, thus becoming acrobats in the world of the Russellian paradox. (p. 25)

The members of this family, in addition to disconfirmation of the other, also disconfirm themselves. Other communicational maneuvers include "partial or total disqualification of the message, sidestepping the main issue, change of subject, non sequitur," and "amnesia" (p. 25).

Hypothesis 2: Each member of the couple in schizophrenic transaction holds a hidden presumption: "that he will sooner or later be able to gain unilateral control of the definition of the relationship." (p. 30)

This is a futile desire, for, in a circular relationship, there is no punctuation of cause and effect, and no one holds the power. The power is in the rules of the game. And this particular game does not allow either winning or losing. Yet each player is urged to continue playing by his or her secret belief that he or she is winning.

The Milan group highlighted certain dynamics present in families in schizophrenic transaction.

1. Each member of the couple wants to define the relationship and receive confirmation, but he or she marries a partner who shares the same problems. This couple's own parents had developed a rigid, repetitive interactional pattern in which they considered it a sign of weakness to give their children approval. Thus, both seek what the other is unable to give.

2. By the time the couple gets into therapy, its members are symmetrical; the game is crystallized. One partner seems to be the "fugitive" from the relationship, whereas the other appears to be the "stable" one; yet these are moves in the game, directed at keeping their opponents engaged in the struggle. The truth is, the couple is inseparable.

3. The schizophrenic message is: "It's not that you should *do* something different; you should *be* different. Only in this way can you help me be what I'm not, but what I could be if you were not what you are" (p. 36). Schizophrenics confuse the categories of *doing* and *being.*

4. Every change is perceived to be a threat to the system. Therefore, it reacts to this threat with greater rigidity, reacting negatively, absorbing the threat in the game. These negative feedbacks are occurring when an adolescent reacts with psychotic behavior.

5. Emotions are considered merely so many more moves in the game. Communication of the double-bind (Bateson) quality (along with disconfirmation as mentioned earlier) is increasingly cryptic, confusing, involutional, and paradoxical.

6. The "guilty" mother, who is "overprotective and pathogenic," contends with the "guilty" father, who is "absent" in order to gain a symmetrical position. Meanwhile, for the patient, "the game has become . . . his very existence. He believes himself to have made the last move, to be in the position of power: he is the one who calls for change but can be changed by no one" (p. 43).

History Taking

The Milan group believes that the best method of assessment is the actual family process as observed during therapeutic sessions. It does, however, consider the initial phone contact the family makes with the center the first step in this process. Therefore, it sets aside specific telephone times during which the therapists talk at length with the families. This interview enables the group to evaluate the type of communication during this initial contact: tone of voice, general attitude, types of demands made, and so on. There is a chart before the therapist during the call on which to record this information as well as other information usual to history taking or the initial interview (name, date, age, address, education, religion, profession, members of family, problem, etc.).

Diagnostic Framework and Classification

The Milan group acknowledges that, although it is interested in the diagnosis of the family as a total transactional system, it is nevertheless forced to classify according to the diagnosis of the identified patient's symptomatology, as no family classificatory system exists at this time. In an apparent attempt to span this gap, the Milan group ordinarily employs terms such as "families with an anorectic member" and "families in schizophrenic transaction," although occasionally it employs terms such as "anorectic family" and "schizophrenic family."

Therapeutic Foci and Goals

As mentioned previously, the Milan group focuses on the family as its unit of intervention and on the rules governing this family transactional system as its specific target. From careful observation, the group attempts to aim its therapeutic intervention at P_s, the modal point of the system at which the maximum number of functions merge. Therefore, it may select underlying issues as a target of greatest efficiency, although one of its initial intervention strategies is the prescription of the symptom itself (the prima facie problem). The therapeutic goal is to transform (change suddenly) the system so that it is less rigid, no longer requires an identified patient, and no longer must play a game. To do this, the therapists learn the system rules; then they change them. "Therapy is an effort to induce a transformation in a structure that has cybernetic properties" (Selvini-Palazzoli et al., 1978b, p. 200).

Therapeutic Process: The Stages of Therapy

The Milan group is quite specific in delineating its stages of therapy. It considers its approach "short–long therapy" because it contracts for ten (to twenty) sessions, which is short, but it conducts the sessions monthly, which is involving the family in the therapeutic process over a long period of time.

The five stages of therapy include

1. The presession, during which the therapists meet to read the chart or the report of the last session.
2. The actual session, which lasts about an hour. During this time, concrete information is gathered, and the family's transactional style is evaluated. Redundancies indicate the existence of secret rules. Two therapists, a male and female team, remain in the room with the family, while another male and female co-therapy team observes the therapy session from behind a one-way mirror. The therapists may excuse themselves at any time to consult with the observers.

3. The discussion of the session occurs in a room reserved exclusively for this use. The two therapists and the two observers unite to discuss the session and to decide how to conclude it.

4. The conclusion of the session consists of the return of the two therapists to the family. They then present a comment and prescription, which is to be paradoxical. If it is the first family session, the therapists (a) indicate whether psychotherapeutic treatment is necessary and (b) agree on the fee and the number of sessions. Monthly intervals were devised because of (a) the long travel distances necessary for most families and (b) the greater impact of the paradoxical prescription on the family if it carried it out for a longer period of time. A paradoxical prescription is unexpected and unsettling and requires time to accommodate to it. The sessions were limited to ten, as the Milan group felt that if changes were to occur they must be provoked quickly. Reassured as to the length of treatment and the cost, the family also feels some responsibility for quick treatment results, as the number of sessions is limited.

5. When the family departs, the four therapists unite to discuss the reaction of the family to the prescription and to formulate and write a synthesis of the session.

Intervention Strategies

The Milan group employs several intervention strategies, many based on paradoxical techniques. Their real contribution has been the rituals, especially the employment of the written messages (L'Abate, 1977). One of the techniques the Milan group employs is that of *positive connotation.* This is done by construing the symptom and the other's reaction to it (and therefore maintenance of it) as positive, because it serves the purpose of holding the family together. By reframing the symptom positively, it involves the whole family, not just the patient, in the problem (defining the family members' relationships as complementary to the system); the therapist aligns himself or herself with the homeostatic function of the system (thus gaining access to the system itself instead of meeting with resistance). Thus, it paves the way for the second technique it uses: prescription of the symptom. This tactic also marks the context as therapeutic and the therapists as leaders.

The prescription is usually given at the end of the first session. This method involves a defined concept: for example, "During the week to come, the parents were to write down, with great detail and care, each in his own notebook, all the utterances made by the child" (p. 69).

The execution (or nonexecution, which also provides the therapists with information) of the prescription allows an assessment of the family's willingness to follow therapeutic injunctions. In addition, it marks the context as therapeutic and structures the process of the subsequent session.

Other methods, which are akin to the prescription, are the *ritual* and the *ritualized prescription,* which the Milan group claims to have developed (Selvini-Palazzoli et al., 1978a; Selvini-Palazzoli et al., 1978b). A ritual concerns formal aspects as well as content specifications; it is defined as

an action or series of actions, usually accompanied by verbal formulas or expressions, which are to be carried out by all members of the family. The ritual
is prescribed in every detail: the place in which it must be carried out, the time,
the eventual number of repetitions, by whom the verbal expressions are to be
uttered, in what order, etc. (p. 95)

An example of a ritual follows:

In the two weeks that were to precede the next session, every other night, after
dinner, the family was to lock and bolt the front door. The four members of
the family were to sit around the dining room table, which would be cleared of
all objects except an alarm clock, which would be placed in its center. Each
member of the family, starting with the eldest, would have fifteen minutes to
talk, expressing his own feelings, impressions, and observations regarding the
behavior of the other members of the clan [extended family]. Whoever had
nothing to say would have to remain silent for his assigned fifteen minutes,
while the rest of the family would also remain silent. If, instead, he were to
speak, everyone would have to listen, refraining from making any comment,
gesture, or interpretation of any kind. It was absolutely forbidden to continue
these discussions outside of the fixed hour: everything was limited to these
evening meetings. (p. 93).

The disadvantage of a ritual is that it is nonrepeatable and, therefore, specific to
each family. In the case of ritualized prescriptions, only the formal aspects are
specified, so that it may be reused in the same format since it aims at a general
dysfunction: for example, that of the parents' trying to define themselves as the
ones who know better with respect to child-rearing practices (which have produced a symptomatic offspring). An example of a ritualized prescription follows; it
is dictated at the end of the session, concerns system functioning, appears un-
expectedly, and is cryptic:

On even days of the week—Tuesdays, Thursdays, and Saturdays—beginning from
tomorrow onwards until the date of the next session and fixing the time between X o'clock and Y o'clock (making sure the whole family will be home
during this time) whatever Z does (name of the patient, followed by a list of
his symptomatic behavior) father will decide alone, at his absolute discretion,
what to do with Z. Mother will have to behave as if she were not there. On odd
days of the week—Mondays, Wednesdays, and Fridays—at the same time, whatever A may do, mother will have full power to decide what course of action to
follow regarding Z. Father will have to behave as if he were not there. On Sundays everyone must behave spontaneously. Each parent, on the days assigned to
him or her, must record in a diary any infringement by the partner of the prescription according to which he is expected to behave as if he were not there.
(In some cases the job of recording the possible mistakes of one of the parents
has been entrusted to a child acting as a recorder or to the patient himself, if
he is fit for the task.) (p. 5)

The Milan group developed its interventions as a means of changing the system
through action, without interpreting to the family what is transpiring: "The devel-

opment of insight can take place after the change has occurred . . . when the consciousness precedes the change, the family will use it in the service of resistance" (p. 4). This level of action more closely resembles the analogic code (nonverbal) on which behavior rests than the digital (verbal) one with which interpretations would be made.

Other interventions employed by the Milan group will be noted briefly.

1. When families have more than one child, and one presents as the identified patient, the therapists use, as an intermediary step to upset the status quo, the assertion that the patient is the sensitive, sane one and the normal sibling is the one who is far worse off and is being protected by the patient. Then the focus is brought back upon the parents: the system has discovered that no one is crazy; they merely play a crazy game.

2. Another method the group employs is to assume the child is fighting against them rather than the parents in order to avoid taking sides. This is effective in treating families of only children. The therapists refer to themselves, rather than to the parents, the conflicts the child has been experiencing with the father and mother. They thus demonstrate that the child's task is not to change the parents and to demonstrate that the child can grow up regardless of what kind of relationship the parents have.

3. If there is a "flight into health," a sudden improvement not accompanied by evidence of substantial system change, the therapists accept this at face value, although they are aware that it is another move in the game. The therapists, still in control, suspend therapy but remind the family of the remaining sessions in the contract, which they may request if their improvement fails to hold up.

4. Usually the Milan group works with the whole family (unless the child is very young or has undergone much previous psychiatric trauma). However, when a member fails to show up for a session, nothing is said. The session, however, is carefully observed (since a member's absence indicates the collusion of the rest of the family), and the concluding comment is carefully worded to include the absent member.

   Finally, the envelope with the final comment is sealed and not read until the family reaches home and all members are present.

5. When the principal weapon is disconfirmation, the Milan group sometimes prescribes this as a symptom, being careful to word the prescription positively.

6. One intervention aimed at the formation of secret coalitions is to give a written prescription, describing the identified patient paradoxically, that is, "saviour" rather than "victim" of the system, and placing the secret coalition on the same plane as the open ones. In addition, the secret coalition is connoted positively, so it cannot be resisted.

7. When the therapists have tried everything, but nothing works, they declare their impotence with reference to the system. However, they also collect their fee and set the date and time of the subsequent session. This forces the family to "help the therapists," because one of the important rules of the game is that no one may leave the playing field. As a result, the system begins to change positively rather than continuing to resist.

8. One way in which the therapists deal with the schizophrenic message "You cannot help me unless you are someone different" is to isolate the paradoxical request, connote it positively, and prescribe it to themselves.

9. In the case in which the children are parentified and then the therapists are placed in that position, the therapists first free the children, then prescribe the parental role, paradoxically, back to them—which all, of course, reject.

Role of the Therapist

The therapists' role in the Milan group is one of active, positive, but neutral, participation. They conduct the sessions in a very serious, impersonal manner befitting the role of "experts." They align themselves with the homeostatic function of the system to be accepted by the system, but they do not allow themselves to be drawn into the "game" or they are rendered impotent. They assume the role of leadership immediately through their methods of positive connotation and prescription. Their role is to discern the rules of the system through the observation of redundancies (repeated behavioral patterns) and to change the system by changing the rules. They act as swiftly and accurately as possible.

More recently, the Milan group has become concerned with the problem of the referring source (Selvini-Palazzoli et al., 1980a) as an "insidious" force kept by the family to maintain the status quo and avoid change. This group synthesized its approach into three major guidelines: (1) *hypothesizing,* that is, formulation of a hunch on how the family is functioning and determination of the specific therapeutic strategies to be followed. If this hunch is incorrect on the basis of additional information, it needs to be discarded in favor of a more accurate hunch with continuous checking on its accuracy with the family; (2) *circularity,* which these therapists define as "the capacity of the therapist to conduct an investigation on the basis of feedback from the family in response to information" solicited about their relationships. and (3) *neutrality,* a specific, pragmatic effect that the therapist's "total behavior" during the session exerts on the family (Selvini-Palazzoli et al., 1980b).

Critique and Evaluation

The Milan group should be applauded for its courage and creativity in providing us with techniques that appear to be highly effective with severely dysfunctional families who have heretofore eluded most attempts to change them. The cost to the family in time and dollars is minimal, as ten sessions (and later twenty, if needed) are contracted for at the outset of therapy. The time and cost to the therapists, however, seems enormous. For each hour spent in therapy (with four therapists involved), several hours are spent outside it rereading records, formulating intervention strategies, and keeping records. This is an advantage to the family, however, as four heads are usually better than one. There have been the usual criticisms of manipulative trickery, coldness and so on, which are applied to paradoxical therapy in general, which could be applied to the Milan group. Its research data still need to be examined against the test of time. We are only seeing preliminary impressionistic results, though they may be, at first, impressive. Perhaps its methods of evaluation and follow-up might be more rigorous, more on the order of Minuchin. Its theory seems to coincide with its practice, as reported, although the full impact of what its members have done is sometimes lost in the excerpts presented in their writings.

A paradoxical approach can be justified on systematic as well as on existential grounds (Soper and L'Abate, 1977). The widespread popularity of this approach, however (Weeks and L'Abate, 1978), should not blind one to its weak and as yet untested empirical basis. If its theoretical grounds are multiple (i.e., existential or systematic), how can accurate testing take place, unless a "crucial" experiment is devised that would support one position versus the other? On the other hand, both positions are stated in sufficiently general terms that it would be extremely difficult, if not impossible, to test one theory versus the other.

As painstaking and noteworthy as the efforts of this group may be, and there is no doubt that they will persist in their project at this point, most of the evidence gathered, even if external to them (other sources such as previous or present therapists, teachers, etc.) is still subjectively and impressionistically evaluated. The lack of external and objective data to support the group's outcomes is probably one of the weakest grounds of the Milan group. This criticism in no way denies the creativity and innovative quality of its contribution. It qualifies it.

References

Boscolo, L. 1979. Personal communication to L. L'Abate, January 4, 1979.

Boszormenyi-Nagy, I., and Sparks, G. 1973. *Invisible loyalties: Reciprocity in intergenerational family therapy.* New York: Harper & Row.

Ferreira, A. J. 1963. Family myth and homeostasis. *Archives of General Psychiatry* 9:457–473.

L'Abate, L. 1977. Enrichment: *Structured interventions for couples, families and groups.* Washington, D.C.: University Press of America.

Montalvo, B., and Haley, J. 1973. In defense of child therapy. *Family Process* 12:227–244.

Selvini-Palazzoli, M. 1970. The families of patients with anorexia nervosa. In *The child in his family,* eds., J. Anthony and I. Koupernick. pp. 319–332 New York: Wiley.

——. 1978. *Self-starvation: From individual to family therapy in the treatment of anorexia nervosa.* New York: Jason Aronson.

——; Boscolo, L.; Cecchin, G. F.; and Prata, G. 1974. The treatment of children through brief therapy of their parents. *Family Process* 13:429–442.

——; Boscolo, L.; Cecchin, G. F.; and Prata, G. 1977. Family rituals: A powerful tool in family therapy. *Family Process* 16:445–453.

——; Boscolo, L.: Cecchin, G. F.: and Prata, G. 1978a. A ritualized prescription in family therapy: Odd days and even days. *Journal of Marriage and Family Counseling* 4:3–9.

——; Boscolo, L.; Cecchin, G. F.; and Prata, G. 1978b. *Paradox and counterparadox: A new model in the therapy of the family in schizophrenic transaction.* New York: Jason Aronson.

——; Boscolo, L.; Cecchin, G. F.; and Prata, G. 1980a. The problem of the referring person. *Journal of Marital and Family Therapy* 6:3–9.

——; Boscolo, L.; Cecchin, G. F.; and Prata, G. 1980b. Hypothesizing–circularity–neutrality: Three guidelines for the conductor of the session. *Family Process* 19:3–12.

Soper, P. H., and L'Abate, L. 1977. Paradox as a therapeutic technique: A review. *International Journal of Family Counseling* 5:10–21.

Stierlin, H. 1978. Foreword. In *Paradox and counterparadox,* eds., pp. vii–ix. M. Selvini-Palazzoli, L. Boscolo, G. F. Cecchin, and G. Prata. New York: Jason Aronson.

Weeks, G. R., and L'Abate, L. 1978. A bibliography of paradoxical methods in psychotherapy of family systems. *Family Process* 17:95–98.

9

The Systems Theory and Therapy of Murray Bowen

"Systems" is one of the most often-used words in the language of family therapy. It is usually taken for granted that everyone who uses the term means the same thing and has the same outlook toward doing "systems" therapy. This is not the case. Various systems theories differ along some very important lines: the focus of intervention, the philosophy of doing family therapy, and the nature of what leads to change. Murray Bowen's theory of family therapy is most closely associated with the ubiquitous word "systems." However, Bowen (1976c) has maintained that his theory of family systems—the Bowen theory—is a specific systems theory about how families function.

Murray Bowen, medically trained in psychoanalytic theory, found, during his early research with families of schizophrenics (conducted in the early 1950s), that, whereas psychoanalytic theory explained the basis of the emotional problems that his patients experienced, psychoanalysis was not an effective therapeutic technique for treating the more severe emotional disorders. Bowenian theory and techniques grew out of an attempt to modify psychoanalysis to treat schizophrenics. From this work, his family systems theory was engendered. Since working at the Menninger Clinic in the 1950s, Bowen has been working in and around Washington , D.C. and has an appointment to Georgetown School of Medicine.

This theory revolves around two main variables: the degree of anxiety and the degree of integration of self. It is the latter on which Bowen places the most importance. He minimizes the importance of anxiety by stating that "all organisms are reasonably adaptable to acute anxiety" (1976c, p. 65). Chronically sustained levels of anxiety help to determine the degree of integration of the self. Such levels of tension can damage either the individual or the relationship system, causing physical illness, emotional, and/or social dysfunctioning: "the degree of chronic anxiety . . . can result in anyone appearing normal at one level of anxiety, and abnormal at another higher level" (1976c, p. 65).

Bowen's theory is a description of emotional illness as it exists in relationships between and among people. He has called his theory a systems approach in that it defines illness as a relationship between people and subscribes to the belief that a change in one person will create a compensatory change in everyone else in that person's emotional interpersonal system (1978).

Bowen has developed a concept of the family system as a system of relationships, forming interlocking triangles, extending over generations. A two-person relationship, he asserts, is not stable. When anxiety rises, a third person is "triangled in" to take some of the strain off the dyadic relationship. The most uncomfortable member initiates the new balance in an effort to achieve the outside position. A new equilibrium is achieved and anxiety is reduced. When anxiety is sufficiently reduced, the relationships return to their previous structures. When little stress is experienced, all members of the triangle may be able to relate as individuals. The ability to relate as a differentiated individual is the primary goal of Bowenian therapy.

Theoretical Background: Self-differentiation in the Family

In contrast to viewing the family as a global system, Bowen's theory enters the family system on the level of the subsystem (typically, the individual or the couple). The focus of Bowen theory and therapy is on the differentiation of the self within the family. Whereas Minuchin (Chapter 7) has focused on the transactional patterns themselves, Bowen has concentrated on the individual and the part that he or she takes in the family's transactional patterns. Bowen works to help the individual differentiate himself or herself on the rationale that, if one component of the system changes (i.e., the individual member), the rest of the system will be forced to change in response. Thus, because of his individual rather than transactional focus, one might argue that Bowen's theoretical and clinical "systems" approach is narrower than that of other "systems" theorists.

However, one may also view Bowen as broader in scope than other systems theorists, because Bowen defines the family as including the multigenerational family network, whereas most systems theorists address themselves primarily to the nuclear family, including others only when they have a direct part in the transactional sequences, which are maintaining the symptomatic behavior (e.g., grandmother's undermining of mother's disciplining her children). Bowen's theory consists of a series of interlocking concepts that account for the process of emotional functioning in the family system. These principles are analogous to what Minuchin, for instance, calls boundary issues: other principles, such as triangles, family projection process, multigenerational transmission process, and sibling position are analogous to the constraints that Minuchin has proposed as means by which boundaries are enforced.

Just as most "systems" theorists, such as Minuchin, propose a continuum of family functioning with enmeshment at one pole and disengagement at the other, Bowen has postulated a differentiation continuum. At the lower end of self-differentiation is a fusion between intellectual and emotional functioning that results in lack of flexibility in responding to life situations. There is also a confusion of pseudoself and real or solid self. A person with a low level of differentiation reacts automatically on an emotional level to situations. He or she has not consciously delineated a set of personal operating principles and beliefs from his or her own life experiences constituting a stable, solid self. Rather, because he or she is controlled by the emotional system "hypothesized to be part of the instinctual forces that govern automatic functions" (Bowen, 1976c, p. 66), the person functions as a pseudoself created by emotional pressure, unstable, and unaware of the inconsistencies resulting from attempts to conform to discrepant principles maintained by different groups in the individual's environment (e.g., family and work situation). In contrast, at the upper end of the continuum, the well-differentiated person has constructed from experience a set of life principles by a process of intellectual reasoning. Because he or she has rationally and consciously made choices about beliefs, the well differentiated person is responsible for self and consequences. Rather than automatic reaction, the solid self of the well-differentiated individual can respond to situations based on a personal framework of values. Thus, the well-differentiated person has a flexibility lacking in the poorly differentiated person whose pseudoself dominates in functioning.

The farther a person is along the continuum toward differentiation, the healthier that person is. The more one thinks, the more one is able to control one's behavior. People at the low end of the continuum (from 0 to 25) are controlled by their emotions. Decisions are based on feelings rather than on the basis of facts or beliefs. Rather than devote their efforts toward independently directed life goals, these people are almost completely other directed. Almost all their energy is devoted to the maintenance of personal relationships. Life goals are expressed in terms of emotional desires, such as happiness and success. People at the lowest end of this scale are usually relegated to life in an institution. They are likely to have problems in every aspect of living.

Although the next grouping of people, those between the levels of 25 and 50, have more flexibility in their life-styles than do those in the first group, they still generally allow their behavior to be determined by emotional responses. Their self-images are extremely shaky, ranging from strong self-appreciation to extreme self-disapprobation, dependent almost entirely upon the approval of others. Decisions are still largely based on feelings. Although these people often have a solid enough thinking ability to do well academically, they are not capable of using this ability in their personal lives. Close relationships and approval are the life goals of these people. Often they are very sensitive and extremely open in their expression of emotion. When the closeness they long for is achieved, however, emotional fusion results. The reaction to this fusion is most often distancing. This, in turn, often leads to another closeness cycle. If they cannot develop a close relationship, two possibilities are most likely to occur: they will either fall into depression or begin to seek a new relationship. When this relationship system loses its homeostasis, symptoms and problems in living arise. When anxiety is minimal, people in this group can function at a fairly high level of differentiation.

People designated as within the 50 to 75 range are quite well differentiated. Some effort is required to maintain the intellect's authority over the emotional system, but generally this effort is successful. These people can allow themselves to react emotionally but are capable of using the intellect when necessary. They are less relationship directed. Generally, they have life goals that are independent of their relationships. Moreover, insofar as people generally marry spouses with similar levels of differentiation, both spouses are capable of functioning independently, "the wife more fully as a woman, the husband more fully as a man; without either having to debate the advantages or disadvantages of biology and social roles" (Bowen, 1978, p. 736). They are able to allow their children to grow independently into independent, differentiated people. They are most able to cope with the normal vicissitudes of life.

The grouping from 75 to 100 is merely hypothetical and would include healthy differentiated people. Bowen has extended the concept of differentiation by establishing the principle of *emotional cutoff*. Not only has Bowen been concerned with the degree to which the individual is capable of differentiating self from his or her immediate, present context, but he has also focused on differentiation from the past. The concept of emotional cutoff proposes that the way in which people differentiate themselves from their pasts bears on the way they conduct their lives in the present generation. The individual who is unable to resolve his or her emotional attachment to his or her parents may separate or cut off from them in a variety of ways (from intrapsychic processes, such as self-denial, to physically running away). Individuals who run away from their families of origin, denying their unresolved emotional attachments to their parents and siblings, are setting up artificially rigid emotional cutoffs between themselves and their families of origin. While such cutoffs may appear to be an example of a disengaged family at first glance, closer observation reveals that a person involved in such a cutoff is emotionally dependent on his or her family of origin and, therefore, is fused to it. Bowen has observed that "the more intense the cutoff with the past, the more likely the individual is to have an exaggerated version of his parental family problem in his own marriage, and the more likely his own children to do a more intense cutoff with him in the next generation" (1976c, p. 84). Thus, the individual who cuts off from his or her family of origin is, ironically, still emotionally involved in it. Thus, emotional cutoff should not be confused with authentic differentiation, which comes only with the conscious defining of a solid self and taking the "I position" (1978, p. 398).

Bowen's distinction between differentiation and cutoff suggests that Minuchin's (Chapter 7) concepts of enmeshment and disengagement may in fact be two manifestations of the same principle (lack of differentiation) rather than qualitatively different principles or polar opposites. Minuchin used the degree of intensity of communication between subsystems as a means of differentiating enmeshed and disengaged families. While enmeshed family members are supersensitive to communications between subsystems, disengaged families are superinsensitive to such communications.

Bowen's framework, with its overarching principle of differentiation, points out that the extent of communication may not be the most comprehensive way in which to understand family functioning. If one is cut off from one's family of origin, there may be no transactions at all between individual and parents; yet, as Bowen points out, the individual, while separated from the family of origin, is not emotionally differentiated from it. Enmeshed and disengaged families are characterized by members who are emotionally fused, although they exhibit this fusion in different ways.

Another comprehensive concept of Bowen theory is that the *triangle* is the basic building block of any emotional system. Although the ideal situation is to have a family of differentiated individuals, each capable of having a one-to-one relationship on the solid-self level, the reality is that, usually, beginning with the parents, these one-to-one relationships are difficult, if not impossible to maintain. Therefore, parents will typically triangulate around a child. The family projection process (whereby spouse conflicts are dealt with by triangulating a child who becomes symptomatic) and the multigenerational transmission process (the extension of the family projection process throughout several generations) are triangles through which lack of differentiation in the spouse or executive subsystem is transmitted within the family.

The central concepts of differentiation and triangles in Bowen theory result in a therapeutic goal somewhat different from Minuchin's and other systems theorists'. Bowen's therapy seeks to assist the individual in differentiating himself or herself from the "family ego mass" in such a way that he or she can establish one-to-one relationships that avoid triangulating in a third party. In describing his work with parents and "problem" adolescents, Bowen found that, by staying out of the mother–father–child triangle, he could understand the family patterns: "Therapeutically, the family did not change its original patterns. The passive father became less passive, the aggressive mother less aggressive, and the symptomatic child would become asymptomatic. In my opinion, the family had not changed, but I had learned a lot about triangles" (1976c, p. 78). Because symptoms in the children are considered by Bowen to be indications of undifferentiation in the parents, symptom removal would constitute an "unmasking" of this lack of differentiation in the spouse subsystem and appears to be the first step in the more lengthy and complicated process of self-differentiation from the multigenerational family.

Bowen's theory presents a series of concepts that apply to the family. Some apply to general family characteristics, others to specific areas of family functioning. The *nuclear family emotional system* describes the basic pattern of relationships in the nuclear family. These patterns are reproductions of the patterns of behavior in past generations and of the patterns as they will continue to be reproduced in future generations.

During courtship, spouses have their most highly differentiated relationship. When they commit themselves to each other, they generally become fused. Fusion can be dealt with in a number of ways: for example, marital conflict, dysfunction in one spouse, or dysfunction in a child. Dysfunction in a child is engendered through the *family projection process*. When anxiety exists between spouses, bringing a child into a triangular relationship displaces the anxiety from the parents to the child. This is often acted out in families with a handicapped child. Most anxiety in the family is directed toward the child, allowing the parents to remain relatively healthy and have a largely conflict-free marriage. This projection process can occur across many generations. Bowen labeled this concept of intergenerational projection the *multigenerational transmission process*. Finally, emotional cutoff from one's family is another possible blockade to differentiation. An extreme cutoff with the past is likely to lead to an exaggerated version of the parental family in one's own marriage and will likely continue in future generations.

Although we have already introduced most of the major concepts in Bowen's theory, it may be helpful to elaborate on each of them, one at a time.

Differentiation of Self

Bowen touts this concept as his "cornerstone." It define individuals as to the degree of "*fusion, or differentiaton,* between emotional and intellectual functioning" (1976c, p. 65). At the low extreme of differentiation are individuals whose intellects are overwhelmed by the emotional system. They are emotionally dependent on others and, according to Bowen, "inherit a high percentage of all human problems." At the other extreme are differentiated individuals who have achieved a relative degree of autonomy between their intellectual and emotional systems. In times of stress they are more flexible, more adaptable, and less dependent on others.

Symptoms and relationships are expressions of the more important, underlying "emotional process" (Bowen, 1978). A problem, indeed the only problem, in Bowen's theory is the failure to differentiate the emotional system from the intellectual system. When this occurs, an individual is said to be "undifferentiated"; when it occurs in a family, the family is said to have an "undifferentiated family ego mass" (1978).

The concept of differentiation of self eliminates the concept of "normal," according to Bowen. He has stated that "It is not possible to define *normal* when the thing to be measured is constantly changing" (1976c, p. 66). Differentiation has no direct relationship with symptomatology. People who are less differentiated have more problems than do people who are more differentiated, but they still may be able to maintain an adequate balance in their lives. Just because one is differentiated does not mean that one cannot be stressed into dysfunction. Bowen has implied that this concept does away with the need for psychiatric categories: "The theoretical concept is most important. It eliminates the barriers between schizophrenia, neurosis, and normal; it also transcends such categories as genius, social-class, and cultural-ethnic differences. It applies to all human forms of life" (1976c, p. 67).

Nuclear Family Emotional System

This concept relates to the single-generational functioning of the family. Bowen contends that behavior patterns between parents and children are recreations of past generations and will be repeated in following generations. He also states that dating, marriage, and reproduction are affected by the two partners' levels of differentiation in their families of origin: "People pick spouses who have the same level of differentiation" (1976c, p. 79). Less differentiated spouses are involved in more emotionally fused marriages. The fusion in these marriages is manifested by emotional distancing of one spouse from another, marital conflict, sickness in one spouse, and/or projection of the problems onto the children.

The *nuclear family emotional system* is a description of how the tension created by a lack of differentiation is dissipated or distributed within the family. The tension can be expressed either in relationships or in individuals, and it explains the occurrence of symptoms in either spouse or a child or the occurrence of marital conflict. In either case, individual or joint expression of symptoms, the basic process is conceptualized to occur between three people. These three people are said to constitute a "triangle." Triangles are more than an arbitrary and functional unit of analysis; for Bowen, they are a basic, naturally occurring, and stable unit of nature in the same way that H_2O is a naturally occurring and stable unit of nature. Relationships occur in triangles or complexes of triangles. This can occur at a societal level as well as at a personal level, as depicted in Bowen's concept of societal regression. Fourth parties, such as normal siblings, can join a triangle at one of its poles but are free to come and go and are not part of the system created by that particular triangle (although they will be involved in triangles of their own).

Family Projection Process

This process was hypothesized as the mechanism for childhood dysfunction via the father–mother–child–triangle. This process starts with anxiety in the mother and is responded to by anxiety in the child, which is then interpreted by mother as a problem with the child. She may then become overprotective or solicitious, grad-usually establishing a pattern of "infantilizing" the child. Stressful periods during childhood may cause symptomatic episodes, or the mother and child may remain in a relatively stable relationship until the child attempts to function independently. If sufficiently intense, mother–child fusion can result in the child's becoming psychotic if the child attempts to move away from the parents. Bowen hypothesizes that schizophrenia is a result of "several generations of increasing symptomatic impairment, with lower and lower levels of differentiation, until there is a generation that produces schizophrenia" (1976c, p. 83).

The concept of the family projection process was one of Bowen's earliest, *concepts* and often it has been subsumed under the concept of differentiation of self. It explains the development of emotional fusion, or an intense relationship, between a child and mother that results in poor differentiation. At a later stage in the family life cycle, the concept of differentiation is related to the degree to which families form cohesive groups or separate, using physical distance in an attempt to break emotional ties. These behaviors are explained by the emotional cutoff concept and are not tied to any higher-level concepts, such as current social structure in the United States.

Triangles

Bowen maintains that "the triangle, a three-person emotional configuration, is the molecule or the basic building block of any emotional system, whether it is the family or any other group" (1976c, p. 76). Two people may be involved in a stable system, but, when anxiety escalates, the most immediate and vulnerable "other" is enlisted to form a triangle. When there is little or no tension, the triangle is made up of a "comfortably close twosome, and a less comfortable outsider." As tension increases, the outside position becomes the more comfortable position. Typically, families become involved in a series of interlocking triangles that may include extended family members, friends, and/or social agencies. The best example of a triangle is the father–mother–child triangle. Usually this triangle is characterized by tension between parents, with father gaining the most comfortable outside position. Mother then aligns herself with the child, who gradually moves toward "chronic functional impairment."

Therapeutically, the family therapist has two tasks with respect to triangles: to stay in emotional contact with the two most significant members yet stay, insofar as possible, outside the emotionality of the triangle. The result is that "the age-old fusion between the family members will slowly begin to resolve, and all other family members will automatically change in relation to the two parents in the home setting. This is basic theory and basic method" (1976c, p. 78).

Emotional Cutoff

This concept explains how individuals separate themselves from their pasts to start their lives in the present. The process is based on an individual's degree of "unresolved emotional attachments" to his or her parents. The less differentiated the child is from the parents, the more intense the unresolved attachments are likely to be. Likewise, the more intense an individual's cutoff with the past, the more likely the individual is to have "an exaggerated version of his or her parental family problem in his or her own marriage and the more likely his or her own children are to do a more intense cutoff with him or her in the next generation" (1976c, p. 84).

Multigenerational Transmission Process

This concept describes the functioning of the family projection process through multiple generations. The child who is the primary object of the family projection process emerges with a lower degree of differentiation than the parents have and does less well in life. Bowen hypothesizes that this child would produce a line of individuals with lower and lower levels of differentiation, eventually resulting in schizophrenia in about eight to ten generations.

The multigenerational transmission process is a description of how individual levels of differentiation are passed down from generation to generation. According to this concept, individuals marry other individuals who have an equivalent degree of differentiation. Their children have an expectation of degrees of differentiation similar to or lesser than that of their parents. Eventually the process produces an individual so deficient in differentiation that he or she must be maintained in dependent relationships or express severe symptomatology. One wonders, given this model, what the process of entropy can be expected to do to a culture as differentiation decreases over generations.

Marital Conflict

Marriages that are dominated by conflict are emotionally intense for both members. Neither has learned to negotiate differences, and the partners usually cycle through periods of closeness, conflict, which provides emotional distance, and making up, which starts the cycle again. This process is not necessarily harmful to the children—if the fusion goes into the marital conflict. It is when the conflict is projected onto the children that it becomes hurtful to them.

Dysfunction in One Spouse. If one spouse must absorb a high amount of undifferentiation to adapt, that spouse is likely to become dysfunctional. The dysfunction can be manifested in "physical illness, emotional illness, or social illness, such as drinking, acting out, and irresponsible behavior." Marriages based on this pattern can be enduring as long as the overfunctioning spouse is willing to be a caretaker to the underfunctioning one.

Impairment of One or More Children. In this instance, the parents project their undifferentiation onto one or more of their children. Bowen postulates two variables that govern this process: emotional cutoff and level of anxiety. Low levels of anxiety tend to decrease symptoms in a child, and decreasing anxiety can be important in opening up a relationship cutoff.

Sibling Position. Bowen has maintained that there is no single piece of data more important "than knowing the sibling position of people in the present and past generations" (1976c, p. 87). This concept is based on Toman's work on the personality profiles of each sibling position (see Chapter 16). The basic hypothesis is that personality characteristics are related to the sibling position within which a person grew up.

Societal Regression

This concept is based on the degree of anxiety present in society. As stated previously about the family, chronic anxiety results in a gradual regression to lower functioning. Bowen postulates that the same process is occurring in society. As we experience more social tension, social structures become dysfunctional and symptomatic. Efforts to effect changes fail, increasing the problem, and the process keeps repeating—"just as the family goes through similar cycles to the states we call emotional illness" (1976c, p. 88).

History Taking: The Genogram

Within the boundaries of this theory, history taking is imperative. Most of one's understanding of how a family works or fails to work is obtained through prolonged, painstaking history taking, which, in this theory, has been elevated to art form, that is, the family genogram (Bowen, 1978; Guerin and Pendagast, 1976).

All the details of past family happenings, attitudes, personalities, habits, deaths, traumas, separations, and divorces are diagrammatically traced through the short-hand of genogram making. This is the major source of understanding how the individual was reared and formed.

The genogram consists of charting (as far back in the past as an individual can remember) all the members in the genealogical tree of the extended family. Myths, rules, secrets, and skeletons are brought out and looked at in terms of their impact on individuals in the family. In this journey the individual may enlist the cooperation of members from his or her extended family of origin to get all these details about functions and roles of the family members, trying to understand how these roles and functions may have had an impact on the searching individual. Thus, "genogramming" is part of the therapeutic process and not a static test that is left aside and forgotten once it is finished. On the contrary, such a genogram becomes the continuous basis of referral and reference to understand one's behavior. It is used throughout the course of therapy, because, in this process, understanding means *history*. How did this behavior develop over the years and through generations?

Diagnostic Framework

Diagnosis is related to an understanding of the degree of anxiety and dysfunctionality in the system. No systematic framework is used, and sometimes psychiatric terminology is used freely. The degree of dysfunctionality is indicated by the psychiatric label pinned on the identified patient (i.e., schizophrenic, psychotic, etc.). Diagnosis means understanding how a certain symptom developed over time.

For instance, out of a genogram (see Figure 9-1) in which father was divorced by mother because of his alcoholism may grow the identified patient. Mother remarried and has had three additional children from her second marriage. The identified patient, broken down two years after the divorce and having become

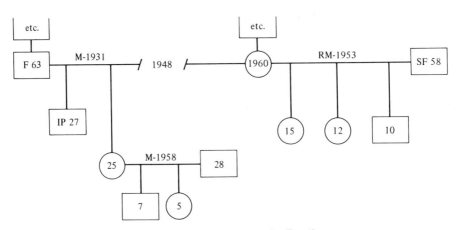

Figure 9-1. Genogram of a Family.

addicted to morphine, was triangularized in the marital conflict, although the sister appears symptom free. However, one of her children, the first-born male, has a "learning disability." And so it goes . . .

Therapeutic Goals

Given the basic problem definition, the goal of treatment is quite easy to define. It is simply differentiation of individuals within their relationships. Bowen saw the goals of therapy as assisting an individual to fulfill the drive toward self-differentiation, step by step. As one member of a family becomes more differentiated, however, repercussions occur in all the interlocking triangles of the family system. Insofar as Bowen believes that patterns of behavior in triangular relationships are completely repetitive, he asserts that he can predict the outcome of changes in any of the family members. Family members will attempt to exert powerful pressures to try to force the differentiating member back to his or her previous fused level; the therapist's intervention is crucial at this point.

The real difficulties arise in Bowen's system when one tries to explain how the emotional process and differentiation become known. The emotional process is defined variously, but never very clearly:

> emotional responsiveness by which one family member responds automatically to the emotional state of another, without either being consciously aware of the process. . . . This "emotional process" is deep and it seems somehow to be related to the *being* of a person. (Bowen, 1978, p. 66)

Bowen (1978) has referred to the emotional process as "basic to life . . . orderly . . . obscured by reason's refusal to accept it . . . deeper than current theory propounds . . . in contact with cellular and somatic processes."

In his 1976 article, Bowen tells the reader that one can get in touch with the emotional process "by knowledge of triangles" (Guerin, 1976). Bowen's students do not seem to be clear about this process either (Fogarty, 1976a; Guerin, 1976). Fogarty has defined it as follows:

> Emotional systems are neither rational nor irrational. They form the undifferentiated background of awareness, apart from any identifiable sensation, perception, or thought. They are like the color in a picture, the setting in a play. They provide the longing for closeness between people, and at the same time are the major source of problems in developing personal relationships. An emotional system is neither true nor false, right nor wrong. It is rated by function. It works or it doesn't. (1976a, p. 146)

What one needs to know is when it works. Bowen and his students seem to be saying that the process is known only by itself, by the emotional process in oneself. This knowledge is gained by experience it seems, particularly by the experience of trying to change one's own family.

Bowen (1976a) provides a statement of his basic approach that summarizes well his principle of change:

> If the therapist is to develop the capacity to stay relatively outside the family emotional system in his clinical work, it is essential that he devote a continuing effort to differentiate his own self from the emotional system of his own family, and also from the emotional system in which he works. . . . It is essential that he always stay focused on process, and that he defocus the content of what is being said. (pp. 396–397)

Unfortunately, here again, our understanding of Bowen's theory depends on understanding the rather diffuse concepts of emotional process and differentiation. Other statements scattered throughout his work give a clearer picture of his method. Generally, it appears that Bowen's point of intervention is the individual family member, preferably the most adequately functioning family member. The initial interview is used to gather information relative to family differentiation on as many generations of the family as possible. Observations on how the family relationships work are not seen as important data in themselves. Following the initial interview, Bowen works with triangles to dissipate anxiety. Once this is accomplished, treatment is focused on creating differentiation within individual family members, often by encouraging the clients to make "I" messages. These messages are presumed to be clear-cut intellectual messages that promote the separation of intellectual and emotional overlaps within the individual (Bowen, 1978). The client can express the "I" position to the therapist, to his or her spouse, or to extended family members. It is presumed that the effect of this change in the individual will reverberate throughout the family system.

Given Bowen's actual approach, it is difficult to distinguish it in practice from a communications-based approach oriented to producing clear messages within the family. Bowen (1978) states, however, that work on family communications is only effective as a short-term method and that it fails to resolve underlying issues. He has also stated that structural rearrangement of family members to different positions on the basic triangle is not improvement. Presumably it leads to change, however, as Bowen earlier described his work in terms of structural rearrangement of triads that led to differentiation.

Given the preceding information, it seems fair to say that Bowen's principle of change is detriangulation of the individual. This can be accomplished in any of the several triangles in which the individual is involved, including that in which the therapist is involved. Detriangulation is aided or accomplished by "I" messages or by the therapist's frustrating the clients' attempts to relate to each other through him or her or any third party. Such detriangulation will only occur in periods of relative quiescence, as anxiety creates the need for a third party in the relationship. How the method of detriangulation differs in practice from a communications-based approach to treatment, which Bowen discredits, remains to be seen.

Bowen uses a variety of levels of analyses in describing his theory. Clearly, the individual level, the family level, and the multigenerational family level are all involved. The individual level is used to analyze differentiation. The familial level relates to triangulation and distribution of anxiety. The multigenerational level is important as father–mother–child triadic behavior is passed down through the family. Without the full multigenerational view, important patterns might be missed.

In terms of time orientation, both past and present are important in Bowen's theory. The past is needed to understand the present, because the past system can cause almost irreversible changes in the individual (Bowen, 1976c) and because the past has been primarily responsible for the degree of differentiation of the present generation. The present is important, because Bowen works in the present, using the past primarily for diagnosing and understanding the present condition of the individual family members and the family system.

Change is evaluated by change in emotional process or degree of differentiation. It is likely that a variety of external cues can be evaluated as indicators of change. One source of information is the degree to which individuals make "I" statements. These are taken by Bowen to be an indication that the emotional process is separated from the intellectual process. Although one does not know what quantity of "I" statements signifies a change in differentiation, one can see whether or not "I" statements are increasing. Another source of information is symptom change. Bowen sees symptoms as expressions of underlying problems that remain in the family until the underlying problems or external stress are removed. A shift of symptoms from the marriage to the child would not be diagnostic, but the total disappearance of symptoms might. Bowen (1978) also presents an expectable pattern of increased symptomatology that reflects one family member's beginning to differentiate successfully from the family.

Role of the Therapist

This differentiation process has several phases, according to Carter and Orfanidis (1976, p. 203). The therapist functions as a coach and first engages the client in the process. Next are the teaching or planning phase, the reentry, the work, and follow-through. Bowen has talked about the importance of the therapist's ability to communicate concern for the clients and to make a connection with the family so that change in family members can be initiated. However, Bowen-oriented therapists would eschew structural methods of therapy because they would seem to offer the possibility of the therapist's getting triangled into the family system. Instead, the Bowen therapist stays outside the family system of triangles by gathering data through history taking rather than by encouraging direct expression of emotions. The therapist emphasizes a matter-of-fact "objective" tone and gradually introduces systems concepts, perhaps suggesting that the client(s) read some professional articles.

Bowen, with his view of the therapist as coach, seems to imply that the client, as well as the therapist, is partly responsible for change. Bowenian therapists appear to engage in "strategy sessions" with their clients, discussing with them what changes they would like to make in their relationships with family members, how they will go about initiating these changes, and what reactions they may expect from other family members in response. In a sense, the Bowen therapist gives the client the tools necessary to become a co-therapist or coach for the client's family as a whole.

Critique and Evaluation

Bowen's major contribution is the organized theoretical framework that describes how an individual develops within a family. In terms of personality functioning, it is a psychodynamically oriented, cause-and-effect theory. In terms of psychopathology, Bowen eliminates the need to pigeonhole individuals by diagnosis and identifies "craziness" as something that "resides" not within individuals but within relationships.

Bowen's theory explains particularly well why problems cluster in particular people, families, and segments of society. It also explains the peculiar relationship between the emotional process in one family member and another that produces dysfunction in one member just as another is beginning to function well. It explains, as well, the complementarity of behavior among family members in many areas other than emotional functioning. The theory does not address the influence of the larger social system on the family (except to see all of society as one large triangle) nor does it address the domain of sibling interaction. It does not address, obviously, a great many other issues and observations.

The concept of differentiation is no better defined than the concept of emotional process. Bowen has presented the subjective scale for rating differentiation of the individual from 0 to 100, but, outside specific descriptions, he has given no directions on how to apply it. He does say, however, that one must understand the emotional process before one can apply the scale (1978). The real problem in understanding both concepts is that they do not seem to be tied directly to cues in the external environment that are readily learnable by others who are trying to learn Bowen's system. As mentioned earlier, they are possibly tied to cues in the internal environment that cannot be communicated through the intellectual process alone. If this indeed were the case, it would be helpful if Bowen would spell out more clearly how one comes to know the emotional process and degree of differentiation of another.

Bowen seems to overemphasize the use of the past in doing family therapy. This is obviously a throwback to his days of psychoanalysis, which looks for all dysfunctioning in an individual's past. His use of a family's history seems somewhat more limited than he describes, although he and his followers make great therapeutic use of this approach.

Bowen does not seem to have a grasp of the word *emotion*. He uses it as a generic, nonspecific term synonymous with stress or arousal. This confusion leads him into mixing emotions with drive states. He acknowledges the use of the term in describing subjective states, such as crying, laughing, fear, and so on; however, he also states that "the emotional system is considered to include . . . all the autonomic nervous system, and to be synonymous with instinct that governs the process in all living things" (1976c, p. 60).

Current emotion theory separates drives from emotions and specifies the nature of "emotional" arousal (Izard, 1977). Drives are cyclic; they result from tissue deficits within the body. However, emotions are experiential and motivational phenomena. They are independent of tissue needs and are not cyclic. Furthermore, the evidence suggests that emotions exist as discrete and preprogrammed neurological, neuromuscular, and phenomenological events rather than as nonspecific arousal states, as Bowen suggests.

An understanding of the emotional system could also suggest new applications for the concept of self-differentiation. A person who is differentiated may be able to experience a wider variety of emotions—and thus may have a much broader perception of the environment than may an undifferentiated person. The latter may tend to jumble together his or her emotion system. Because he or she cannot distinguish accurately what he or she is feeling at any particular moment, that person tends to over- or underrespond to situations. Specific emotions may threaten the undifferentiated person, so he or she lumps them all together and narrows his or her response options—thus limiting his or her perception of reality (L'Abate, 1976).

Applying this criticism to Bowen theory may clarify some of his concepts and may suggest new hypotheses. His concept of "emotional illness" is a vague term that may be difficult to grasp. Does it mean that there is a dysfunction of the drive and emotion system or a dysfunction in how the person responds to emotion-eliciting events? Furthermore, the use of the term "anxiety" is equally vague. Anxiety is made up of a variety of emotions, which may vary depending on what the author means. Bowen seems to use it to mean "stress," which is *not* an emotional response but a global physiological response. It becomes anxiety when emotions such as fear, guilt, distress, or anger become associated with it. For example, we experience stress when our environment changes; if it changes too much and too rapidly, we may experience fear or anxiety.

In assessing which approach to take with a family, one must take into account the capability of the family to absorb and respond to stress. There may be situations that a family experiences as stressful but that it can absorb and tolerate. In these cases, extended family history work may be valuable. However, if a symptom is causing so much stress that the system's equilibrium is seriously jeopardized, then another systems approach (e.g., structural, strategic, or paradoxical therapy aimed at symptom removal) may be in order. Thus, at crisis points, at transitional points in the family life cycle, structural maneuvers may be more appropriate. Once the crisis subsides, it may then be appropriate to use systems coaching methods.

In his article on "Family Reaction to Death" (1976b), Bowen seems to indicate that his approach was to get the father, who had been a peripheral figure in the family, involved with his children in the grieving process after the death of the mother. In essence, he was involved in helping the family restructure itself in response to the loss of the mother. In contrast, Minuchin (Chapter 7), in his interview, probed each of the spouses for data concerning their families of origin, helping them to see continuing patterns from family of origin to present marital and family situation. This approach is essentially the one advocated by Bowen. It was used appropriately by Minuchin with a couple who presented with no stated problems. However, it was clear that the interview was therapeutic for the couple. Thus, it does not seem productive to try to characterize one of these therapeutic systems as "better" than the other in an absolute sense. Rather, it is more productive to see the two approaches as useful at different points in the family process.

It seems that part of the difficulty with Bowen's concepts of differentiation and emotional process is that Bowen has reified the convenient fictions he uses to explain and predict how people behave in relationships. As a result, we lose touch with the actual observations that the theory is created to explain. More attention is spent on what the emotional process is than on how it can be used to explain how people act. The emotional process is almost impossible to define without knowledge of exactly which behavior it is related to. An explanation simply will not make sense when it is not connected with that which it was created to explain. When Bowen's concepts are reconnected with the behaviors they explain, it should be easier to find cues in the external world with which to align the theory.

A related difficulty is inherent in theories about relationships. Because relationships are themselves inferences that are once removed from actual observation, explanations of relationships are twice removed. This leads to some very complicated theorizing and requires a great deal of intellectual effort to return to the actual observations on which the theories of relationships are based. Haley (Chapter 6) has simplified this problem by talking not about relationships but about sequences of observable events. He intervenes in sequences, not in relationships.

One of the most important questions asked of any theory—under what conditions will it apply? (or to what region of experience does it apply?)—is left unanswered by Bowen. He has told us that his method will not work if the system is experiencing too much anxiety or if the treatment is basically emotionally rather than intellectually centered (1978). However, there is no other limitation imposed on the method, and supposedly it is universally applicable. This indicates that the author of the theory has declined to specify the region of experience upon which the theory was developed, assuming that it will generalize to an entire universe of experiences.

Data for Bowen appear to be supplied primarily by the therapist's emotional responses in therapy and by the client's report of feelings. The structure of a patient's verbalizations appears to count as data as well in that it can be used to discriminate degrees of differentiation. Symptomatology in family would appear to be Bowen's final source of data. Data are obtained by direct observation of the family and family members as well as by reports of family members by other family members.

One of the worst shortcomings of this approach is its possible misapplication in the hands of unqualified therapists claiming "to do Bowen's therapy." In one case heard by this writer, the presumably Bowenian woman therapist asked a mother to sell her house and move from the West Coast to the East Coast so that the daughter could "differentiate" herself from her. Although this woman therapist claimed that the process was still in progress, the results for the older woman seemed disastrous and her daughter was totally insensitive to her plight.

Regardless of the theoretical niceties that can be levied against this or any theory, it is important to acknowledge that Bowen has been influential in producing top-notch family theorists and therapists (Fogarty, 1976a, 1976b; Guerin, 1976), who, with their master, have left an indelible imprint in the path of family therapy.

References

Bowen, M. 1976a. Principles and techniques of multiple family therapy. In *Family therapy: Theory and practice,* ed. P. J. Guerin, Jr., pp. 388–404. New York: Gardner Press.

——. 1976b. Family reaction to death. In *Family therapy: Theory and practice,* ed. P. J. Guerin, Jr., pp. 335–349. New York: Gardner Press.

——. 1976c. Theory in the practice of psychotherapy. In *Family therapy: Theory and practice,* ed. P. J. Guerin, Jr., pp. 42–90. New York: Gardner Press.

——. 1978. *Family therapy in clinical practice.* New York: Jason Aronson.

Carter, E., and Orfanidis, M. M. 1976. Family therapy with one person and the family therapist's own family. In *Family therapy: Theory and practice,* ed. P. J. Guerin, Jr., pp. 193–219. New York: Gardner Press.

Fogarty, T. F. 1976a. System concepts and the dimensions of self. In *Family therapy: Theory and practice,* ed. P. J. Guerin, Jr., pp. 144–153. New York: Gardner Press.

Fogarty, T. F. 1976b. Marital crisis. In *Family therapy: Theory and practice,* ed. P. J. Guerin, Jr., pp. 325–334. New York: Gardner Press.

Guerin, P. J., Jr., and Pendagast, E. 1976. Evaluation of family systems and genogram. In *Family therapy: Theory and practice,* ed. P. J. Guerin, Jr., pp. 450–464. New York: Gardner Press.

Izard, C. E. 1977. *Human emotions.* New York: Plenum Press.

L'Abate, L. 1976. *Understanding and helping the individual in the family.* New York: Grune & Stratton.

10

The Social Learning Approach of Gerald R. Patterson and the Oregon Project

Gerald R. Patterson (Ph.D., University of Minnesota), who has spent most of his professional career in Eugene, Oregon, has applied behavioral principles to research and therapy in the area of behavioral disturbances in children. His work has dealt with changing behaviors, such as aggression, hyperactivity, and other undesirable social behaviors, as well as with some factors that can lead to these and to socially accepted behaviors. Patterson's work has been controlled rigorously and supported experimentally. Although he has stated no general theory of behavioral disturbances in children, his research is derived from a specific theory and lends itself to placement within the framework of a behavioristic theory.

In Patterson's approach, research and practice are completely overlapping, or at least as overlapping as is humanly possible. Thus, his approach not only helps to demonstrate the usefulness of behavioral methods of intervention, but, even more important, it helps to demonstrate the usefulness of an empirically grounded approach, one that can form the basis for feedback and change in the system itself, as Patterson and his co-workers have demonstrated repeatedly. This feedback and consequent change is lacking in most of the therapeutic approaches reviewed in this book. Perhaps other therapists use a more subjective and impressionistic kind of feedback. However, they have failed to demonstrate significant changes in their techniques to the extent and with the detail demonstrated by Patterson and his co-workers. He has exercised widespread influence not only within an "inner circle" of loyal co-workers but also outside this circle. Among his co-workers, Weiss (1978), for instance, has applied most of the experiences learned from the Oregon Social Learning Project to behavioral intervention in marriage and marital conflicts. Patterson's influence is extended through his published work and a great many studies, Ph.D. dissertations, and unpublished reports that have sprung up because of his influence.

The Social Learning Project was begun in 1965, its primary objective being to develop an empirically based, low-cost treatment approach for use with families of aggressive and predelinquent children. In addition, the project was designed to implement procedures for evaluating the impact of behavioral treatment. The paper by Weinrott, Bauske, and Patterson (1979) is one of various progress reports that reviews their earlier work, describes in detail recent innovations, and indicates future directions for the project.

From 1965 to 1968, the project followed a course of simple case studies, which served as vehicles for developing treatment and assessment technologies. Their major premise was that the social environment of the child is paramount. Through case studies, Patterson and his co-workers began attempts to teach parents how to reduce the amount of deviant behavior displayed by children through the use of operant techniques. In the initial years there was an over-reliance on tangible reinforcers as well as on the use of contingent parental attentions. These treatment components were soon increased by observation training, data collection, and more discriminative incentives: "time-outs" and "modeling."

The group developed a prototype of a multicategory scoring system to generate data to evaluate five consecutive referrals in the first multiple-case study. In this study (Patterson, Ray, and Shaw, 1968), problems included withdrawal, isolation, school failure, separate activity aggression, setting fires, and so on. Prior to the onset of treatment, observations were conducted by highly trained observers and scorers. Observations were also scheduled throughout intervention and follow-up. Child treatment then consisted of having parents learn the program through a learning text (Patterson and Gullion, 1968) designed to teach principles and applications of social learning theory. This learning was followed by training parents in observation and data collection.

After the initial tryout of three families, a more stringent test of treatment was designed. It was characterized by relatively large numbers of referrals, with evaluation based on multiple outcome measures. Evaluations included data showing the cost of professional time, both during treatment and for booster shots thereafter, and a follow-up of one year. From January 1968 to June 1972, twenty-seven families were referred to the project from outlying agencies. Families were accepted for treatment because at least one boy in the family had been identified as a conduct problem for a number of years. Families with severely retarded, acutely psychotic, or clearly brain-damaged children were excluded from treatment. Ages of children accepted for treatment ranged from five to fourteen years. The sample contained eight father-absent families. The majority of these families were economically disadvantaged. Treatment consisted of training, in which parents learned to apply skills necessary to reduce rates of deviant behavior and increase rates of pro-social responses. Treatment components included contingent attention, a point incentive system, time-outs, and contingency contracting (Patterson, Cobb, and Ray, 1973). Multiple measures of family behavior attitudes and personality were obtained prior to, during, and following treatment.

The two principal forms of assessment were in-home observation conducted by trained professionals and parents' reports of preselected noxious behaviors displayed by the identified patient (Patterson, 1980). The results indicated that independently observed deviant behavior rates were reduced significantly from base line to termination. This improvement persisted through to a one-year follow-up period. Parents also reported that child-coercive behavior also declined significantly from base level to termination. The data indicated that 75 per cent of the families showed considerable improvement. These gains were realized at an average cost per family of 31.4 hours of professional time during formal parent training and 1.9 hours for periodic "booster shots" during follow-up.

Although these overall findings were clear, albeit not conclusive, evidence of persistent treatment effects, there were compelling rationales for systematic replication. The original sample was a mixture of high-rate, socially aggressive children and a second subgroup referred for low-rate but rather serious offenses, such as stealing and fire setting.Not only might the two types of children require different forms of treatment, but statistical problems also existed in combining them for group analyses. Of the twenty-seven target children, eleven showed deviant behaviors that were within the range displayed by normal, unreferred children. For these families, the variables extracted from observation data were simply not appropriate for measuring the impact of treatment. The second problem was a rather high attrition rate during follow-up (Kent, 1976). Of the twenty-seven families discharged, eleven (41 per cent) were either unwilling to provide data or were impossible to locate one year after termination. Families with higher rates of deviant behaviors during base line showed a greater tendency to drop out.

Because of the high attrition rate, an important objective of the next replication study was to reduce the attrition rate during the posttreatment period. Another objective was to reduce the amount of professional time needed for treatment. Two cost-effective procedures were implemented in the replication to reduce costs. First, parents were treated in groups, and, second, much of the training occurred by means of videotaping. Recordings structured and paced each group session and further obviated the need for advanced-level training. The sample of twenty-seven families and the cases that preceded them were treated directly by Patterson and Reid (1970) and a few other advanced-level therapists. It was important to replicate the first study using an entirely different group of therapists. To achieve this goal, the Family Center was created as a semiautonomous unit, which was to serve as demonstration replication site for treatment of aggressive children. This replication sample was made up of twenty-six consecutive referrals to the Family Center who fulfilled the following criteria: (1) the child, male or female, had to be between three and twelve years of age; (2) families had to reside within a twenty-minute drive of the Family Center to accommodate observers and occasional home visits by therapists; (3) neither parent nor child could have been diagnosed previously as psychotic, severely retarded, or autistic; (4) the primary referral problem had to be social aggression, physical or verbal or both; (5) parents had to agree to home observation, telephone interviews, and attendance at therapy sessions; (6) parents could have no plans for divorce, moving to another community, or placing the child in foster care or residential treatment; and (7) the base-line deviant behavior for the target child had to be equal to or exceeded .45 per minute. A deviant behavior rate of .45 per minute is half the standard deviation of the mean rate for normal referred children. Of the twenty-six initial families, eight dropped out during base line on the first few weeks of treatment. The remaining eighteen families attended ten or more weeks. Of these, fifteen children were boys and three were girls. The mean age at intake was seven years; nine families were intact and nine had only a single parent.

Treatment consisted of parents' meeting in groups of three to four families for a ten-week core instruction program. Following this instruction, families were placed on a low-level maintenance schedule to maximize long-term gains and cooperation with the data collection activity during follow-up. A detailed description of the instruction sessions for the parents will be given later. In cases in which families had achieved some gain but still experienced an occasional relapse, more intensive individual family sessions were added. The content of such sessions varied substantially from family to family but usually involved further negotiation training and careful probing by the therapists regarding application of various components. Occasionally, a family would be referred elsewhere if behavioral techniques did not seem to be helpful.

Family Concepts

Personality is learned as a result of small events that happen to a child thousands of times each day and that are reinforced in small steps, positively, through presentation of a rewarding stimulus, and, negatively, through avoidance or termination of painful events (Patterson and Gullion, 1968). Most behaviors are learned as a result of social stimuli. In the first stage of personality development, the child is taught to respond to social stimuli. Younger children are more responsive to social stimuli (Patterson, 1969) and learn responsiveness through pairing of social stimuli with high-incentive stimuli, such as food, candy, and preferred toys (Patterson, Littman, and Bricker, 1967). A child who is being trained to respond to the eliciting and reinforcing aspects of the behavior of others provides a basis for acquiring both adaptive and deviant behaviors (Patterson, 1969).

The family is, of course, the primary center for learning this social responsiveness. The family consists of "mutually interdependent dyads" (Patterson & Reid, 1970). The behavior of one member of the dyad determines behaviors that the other will develop and the extent to which such behaviors persist (Patterson and Cobb, 1970). Two individuals in a functioning dyad attend to each other partially because they have influenced each other to develop overlapping repertoires of social behavior (Patterson and Reid, 1970). Behaviors that parents consider "good" are assumed to be reinforced through parental approval (Patterson, Littman, and Hinsey, 1964). Parental love, interest, and attention are powerful reinforcers (Patterson and Gullion, 1968) and account for development of much behavior and responsiveness to social stimuli.

Social reinforcement of behavior is a prime component of effective functioning in the child's behavior. Certain classes of child behaviors, those valued by the parent or peer group, are more likely to elicit social approval for them. The greater the child's social responsiveness, the more likely the child is to acquire the valued behavior (Patterson, 1965a). A well-functioning social dyad is a reciprocal one, that is, the two members of the dyad positively reinforce each other's behavior at an equitable rate, maintaining the behavior. One member's behavior is reinforced until that member is satiated and the reinforcing member becomes habituated; then the roles are reversed. The reciprocal pair reinforce each other to become more alike (Patterson and Reid, 1970).

Some other factors are associated with effective functioning of the child's behavior. There is a relationship between the activity level of the child and his or her acquisition of acceptable social behavior. Up to moderately high activity levels, the child's behavior will result in an increasing number of reactions from adults and peers. A very active child (assuming that the reactions of others are positive) will acquire social skills more rapidly than will a less active child (Patterson et al., 1965). There is also a relationship between responsiveness to social approval and the acquisition of socially acceptable behaviors. The normal child is responsive first to parents and then to peers (Patterson et al., 1964). Those people to whom the child is responsive are of importance also. The acquisition of socially acceptable behaviors in boys is related to responsiveness to males and that in girls to females (Patterson and Fagot, 1967). In most instances, socially acceptable behavior inhibits other incompatible behavior (Patterson and Cobb, 1970) and does not have a demand characteristic associated with dysfunctional behaviors (Patterson, 1969).

Dysfunctional behavior, like functional, is learned. A problem child behaves that way because the child was taught to. Most behavioral disturbances in children are undesirable behaviors taught accidentally. Problem behaviors are reinforced accidentally, both positively and negatively (Patterson, 1971). Aggressive, negativistic, hyperactive, frightened, withdrawn, and dependent behaviors are learned (Patterson and Gullion, 1968).

One factor in the early development of dysfunctional behavior is the child's failure to learn to respond to social stimuli. For example, the autistic child is one who fails to develop social behaviors because the process of learning this responsiveness has been omitted or is incomplete. Another type of this nonresponsiveness is selective, that is, the child chooses the person to whom he or she will respond. Some deviant behaviors seem to be associated with selective nonresponsiveness of the child to adults of the same sex. For example, boys who respond only to social reinforcement by the mother often have dysfunctional behaviors (Patterson and Fagot, 1967). Since, in most of Patterson's observations of families, the father was the most uninvolved family member, providing the fewest social reinforcements (Patterson and Reid, 1970), there seems to be considerable opportunity for deviant behavior, particularly in boys. In general, then, it is probable that behavior problems may be found in those children who are responsive only to some aspects of the social environment and whose behavior is not being conditioned by some agents, such as peer group, parents, or other adults (Patterson, 1965b).

This selective nonresponsiveness may be one factor that places the child on extinction schedules (i.e., periods in which behavior is not reinforced). These periods provide the opportunity for development of other behaviors, which may be deviant (Patterson and Reid, 1970). Although parental emotional adjustment is not necessary or sufficient for deviant behaviors in the child (Patterson and Cobb, 1970), not all parents who reinforce deviant behavior are emotionally disturbed (Patterson, 1965a). However, parents of children referred to clinics have had MMPI profiles that are more deviant than those of "normal" groups (Liverant, 1959). It is possible that these parents are more likely to have children on extinction schedules (Patterson and Reid, 1970).

One prominent type of dysfunction, often established by dyadic interaction in "normal" families, is frequent use of coercion in too many situations, which may produce a conduct disorder. Coercion is a social relationship in which the behavior of one member of a dyad is controlled by positive reinforcement and behavior of the other is controlled by aversive stimuli (Patterson and Reid, 1970). Like other types of dysfunction, coercion is a result of the accumulation of numerous small events (Patterson and Cobb, 1970). The most common example of coercion is the one in which the child trains the parents to respond to his or her wishes to escape or avoid aversive behavior. Coercion begins with conflict, which is "a demand for immediate change followed by a noncompliance" behavior (Patterson, 1971, p. 102). However, not all children are equally responsive to social reinforcers or aversive social stimuli. This difference influences the children's rate of acquisition of social behavior. Responsiveness to social stimuli has three components: responsiveness to social approval and disapproval, imitation, and ability to discriminate among social cues (Patterson, 1965a, 1976).

The child is first taught by the family to respond to social stimuli. As the child gets older, he or she is increasingly responsive to social reinforcers delivered by the peer group, and reinforcement by friends is more effective than reinforcement by nonpreferred peers (Patterson and Anderson, 1964). The child is reinforced for certain behaviors, depending on the group in which he or she operates and may select friends and groups on the basis of the reinforcement they provide. This reinforcement is contingent on behaviors valued by the group (Patterson et al., 1967).

Besides peer status, other variables affecting social responsiveness of the child are his or her age and the interaction between the child's sex and that of the parent (Patterson, 1965a). In observation of families in a laboratory situation, Patterson found that mothers had a greater influence on their sons and fathers on their daughters (Patterson et al., 1964).

Social responsiveness is a determinant of personality traits (Patterson and Anderson, 1964). One set of personality traits is correlated with responsiveness to parents and another with responsiveness to the peer group. The child's acquisition of a wide range of personality traits may be a function of responsiveness to social stimuli (Patterson, 1965a). Responsiveness to social approval is related to acquisition of socially acceptable behaviors. Failure to acquire these behaviors is due in part to a lack of responsiveness to social approval, first from the parents and later from the peer group (Patterson et al., 1964). These behaviors are reinforced because they are valued by the parent or peer group.

Personality traits associated with responsiveness to disapproval are considered a kind of avoidance response, learned in conjunction with punishment (Patterson, 1965a), and punishment is generally followed by emotional disturbance (Patterson, 1971). Therefore, responsiveness to social disapproval is related to maladjustment, just as responsiveness to approval is related to adjustment.

Two procedures that elicit behavior—persuasion and modeling—have the catalytic effect of accelerating the acquisition and change of social behaviors, both adaptive and deviant. Modeling is reinforcement of another person for some behavior in the presence of the subject. In persuasion, the social agent is not reinforced (Patterson, 1969). These procedures are related to social responsiveness in that responsiveness helps to determine the effect of persuasion and modeling.

The amount of social interaction is often an important variable in establishing and maintaining behavior. A child who interacts with his or her peers at a high rate has been conditioned to be highly responsive to reinforcers dispensed by peers as well as having a high activity level. The amount of the child's interaction is determined in part by the reinforcement received for this interaction (Patterson et al., 1967). The amount of interaction may be a variable associated with aggression, which is the specific area in which Patterson's contribution is paramount.

Aggression is one of the most frequent behavior problems for which children are referred to outpatient clinics. For a child to be considered clinically aggressive, there are two necessary conditions. First, the child is aggressive at higher rates and in situations in which it is not acceptable. Second, the child's conditioning process is characterized by a variety of motivational states' becoming eliciting stimuli for aggressive behaviors, with the termination of these states strengthening aggressive behaviors (Patterson et al., 1967).

Aggressive behaviors are a high-amplitude subclass of assertive behavior, which is a broader class of behavior consisting of motor and verbal behaviors all characterized by a demand feature, as in coercion. Assertive behaviors are coercive because they demand environmental reaction, which is often reinforcing. Aggressive children are well trained in assertive behaviors. Besides the demand for immediate reaction, another characteristic of assertion is aversive behavior contingent on noncompliance with the demand (Patterson et al., 1967).

There are two factors in the process of the acquisition of assertive behavior. First, there is social reinforcement from parents and peers to shape the behavior; second, there is accompanying high-intensity emotional or motivational states. Aggressive behaviors are reinforced because the reinforcement removes unpleasant situations (Patterson, 1971). The first phase in the reinforcement of aggression in the child is assertion toward parents to obtain high-incentive reinforcing stimuli. The second phase is the generalization of this behavior from the parent to a sibling or peer of the same age or younger, who is more likely to reinforce aggression by giving up a desired toy, crying, moving out of the way, and so on (Patterson et al., 1967).

Most children develop assertive behaviors as a function of interaction with peers (i.e., as a result of normal, healthy, social interaction). Because the stimuli that set up the occurrence of reinforcement are primarily social, they are of short duration and low amplitude in the young child. The more intense, high-amplitude behavior that leads to parental concern and a desire for professional help may sometimes be a result of punishment. The correlation between punishments by parents and aggressiveness in the child could be a result of punishing or extinguishing aggressiveness in the home but having it reinforced in the peer group (Patterson et al., 1967).

The rate of aggressive behavior may fluctuate as a result of several variables, even within a given setting. One variable is the behavior of the victim of an attack, as he or she provides both the cues and the reinforcement for the attack (Patterson and Cobb, 1970). There are also individual differences in the generalized reinforcers for aggressive behaviors, as well as differences in activity level (Patterson et al., 1967). Some other factors that may increase the likelihood of an aggressive attack are frustration (because of nonreinforcement), negative evaluations (verbal insults, unfriendly acts, etc.), confining space, fatigue, and hunger. Certain family members and peers may function as stimuli that can either facilitate or inhibit aggression by virtue of their size, skills in counteraggression, and so on. An event will facilitate aggression only to the extent that the family member who dispenses it can be conditioned to terminate the behavior. Children with assertive older siblings are more likely to be assertive, because their assertion is learned through modeling and reinforcement of counterassertion (Patterson and Cobb, 1970).

Aggression usually decreases with age. As the child grows older, the consequences of aggression become more aversive. Peers become larger and counterattacks longer and more painful, and adults are more liable to punish aggression physically and psychologically. Social stimuli that were cues for aggressive behavior become cues for nonaggression. For example, the parents are likely to punish aggression and not let themselves be victims (Patterson et al., 1967). Aggression is, therefore, learned behavior that may fit, in varying degrees, at different points along the continuum from functioning to dysfunctioning. Because behavior is learned through reinforcement and punishment and, when dysfunctional, may be changed in the same manner, the first step in changing behavior is to observe it to determine what the behaviors are, how they are maintained and how frequently they occur (Patterson and Gullion, 1968).

The most likely antecedents of coercive behaviors occur with what Patterson labeled "diffusion parent." The parents are only peripherally involved in tracking and arranging contingencies for the behavior of their children. There may be a second pattern of interaction. The parents are involved and do track child behavior. They may do a good job of rearing several children. For this particular child, however, they neither track nor apply contingencies. The process is labeled "selective diffusion." This may be the case of the working mother who feels some guilt about depriving the child of "mothering" and allows his or her coercive behavior to occur. For other parents under stress of illness or crisis, the same process may occur. Each results in a loss of control over the behavior of the child and a lack of consistency.

Effective behavior modification, therefore, can alter the output of deviant behaviors within the family system by increasing the frequency of reciprocal interaction. As Patterson and his co-workers have shown repeatedly, deviant children and deviant parents do not have reciprocal interactions. Instead, one member of the dyad typically coerces the other. To prove this hypothesis, a retarded ten-year-old boy from a family of eight was used as a subject for reprogramming the entire family. The intervention involved the use of Patterson's *Living with Children* and a record or graph of three events that counted the frequency with which children fulfilled or resisted requests, frequency with which each spouse positively reinforced good behavior, and frequency with which each parent received positive reinforcement from the family. Two of these helped the child, whereas the last one involved reciprocity for the entire family. The child was given M&Ms as rewards for his good behavior. The mother received points toward driving lessons, and the children received points toward ice cream cones. As a result of these techniques, the target child decreased the rate of his deviant behaviors in the home. The family, in turn, supplied less support for these behaviors. Along with this home intervention, there was some accompanying intervention in the school. Through the use of shaping procedures that reinforced each gain in desirable behavior, another boy taught the target child to play football. He was instructed to use praise only—never criticism—and to use small, easily accomplished steps. (The ball was thrown only three feet at first.) The difficulty of the steps was gradually increased, and the whole class was let out fifteen minutes earlier each day that the target child's score improved. This success produced a throng of interested and reinforcing spectators. As a result of both intervention programs, the target child adjusted better in school and at home.

Patterson (1979) has found repeatedly that socially aggressive boys referred to treatment engaged in two to three times more coercive events than did boys from nonproblem families. They were also more likely to engage in longer sequences of coercive acts. Patterson argues that the tendency to engage in extensive coercive behaviors represents the critical difference between conduct disorder and nonproblem children. He reports data that show that it was the reaction of family members during a coercive episode that determine whether a child will be involved in a chain of extended or short duration. Members of distressed families are much more likely to engage in reactions associated with longer sequences; that is, their behavior reinforces the child's coercive behavior.

In a sophisticated and complex paper (1977), Patterson reviews the role of the mother from the perspective of cohesion theory. Within this context, Patterson assumes that mothers of preschool children are usually exposed to high intensities of aversive events. In fact, it seems that the younger the child, the higher the rate of aggressive behaviors. Mothers' satisfaction in their roles may vary as a function of these inputs: the greater the aggression, the lower the satisfaction in the motherly role. Mothers of aggressive children encounter higher rates of aversive events than do mothers of normal children. In a normal family, fathers function as social facilitators and resident guests, mothers serve as caretakers, and both parents share in child management problems. In distressed families the same goals take place; however, the mother's role is expanded to include that of a crisis manager, whereas the father seems to be much less involved in the day-to-day details of child management. With aggressive children, the behavior seems to be more an attack against the mother than a reprisal against the mother's behavior.

Patterson hypothesizes that prolonged experience of aversive systems will produce low self-esteem and that mothers of socially aggressive children may be more exposed to higher rates of aversive events than are the mothers of normal children. Consequently, mothers of aggressive children may show lower self-esteem than may mothers of normal children. He tested this hypothesis by using the Minnesota Multiphasic Personality Inventory. Mothers of socially aggressive children showed significantly higher scores on the Depression scale, with borderline elevations on Hysteria and Social Introversion and lower scores on Psychosthenia; mothers of children who stole had MMPI profiles similar to those of classic profiles for adolescent delinquents, who had elevated scores on Psychopathic-Deviate and Hypomanic scales. Following training and supervision in child management skills, there was a significant decrease in Depression and Social Introversion and an increase in the Hypomania scale for mothers of socially aggressive children.

History Taking, Diagnostic Procedures, and Framework

In this system, emphasis is on the here and now, namely, that which can be controlled and changed. Hence, historical antecedents, although important, are not as relevant as are *present* circumstances. The past cannot be changed. The present can and should be changed if it is dysfunctional for a family. The past is relevant insofar as having information about past methods of discipline, reinforcement history, and coercive efforts used to control the child's behavior.

Diagnostic procedures consist of the behavior recording system. It is an exhaustive nineteen-category observation system, which provides a sequential record of noxious and pro-social behavior displayed by family members, such as those listed in the checklist to be presented later in this chapter. Each family in this study serves as a subject for two five-minute segments, which were assigned on a random basis. Coded entries are made by observers every five seconds through a portable audio-pacer that generates signals delineating intervals. Observations are usually conducted just prior to the dinner hour, a time when most parents report difficulty in managing their children. The behavior coding system provides scores for each category of behavior and for each family member. These scores have generally been expressed in terms of rates per minute, and they can be combined to form composites. For instance, by combining scores for fourteen division categories, a measure of total deviant behavior is obtained. Follow-up probes consisting of two sessions on consecutive days are scheduled four, eight, and twelve months after termination. Most of these observations have high observer reliability, as evidenced by a variety of data presented by Patterson and his associates.

The telephone interview report is used to measure the daily occurrence of behavior classifiable as socially aggressive and to document low-rate events, such as stealing, fire setting, bed wetting, and refusing meals. Because in-home observations are expensive and hence relatively infrequent, they are unlikely to produce data on these low-rate events. Parents' reports support this conclusion, although the dependability of such reports is difficult and apparently not ascertained by this group.

Behavior categories and definitions for the behavior coding system consist of first-order categories, such as verbal behaviors (commanding, crying, humiliation, laughing, whining, and yelling); nonverbal behaviors (destructiveness, physically negative, physically positive); and verbal or nonverbal behaviors (approval and compliance, disapproval, dependency, indulgence, noncompliance, play, teaching).

Second-order categories consist of verbal behaviors (talking) and nonverbal behaviors (attention, touching, etc.). Self-stimulation is a class combining both verbal and nonverbal behaviors. Telephone calls are conducted in a structured way, using the behavior checklist shown. The reliability of telephone calls for coding seems to be extremely high among interviewers.

1. Arguing/talking back to adults
2. Bed wetting
3. Competitiveness
4. Complaining
5. Crying
6. Defiance
7. Destructiveness
8. Fearfulness
9. Fighting with sibs
10. Fire setting
11. Hitting others (not sibs)
12. Hyperactiveness, running around
13. Irritableness
14. Lying
15. Negativeness
16. Noisiness
17. Noncompliance
18. Not eating (meals)
19. Pants wetting
20. Pouting, sadness
21. Running away
22. Soiling
23. Stealing
24. Teasing
25. Temper tantrums
26. Whining
27. Yelling

Of the eighteen families who terminated treatment after ten or more weeks, fourteen provided data on follow-up at four months, eleven at eight months, and eight at twelve months; four were not available or were unwilling to participate after treatment had ended. The attrition pattern was similar to that observed in the original studies (Patterson. 1976). In families who completed ten or more weeks of treatment, there was a reduction in the rate of aggressive behavior from .83 per minute in base line to .36 at termination. For these families, some follow-up data were obtained: a decrease in target deviant behavior from .90 base line to .31 at termination. Many of these results and changes that occurred in aggressive behavior at the end of treatment were maintained after follow-up. In 69 percent of the families, significant trends showed from base line to observations as measured by telephone interviews, with no dissipation of effects during follow-up. It should be mentioned that the 69 per cent improvement rate is not different from rates reported for individual psychotherapy outcome. Essentially, treatment was successful in reducing parent-reported negative behavior below base-line levels and the level during follow-up was also well below that reported in the baseline.

Therapeutic Foci and Goals

The goal of any intervention for Patterson, as well as for other behavioral therapists, is to bring the identified patients behavior under stimulus control. The unruly child should learn to comply; the inattentive child should learn to pay attention and "mind." Thus, in this respect, the therapist accepts the symptoms brought in by the parents at their face value, concentrating on them, often ignoring the rest of the family context (i.e., why is Mother so overinvolved with the child's behavior while Dad stands idly by?). The goal is to control the behavior, *not* to deal with the family system.

The goal of intervention is to reprogram the social environment to decrease the occurrence of dysfunctional behavior and increase the occurrence of competing behavior (Patterson and Brodsky, 1966). Changing the reinforcement schedules of parents or peers is the main focus. The parents must be instructed on how and what behaviors to reinforce (Patterson, 1965b).

Intervention Strategies

One method of instructing parents on what behavior to reinforce is called "time-out." This method is used to decrease the occurrence of behavior, a procedure that removes the possibility of any behavior's reinforcement by placing the child in a nonreinforcing environment. The second method is conditioning more socially adaptive behaviors through positive reinforcement (Patterson et al., 1967). Another method is to set up "contracts" whereby the child, through certain clearly specified behaviors, earns points that are redeemable for certain rewards. In this manner, small increments of behavior are rewarded, but numerous small increments are necessary to obtain the desired reward. This method operates on what Patterson (1971) calls a "first-and-then" notion: first, the child omits certain behaviors already in his or her repertoire; then, the child is rewarded.

An important point to remember in changing behavior is that new behaviors are not shaped but that small increments of change in existing social behaviors are elicited. For this treatment to be effective, stimulus generalization must exist, although this generalization cannot totally account for the persistence of treatment effects (Patterson et al., 1967).

Some children seem to be deviant due to lack of social responsiveness; that is, their behavior is difficult to change because social reinforcers are ineffective. The first step in behavioral change is to alter their social responsiveness. If they are selectively nonresponsive (i.e., responsive to only a few classes of social agents), their behavior should be brought under the control of a wider range of social agents. The person responsible for dispensing social reinforcement is, of course, a vital element in behavior change. High-prestige agents are more effective in altering behaviors; male adults are more effective in altering behaviors in girls and female adults are more effective in altering those of boys (Patterson, 1969).

These counterconditioning methods are, in some instances, quite difficult to use effectively. The most difficult types of behavior to change are those involving command behaviors because they were probably established on a variable ratio schedule (reinforcements given after a number of responses, with that number varying from reinforcement to reinforcement) and increase in intensity during extinction (frustration), making nonattending to these behaviors difficult (Patterson and Reid, 1970). However, some children may be socially harmed by other methods of controlling behavior, such as punishment. Some behaviors, such as hyperactivity and aggression, are partially a function of amount of social interaction; punishing these behaviors may result in a slower rate of social development, as rate of interaction may be decreased also. Therefore, Patterson's method of behavior change through positive reinforcement is, in the long run, more effective than is punishment (Patterson et al., 1965).

Several applications of operant conditioning can be found in the work of Patterson (1971) in the area of home management. This contribution is within the framework of the normal family and involves routine discipline problems that stem from the assumption that consequences control behavior. We can teach parents methods that will encourage desirable behavior in their children and eliminate undesirable behavior with the techniques of operant conditioning. Patterson and Gullion (1968) provided a step-by-step method in which they described the use of social reinforcers, such as praise, approval, attention, and nonsocial reinforcers, such as food, money, toys, or points. It is a very down-to-earth, easily understood program. They explain to the parent that behavior followed by positive reinforcement will recur in the future and gives a helpful guide toward establishing new behavior. The parent is instructed to break down the desired behavior into concrete steps small enough for the child to receive reinforcement along the way to a larger goal. For instance, if the objective is to be a good student, small steps must be identified along the way toward that goal. If this method does not work, either the steps are too large or reinforcement is not meaningful to that particular child. Later, larger steps and, finally, intermittent reinforcement stabilizes the behavior.

Retraining involves strengthening the competing behavior while weakening the undesirable behavior. For instance, in the case of the "I don't want to" child, whose patterns have been reinforced by the attention mother must give him or her in repeating her requests, the competing behavior of cooperating or playing nicely must receive rewards. At the same time, weakening the negative behavior can be accomplished by a "time-out." The child is sent to a bare room, perhaps the bathroom or the dining room, for fifteen minutes. (Five minutes is long enough for a young child.) The child must remain in time-out without misbehaving for the entire fifteen minutes. No scolding or punishing can be done on the way to the time-out room, as the upset parent is very reinforcing. One must explain to the parent that spanking the child does not get the best results. In fact, the one thing that is most reinforcing to the child is attention, whether it is good or bad. The pain of spanking is often worth the attention to the child, and the accompanying highly charged emotional scene gives a sense of power. ("Look how angry I can make mother!") To some children, spanking is like paying a monthly bill; they have cleared their accounts and are ready for more undesirable behavior. One of the most important benefits from the use of the time-out is that the child begins to realize that his or her own behavior will determine the enjoyment or withdrawal of privileges. Because the parent usually feels guilty after spanking the child, he or she is sometimes overindulgent. There is no guilt about short periods of isolation. It is impersonal. The parent gets fifteen minutes' relief from annoying behavior, and a great source of friction between parents and children is removed. Through the time-out, the undesirable behavior is weakened, whereas the desirable behavior is strengthened with rewards.

Members of the family acquire and maintain mutually supporting roles of "victim" and "aggressor." The victim of the aggressive act provides positive reinforcement for the very response that produces pain for him or her. For instance, a mother and child are shopping in a supermarket when the child begins to cry for an ice cream cone. If the mother tries to ignore the demand, the volume and intensity may escalate until the mother, too embarrassed to prolong the scene, complies by buying the cone. In this coercive interaction, noncompliance is punished by the temper tantrum, whereas compliance is reinforced. The mother has strengthened the very tantrum that makes her miserable. A coercive demand makes the world more predictable for a child, in that it produces an immediate and specified consequence. It is typical of preschool children and also typical of the child who is labeled deviant.

"Pathology" begins when the family will no longer tolerate forms of coercion. In other words, there is a saturation point, which varies from family to family, beyond which the members of the family refuse to be coerced. When Patterson (1980) observed a family, he found the rate of hitting among family members to vary daily according to the stimulus, the responses, and the reinforcement. In other words, whether a child hit or talked back was based on the consequences. Therefore, because aggression is the result of social stimuli, behavior in a dyad can be controlled by the withdrawal of aversive stimuli, usually compliant behavior.

Therapy Process

In Patterson's approach, ten sessions are used to train parents of aggressive children.

Pinpointing, Observing, and Recording Behavior. Session 1 is designed to teach parents to pinpoint, define, observe, and record behavior. These parents are taught to observe the child's behavior because parents of aggressive children often overlook the kinds of behavior that quickly become obnoxious. Through close observations, these parents can learn when and how their children whine, kick, or demand attention. At the end of this session, parents are assigned to observe the child's behavior closely for one hour a day. During this period of observation, they have to record whatever they see and how often they see it. These behaviors have already been identified during the first class and some instruction has been given at the end of the class. In the class, parents practice observation techniques using a short story about Heidi, a problem child. They are asked to pretend that they are Heidi's parents and they must count how often Heidi plays cooperatively, teases, does what she is supposed to do, and does not do what she is supposed to do.

It is a quiet Sunday afternoon at the Blake home. Mrs. Blake stands over a counter in the kitchen preparing the noonday meal. Mr. Blake sits in his easy chair in the living room reading the sports section of the newspaper, with Heidi and Debbie at his feet reading the comics. Mrs. Blake enjoys hearing the two children laughing and giggling at the funny papers. However, lunch must be served. So Mrs. Blake asks Heidi to help her set the table. Heidi replies she will, but returns to the comics. Suddenly Heidi sees a comic strip she wants to read on the back of the paper Debbie is reading and she grabs the paper away, calling Debbie a slowpoke. Debbie yells at Heidi to give it back, then takes the paper back. Then the children return to reading the comics together and everybody relaxes. That is, until Heidi tells Debbie she takes up too much room because she's fat. Hearing that, Mrs. Blake asks Heidi again to help her. This time Heidi goes to the kitchen and begins setting the table. The soup smells good to Mr. Blake, who settles down even farther into his chair. Heidi laughs at Debbie, though, and says she is too fat to have any lunch. Mrs. Blake asks Heidi not to say such things to Debbie and the children are quiet during lunch.

This vignette illustrates three teasings, one playing cooperatively, two complies, and one noncomply. With their weekly observation sheet, the parents go home to observe the children; during five- to ten-minute daily telephone conversations, the therapist tries to find out from these parents how their assignment is going. Worksheets (see Figure 10-1), complete with checkmarks, are tickets for the next class.

	M	T	W	TH	F	S	S
Behavior definition							
Behavior definition							
Behavior definition							
Behavior definition							
Actual time observing: Mother From To							
Father From To							

Figure 10-1. Weekly Observing Sheet.

Point Incentive System. Session 2 is used to teach parents a basic point incentive system. In this class, teachers help parents to identify behavior for rewards and punishment by initiating a point system. Parents are to specify and put a value on certain behaviors and accomplishment of certain chores. If a child earns a certain number of points, the child gets a reward of something desired, such as money, food, or a special late television show. Losing points means that what the child wants is taken away. Praise should accompany the awarding of positive points. Although the point system may sound complicated in the beginning, apparently most children like the idea and treat it as a novelty game that they try to win. In this class, the parents watch videotapes that present examples of a point system in practice. When parents balk at the time it would take to manage such a point system, they are reminded of how much time it takes to try to control their children. Eventually, the point system should be replaced with natural rewards, such as praise, approval, hugging, and kissing.

Time-outs. Session 3 is to practice time-out procedures, one of the most popular behavioral techniques for changing a child's behavior. Whereas spanking and yelling usually mean that the parent is angry, time-outs can be used quickly and consistently to signify disapproval without anger. Instead of spanking or nagging, a parent sends the child to a neutral room, a setting that does not offer as much personal gratification. For example, five minutes in the bathroom would be a time-out when a child does not choose to go there because it is not that much fun. At first, parents should apply time-outs to the most frequently occurring problems and keep a record of each time they use the time-out alternative. Young children usually grasp the concept easily. When the mother says, "John, that's the second time you've interrupted me," John knows that this activity is about to be interrupted. "Time out," says mother. "Two minutes this time. Set the timer on the stove and go." The time-out procedure is clearly one of the most frequently used behavioral methods of controlling a child's behavioral problems without yelling, screaming, pleading, or spanking the child. Since this is a rather controversial use of discipline by behaviorists, it is perhaps better to describe it in some detail. There are three steps in the procedure: (1) the child should be informed of what is expected of him or her as well as the consequences of whatever misbehavior will determine use of the procedure; (2) commands must provide information about what the child wants to do or stop doing: "Johnny, please stop screaming"; (3) the time-out warning, which is given when the child does not comply with the command, should warn the child of the consequences of continued noncompliance with the parent's order: "Jimmy, if you don't pick up your toys right now, you will have to go on time-out." What is important, of course, is that the parent does not yell or physically interact with the child. The consequence might be stated unemotionally but firmly. Use the time-out instead of yelling. For time-out, if the child does not comply after the time-out warning, the child is then placed in time-out. The parent instructs the child to go to time-out, unemotionally or with little verbal interaction between the parent and the child. This procedure, of course, is considered by behaviorists to be better than yelling or other negative behavior, which is usually ineffectual for parents. The child is usually controlled by the consequence of being placed in time-out, which must follow the particular misbehavior.

Program Evaluation. Session 4 is used to evaluate how the program is going in the home. The parents learn to graph increases or decreases in problem behavior; they also learn to keep a checklist for themselves; they are also prodded into questioning whether they remembered to praise the child when he or she acted the way the parents wanted him or her to act, whether they kept the point sheet in a place where the child could readily look at it, whether the parents remained calm while sending the child to time-out, and whether the parents remembered not to nag or bring up the bad behavior after time-out. The checklist not only helps the parents to act consistently with their children but apparently helps them to focus on the children in a new way. They begin to see behaviors they had never noticed before.

Program Presentation. Session 5 is used for review of class progress and for the selection and solution of new problems. In this session the parents present experiences, the results of the new handling of the children's behavior, and the consideration of new problems. This is essentially a free-wheeling session designed to solve other problems. The home assignment for this session is to select new behavior problems, define the behavior and its positive opposite, collect data for three days, and then work out a reward system while using time-out to eliminate it. Essentially, these procedures in the final session represent an important behavioral aspect of rewarding what needs to be changed and either ignoring or putting on time-out that behavior that needs to be eliminated (see Figure 10-2).

Attending and Ignoring. Session 6 is used to continue review and to permit case presentation by the parents, who share their successes. Parents present their graphs and review the progress with their children. The trainer decides on a future

Name _____   Date _____

M	T	W	TH	F	S	S

A gold star means _____

Behaviors	M	T	W	TH	F	S	S
Teases							
No teases							

Figure 10-2. Gold Star Chart.

agenda for each parent, which may vary according to progress. Some families will require daily telephone calls and some home visits; others will use the therapist only as a consultant, calling him or her with very specific problems. Parents who have continued trouble with their children may require additional sessions. In the extra sessions they learn other behavioral techniques and practices that they were unable to learn initially. If the treatment at this point fails to turn up any changes, either because the parents has not participated fully or because the child's problems are too complex, the family is referred to other sources for other kinds of treatment. There are, of course, dropouts, but the Oregon group has experimented with parents' salaries as a way to cut the dropout rate. In one case, a family was paid a dollar for each day it followed the teaching instruction, such as observing and recording the child's behavior. Salary had a dramatic effect in reducing dropouts, particularly in low-income, single-parent families. Originally, parent training consisted of six sessions, which were then extended to ten. The purpose of the sixth session was changed to teaching parents (by watching videotaped vignettes) to ignore irrelevant behavior; the art of ignoring is espoused so that parents may use attention for appropriate behavior.

Shaping. Session 7 is devoted to shaping. Parents are instructed how to help the child face new learning skills. Illustrative task analyses and presentations are depicted. Special emphasis is placed on strategies that prevent teaching sessions from degenerating into arguments.

Problem Solving. Session 8, using a typical problem-solving approach, helps parents to define a minor problem, pinpoint target behaviors, list possible solutions and the consequences of them, speculate on the consequences of each alternative, select the most appropriate course of action, and decide how to evaluate the effectiveness. Emphasis is placed on specific goals, which include not bringing up the past.

Contingency Contracting. Session 9 teaches contingency contracting for use with children ten years of age and older. Contingency contracting requires reviewing the rules of negotiations, stating the child's responsibility, listing privileges that appeal to the child, drafting a preliminary agreement, reviewing terms of the agreement, finalizing contingencies, and agreeing on the length of the contract and its subsequent renegotiation upon expiration.

Fading. Session 10 gives parents suggestions for gradually eliminating the point system (fading), including intermittent reinforcement, operating the program during progressively fewer days each week, and removing from the system certain behaviors that are no longer of concern and not worth replacing. Although the use of time-out, contract negotiating, shaping, and contingent attention are to be maintained, the final structure of the point system is fading.

Role of the Therapist

In the behavioral social learning approach, the therapist is first and foremost a *trainer* who actively educates parents in what they need to learn. The therapist is involved but the approach is simple, concrete, and linear. The therapist deals with observable and measurable behaviors and avoids dealing with hypothetical, inferred, or "invisible" intrapsychic constructs. Patterson, to his credit, is not as rigid as other behaviorists and sometimes uses terms that indicate a broader perspective than that of the orthodox behaviorist.

Hypothesis Testing of Social Stimuli

Interventions and hypothesis testing are one and the same in Patterson's approach. Thus, intervention and experimentation go hand in hand. For example, we shall review some of the hypotheses that he and his associates have tested for responsiveness to social stimuli.

Hypothesis 1. There may be a sex difference in the relationship between responsiveness and personality traits. In one study (1965a), Patterson found that girls' responsiveness to parental reinforcement was related to development of a large variety of personality traits, whereas responsiveness to the peer group was not. The reverse was true for boys.

Hypothesis 2. Responsiveness to peer group reinforcement increases with age. The data from one study (Patterson and Anderson, 1964) supported the hypothesis.

Hypothesis 3. The father's anxiety affects responsiveness of the children. In one study (Patterson, 1965d), the data indicated that fathers who were determined to be more anxious from MMPI scores had both boys and girls who were more responsive to his disapproval.

Hypothesis 4. There is a relationship between responsiveness and the type of home of which the child is a part. In general, a warm, permissive home has been found to be related to boys' responsiveness to their fathers and girls' responsiveness to their mothers; restrictive, punitive homes were related to responsiveness of both sexes to the opposite-sex parent (Patterson, 1965a; Patterson et al., 1964). The former type of home is also related to responsiveness of boys to parental disapproval (Patterson, 1965d).

Hypothesis 5. Responsiveness to parental disapproval is associated with behavioral disturbances. In one supporting study (Patterson, 1965d), girls most responsive to parental disapproval were described as being emotionally disturbed and inefficient in the classroom. Boys most responsive to disapproval were described by their parents as being immature. In another study (Patterson, 1965a), girls most responsive to parental disapproval were described as being difficult to control.

Hypothesis 6. Related to both responsiveness and eliciting procedures is a factor known as "negative set," which mediates the effects of social stimuli on behavior. A child with a negative set would, in modeling procedures, attend less frequently to the model's behavior, or might delay performance until the model was no longer present, or might behave in a way opposite from the model. This hypothesis is supported and the construct of negative set defined operationally (Patterson, Littman, and Brown, 1968).

Hypotheses associated with eliciting procedures state that high-prestige social agents are more effective in altering behavior: Male adults are more effective in altering behavior in girls than in boys, and female adults are more effective in altering behavior in boys than in girls. Both hypotheses were supported in laboratory studies (Patterson, 1969).

Patterson's approach also contains two hypotheses related to amount of social interaction. The first is that the amount of social interaction is related to development of dysfunctional behaviors. Observational data (Patterson et al., 1967) indicate that passive children who interact at high rates are more likely to increase aggressive behaviors, and highly aggressive children interact at a high rate. The second hypothesis is that the amount of social interaction is related to the acquisition of socially acceptable behavior. Observational data again support this hypothesis (Patterson et al., 1965).

Three hypotheses of Patterson's theory are related to the axiom of aggression. The first is that the discriminative stimuli that set up the occurrence of reinforcement of aggressive behaviors are primarily interpersonal and social rather than emotional, such as frustration, anger, and anxiety. Patterson et al. (1964) quoted Bandura and Walters's conclusions that frustration does not effectively elicit aggressive behavior and that aggression is probably a result of direct training.

The second hypothesis, tested in the same study in a nursery school setting, was that a positive reinforcer provided by the victim of an aggressive act would increase the likelihood of immediate repetition of the same aggressive behavior. If the child were counterattacked or the teacher intervened, it was hypothesized that the aggressive behavior would be temporarily repressed, and the aggressor would change either his or her response or his or her victim. For a total of 1,641 assertive–aggressive events with nine subjects, the predictions made from the preceding hypotheses for seven of the nine were significant at the .10 level, six at the .01 level, and five at the .005 level, even in the continuously changing stimulus situation in the nursery school.

The third hypothesis, also in the Patterson, Littman, and Bricker study (1967), was that contingencies in the nursery school setting affect aggression. In twenty-eight subjects who showed passive and moderately aggressive behaviors, the number of these behaviors increased in their first five sessions in the nursery school. The data indicate that the increase in aggressive behaviors in more passive children is a function of the amount of interaction with peers, the frequency of being attacked, the frequency of counterattacks, and the proportion of counterattacks that successfully terminated the aggressive behavior.

Patterson has also hypothesized that laboratory methods may be used in assessment. He supports this hypothesis by using an instrumental-conditioning procedure with rate of response in a task related to aggression as the datum used to predict which children were most often the victims of aggressive attacks (Patterson, 1967).

One hypothesis related to learning of some higher-order behaviors is that high levels of anxiety will impair the acquisition of complex verbal responses. Patterson, Helper, and Wilcott (1960) conditioned two groups of children to increase the frequency of verb usage. The group that was more anxious, as determined by clinical judgments and measures of skin conductance, showed less learning.

There are several hypotheses and case studies related to Patterson's method of behavior change. The first is that changing reinforcement schedules of parents and peers will affect the dysfunctional child's behavior: this hypothesis was supported in case studies utilizing this method (Patterson and Brodsky, 1966; Patterson et al., 1967; Patterson et al., 1965).

A second hypothesis is that using primary reinforcers, such as candy, in treatment sessions will increase the effectiveness of the therapist as he or she and his or her approval become secondary reinforcers. This is not a new approach, nor one used strictly by behavior modifiers. Play therapists use the pairing of primary reinforcers, such as candy, to create a relationship with the child. Generalization is then expected to occur from behavior change in the therapy situation to change in the natural environment. This hypothesis was supported in the pairing of candy with social reinforcers of praise from the therapist in the successful treatment of a seven-year-old school-phobic child (Patterson, 1965b).

Another hypothesis is that one factor that helps children to change their behaviors is teaching them to discriminate among behaviors that lead to rewards. Evidence for this hypothesis is found in a study (Patterson, 1965c) in which acceleration in conditioning attending behaviors in a child occurred when the child was reinforced for identifying inattentive behaviors in other children and recording them on a data chart.

Critique and Evaluation

The behavioral principles upon which Patterson's theory is based are well known and widely published. His work has not attempted to lay out an all-encompassing theory of child behavior, but to put into effect these behavioral principles in a practical manner for dealing with behavioral disturbances in children.

Patterson's theory is logically derived from experimental evidence. The theory produces evidence for the establishment of both adaptive and maladaptive behavior in observing factors that seem to be relevant to certain behaviors, controlling for other factors in experimental manipulations, and changing maladaptive behaviors through well-controlled manipulations.

Any data are accepted that are relevant to the particular subject matter, including accurate, well-planned observations and control of nuisance variables. In other words, only empirical evidence is accepted. Hypotheses, axioms, postulates, and assumptions are derived logically from empirical data.

Patterson's work is extremely systematic, but not a complete theory. He does not use energy, experimental time, or publication space on the principles underlying his work. From this viewpoint, his may not be considered a theory at all, but merely an application of theory to specific behaviors.

Patterson's approach is parsimonious in terms of its simplicity. Behavioral principles are relatively simple to understand, as only observable behavior is considered relevant. With an understanding of these principles, the approach is understood; even terms not specific to behavioral theories, such as reciprocity, coercion, and negative set, are explained in behavioral terms.

The approach is useful when all its components are considered. Accurate and well-recorded observations should reveal the source of social reinforcements, the behaviors that are reinforced, and the child's responsiveness to them. The target for change should then be evident. Change is easily detected through simple observation, and this change is the criterion for procedural effectiveness. If behavioral change is not forthcoming, the procedure may be changed.

The testability of this approach is obvious: all segments of it have been tested in Patterson's work and its basic principles have been laboratory tested. All components of the theory may be tested and the research that has been done is generally susceptible to all types of replication.

The range of Patterson's approach is limited in the work that has been done. He has dealt with only a few types of behavior, how they develop, and how they may be changed. The implications for applicability to other behaviors, as well as related research done by others of similar theoretical orientation, increase the range of the approach. The necessity of controlling irrelevant variables limits the behaviors that may be examined in one study, making accumulation of data somewhat slow, particularly for one investigator. Patterson's approach is not directly applicable to some disturbances, such as those organically caused. However, the problems of observable behavior associated with organic difficulties are of relevance. In short, the range of Patterson's approach is ultimately quite wide, but research has not yet covered the whole range.

Patterson's work has also had considerable influence. The practical, common-sense, exact specifications of ways to change undesirable behavior appeal to practitioners and parents. Therapists, educators, corrections people, and others have used the principles, and numerous parents have made use of the programmed text (Patterson and Gullion, 1968). In short, Patterson's approach, although not a theory, is well constructed, well supported, and useful. Above all, the treatment method which is a part of it, is effective, and that is where the value of the theory really lies. To be more specific, there are many positives about Patterson's approach that set it apart from any of the other approaches reviewed in this book:

1. Healthy concern and correction for lack of empirical research in family therapy: data oriented rather than personal impression oriented, demonstrative rather than dialectical.

2. Self-correcting system based on results of observations. Although the endpoint of this process may be consideration of the family as a system, the process has been different and the outcome of this process, for Patterson, is going to be different. He provides a much-needed correction for the data-poor, impression-rich field of family therapy. With the exception of Minuchin (Chapter 7), Patterson is the only one who has empirically followed up the outcome of his interventions.
3. In spite of the narrow conceptual base, his empirical approach is inherently sound and eventually will pay off for him and for all of us involved in the same enterprise.
4. Another positive is the broad, unorthodox, and open behavioral approach that changes when results indicate a blind alley or the need for a detour. It is unfortunate that the end result (i.e., awareness of the family as a system of interrelated influences) took many years of trial and error (Patterson and Fleishman, 1979). Regardless, the reader can be assured that Patterson's view of a system will be different from concepts derived from general systems theory and that his empirical determination will eventually prevail over impressionistic efforts. Although the ultimate conclusions may be the same, behavior is extremely variable and complex; it takes more than one therapeutic approach to encompass such variety and heterogeneity; one approach, no matter how sophisticated and empirical, like his, can help only a certain percentage of families; and certain families cannot be helped no matter what approach is used.

On the more negative side, the following points need consideration:

1. Failure to consider the family as a system (i.e., lack of consideration for the role of parents and siblings, whereby the parents' inability to control a child may stem from a variety of *system* failures).
2. Scapegoating the child by accepting at face value his behavior as a symptom *in* the child rather than a symptom of systemic ineffectiveness (i.e., accepting the child's "misbehavior" uncritically without considering the *function* of the behavior in keeping the family in a no-change situation.)
3. Compliance of the child's behavior allowing parents to use their control to avoid creativity in the child and in themselves.
4. A father's "returning to his previous uncommunicative self" as an example of failure to pay attention to the role of the father (Eugeln et al., 1968).
5. Nonattention to individual differences among families' socioeconomic, educational, and intellectual levels.
6. Nonattention to the degree and type of pathology above and beyond the referral symptom.
7. Failure to differentiate among intensity, function, and degree of symptoms (i.e., destructiveness equated with pouting).
8. Failure to observe the family *as a system at various levels of functioning and interpretation* (L'Abate et al., 1978), for example, by not allowing Patterson to consider that the mother's punitive behavior toward the target child can be, and usually is, an indication of (a) failure in the coalition with the husband, (b) his lack of emotional support for her, as well as (c) her low self-esteem and depres-

sion at having to be cooped up in a house for hours with three or four children. Although Patterson deals with her as a "victim," he fails to make the subtle dialectical distinctions that would allow him to recognize that victims can also be victimizers and that rescuers can also be persecutors (L'Abate et al., 1979).

In conclusion, it is clear that Patterson is aware of some of the limitations in his approach. In a review of maintenance and treatment effects (Patterson and Fleishman, 1979), Patterson has made various comments about incompleteness of analysis. This conclusion is important because it indicates that, after so many years, those using the whole behavioral approach may have become aware of failure to consider the family as a system.

The findings indicate moderate support for the idea that treatment brings change in the behavior of the problem child and other members of the family, as well. Second, the data illustrate that treatment effects persist. This latter effect was obtained in a group of studies from different settings, using a wide range of criteria measures. The question now is whether one finds these data valid.

Johnson, Bolstad, and Lobitz (1976) have taken the position that the case for parent training needs further investigation. The fact is that at least three different groups of researchers have not been able to obtain significant results in treatment. This conclusion could mean that various groups are doing things differently and are calling it parent training and/or that the criteria measures in some samples are not appropriate for the subject.

The preliminary follow-up data summarized by Patterson and Fleishman (1979) are supportive. These follow-up data, along with comparison designs, provide the essential data for the solution to this problem. The decision about persistence of treatment effects must be based upon comparative follow-up studies now being conducted.

Aside from the incomplete state of the follow-up data, Patterson and Fleishman believe that "there is another type of important analysis which is needed." It could be called a multiple regression (a linear distant function's format), in which success during follow-up and process changes during treatment are correlated. For example, two variables, such as less parental punishment, fewer noxious intrusions by siblings, low or negative reinforcement schedules, or increasing responsiveness of parental enforcement, could determine significant variance in measures of success follow-up. Some of the findings of Wahler, Lesky, and Rogers (1976) indicated that lower-class, father-absent ghetto families with children who steal and are truant may not show continued follow-up effects. This suggests the necessity for analyzing demographic and process variables in doing research, as we have suggested.

"If and when persistence of treatment effects becomes an acceptable fact, it will be necessary to show that these effects were created by *process changes in the family as a system*" (Patterson and Fleishman, 1979). It took Patterson and his co-workers more than fifteen years to reach a conclusion already reached by others in the field. Perhaps science is discovering the obvious. In this regard, then, Patterson is very much a scientist.

As an example of an empirical approach to family therapy, Patterson's work remains unequaled ("In the land of the blind, the deaf is king . . ."). His theorizing has changed as a result of empirical inputs. His final conclusion, that the family functions as a system, can only bring about a faster combination of behavioral with systemic (structural, strategic, contextual) approaches.

References

Eugeln, R.; Knutson, J.; Laughy, L.; and Garlington, W. 1968. Behavior modification techniques applied to a family unit: A case study. *Journal of Child Psychology and Psychiatry* 9:245-252.

Johnson, S. M.; Bolstad, O. D.; and Lobitz, G. 1976. Generalization and contrast phenomena in behavioral modification with children. In *Behavior modification in families,* eds. E. J. Marsh, L. A. Hamerlynck, and L. C. Handy, pp. 160-188. New York: Brunner/Mazel.

Kent, R. N. 1976. Interventions for boys with conduct problems: Methodological critique. *Journal of Consulting and Clinical Psychology* 44:292-296.

L'Abate, L.; Weeks, G.; and Weeks, K. 1978. Psychopathology as transaction: A historical note. *International Journal of Family Counseling* 6:60-65.

——; Weeks, G.; and Weeks, K. 1979. Of scapegoats, strawmen, and scarecrows. *International Journal of Family Therapy* 1:86-96.

Liverant, S. 1959. MMPI differences between parents of disturbed and non-disturbed children. *Journal of Consulting Psychology* 23:256-260.

Patterson, G. R. 1965a. Responsiveness to social stimuli. In *Research in behavior modification,* eds. L. Krasner and L. P. Ullman, pp. 157-178. New York: Holt, Rinehart and Winston.

——. 1965b. A learning theory approach to the treatment of the school-phobic child. In *Case studies in behavior modification,* eds. L. P. Ullman and L. Krasner, pp. 278-284. New York: Holt, Rinehart and Winston.

——. 1965c. An application of conditioning techniques to the control of a hyperactive child. In *Case studies in behavior modification,* eds. L. P. Ullman and L. Krasner, pp. 370-375. New York: Holt, Rinehart and Winston.

——. 1965d. Parents as dispensers of aversive stimuli. *Journal of Personality and Social Psychology* 2:844-851.

——. 1967. Prediction of victimization from an instrumental conditioning procedure. *Journal of Consulting Psychology* 31:147-152.

——. 1969. Behavioral techniques based upon social learning. In *Behavior therapy: Appraisal and status,* ed. C. M. Franks, pp. 341-374. New York: McGraw-Hill.

——. 1971. *Families: Applications of social learning to family life.* Champaign, Ill.: Research Press.

——. 1973. Changes in status of family members as controlling stimuli: A basis for describing treatment process. In *Behavior change: Methodology, concepts and practice,* eds. L. A. Hamerlynck, L. C. Handy, and E. J. Marsh, pp. 167-191. Champaign, Ill.: Research Press.

——. 1976. The aggressive child: Victim and architect of a coercive system. In *Behavior modification in familes,* eds. E. J. Marsh, L. A. Hamerlynck, and L. Handy, pp. 267-316. New York: Brunner/Mazel.

——. 1976. Mothers the acknowledged victims. In *Mother-Child, Father-Child Relationships,* eds. J. H. Stevens and M. Mathews, pp. 146-162. Washington, D.C.: National Education Association.

——. 1979a. A performance theory for coercive family interactions. In *The analyses of social interaction: Methods, issues, and illustrations,* ed. R. Cairns, pp. 193-210. New York: Wiley.

———. 1979b. Personal communication, August 3, 1979.

———. 1980. *Coercive family processes.* Eugene, Ore.: Castillia Publishing Co.

———; Helper, M. E.; and Wilcott, R. C. 1960. Anxiety and verbal conditioning in children. *Child Development,* 31:101–108.

———, and Anderson, D. 1964. Peers as social reinforcers. *Child Development* 35: 951–960.

———; Littman, R. A.; and Hinsey, W. C. 1964. Parental effectiveness as reinforcers in the laboratory and its relation to child rearing practices and child adjustment in the classroom. *Journal of Personality* 32:180–199.

———; Jones, R.; Whittier, J.; and Wright, M. A. 1965. A behavior modification technique for the hyperactive child. *Behavior Research and Therapy* 2:217–226.

———, and Brodsky, G. 1966. A behavior modification programme for a child with multiple problem behaviors. *The Journal of Child Psychology and Psychiatry* 7:277–295.

———, and Fagot, B. I. 1967. Selective responsiveness to social reinforcers and deviant behavior in children. *The Psychological Record* 17:369–378.

———; Littman, R. A.; and Bricker, W. 1967. Assertive behavior in children: A step toward a theory of aggression. *Monographs of the Society for Research in Child Development* 32 (Serial No. 113).

———; McNeal, S.; Hawkins, N.; and Phelps, R. 1967. Reprogramming the social environment. *Journal of Child Psychology and Psychiatry* 8:181–195.

———, and Gullion, M. E. 1968. *Living with Children.* Champaign, Ill.: Research Press, 1968.

———; Littman, R. A.; and Brown, T. R. 1968. Negative set and social learning. *Journal of Personality and Social Psychology* 8:109–116.

———, and Cobb, J. A. 1970. A dyadic analysis of "aggressive" behaviors. *1970 Minnesota Symposium on Child Psychology,* pp. 72–129. Minneapolis: University of Minnesota Press.

———, and Reid, J. B. 1970. Reciprocity and coercion: Two facets of social systems. In *Behavior modification in Clinical Psychology,* eds. C. Neuringer and L. Michael, pp. 133–177. New York: Appleton-Century-Crofts.

———; Cobb, J. D.; and Ray, R. S. 1973. A social engineering technology for training the families of aggressive boys. In *Issues and Trends in Behavior Therapy,* eds. H. E. Adams and I. P. Unikel, pp. 193–210. Springfield, Ill.: C. C. Thomas.

———, and Fleishman, M. J. 1979. Maintenance of treatment effects: Some considerations covering family systems and follow-up data. *Behavior Therapy* 10: 168–185.

Skinner, B. F. 1957. *Verbal behavior.* New York; Appleton-Century-Crofts.

Wahler, R. G.; Lesky, G.; and Rogers, E. S. 1976. *The insular family: A deviant support system for oppositional children.* Paper presented at BANFF: International Conference on Behavior Modification.

Weinrott, G. R.; Bauske, B. W.; and Patterson, G. R. 1979. Systematic replication of a social learning approach to parent training. In *Trends in behavior therapy,* eds. P. O. Sjoden, S. Bates, and W. S. Dockens, III, pp. 331–351. New York: Academic Press.

Weiss, R. L. 1978. The conceptualization of marriage from a behavioral perspective. In *Marriage and marital therapy: Psychoanalytic behavioral and systems theory perspectives,* eds. T. J. Paolino and B. S. McCrady, pp. 165–239. New York: Brunner/Mazel.

11

The Family Group Therapy of John Bell

John Elderkin Bell originally developed an interest in family therapy during a sojourn in London in the early 1950s. His interest in the area was stimulated by learning of clinical experiments in family therapy conducted at the Tavistock Clinic. Prior to 1951, most of Bell's experience was obtained in child guidance clinics, where his main focus was on the individual child. His belief, at that time, was that the child's behavior was the result of the parent's handling of the child. Bell began some tentative work with families in 1951. His first case involved a thirteen-year-old adopted girl who had severe behavioral problems. The father's alcoholism complicated the case. Bell met with this family for one and a half years. Progress was slow, but gains were made. Bell admits to learning some worthwhile facts from this family, namely, that (1) "this method of handling a disturbed child is feasible, (2) it's possible for the whole family to come together and talk about problems and resolve them" (1975, p. 106). Bell began to devote his efforts toward research in this area.

Bell's theory of family therapy has developed from his experience with families and from a basic assumption that equates the family to a small group. Bell (1975) defines the family as a social unit. In this definition, emphasis is placed upon the unity of the family and not upon individuals who compose the family. Bell states that "this approach leads to theories concerning communication in the family, group attitudes and ideals, family group decisions, and family group activities" (1975, p. 172). Bell's theoretical approach is, therefore, based on small-group theory, and the process of family therapy employs knowledge of small-group functionality to effect change in the family.

The family does have some features that distinguish it from other small groups. It goes through a longer history of group formation than do other groups. Its members have relational ties uncommon in most other groups. The family remains together, as a group, between and after the termination of therapy sessions.

Family group therapy is an effort to change the behaviors and attitudes within a total family through a series of meetings with the entire family unit made up of parents and children nine years of age and older. Therapy generally begins with the referral of a child who is disturbed; however, the therapeutic goals are family centered rather than child centered. The primary intent of the therapist is to change the functioning and structure of the family as a group. The basic assumption of Bell's therapeutic approach is that the family is the unit to be treated. The family is considered a biological, social unit and the problem for which the family is accepted for therapy is thought to be a problem of the family, not a problem of the child. Bell's family group therapy is one of the earliest methods of family therapy, and he is unique in emphasizing attention on child's complaints and requests for changes in the family in the early sessions of therapy.

Presently, Bell is a psychologist with the V.A. hospital in Palo Alto, California and an associate professor at Stanford University School of Medicine. In recent years Bell has defined an approach that moves the center of family interventions from the clinical office into the larger society to helping agencies and institutions, which may become the site for therapeutic effort (1978). Family context therapy attempts to modify environmental conditions that contribute to family difficulties and to construct contexts that promote family well-being. It is an extension of family therapy that seeks to alter contextual physical, economic, and social factors to lessen or remove problems that are caused or accentuated by the environment and to assure the external resources needed for family well-being.

In family group therapy the therapist is concerned essentially with affecting directly the processes within one family. As a family context therapist, the therapist is a planner and coordinator. The therapist becomes a strategist mobilizing the community, its institutions, and its resources to center attention and effort on family change. The therapist directs the community toward change through providing settings for family problem-solving modifications in the environment that are induced by the therapist as a change agent. Change may be experienced by a family without any direct association with a therapist. A team of people working together or an institution may take the initiative for family change and, by modifying the environment, provide the requisite environmental resources to achieve therapeutic aims.

The focus in this chapter is on Bell's concepts of family group therapy. These are the foundation of his position that eventually led to his innovating ideas of families' interfacing with hospitals and community agencies. Family group therapy is a pioneer approach in family therapy, and John Bell has continued working with the concepts.

Family Functioning

Family group therapy focuses on the family by applying small-group theory from social psychology to the family as a natural group. Bell (1975) claims that to understand the processes of family therapy it is necessary to attend to four social units in the family and to examine the family as a group.

The first social unit is the single collective composed of parents and children. This unit is founded at the base of a biological relationship and even an adoptive family is modeled on the biological model. This unit is typically referred to as the nuclear family, and it is this group that is normally involved in family group therapy.

Second, within this collective unit of the family there are a series of subgroups that are not static but are forming, expanding, and dissolving. While the collective unit of the family has an identity and a structured entity, the subgroups are characterized more by their functional aims and action than by a defined structure as social units. The subgroups may be seen as individuals' forming coalitions or cliques. The process of family life as described by Bell is a sequence of emerging subgroupings within the collective nuclear family. The total family group may be regarded as an assumed system of subgroups that may be separately identified at various times.

Third, family members interact with extended family members and other significant individuals who influence individual family members and the family as a whole. These relationships offer gratifications that extend the limitations of the family and compensate for problems within the nuclear family and at other times form the rationalizations for behavior in criticizing the family. Family members also react to community pressures, and the external pressures complicate interpersonal relations within the family and force members toward holding relationships with each other. Although individual members choose goals or actions outside the family, there is always some degree of relationship within the family group. There is always a boundary around the family that keeps it together.

Bell identifies a fourth social unit that involves the family members and the therapist. The therapist becomes a part of the group in the therapy situation and helps the family to focus on the total social group.

Group Formation

Bell describes the processes of group formation in the family. The formation of the relationships in the family begins when the aims of an individual confront those of others in the situation. Bell defines aims as a general term encompassing the meanings of "instinct," "drive," "motive," and goal." Two consequences may follow the situation in which one individual's aims confront those of another. First, if one person's aims are complementary to those of another, that person will receive support for his or her goal-seeking behavior and action will ensue. Second, if the individual's aims are not complementary with those of others, an ambiguous situation is created and the individuals or subgroups seek appropriate resolutions. This situation involves oscillation of action and reaction, with individuals' moving together and apart, which Bell has called transitive actions.

The family typically goes through a longer and more varied history of group process development than does any other small group in society. In the beginning the interrelations are situation specific; however, interrelations may be conscious, because the family chooses to keep doing things in the same familiar pattern, or sometimes unintentional, because the patterns have become familiar ways of doing things.

The family consists of adults and children; therefore, there are individuals at different ages developing at different maturational rates and with different values. Individuals at different stages of physical and psychological maturity are apt to produce dissimilar requirements for change and possibilities for action. Obviously, the kinds of problems with which the family must cope keep changing.

Health and Pathology

Health and pathology are considered value judgments applied to the behavior of individuals or the family group by either those inside or those outside the family. Actually, the judgment that a behavior is pathological is a demand for change whether or not it is possible. In the same sense, health represents behavior that is socially acceptable within the family group as well as outside of it. Although behavior may be called healthy or pathological, it is not clearly one or the other as the judgment is related to personal standards.

A healthy and efficient family implies some broad concurrence on the characteristics of the family, and Bell (1975) suggests the following traits: (1) the family shows that complementarity aims exist and are supported by the functions and structure of the family as a group; (2) the family has multiple methods available for accommodating the mutually incompatible demands of individual members; (3) the family has means of continually evaluating the consequences of its achievements of accommodation; and (4) the family chooses to behave flexibly so that new methods of accommodation may be found and used when radical shifts are necessary.

In contrast, the disturbed family has developed patterns of interaction that are rigid. Individuals are assigned roles that are often stereotypic and little opportunity is given to assume more realistic ones. Communication within the family is constricted, and one person is then cast in the role of carrying the pathology of the entire family.

An example of this rigidity is the reduction in communication. Behaviors that are disturbing to other people become intensified and the individual may become a problem in the community or school as well as in the family because there are few ways in which the individual can communicate about the things happening inside the family group. A characteristic of a pathological family is that one individual may carry the pathology for the system. One individual is referred because he or she has a problem, where in fact that person has carried the pathology for the whole family. This does not mean that the scapegoated individual is less competent or adequate than other family members but only that this person has been cast in the role of being bearer of the family problems. For this reason, the whole family must be a part of the therapeutic group.

There is no simple explanation of why people become disturbed. In the past, mental health specialists thought the major causes of disturbances could be explained by knowing what was happening inside the individual. Much of the pathology was regarded as happening within the individual; however, much of the systems theory that is prominent in family therapy has added emphasis to the social situation of the person and has involved his or her family's interaction. Bell does not think that every evidence of emotional disturbance in an individual is a product of a disrupted family interaction or that the responsibility must be placed on the family. In some cases pathology involves physical or organic problems, and, in other situations, larger social groups such as the neighborhood or community are contributing variables. Bell (1975) shifts explanations of pathology away from the types of interpretation that it is a product of what the families have done to an individual toward describing pathology as a behavior of an individual embedded in the family. The manner in which an individual is functioning in a family that itself is not functioning adequately may account for the individual's disturbances. Bell believes that this concept does not supplant, but rather supplements, individual-oriented theories of pathology.

Bell (1975) suggests that it is necessary to differentiate the conditions within which acute symptoms are developed and those in which chronic behavior is produced. He states that an acute crisis in a family is evidenced when an individual is first showing disturbed behavior, when symptoms suddenly break out, or when the individual's behavior has newly become a cause for family anxiety. In most cases this occurs when there is a demand on the part of one individual for change in the family constellation. The acute symptoms are a sign of the individual's need and desires. Actually the symptoms are an attempt to communicate in such a manner and intensity as to effect disturbance in the family group. Often the demand for change in a family occurs because of developmental changes taking place as a child matures. There is a tendency, when a person's demands for change are not being met, for that person to use more primitive language because more mature language is not functional. In practice, then, the acute symptom is frequently nonverbal rather than verbal in that nonverbal communication generally takes precedence over verbal communication in the family. Bell indicates that in family group therapy the appropriate exploration is into the communicative intent and meaning of the symptom within the present relationships.

If acute symptoms are not resolved, then the symptom processes are incorporated into the patterns of family life. The symptom is then perpetuated as a role that is partly developed and partly assigned. Such a role may retain a certain amount of its communicative purpose but tends to lose this purpose as it is reinforced by the pressures of the family and therefore becomes habitual. This is how Bell sees the development of chronic behavior problems. The symptom behavior becomes perpetuated because it has become integrated into an established pattern of family interaction and its persistence is functional and necessary to the continuation of the family structure.

When chronic symptoms are deeply entrenched in the pattern of an individual, Bell suggests that certain conditions or situations may be observed in the family. First, there may be a limitation in the range of accommodating conflicts between family members. Patterns of behavior tend to become stereotyped and the manners of relating become fixed and unresponsive to modifying influence. There is considerable inflexibility in terms of goals, behaviors, and interchanges in subgroups. Second, there is a decrease of symbolic language and an increase in the use of simple signs. Therefore, messages that can be transmitted are fewer and contain less quality. In addition, individuals do not listen or watch for gestures that may improve the communication. Third, there is a breakdown in the evaluation process by which individuals can revise their perceptions of others, the awareness of their own methods of behaving with others. Consequently, they behave in a manner to perpetuate the pathological behavior as though it were impossible to change. Fourth, the family may value change insufficiently or excessively. If the family clings to old behaviors too strongly, the family will face disruption because of the conflict in values with the culture and the internal rigidity of the family. However, if change is overvalued, the family cannot take advantage of the economy of stable patterns.

History Taking and Diagnosis

In family group therapy, there is no history taking in the traditional sense. The therapist does, however, meet with the parents alone for the first session. Bell refers to this session as an orientation. In addition to allowing the therapist to delineate his or her role and to arrange practical details for future conferences, the therapist uses the session to hear the parents' story of the child's problems. The therapist may also ask for the history of the child's development at this time. Bell suggests that this information may not be particularly relevant, but, by allowing the parents to discuss the child, the therapist begins establishing a relationship with the parents. The therapist also has the opportunity to compare what is expressed when the child is not present with what the parents say directly to the child at a later time.

Diagnosis as a tool for understanding the individual members of the family is not used. Because the family unit is the patient, Bell does not believe that diagnosis of individuals is useful to the therapist in helping to understand the family. The therapist needs information about the interaction patterns of family members. This information can only be obtained properly from the therapy sessions. Diagnosis, then, is an ongoing process, with the therapist evaluating and reevaluating the family as the therapy progresses. He believes that useful diagnostic understanding occurs through actual exposure to the family and cannot be gained before.

Therapeutic Foci and Goals

Family group therapy aims to effect behavioral and attitudinal changes within a total family through a series of conferences attended by the parents, the children nine years of age and older, and the therapist. An underlying element of this effort is the therapist's attempt to help the family to develop and improve modes of communication and interaction patterns within the family.

The focus of family group therapy is upon the family unit. Individuals are important, only as they relate to other members of the family. The therapist continually directs the treatment process to what is happening between individuals, not inside them. The content of the sessions focus on family interaction, what they are like as people, the kinds of feelings produced as they talk to one another, the ways in which they would like one another to act, the things they would like to accomplish with each other, and what is necessary from each person to accomplish these things.

The end goal(s) of therapy is left to the family. Bell believes that the family will set its own goals in accordance with its own values. The therapist encourages the family to clarify its goals and to set new and/or appropriate goals that coincide with group and individual needs.

While the family is expected to assume the major responsibility for goal setting, the therapist considers the setting of process goals as his domain. Bell (1975) lists the following as process goals:

1. To release the respective family members from inhibition about the expression of feelings, wishes, ideals, goals, and values.
2. To develop new forms of expression to channel the interpersonal communication.
3. To make the family conscious of the roles that the various members play in relation to one another.
4. To demonstrate to the family its essential unity and the mutual interdependence of each with the other and with the family as a whole.

Stages of Therapy

The process of therapy normally takes place in four stages. These are identified as the orientation phase, the child-centered phase, the parent-centered phase, and the family-centered (termination) phase.

The Orientation

Treatment is initiated with the orientation phase. Actually two orientation sessions are held. The therapist meets with the parents alone for the first session and with the entire family for the second. During this phase the therapist defines his or her role and emphasizes his or her intention to meet with the family as a whole only.

In the first session the therapist warns the parents that the child will probably demand changes in the home routine and that initially the therapist will be especially supportive of the child. The parents are prepared for the child's hostility, and the therapist reassures them that this is a phase preliminary to the expression of positive feelings. The parents are assured that they will be given an opportunity to express their feelings, but in the beginning it is important to give the child the opportunity to speak. Some practical details are worked out in this session, such as who will attend future conferences and the time for these conferences.

In the next session with the entire family, the children are told about the content of the first session. At this time the therapist attempts to structure his or her remarks to convey to the children that he or she will help them to explain to their parents what they feel. The therapist reviews his or her role, placing emphasis on the referee status and the intention to give support and encouragement for expressions of feeling to all family members.

The Child-Centered Phase

During this phase the child is encouraged to tell why he or she thinks the family is unhappy. Very often the child will begin with complaints and demands for changes in rules that govern his or her behavior in the family. The therapist responds to these issues by asking the child to suggest resolutions to these problems. The parents are discouraged at this point from voicing their own ideas about the problems for fear that they will inhibit the child. The response of the parents to the child's demands is tempered by their ability or willingness to compromise or accept the child's wishes. The pace of the treatment in this phase is determined by the acceptability of the parent's responses. After the child's demands are exhausted, therapy enters the next phase.

The Parent-Centered Phase

The parents enter the discussions in this phase, actively voicing their complaints or problems with the child. Bell (1975) indicates that complaints or problems with considerable hostility have been building up in the parents during the child-centered stage and are released at this time. The child is put on the defensive and counterattacks with his or her own expression of hostile feelings. During this stage the family members begin to develop a deeper understanding of their behaviors. It becomes apparent that, in spite of the hostility generated in the sessions, the family members begin to develop a greater tolerance for each other and positive feelings begin to be expressed as well.

During this stage the parents may also begin to discuss their interaction openly. Parents approach resolution of their difficulties as the focus shifts to an analysis of the mother–father relationship. There is a loosening of communication, and family members interact more freely, expressing both negative and positive feelings.

The Family-Centered Phase (Termination)

This stage is usually marked by the disappearance of the referral symptoms. A series of other indicators is also evident. The family begins to laugh together more frequently. Reports are made of incidents during the week in which the family has worked to resolve to the mutual satisfaction of all, and an increase in the number of family-oriented activities may be reported. The family agrees that the conferences are no longer needed because its members now feel that they can manage without the therapist. There is greater acceptance by the family of the independent activities of each member.

By the time the family-centered stage is reached, the therapist has become less active in the sessions. Each member is actively involved and there is little support from the therapist. The therapist concludes the sessions by recapitulating what has taken place by summarizing some of the features of the treatment. The therapist also discusses future steps for the family.

False Recovery

The family members may insist that they are ready to terminate. Bell states that they are probably actually covering over new difficulties. The therapist must evaluate the signs of readiness for termination. If these are not apparent, the therapist may suggest that the family meet for an additional session.

Follow-up

Families may return for follow-up treatment if they so desire. Bell states that, thus far, he has not had any families return.

Process of Therapy

The process of family group therapy moves through phases similar to other ongoing groups. Bell (1976) identifies seven phases that comprise the process: initiation, testing the parameters, struggling for power, settling on a common task, struggles toward completion of the common task, achieving completion, and separation.

The process of therapy begins with a referral that is typically a request for change in one individual. The first problem in family therapy is to convert this request for change in one individual to an awareness of change for the total family. Many family members will not accept this assumption, but the therapist supports it when he or she insists on seeing the whole family as a group. It is important to note that the family is already a group that has been functioning for many years and that in therapy the group will continue not only as an instrument of therapy but as an end in itself throughout the whole week. Therefore, change that begins in the therapy session may have a transfer effect into the continuing life of the family.

When the family accepts the concept, the therapist forms a group with the family in which he or she plays a planned, controlled, and communicated role. This is a new group that is formed in the therapy sessions. The therapist does not try to find out what has happened within the family; rather the therapist wants to see what happens between himself or herself and the individuals, subgroups, and total family. The therapist uses a conscious and disciplined technique to help the family in solving its problems. The difference between a family's meeting alone to discuss its problems or even with friends is that the therapist is following a technique. The therapist is using himself or herself in a predetermined way, as an instrument in helping; therefore, it is the therapist and his or her technical confidence that can be used to change the family interaction. Within this family group the therapist becomes aware of how the family moves toward mutual goals, how its members reduce tension and conflicts when their goals are incompatible, and how the members deal with goals that are incongruent and in conflict with each other.

It is important for the therapist to develop and maintain the clear definition and presentation of his or her own functions. The more consistent the therapist is in bringing his or her own ways of acting and responding to the discussion, the clearer the family will be in understanding what the therapist is trying to communicate, which will lead to more progress. Bell suggests that a therapist needs to make clear to the family that the therapist is aware of the formal responsibilities that he or she will undertake. The therapist should also define the manner in which these responsibilities will be accomplished, the limits of his or her participation, and his or her expectations for the family. The therapist should also make clear the relationship between what he or she says and what he or she does. The more the therapist's behavior is predictable, the more rapidly the family testing of what the therapist says will be reduced and the more the family group will structure itself to a meaningful session.

In the group sessions the therapist establishes a relationship with each individual within the presence of the whole family. Through this process the individual can interact with the therapist as a nonmember outsider. Bell assumes that most individuals have available to them potential patterns of behavior beyond the ones they typically use in the family. By interacting with the therapist as a nonfamily outsider, the rest of the family can see the different kinds of patterns that may not be shown at home. This may introduce new perspectives for the family members, as they can see the behavior of various individuals in new ways and with new potentialities.

With the therapist and family joined in working together, the members can perceive the new possibilities of action that are available to them and try to incorporate them into their joint behaviors. As they see new behavior patterns in each other, the family members can revise their stereotypes about each other and reevaluate each other, thereby responding with new attitudes and new accommodations to each other. This involves a testing out of the potentialities for relations that incorporate changes. Through this testing period, some behavior will not be liked and the members will need to work within the family to keep some behaviors from occurring at home while other behaviors may be adopted into the family. This testing-out process may begin with two-person subgroups and then involve larger subgroups until the whole family is involved in the action.

Bell describes the therapist's overall activity as an effort to promote social integration through communication in the family, permitting the family to experience, appraise, define, and reorder its interrelationships. The therapist works toward building social action on the basis of his or her own methods of participation. The therapist conducts relationships with individuals, subgroups, and the total family. The therapist attempts to disrupt unsatisfactory patterns of interaction and permits individuals to reaffirm old intentions that have been frustrated. The family is encouraged to clarify its goals and to choose goals more appropriate for the whole family and more appropriate for life outside the family. The therapist demonstrates through the interaction of the individuals in the family that the family has within itself an increased flexibility to communicate and carry out roles. Through this process the therapist promotes new evaluations within the family of the potentialities and skills of the individuals. Therefore, the content of the therapy session is focused on the family members' interactions with one another, what they are like as individuals, the kinds of feelings produced as they interact with each other, the ways in which they would like to have each other behave, the things they want to accomplish, and what is necessary for each one to accomplish these things.

Through this process of family group therapy, the family should experience an increased fluency in conversation in which the individuals can communicate with increased range of content and manner of communication. There should also be an increased understanding about the roles that are required and permitted for individuals within the family. The range of roles that individuals can perform should become more apparent. Greater flexibility is generally permitted for individuals to choose the roles that they will play within the family. Another form of change that occurs in family therapy is the reevaluation of who is responsible for the problems within the family. After the family has become committed to the counseling process, it becomes apparent that not just the referred individual has a problem but that the family members are able to understand that their behaviors have contributed to the inappropriate behaviors. Through the therapeutic discussions, the family discovers what changes are needed, who must make the changes, and that the changes are possible.

Insight and Action in the Process

Bell proposes some revised theoretical concepts regarding insight and action in the therapeutic process. At one time he used interpretations freely, relying on personality theory and direct observations of family interactions. However, he reached the conclusion that interpretations based on his inferences about intrapsychic conditions were not useful in producing behavior changes in the family members. As a next step he used a more supportive assertion, assuming that the person had good reasons for what he or she was doing and asked the person to tell about the significance of the internal experience that justified the behavior. Although this was valuable and therapeutic in some situations, it was not sufficiently predictable for indiscriminate use. Finally, he used a technique to report on the sequences of the behavior he observed during the family interaction. When the verbal participation was reduced he would merely make observations about the nonverbal behaviors to move the interchange along. He claims that these were not interpretations of intrapsychic events but rather were statements that mirrored observable behavior. He found that this kept the action focused on the family group and led the members to verbalize content relating to their interaction and that the content was frequently interpretative, that is, expressing formulations about the family's intrapsychic life.

As a result of this technique, Bell revised his theories about the relationship of insight to action and has concluded that action comes before insight. More significantly he believes that the action that leads to insight takes place in the process of a social group rather than within an isolated individual. Insight appears to happen with an individual because it is abstracted from the social action and is seen from the point of view of a person who is acting; therefore, to call it intellectual insight is appropriate. However, Bell believes that psychologists have traditionally overlooked the social matrix within which it occurs, forgetting that the individual is never independent. This is particularly obvious within a family group.

Bell has concluded that intellectual insight does not consistently lead to changes in behavior because the insight is a result of past action. The insight is a reference to an action that has already been completed. When he examines the effect of a person's intention on that person's actions, he believes that a person's intent leads to changes in action but not necessarily to specific changes. It cannot produce desired changes in action if the other people do not cooperate and, before the cooperation, the intention must be communicated. Therefore, intention leads to new behavior through directing other people by dissolving or reducing resistence or through mobilizing another person's support. Therefore, it is important to recognize action as a social behavior rather than as a behavior of an individual.

Role of the Therapist

The therapist plays an important and active role in family group therapy. Bell (1976) perceives the therapist as an essential element in family therapy—an agent of change. He admits, however, to having no satisfactory explanation for the impact that the therapist makes. The therapist is seen both as an outsider to the family group and as a member of the group. In the role of the "referee" or "umpire," the therapist ensures that everyone has a chance to speak. The therapist is particularly supportive of the children who need protection to aid the development of their confidence during the initial stages of treatment.

During the orientation sessions, the therapist communicates to the family the structure of his or her role. The therapist emphasizes his or her relationship to the family as a group. The therapist tells the family that he or she will not give advice or offer solutions to its problems. The therapist also avoids being placed in or assuming a parental role. The family is given the responsibility of setting the goals of the therapy.

The therapist resists any attempts on the part of individual family members to meet in private conferences. If the therapist develops relations with any family member, the others may feel left out and resentful. If the therapist feels that a family member may need individual therapy, the therapist may offer to arrange an appointment with another therapist. For similar reasons, the therapist also avoids meeting with only part of the family. Conferences at which only partial attendance of the family is possible are canceled or rescheduled.

The therapist attempts to remain focused on the interrelations of family members. The family may respond with hostility to the therapist or to the interaction in the therapy session if the therapist concentrates on one family member and what is going on intrapsychically with that member.

The Therapist as Group Leader

The family group therapist acts as a leader in much the same way as the leader of other small task-oriented groups. He fulfills this leadership role by engaging in the following behaviors:

1. Stating and legitimizing a leader role.
2. Concentration of attention to what is going on between family members.

3. Directing his private analyses of what is happening in the family to the meaning of what he perceives for characterizing the components of his relations.
4. Bridging gaps between family members.
5. Modeling the act of listening.
6. Distributing opportunities for family members to speak.
7. Confining the content in most stages to intra-family matters.
8. Firming up the boundaries around the family in a related way.
9. Adapting the pace of development of the group to that which emerges with each particular family.
10. Affirming the importance of each individual and of the family as a whole.
11. Assisting them to explore what will now work out of what they know how to do.
12. Encouraging trails of new interactions regarded as promising by family members.
13. Facilitating termination of the therapy. (Bell, 1976, p. 141)

Practical Considerations

The therapist also has ascribed to his role a number of practical details for which he is responsible. These include arrangement of the form of the conferences, their setting, the time of the conferences, and the composition of the group.

The Conferences. The conferences are held weekly for an hour. Eight to twenty conferences are the norm, but more may be scheduled depending on the severity of the disturbance within the family.

The Setting. Conferences are generally held in the therapist's office or designated room. Earlier, Bell attempted to be flexible on the setting, but he found too many disruptions in other settings. He recommends a room equipped with a table around which chairs are arranged. Assignment of seats is not customary, but one additional chair over the number needed is present. Bell believes that this arrangement reduces the authority of the therapist by making him or her equal in seating with all other members of the family.

Group Composition. The therapist asks "Who makes up the family?" and helps the family to decide who should attend the meetings. Bell has found that children under nine years of age are not amenable to this therapy because of its dependence on verbal communication. The therapist explores the nature of the relationship and the suitability of including various individuals in the conference group.

Time. The therapist helps the family to find a time to which all members can accommodate their schedules. It is the family members' responsibility to secure release from work or any other activity that may infringe upon the conference time.

Sex of the Therapist. The sex of the therapist does not seem to affect the therapy. Bell has noted, however, that the male therapist may threaten the father. The father may be hesitant, at first, to join the discussions until he is assured that the therapist is not assuming a parental role. Female therapists may encounter similar reactions with mothers.

Co-therapists. Although Bell has not worked with a co-therapist, he believes that at times this approach may be suitable. The therapists are cautioned against appearing as parental models, especially if one is male and one is female.

Transference. Transference in the traditional sense does not occur in family group therapy. Bell believes that the transference phenomenon does not occur because the significant others are present during therapy and the child can express his or her feelings to the parents directly. Therefore, the emotional involvement with the therapist is not developed to the extent that it takes place in individual therapy. Bell also sees the formality of the conferences as contributory to the lack of transference.

Control of Content. The therapist does not choose the content for the therapy conferences. Rather, the therapist assumes that when the family is ready someone will bring up content relevant to its problems. The therapist does, however, control the content by not allowing for discussion material that involves individuals outside the family. The therapist keeps the focus of conversation on the interrelationships between family members.

Techniques of Therapy

A prerequisite of the therapist's beginning work in family therapy is what Bell refers to as the development of a mind set. The therapist must utilize techniques that focus on the family as a whole. The temptation to use techniques appropriate to individual therapy should be avoided. The emphasis in family group therapy remains on the family and the individual only as that person relates to the family unit.

Bell states that the techniques he has learned about range from an emphasis on the therapist's asserting himself or herself and an emphasis on the therapist's affirming the family in facilitating its use of its own strategies toward problem solving and attaining its members' goals. The intervention strategies used by a family group therapist are designed specifically to offer support to the family members and to facilitate communication process.

Interpretation

Bell relies heavily on interpretation as an intervention strategy. He distinguishes this technique, however, from the interpretation used in individual therapy. The therapist does not attempt to interpret intrapsychic events within the individual. Early attempts to use this form of interpretation seemed to result in the family's ignoring the interpretation, the family's unanimously denying the truth, or only part of the family's agreeing with the therapist while the other part disagreed. Hence, Bell concluded from his experience that this form of interpretation was not helpful as a part of the treatment process.

He developed a technique that allows the therapist to "mirror" the behavior that he or she sees taking place in the conference. This technique should protect the therapist from partiality toward any individual or segment of the family and promote a desire for the family's interaction and change. When the family's verbal participation is reduced and the therapist senses that others are seeking to take part more actively, the therapist can describe an observation of what he or she sees going on. The therapist merely reports on the sequences of behavior that he or she observes at the moment in the family. This technique does not engage the therapist in a one-to-one relationship with a family member, but it does keep the center of action in the family group and leads family members to verbalize content relative to their interaction. Most important, the content that the members discuss is frequently interpretive formulations about their intrapsychic life such as their feelings, experiences, and ideas. In other words, the type of responses made by the members are similar to statements that the therapist might have used as an interpretation.

Early in his family group therapy work Bell outlined four types of interpretation. The four types of interpretation do not involve in-depth interpretation but are techniques used to provide support for the family.

The Reflective. The therapist verbalizes his or her observations on the current state of family affairs and especially on the immediate occurrences in conferences. This interpretation mirrors the activities the therapist sees. In a sense the therapist confronts the family with aspects of its own functioning.

The Connective. The therapist makes statements that point out unrecognizable links between acts, events, attitudes, and experiences. Links may be observed in reciprocal behaviors between family members. Interrelations may be causal, and theories may be developed for the family about the intercommunication between causal and consequential actions. This approach expands the information available to the family.

The Reconstructive. The therapist recalls the history of the family, its relationships, and its peculiar ways of reacting. This is important as a review of this history may produce new facts, memories, and ideas about the family. This becomes useful to the family for its present and future reference as well as to its immediate and potential goals for action.

The Normative. The therapist comments on parallel or contrasting relationships or on behavior observable in other families. The therapist uses this technique to overcome blocks, to relieve guilt, or to support an individual in speaking freely. The therapist is cautioned, however, to use this technique sparingly, as such statements may be perceived by the family as instructions or expectations for them (Bell, 1975, pp. 90-92).

Communication Techniques

The therapist uses a number of approaches to provide support to the family. This is particularly true in the initial stages of therapy as the children need the therapist's support and courage to speak freely. The therapist may provide this support with the following communication techniques. The therapist tries to create openings when they may not otherwise occur so that individuals are able to speak in the family group. The therapist also helps individuals to put ideas, wishes, and feelings into words; this may be done by rephrasing what the individual has said and drawing the attention of the rest of the family to the individual behavior. The therapist prevents the parents from asserting their authority except in the control of the child's motor activity during the session. However, the therapist refrains from imposing controls so that he or she will not seem to the family to be taking over a parental role. The therapist does support the child when the child is verbalizing, thereby helping to reduce the child's anxiety and the consequences of talking.

Process, Role, and Technique

There seems to be a great deal of overlap between the role of the therapist and specific techniques used in the process of family group therapy. Bell (1975) summarizes six points in the therapist's behavioral repertoire.

First, the therapist orients the group by establishing his or her expectations about the way in which the family members will behave and the rules by which therapy will be conducted. The therapist describes what work will be done and the methods by which it will be performed.

Second, the therapist structures his or her own role. Although he or she cannot engineer his or her impact on the family, the therapist can discipline himself or herself to adopt certain behaviors and become predictable to the family members, which will reduce their anxiety about working with a therapist.

Third, the therapist limits the content of discussion to understandable and solvable problems and for developing ways of solving them. Actually, the content is restricted to what pertains to the action within the family.

Fourth, the therapist depends on the family's capacity to develop insight. The therapist is not an instructor. If the action among the members changes, the understanding of their behavior is changed. Bell does not depend on interpretations from an outside source's talking to the family but rather in having the individual's act and from those interactions gaining insight. With this premise the therapist only promotes the interaction among the family members and describes the family's behavior with each other; then new insights can be generated within the family.

Fifth, the therapist endorses the family's right to work out its problems within its own value system. It is important that the therapist not promote his or her own value system or solutions among the family. The therapist consciously adopts the position that there are other agents in the community whose function it is to promote value systems and that his or her role as a therapist is to help the family live more adequately together according to its members' own values.

Sixth, the therapist accepts the limits of what he or she is able to do. Family therapy can affect the interpersonal action in the family that has caused problems or has been derived from the problems. However, it is not able to affect all problems associated with the family members as individuals or the total family.

Limitations of Family Group Therapy

Under certain circumstances the use of this therapy is limited. Bell outlines some of the limitations he has found.

Age of Child. This approach is not adaptable to very young children. The highly verbal nature of family group therapy makes it difficult for children under the age of eight to benefit from this treatment approach. A child of seven or eight has not yet developed the ability to conceptualize at the level necessary for full participation in the therapy sessions. There is, however, no upper age limit so long as the child is still living with the parents.

Time. Time can be a limiting factor. The therapist is called upon to remain flexible and to make allowances for the demands placed upon the time of individual family members. For example, a conference may have to be postponed due to illness of a family member. As a result, the therapist adjusts the standard conference time to ensure the continuity of the sessions and to prevent a prolonged lapse of time between sessions.

Economic and Cultural Background. Bell notes that the effects of the family's economic and/or cultural background upon the therapy are still unexplored questions. With one exception, all Bell's families have come from a middle-class background and have had above-average education and intelligence. In the case of the one lower-class family, considerable modification of the therapy technique was required. This is an area in which future research is indicated before any questions are answered.

Level of Parental Adjustment. Difficulties may surface in therapy stemming from the marital difficulties of the parents. It is not uncommon for the parents to explore and resolve some of their problems during the therapy. Serious parental adjustment problems, however, may hamper treatment. All the parents that Bell has treated have been suffcently motivated to work at keeping their marriage and family together. Bell states that he is unsure of what effects an imminent separation would have on the treatment.

Technical Limits. Bell states that many issues regarding family life and adolescence emerge that need to be dealt with specifically. Often the best technique for handling these issues is not clear. The complexities of and the lack of detailed normative data on family adjustment patterns restricts the therapist. Sometimes the therapist cannot anticipate and may not be prepared to evaluate or interpret these patterns. Bell perceives this limitation as being reduced by the experience level of the therapist and ultimately by research on familial patterns.

Size of Family. The size of the family is not a limiting factor in family group therapy. The largest family that Bell has worked with was composed of five members, although family group therapy has been successfully used with a family of nine.

Referral of Adult. Work has been done in family group therapy when an adult was the referral problem. In many instances the problem is alcoholism. Family group therapy seems to be an appropriate means for dealing with this problem as the family can be very supportive to the recovering alcoholic.

Critique and Evaluation

John Bell pioneered in the field of family therapy and has remained independent. His early ideas challenged previous thinking about psychotherapy. He claims to summarize his experiences more for himself than for others, although many have used his ideas. He developed his rationale for family group therapy from his experience and private reflections. He remains aware of deficiencies in all approaches and has a refreshing tone of self-criticism regarding his own theoretical work. Therefore, he continues to examine and modify his thinking and practice.

Bell's emphasis on the similarity of the family to a group is unique. Certainly, all family therapists recognize the family as a special group with group dynamics, but Bell emphasizes similarities and differences in respect to group dynamics, life stages of development, process of group interaction in therapy, and the role of the leader. He talks about changing the structure in the family but not in the same way as the systems approaches. His techniques have the appearance of negotiation between family members, but not specifically side taking and the go-between of Zuk. His seems to be more gentle and less directive than most approaches indicate for a therapist.

The evaluation of this approach has been citing cases. Bell acknowledges that it does not work in all cases, but the approach generally leads to satisfaction for the family.

References

Bell, John E. 1975. *Family therapy*. New York: Jason Aronson.
——. 1976. A theoretical framework for family group therapy. In *Family therapy: Theory and Practice,* ed. P. J. Guerin, Jr., pp. 129–143. New York: Gardner Press.
——. 1978. "Family context therapy: A model for family change. *Journal of Marriage and Family Counseling* 40:111–126.

12

The Triadic - Based Family Therapy of Gerald Zuk

The go-between process is a triadic-based approach to family therapy that explores and works to shift the balance of pathogenic relating among family members so that new, more appropriate behaviors become possible. Gerald Zuk developed the approach through his experience as a therapist, researcher, and trainer. He is a psychologist affiliated with the Eastern Pennsylvania Psychiatric Institute in Philadelphia where he has served as the associate director of training. In addition to influencing the field with his teaching and writing, he serves as the editor of the *International Journal of Family Therapy.*

Although he had worked as a family therapist for many years, it was in 1967 that Zuk began focusing on a triadic-based approach. Up to that time he stated that most family therapists focused on dyadic interaction, basically because the majority of therapists and researchers had been analytically oriented and the psychoanalytic model has its most direct extension in two-person interactions. Although some analytically oriented therapists have referred to a triadic-based concept, Zuk believes that their interest in triadic-based interaction was marginal to the primary focus on dyadic interactions. Communication theorists have addressed themselves more to the triadic-based interaction concepts; however, Zuk believes that they too focus on the dyadic interaction.

In the triadic-based approach, the therapist examines the processes of coalitions, alliances, and cliques as well as the processes of mediation and side taking. Coalitions and mediation do not occur in groups of two; however, they may occur in groups composed of three or more. In coalitions, at least two individuals join against at least one other person. In mediation, at least one person acts as a mediator between at least two other individuals.

Concept of Family

Zuk does not describe the characteristics of a normal or healthy family but focuses most of his attention on pathogenic relating in the family. He does describe some characteristics of the American family and how such characteristics may contribute to difficulties within a family.

He believes that the American family is female dominated whereas the other institutions in the society are primarily male dominated. He describes the key characteristics of institutions dominated by men as "paying close attention to orderly procedure, regulation, and process; establishing a clear-cut chain of command; developing codes of acceptable behavior for performance, with rewards defined; and establishing concrete goals and delineating depths necessary to achieve them" (1971, p. 118). He believes that females in their roles as wives and mothers place a relatively lower value on these characteristics and therefore that these characteristics tend not to characterize family life.

He follows some stereotypical differences between the functions of husbands and wives in the family by describing the wife-mother as dominant in the expressive function in the family and the husband-father as dominant in the instrumental function. The management of children is primarily a wife-mother's role, with the husband-father's role being primarily away from the family and on the job. The wife-mother's role is primarily responsible for the control and management of the children; the husband-father occupies a peripheral role in the American family. Hence, Zuk believes that children are more apt to model the expressive behavior of their mother, and not enough of the instrumental function of the father because the wife-mother is the predominant teaching agent.

Due to the increasing isolation of the nuclear family from its relative network, the family is increasingly fulfilling a more specialized function than in previous years. The high incidence of rebelliousness in today's youth and the high incidence of mental disturbance and lawlessness may be attributed in part to the family's structure. The extended family system has decreased in its role, and the nuclear family has emerged with increasing pressure on the parents to provide training for their children. However, the training process has been centered primarily in the mothers. Zuk believes that a major source of problems facing youth has been the overabundance of the mother as the teaching agent at the expense of the father's role. Because the father is a peripheral figure in the family, children tend to distrust him and what he stands for. Particularly in adolescence and young adulthood, children have difficulty and confusion in handling their encounters with institutions because the social units reflect, to a higher degree, the thinking of the male-dominated world. Zuk states that the father is a primary teacher of children about the male-dominated institutions but that father has lost his credibility. He believes that the unavailability of fathers to serve as a bridge between the family and other institutions sets the stage for adolescent challenge of the credibility of the institutions and for rebelliousness that one observes in adolescents.

Zuk calls attention to the similarity between his thinking and that of Keniston's in *The Uncommitted: Alienated Youth in American Society*. Keniston (1965) also described the wife-mother as a central figure in the family and stated that "American boys are increasingly brought up by women-mothers and teachers—who have the greatest power and authority over them. This matriarchal situation tends to encourage identification with women, their functions and their activities" (p. 305).

Keniston believes that a developmental discontinuity is presented to children in that their enormous dependency on their mothers does not prepare them for independence. This is particularly true of males because their mother dependency interferes with the establishment of a masculine identity. Interestingly, Keniston drew his conclusions regarding the American family from his observations of a bright, privileged young people whom he described as alienated. Zuk's ideas were based on a very different sample whom he had seen in therapy—primarily the lower-class families. Zuk concluded that different solutions are found by youths whose estrangement from their fathers and overdependency on their mothers did not prepare them for the adult society. Keniston's population with high intelligence and affluence used a behavior described as alienation, whereas Zuk's lower-class population used aggressive behavior, stealing, poor school achievement, and truancy. The ideas of Zuk and Keniston were both presented originally in the mid- to late 1960s, and one must bear in mind the tenor in American society during the late 1960s.

Zuk (1975) categorizes three apparent antagonisms that generate pathogenic relating. First is the male–female struggle that is particularly evident in husband and wife conflicts. Second is the parent–child struggle that occurs more frequently between the male children and parents. Third is the social status struggle that occurs in conflicts of the husband at work or in family–neighborhood conflicts.

The conflicts between husband and wife can cause pathogenic relating when one parent consolidates the loyalty of the children against the other. This occurs more frequently when the wife and children oppose the husband. The conflict of the husband and job fits into this situation, as the husband comes home and does not get support from the wife. In fact, Zuk observes that many problem situations arise because the father is peripheral or absent. During the past two decades, as a result of pressures from the economy, technology, and an information explosion, the husband-father's role in the nuclear family has deteriorated. He is more alienated from the children and wife, and the children are primarily under the wife's control. The attitudes, emotional tone, and values of the wife influence the children; those of the father are more distrusted.

Zuk (1975) has a graphic presentation of his hypothesized changes in the U.S. nuclear family over the past few decades. Figure 12-1B as compared with 12-1A shows that the "buffer role" exercised by a combination of the father and extended family between the mother–child unit and social organizations has been reduced. The father and extended family once served as a check on the mother's values to her children; however, mothers have become increasingly dominant teaching agents. Zuk believes that the mother's values have traditionally been at odds with those of societal institutions and agencies that are more dominated by male values. Therefore, children are growing increasingly at odds with the social agencies and institutions. Particularly when children move into adolescence, the antagonism between their mother-dominated values and the male-dominated society will be evident.

The explanation of value conflict has been made more explicit with the introduction of the terms "continuity" and "discontinuity." Zuk (1975) uses these terms to refer to the contrasting values that may degenerate into pathogenic relating between spouses, parents and children, or the family and social institutions.

Continuity values tend to deemphasize "order, system, hierarchical arrangements, etc., and stresses egalitarianism but mixed with an antiuniformity" (1975,

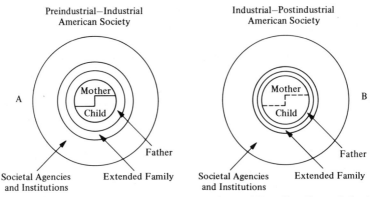

Figure 12-1. Changing Relation of Mother-Child to Other Family and Social Systems. (*Source:* G. Zuk, *Process and Practice in Family Therapy.* Haverford, Pa.: Psychiatry and Behavioral Science Books, 1975, p. 22.)

p. 28). Continuity values take the special case or unique incident to be important. Discontinuity values emphasize the "goodness of order, system, hierarchical arrangement or taxonomies, rules and procedures, analysis, selectivity and exclusivity" (1975, p. 27). Table 12-1 presents the value categories and the primary expression.

In major conflicts there is a commonality in the values expressed by husbands, parents, and community versus those of wives, children, and family. Zuk labels the values expressed by wives, children, and family as continuity and those of husbands, parents, and community as discontinuity.

Table 12-2 summarizes the value conflicts. In conflicts between spouses, the husband usually espouses the discontinuity values to the wife who expresses continuity values. For example, in a conflict over child discipline, the husband claims

Table 12-1. Categories of Contrasting Values Expressed in Family Interviews

	Values	
Categories	*"Continuity"*	*"Discontinuity"*
1. Affective/attitudinal	Empathic, sympathetic, "warm"	Distant, reserved, "cool"
2. Moral/ethical	Anticonformist, Idealistic, egalitarian,	Disciple of law, order, and codes; Pragmatic; elitist
3. Cognitive/conceptual	Intuitive, holistic	Analytic, systematic
4. Tasks/goals	Nurturing, caretaking	Achieving, structuring

G. Zuk, *Process and Practice in Family Therapy* (Haverford, Pa.: Psychiatry and Behavioral Science Books, 1975), p. 28.

Table 12-2. Contrasting Values Expressed by Various Conflicted Parties in Family Interviews

Conflict Between	Values	
	"Continuity"	"Discontinuity"
1. Mates	Wife	Husband
2. Generations	Children	Parents
3a. Family and community	Family	Community
3b. Family and community—race as a central factor	Black	White
3c. Family and community—social class as a central factor	Lower class	Middle class
3d. Family and community—politics as a central factor	Liberal	Conservative

G. Zuk, *Process and Practice in Family Therapy* (Haverford, Pa.: Psychiatry and Behavioral Science Books, 1975), p. 30.

that the wife is too permissive or lax and does not hold to the rules, whereas the wife claims that the husband is too rigid and severe. In conflicts between parents and children, the parents espouse the discontinuity values, whereas children express the continuity position. Parents set rules and procedures, and children are described as rulebreakers who have ready excuses. When the family and community are at odds, the community is accused of being too restrictive and demanding in regulations, whereas the family expresses unique and special interests. Zuk elaborates on the family–community conflict with examples of race, social class, and political factors (1979).

Diagnosis

The therapist must formulate a concept of what is "wrong" with the family, that is, the nature of its pathogenic relating. Actually, pathogenic relating refers to the formulization that the therapist makes about the distortions in the patterns in relating among the family members that are important in producing symptoms in one or more members. Examples of pathogenic relating involve silencing strategies that families use as well as scapegoating and inappropriate labeling of members' behaviors.

Zuk also suggests that the family's pathogenic relating is communicated to the family. He does note that no one should expect miracles from this communication because the family is not likely to accept or use the therapist's insight without a period of testing.

One of the first interests when starting to work with a family involves silencing strategies, because these can usually be observed fairly early in the process. Zuk tries to observe the coalitions among members to shut out another member and also the nature of the particular technique employed by the coalition to shut up the member. The therapist also observes how a person responds to being shut up and the coalition's response to the therapist's label of its behavior in describing its silencing strategy. When the therapist finds an intermeshing of types of psychogenic relating such as silencing, inappropriate labeling, scapegoating, and promoting inappropriate family myths, it is necessary to describe and challenge them together as well as separately (1971).

Prior to the first meeting, Zuk does not review material that is available about the family or the identified patient because it may set up a bias and interfere with a proper evaluation during the family interview. He may review available material after the first interview, as the effect of bias would be reduced. In the first interview he asks about the problem and who referred the family and takes keen interest in who initiates the answers to these questions. A primary motive in the first meeting is to create an interest for the family to attend a second meeting; therefore, he is not so interested in eliciting a detailed history as he is in mobilizing positive motivation to seal the engagement and be able to continue therapy. He explains to the family that one meeting is not enough to establish a basis for therapy and that several meetings will be needed after which it is possible to state the way he views the problem and whether therapy will be recommended. He stresses to the family the importance of passing through a brief series of evaluation meetings.

During these first few meetings, each family member is encouraged to give his or her views on the problem and to comment on each other's views because interesting differences may appear regarding the nature of the problem. Interesting concepts regarding the family dynamics can be gained by observing who corrects, revises, amends, or monitors other persons' communications.

Because diagnosis is an ongoing process, Zuk begins continuing interviews by asking the family members to tell what happened to them during the preceding week. Families are expected to describe the problems that arose and the arguments or anything else that was unusual that occurred during the week. If nothing special occurred, the families are encouraged to describe what happened anyway. The description of and working through what happened during the week may involve the entire time or very little.

The therapist's concepts about the family's pathogenic relating are not derived only from the verbal report about the family conflict or from the past history but are an outgrowth of the relationship that develops between the therapist and the family. When unable to observe directly, the therapist can stimulate pathogenic relating by suggesting, teasing, prodding, exhorting, side taking, silencing, task assigning, and threatening to suspend the session or terminate therapy. There are times when the therapist will find himself or herself involved in the pathogenic relating. Family members may put pressure on the therapist that he or she experiences as tension, or the therapist could find himself or herself restrained from introducing certain topics or confronting the family on certain issues. Pathogenic relating directed toward the therapist by family members usually takes the form of pressuring the therapist to take sides prematurely. The therapist may be pressured to take the family's side in viewing a problem particularly when the family wishes it to appear that there is no problem. At the end of each interview Zuk suggests that the therapist ask himself or herself two questions: First, with whom and on what issue did they expect me to take sides and, second, what did they tell me that was new today? The therapist's ordering of the questions illustrates the importance of the relationship of the therapist to the family members in taking precedence over other information.

When Zuk concludes his diagnosis he believes that, despite a wide variety of conflicts expressed in the interviews, there are generally three major problem areas (1975). The first involves the conflict involving appropriate sex roles, particularly as enacted between husband and wife. The second is the conflict regarding appropriate age roles, particularly between the parents and children. The third involves the conflicts regarding the appropriate relationship of the family to the community and includes frictions related to a cluster of social class variables including race, religion, education, and jobs.

After the three or four interviews, which Zuk uses as an evaluation, a decision may be made regarding continuing therapy. By that time it is generally clear that the family will be cooperative and that it is capable of responding appropriately in the therapy situation. The decision to continue in therapy may not be communicated formally; in such cases continuing sessions are scheduled and the therapist gives an indication of the number of sessions and periods of time required for successful change to occur. It is helpful for the therapist to indicate how long he or she believes therapy will continue and what changes he or she hopes can occur. In addition, the therapist may want to explain the conditions that can affect the length and outcome of therapy.

Contraindication and Limitations of Therapy

Zuk states that family therapy is contraindicated only when the family appears to have an attitude that the therapist is serving one person or institution to carry out disciplinary actions with a family member or the family as a whole. The therapist may be perceived as an agent of the schools, the court, or the welfare department. In some situations children may perceive the therapist as an agent of the parents. In these situations the therapist is not free to introduce change that he or she believes is necessary and useful. The purpose of the therapy is essentially compromised and subverted, and therefore it is better not to begin the therapeutic process.

In addition to these conditions that make family therapy contraindicated, Zuk describes some factors that limit the applicability of family therapy. These factors limit the likelihood that the family will become successfully engaged in the process and, if they do, that they are less likely to experience a successful outcome (1971). Such factors do not carry the risk that the course of therapy, if decided upon, would have an undesirable side effect.

Zuk believes that a major limiting factor is grounded in the rule that, as one descends the socioeconomic ladder, the level of family disorganization increases. He believes that lower-class families are less interested in opportunities for an extended interaction with the therapist and that they have less ability to speak skillfully in the language that increases their sense of inadequacy in therapy. Often the job demands of lower-class parents tend to disrupt the schedules for meetings.

Another limitation to family therapy involves the refusal of a family member to attend or the absence of a member who has attended previous meetings. Zuk suggests putting pressure on the families to secure the presence of members who refuse to attend.

A third limiting factor involves the relationships in working with single-parent families, usually with the mother as the remaining parent. When the therapist is a male, Zuk believes that the therapist becomes cast in a father-substitute role and must be concerned lest he build up too much dependency as a substitute father; Zuk suggests working toward a relatively concrete, practical, short-term goal and then offering further consultation.

Goals and Therapeutic Foci

Zuk (1975) states there are many desirable goals in family therapy, including conflict resolution, improved communication and understanding among family members, and enhanced family solidarity as well as a greater tolerance for appreciation of individuality. Although there are many specific goals for a family in family therapy, Zuk believes that there is only one central goal: that of reducing and replacing pathogenic relating among the family members. He does not believe that the therapist should move toward larger, more pervasive goals such as personality transformation. He believes that subgoals such as restoration of the marriage, job improvement, or better school achievement may occur as pathogenic relating is reduced; however, the therapist should not side prematurely to save the marriage or job or to increase the student's school performance. He recommends that therapists steer clear of communicating goals to families in terms of preventing situations such as divorce or improving situations such as jobs or school performance. It is through the central goal of reducing and replacing psychogenic relating that more specific goals of individual members may be accomplished.

The overriding goal for the therapist is to return the family to functioning within normal limits. Zuk believes that it is up to the therapist to decide what constitutes normal limits for each family. He believes that "within normal limits" does not mean the absence of friction, rivalries, or competition between members of the family or between the family and the community. Nor does it mean the absence of anxiety, guilt, frustration, or anger or that family members always behave fairly with each other. In fact, family members may not feel a common bond or develop a sense of solidarity. Zuk's definition of within normal limits means that these malevolent, intimidating, disruptive, and inflammatory processes, which he describes as pathogenic relating, are no longer observed by the therapist or that they have been reduced sufficiently so that there is noticeable improvement in the family relations and individual functioning.

Zuk (1971) describes a major process goal of therapy as obtaining the commitment of the family to be treated on the therapist's terms. He believes that the family's involvement in therapy according to the therapist's ideas is a major determinant of the outcome of therapy, not just a precondition for it. In essence, the commitment of the family to the therapy on the therapist's terms would be considered the major process goal of the therapy. Two other process goals consistent with outcome goals are stated. One involves negotiation of the therapist and family about the manner of pathogenic relating in an attempt to bring pressure on the family to reduce its pathogenic relating. The other involves the type of negotiation involved when the family therapy has started to be effective and the family and therapist work with each other on the issue of termination. With a favorable change, a positive outcome of this negotiation is possible, too.

Types of Family Therapy

Zuk describes the characteristics of four types of family therapy. Family therapy may be very brief, as in a crisis-resolution situation; short term, with ten to fifteen interviews; middle range, with twenty-five to thirty interviews; or long term, with forty or more sessions. He presents some conditions (Table 12–3) that describe the family characteristics and goals of the four types of family therapy (1975).

Crisis Resolution. A crisis precipitates many families' coming for the first therapy session. One member of the family may have developed a serious symptom, or one person could have become unmanageable, or one member may have experienced serious difficulty with a community agency. Such a family generally presents a picture of disorganization. The therapist's goal is to reduce the tension and, if possible, resolve the crisis. Zuk states that, despite the best efforts of the therapist, most of these families will not continue in therapy once the tension has been reduced or the crisis resolved. These cases usually exist for one to six interviews over a period of one to six weeks.

Short Term. Zuk describes short-term therapy as being determined by the family rather than by the particular type of problem. Some families are reluctant to be involved for a long period of time with the verbal type of interaction involved in therapy. The short term of verbal psychotherapy with lower-class clients has long been known. Families who are willing to participate in short-term therapy generally see the goal of therapy as limited to symptom reduction, and they are seen from ten to fifteen interviews up to a period of four months.

Middle Range. The middle-range family therapy on Zuk's chart typically runs from twenty to thirty interviews over an eight-month period. He finds that it is mostly middle-class families who are willing to invest more time. They do not set such strict limits on the time for therapy and have a broader goal for the process than do the lower-class families.

Long Term. More sophisticated middle- and upper-class families whose culture values words and are skillful in exchange of words may be more disposed to a

Table 12-3. Characteristics of Some Types of Family Therapy

Types	Number of Contacts	Family Characteristics	Goals
Crisis resolution	1–6 interviews over 1 to 6 weeks	Disorganized; poor minority, especially black or single parent	Primarily to reduce tensions
Short term	10–15 interviews over 2½ to 4 months	Lower middle class	Primarily symptom reduction
Middle range	25–30 interviews over 6 to 8 months	Middle class	Better communication and understanding among family members
Long term	40 or more interviews over 10 to 15 months	Middle and upper middle class, especially Jewish; the more socially sophisticated	Increased solidarity but with better acceptance of individuality in members

G. Zuk. *Process and Practice in Family Therapy* (Haverford, Pa.: Psychiatry and Behavioral Science Books, 1975), p. 4.

longer-term therapeutic process. The goal of this therapy requires a family that exhibits a fair degree of solidarity even though solidarity may be part of the problem. The goal of long-term therapy is to enhance the solidarity but with increased tolerance and understanding of individuality. Working with and attempting to alter member's values is a part of all family therapy but especially so with long-term therapy.

Phases in Family Therapy

The usual schema in psychotherapy is to organize it into a beginning, middle, and ending phase; however, Zuk believes that family therapy has transitions that occur too rapidly to divide meaningfully. Because he divides family therapy into four different types with different goals to be accomplished, often there is only a beginning and ending phase. In his view it is only in the long-term family therapy that the beginning, middle, and ending phases actually occur. Therefore, when he discusses phases of family therapy, he concentrates on two: the engagement and the termination.

Zuk views family therapy as a series of critical incidents beginning with the engagement. Engagement is such a significant critical incident in family therapy because many that attend do not consider themselves the patient. Therefore, they have a high level of anxiety, and it is important for the therapist to help control that anxiety or it will drive them away from therapy. He considers the engagement incident the prototype of critical incidents that will occur in family therapy. In a sense, all other critical incidents are reenactments of the engagement. During each incident there is a time of rising tension and anxiety as the therapist and family negotiate the specific issue, that is, the substance of content of the particular incident. There are always times that may lead to termination. In fact, termination is a specific critical incident in family therapy and a phase of active negotiation between the therapist and family that is particularly important.

The Engagement

The procedure of engagement does not vary depending upon the type of therapy that may occur. It is used with all families and is designed to encourage continuation beyond the initial stage. It is also intended to test the family's motivation for therapy and to gain basic information for the therapist's judgment regarding the course of therapy.

Although not all family members accept the idea that they are patients in the same way in which the identified patient is, everyone has anxiety at the beginning of the therapy session. The fact that the therapist insists that every family member participate in the interview is a strong message regarding his or her idea of causation. By accepting to participate, the members are, at least to some degree, accepting the therapist's message and the burden has started to shift from the identified patient.

The first interview begins by asking what the problem is and who referred the family for therapy. The primary interest with this question is who takes the initiative in answering inquiries. Typically it is the wife-mother who tends to answer and be the spokesperson for the family, probably reflecting the centrality of the wife-mother in the nuclear family. Generally the husband-father is more peripheral. All family members are encouraged to give their views on the problem and to comment on each other's viewpoints, for there may be interesting divergencies regarding the nature of the problem. It is important to notice which member typically corrects, revises, amends, or otherwise monitors other members.

It is usually explained to the family that a series of three or four interviews will be used to evaluate the family. At that point a decision will be made regarding continuation. The motive in the initial interview is to create interest for a continuing meeting rather than eliciting detailed information. Zuk's primary interest is to mobilize a positive motivation and involve the family in the engagement process. After a few sessions the family may be cooperative and capable of responding in a therapy situation.

In the early sessions the therapist tries to establish a friendly relationship with the family as well as establish the legitimacy of his or her role as an expert and authority. Some families will test and challenge the therapist's expertise and authority; other families may invest the therapist with too much power, more power than is appropriate. Zuk believes that the therapist who shares a religious, ethnic, or religious background with the family has an advantage over one who does not. However, sharing similar characteristics does not solve the real issues in establishing the relationship.

Some administrative issues are covered in the first interview, such as the hour and day of sessions, the fee and frequency of sessions, and the determination of which family members must be present. The resolution of these seemingly administrative issues such as the father's complaint of not being able to take time from work to attend sessions may have a significant effect on the outcome. Zuk believes that all issues that require negotiation between the therapist and the family are significant in the engagement process. He states that every family therapy is really a contest between therapist and family as to who will change the other and how and under what circumstances. Change occurs from the various contests between the therapist and family, and sometimes families change only after they believe that the therapist has also changed or that they have won some part of the contest with the therapist.

Zuk conducts a series of three or four interviews to learn about the family and to permit them to become acquainted with the therapist. This process also discourages premature termination. The three or four evaluation meetings are short enough to control the anxiety of the family members regarding a long-term involvement, yet long enough to generate an attitude of interest and a liking for the therapist and therapy. After the evaluation series, a decision may be made that therapy is not needed at the time or that a referral is indicated. The therapist may decide that therapy of a certain length of time or number of interviews is appropriate and can determine if he or she is going to work with just the parents, part of the family, or the entire family together.

Termination

Zuk emphasizes that termination is, like the engagement phase, an active negotiation between the therapist and family that provides potential for therapeutic change. Termination is not viewed as a weaning period but as another content in a series of contests between the therapist and the family regarding needed changes.

A family or family members may terminate or threaten to terminate when some change occurs or when change is absent. When there is a disagreement between the therapist and family about the behavior or individuals who need change, this may also initiate a discussion about termination. The family may talk specifically about termination. Individuals or the whole family may not attend interviews. Zuk advocates a policy that takes the decision to terminate out of the hands of the family. He suggests calling the family that misses appointments and stating that the therapist is not obligated to work with the family. This reverses the position and takes the initiation for termination away from the family members. It may also have the effect of a more constructive attitude toward continuation. Because some families test the therapist's need for them by threatening termination, this poses a problem for the therapist by testing his or her self-assurance and sense of self-worth.

The therapist should make decisions regarding termination when the family has accomplished the intended goals. Termination may be discussed when one or some, although not all, of the goals have been achieved. This decision may be made when the therapist assumes that the family is not ready for the direction that is needed to achieve some of the other goals. The therapist may describe the situation to the family while offering to work at a later time when the entire family is ready. The therapist does not use the idea of termination lightly or as a trick to overcome resistance. The therapist initiates the idea of termination only when he or she has completely exhausted all other available sources of leverage or when he or she is convinced that an impasse seriously interferes with effectiveness (1975).

Zuk states that occasionally families report the occurrence of significant change after termination, which he believes is a result of termination and having been in therapy. He suggests that there is an increasing potential for change during the course of therapy that does not materialize or a goal that the therapist desires is not achieved. He believes that termination may free the family or individual members for change that for various reasons could not occur while they were in therapy.

Zuk also describes excluding one family member from attending further interviews as one type of selective termination that has powerful therapeutic effects. He describes the case in which he requested the identified patient to remain home while working with the parents. This selective termination was used to reinforce the concept that had previously been communicated that the central problem was with the parents and that the son's inappropriate behavior was merely an offshoot (1975).

The numerous examples that Zuk uses to describe the termination phase clearly indicate that termination is not viewed as a weaning period but that therapy continues to be a negotiating contest right to the end. It is this negotiating process as a part of termination that is still part of the learning process in family therapy.

Zuk describes his technique of family therapy as a go-between process because the therapist takes and trades the roles of a mediator and a side taker. The process involves the therapist's applying leverage against the psychogenic relating in families in an attempt to break up and replace it. This involves the therapist's ability to catalyze conflict followed by his or her movement into the role of go-between or side taker. The therapist does not aim to resolve the conflict; in fact conflict facilitates the go-between process as it provides a climate in which the therapist can intervene forcefully. Conflict provides a crisis situation that is favorable for a change to occur, and the go-between process attempts to reduce and replace the psychogenic relating that occurs rather than resolving the conflict.

In beginning family therapy, two questions occur to the family: "Is there something wrong with us?" and "If there is, how will you treat us?" Often the family and therapist are opponents on these questions. The therapist begins the process when he or she explores these questions with the family for areas of expected agreement and disagreement. Some families will try to convince the therapist from the beginning that nothing is wrong with them and in fact that this process may bring about some improvement. This change is really a function of the bargaining transaction between the therapist and family on the question of whether or not something is wrong with them. The family changes in an attempt to change the therapist's expected position. In fact the change is expected to be the least necessary to secure a change in the therapist's expected position. By means of judicious siding, taking the role of go-between, or shifting between the two positions, the therapist hopes to control the bargaining transactions in accordance with his or her therapeutic goals (1971).

Zuk (1971) states that the therapist conducts the go-between process when he or she probes issues in the family and establishes the existence of conflict by eliciting expressions of disagreement and encouraging the open expression of a disagreement. He also exposes and resists the family's efforts to deny or disguise disagreements. The therapist encourages the expression of recent and/or current disagreements rather than the rehashing of old issues. The therapist focuses on the expression of conflict between present members rather than between those who are absent from the session.

The therapist conducts the go-between process by selecting specific disagreements that he or she deems worthy of discussion, rejecting others as not worthy, and resisting the family's expected efforts to establish its own priorities. This selection of appropriate conflicts is a part of the therapist's move into the role of go-between in which he or she seeks to establish authority and resists the family's expected efforts to displace him or her.

In conducting the go-between process, the therapist sides either implicitly or intentionally with one member against another in a particular conflict. Siding is unavoidable; even if the therapist thinks that he or she is maintaining a neutral or objective position, the family will judge the therapist as siding. It is important for the therapist to decide when and with whom to side intentionally as a therapeutic tactic. It is also important for the therapist to know with whom the family believes he or she is siding. It is possible for the therapist to side with or against the entire family unit in a particular disagreement as well as with or against individual members. Zuk believes that siding is a legitimate tactic of therapeutic value in shifting the balance of psychogenic relating among family members. "By judicious siding, the therapist can tip the balance in favor of more productive relating, or at least disrupt the chronic pattern of psychogenic relating" (1971, p. 73). While siding with one family member in a conflict with another member, the therapist adds weight to the position of one. The effect of the therapist's being against all members causes the members to minimize the extent of disagreement but it also pushes them to examine more carefully the basis of the disagreement. It is probably unwise for the therapist to give the message that he or she consistently sides with one member against others. The therapist needs to be flexible in the face of the family's efforts to get him or her to side in a systematic manner so that the therapist will become more predictable and in Zuk's opinion, therefore, a less effective therapeutic person.

The go-between process involves the concept of therapeutic power, meaning the capacity of the therapist to define the therapist–patient relationship and to initiate action to increase control of the relationship in ways that the therapist believes will be in the best interest of the family. The go-between process presumes that conflict is a characteristic and inevitable part of family life and that it is in the interest of the principals to take steps to check its magnitude. The go-between process in family therapy presumes that conflict erupts not among strangers but also among individuals who have had a long history with each other and who have worked out a complex process for mediation or pseudomediation of the conflict. The therapist enters this existing situation and brings his or her expertise. Zuk points out a partial paradox that families will tend to follow the therapist directions but resist the directions that appear to challenge the family's status quo. In addition, while families wish the identified patient's improvement, they resist the idea that the identified patient's improved condition rests in their acceptance of their own causal involvement in the condition.

The go-between process involves a shift in that it denotes a phase of eruption of conflict and a phase of diminution and involves a sequence in that a diminution follows the eruption in a regular fashion and as separately describable phases.

Steps in the Process

Four key steps in the go-between process in family therapy are outlined by Zuk (1971). First, the therapist or a family member introduces an issue on which there are at least two identifiable opponents or principals. Second, there is an intensification of the conflict and the beginning of movement of a person, either the therapist or a family member, into the role of go-between. Third, there are attempts by the principals and go-between to define and delimit each other's roles or positions. Fourth, there is a recession or secession of the conflict associated with the change in the positions of the principals or a redefinition of the conflict, or both.

The therapist introduces issues as potential sources of conflict and then directs the go-between process. He observes the family to see if the issue produces a conflict and if the conflict produces principals and then decides his or her own orientation regarding the contending principals. That is, the therapist decides whether to enter the conflict in the role of go-between or principal. As the go-between process continues, a struggle ensues over the definition and limitation of differing positions. Even though the family may have empowered the therapist to act as such, different members take steps to deny and limit the go-between's power to mediate in the conflict. To the extent that the therapist accepts the family definition of his or her role, the therapist's powers are limited.

Variations of the Process

Zuk points out that the go-between process may be conducted either by the therapist or by the family members. When conducting the go-between process, the therapist aims to change the family in ways that he or she deems beneficial, whereas the family members' conduct of the go-between process typically attempts to maintain the status quo and resist the therapist's attempt to change them. Four variations of the process are (1) a family member's acting as go-between with other family members as principals, (2) a family member's functioning as go-between with another family member and therapist as the principals, (3) the therapist's focusing as go-between with family members as principals, and (4) the therapist's acting as go-between with family members and a community agency as opposing principals.

An example of the first variation, in which a family member acts as go-between with other family members as opposing principals, may be seen when a mother pits her husband and children against each other and plays the role of benevolent go-between. In this type of situation, the mother explains the children and husband to the therapist, reporting that they have never gotten along and that she has had to keep them apart. The mother employs the go-between process to control relationships with both the children and her husband. The therapist may play into this situation during the therapy session by asking the mother for further understanding of the family situation, channeling direction or advice through her, or identifying her as an ally since they do report more information. Actually, this person is seriously undermining the therapist's efforts, for as go-between this person is able to alter and rearrange messages to the other family members. In such a case, this person would actually be a strong resister of change in the family.

Zuk proposes three gambits that a therapist might apply in such a situation. First, the therapist may define the mother as a principal in a conflict with another member such as a child and interpret and confront her in an attempt to move back into the go-between role. Second, the therapist may encourage another family member to confront the mother as an opposing principal. Third, the therapist may consistently support a different family member from the mother to assume the role of go-between and confront the mother in her efforts to usurp that role. Each of these gambits makes it possible to expose and limit the mother's control of the go-between process.

The second variation involves a family member's working as go-between, with other family members and therapist as the principals. This variation occurs when a family member plays another family member against the therapist, which reduces the therapist's effectiveness in changing the family, as when a member is absent from the therapy session. This often makes another family and therapist as principals in conflict. The therapist may demand the return of the absent child, and the parent may claim that it is impossible. Zuk indicates that parents may play a go-between role with acting-out children and the therapist as the principals or the parents and therapist may be the principals with the child's functioning as a go-between.

Two therapists' resolutions may be suggested. First, the therapist may refuse to accept the parents' idea of helplessness and confront them with their intent to resist the therapy by using their children against him or her. Second, the therapist may arrange to see the parent and children separately in an effort to explore the nature of their secret alliance and attempt to split that alliance.

The third variation involves the therapist as a go-between, with family members as opposing principals. This is actually the primary process by which the therapist can employ his or her efforts to produce change. The major concern for the therapist in this position is to avoid being trapped into a too rigid go-between role so that he or she may become a family judge. The therapist could lose important therapeutic leverage if the family can induce him or her into a specific type of go-between. Successful management of the process requires the therapist to use the element of surprise; that is, the opportunity to change from one kind of go-between to another or even from a go-between to a principal. The therapist is certainly in a position to take the role of go-between because the therapist is the professional authority in the counseling session. The therapist can help describe issues and assign members as principals. By eliciting individuals as principals in the conflict, the therapist can assume the role of go-between for himself or herself or assign another member of the family as go-between. In any event, the therapist takes the initiative in conducting the go-between process.

The fourth process in the go-between process involves the therapist as the go-between, with family members and a community agent as opposing principals. When a family or family member is in a serious conflict with a community agency, the therapist may secure an agent of that agency to act as a principal and permit the therapist to work as a go-between. In this situation the therapist describes the issue between the family and the agent of the community. An example of this procedure may involve the therapist as a go-between with a member of a school representing the community agency in conflict with a student and the family. The therapist may be viewed by the family as an ally with the school system and sometimes by the school as an ally of the family. It is important that the therapist is seen as an independent force mediating between the family and the school.

Role of the Therapist

The general role of the therapist is to apply leverage to displace the pathogenic relating in the family. The therapist's roles permit his or her initiating changes in the family interaction. The three sources of leverage for the therapist involve acting as a celebrant, acting as a go-between, and acting as a side taker.

The Celebrant

Zuk (1975) describes the celebrant as a transferencelike phenomenon in which the therapist is invested by family members with a mantle like the six well-known institutional father figures: (1) the priest, minister, or rabbi; (2) the judge; (3) the physician; (4) the police officer; (5) the lawyer; and (6) the politician. These are celebrant roles assigned to a male therapist, and Zuk believes that a female therapist may also assume the mantles of a school teacher and/or a social service agent. Transference in this situation is limited to giving authority to the therapist, not to transference in the usual psychoanalytic concept as something to be worked through.

There are two types of cases in which the therapist is most likely cast as a celebrant: the lower-class family and families interviewed at a crisis point. These families typically allow the therapist access for a limited period of time and do not involve long-term situations. There is apt to be an awe as well as distrust of the therapist's expertise and an unwillingness to enter a long-term therapy with an outsider who has superior education.

Short-term therapy with lower-class and crisis-oriented cases is prone to demand a specific type of short-term therapy. Within the restrictions imposed on the therapist's power and authority. The overinflation takes the form of the therapist's having indefinite authority to attribute to him or her qualities of familiar authorities such as the priest, judge, physician, or lawyer. To invest the therapist with this high as the priest, judge, physician, or lawyer. To invest the therapist with this high mantle of respect helps to provide closure for the short-term therapy family.

The therapist must recognize that as a celebrant he or she has a very powerful therapeutic position; however, the therapist has this position only for a brief time and does not so much introduce change into the family as "celebrate" the fact that a change has occurred or is about to occur. The family empowers the therapist to certify that something has happened or is about to happen that is important to them and therefore requires the presence and observance of a quasi-representative of one of the powerful institutions of our society.

Whether the therapist wishes it or not, families will view him or her as a celebrant on certain occasions. In fact, with certain families and in certain situations, that is the only role available to the therapist, and he or she must make the most of it if he or she is to have impact on the family. There are times when the therapist can move from the celebrant role to that of the go-between or side taker. There will be other occasions when, after the family has explored some conflicts and the therapist has developed the go-between process by moving back and forth with the go-between role and the side-taker role, that the family will view him or her in the celebrant role.

Zuk (1975) believes that the ethnic or racial factor is significant in determining the therapist's celebrant role. He suggests that with black, lower-class families the therapist is often viewed as a quasi-political figure, whereas Jewish families are more likely to cast the therapist as a lawyer or judge and catholic families may view the therapist as a quasi-priest.

Zuk argues that the therapist is cast as a celebrant because the family is a conservative unit and that the conservatism requires families to expect the therapist to function as a quasi-representative of a powerful institution in the society. Therefore, the therapist is expected to act like the priest, physician, or judge. This conservatism of the family's experiencing a problem indicates that it will not tolerate very well, especially in early interviews, a therapist's wide departure from its expectations about him or her as a quasi-priest, judge, or physician. Zuk's position is that families do not tolerate very well the therapist who uses profanity, is overly clumsy, whose attire varies too much from the norm, and whose suggestions seem too foolish or diverse from the family's values. Additionally, he believes that the family's conservatism leads its members to prefer a therapist over forty, male, and white. He does say that, although age, sex, and race of a therapist may turn some families off, in a majority of cases this is not the fact. He does not believe that a family therapist should be "a square," but he does think that a therapist should take special effort not to violate the conservatism that the family denotes.

The family therapist's role of a celebrant is a change agent in that he or she helps to seal a step in the process of change. The therapist testifies that a change has occurred or is about to occur, and with some families that may be the only function that the therapist is permitted.

The Go-between

The go-between process presumes that conflict is a characteristic part of the situation and that most individuals will take steps to check its magnitude. One of the major steps is to search for and select someone empowered to mediate the conflict. The power of this person, this go-between, to change the nature of the conflict and also to promote change in each principal is an important role for the therapist.

The role of the go-between is generally more than that typically associated with the role of the mediator. The mediator typically seeks to clarify issues; however, the go-between in family therapy may intentionally confuse issues. The mediator is generally one who claims and is assigned the role whereas the go-between role may shift among the participants in family therapy and also the go-between specifically denies that he or she is acting as such.

The go-between may be very active, obtrusive, and confronting or be inactive and passive. The person may move into the role of go-between by attacking two parties that he or she hopes to have become principals, or the person may move into the role by pointing out the differences between two parties. The person can become a go-between by refusing to take sides in a dispute or by presenting a new view of a disagreement.

The go-between decides if he or she will ask the principals to change their positions. The go-between may also decide that his or her position is not strong enough for him or her to ask for changes. Obviously, then, the go-between may be weak or strong. The go-between may be weak if he or she has been seduced into taking the role of go-between by a principal who wishes to split an already established alliance. The power will be in the hands of the individual in family therapy who controls the go-between process. This does not necessarily go to the individual who takes the role of go-between. Therefore, the therapist can cast himself or herself as a principal in the conflict, hoping that a family member who might otherwise be a strong, opposing principal will become a relatively weak go-between. The therapist, therefore, rearranges and, it is hoped, diminishes the resister force in the family against him or her.

The go-between has considerable therapeutic power because the principals empower the go-between to secure certain changes in their positions with each other. Their acceptance of the therapist as go-between signals a readiness to move from their fixed positions. Certainly each principal hopes the go-between will act mainly in his or her interest against an opposing principal. This permits the go-between to exert leverage against the opposing principals with the aim of securing significant changes that he or she deems therapeutic. In the go-between role, the therapist can introduce initiatives not suggested by the principals and can use therapeutic power by delaying or speeding up his or her arbitration.

In summary, the go-between focuses on the current issue on which the family members are in conflict. He or she encourages the family members to define and change the areas and terms of agreement and disagreement among themselves. He or she establishes limits and rules out certain behaviors during the discussion of the conflict. A major source of leverage of the go-between is the therapist's capacity to introduce initiatives and alternatives not proposed by the principals. Behavioral assignments are used to bring family conflicts into sharper focus. The family can be asked to remember or to recreate conflicts, thereby permitting the therapist to confirm or revise his or her concepts of their psychogenic relating as the therapist sees it during the interview (Garrigan and Bambrick, 1975).

Side Taker

In the role of side taker, the therapist directly supports the position of one family member to shift or reduce the pathogenic patterns. The therapist may take sides on an issue with one family member and observe how the family members realign themselves in coalitions, alliances, or cliques to maintain the status quo of pathogenic relating. Through this maneuver the therapist gains knowledge about how to intervene more effectively at other opportune moments.

The therapist will be called upon to take sides with regard to the three main problem areas: conflicts between husband and wife, conflicts between parents and children, and conflicts between the family and community agencies. The therapist will not be able to avoid taking sides; therefore, the therapist should be prepared to respond according to a rational scheme. When siding with a husband in a conflict with his wife, parents in a conflict with their children, or the community in conflict with the family, the therapist expresses what Zuk refers to as "discontinuity values." When siding with the wife, the children, and the family in the conflicts, the therapist is supporting "continuity values." It is apparent that the therapist's personal values will be involved in his or her side taking; however, these must be applied in a manner that will be productive for the particular family.

Critique and Evaluation

Zuk developed his approach from his own experience, and the concepts of therapy seem logical. The idea of taking sides and negotiating between people has a commonsense aspect. In fact, there has been some research to evaluate Zuk's go-between approach. Two studies by Garrigan and Bambrick (1975, 1977) report research using short-term family therapy for families with emotionally disturbed children. They report outcomes in which the identified child's symptoms were significantly reduced in the classroom and at home. Parents were also able to reestablish communication on a more meaningful level. This therapy was conducted by doctoral students who received 150 hours of training in Zuk's approach, which suggests that the techniques can be taught in a relatively brief training program.

The disturbing aspect of Zuk's approach is the elitist position of superiority attitude regarding people. One could say there are tones of class, race, and sex bias. His delineation of the groups for whom the various types of therapy are appropriate indicates class and racial biases. His views of the family indicate sexism. The generalizations about people are too broad and not true for too many.

It seems reasonable to not use the generalization but to examine the techniques and apply them with the specific family. The process and techniques seem a viable approach to family therapy.

References

Garrigan, J., and Bambrick, A. 1975. Short-term family therapy with emotionally disturbed children. *Journal of Marriage and Family Counseling* 1:379–385.

——, and Bambrick, A. 1977. Family therapy for disturbed children: Some experimental results in special education. *Journal of Marriage and Family Counseling* 3:83–93.

Keniston, K. 1965. *The uncommitted: Alienated youth in American society*. New York: Harcourt Brace.

Zuk, G. 1971. *Family therapy: A triadic-based approach*. New York: Behavioral Publications.

——. 1975. *Process and practice in family therapy*. Haverford, Pa.: Psychiatry and Behavioral Science Books.

——. 1979. Value systems and pyschopathology in family therapy. *International Journal of Family Therapy* 1:133–151.

13

The Multiple Family Therapy of Hans Peter Laqueur

Hans Peter Laqueur is best known for starting multiple family therapy (MFT). The composition of this group is emphasized more than his method, although he used an eclectic systems approach with humanistic–existential touches emphasizing changes of behavior followed by "insight." The frequency and diversity of use of this procedure, which involves a number of families meeting together with a therapist or therapists, is increasing rapidly. MFT is currently used to treat a motley of family types, for example, families with schizophrenic members (Laqueur, Wells, and Agresti, 1969); with prisoners (Ostby, 1968); with problematic adolescents (Leichter and Schulman, 1968; Paul and Bloom, 1970); with drug addicts (Bartlett, 1975); and with "well" members (Papp, Silverstein, and Carter, 1973), in addition to taking on a variety of forms and structures. Although Laqueur worked mostly with young, hospitalized, schizophrenic patients, his method has also been used in child guidance centers, outpatient settings, day treatment centers, postdischarge follow-up, family service institutes, and correctional institutions (Benningfield, 1978; Laqueur, 1977).

Laqueur was born in 1909 in Koenigsberg, Germany. He was educated as a psychiatrist at the University of Amsterdam. He spent the World War II years as a captain in a Dutch army hospital in Buenos Aires, Argentina. After the war he continued his training at Columbia University. He held academic appointments at Adelphi College, Mt. Sinai School of Medicine, and University of Vermont. His experience was at La Fargue Clinic, Mt. Sinai Hospital, Morningside Community Center and West Queens Child Guidance Center, all in New York City; at Creedmore State Hospital; and, before he died (in 1979), at the State Hospital at Waterbury, Vermont.

The practice of MFT began almost by accident around 1960. Dr. Laqueur was in charge of a seventeen-bed insulin therapy ward at Creedmore State Hospital. He began meeting with the families of patients after visiting hours on Sundays to explain treatment. The families continued talking among themselves outside on the lawn. The talks evolved into open meetings with families and patients. The patients did not want to be left out. They felt that something secretive was going on without them. Dr. Laqueur then organized the Auxiliary Council, structured along the lines of a PTA. Its members volunteered time, provided funds and equipment, and helped other family members. When he took over a one hundred-bed intensive treatment wing, Laqueur accepted only patients whose families would be willing to come to the family meetings. The council scheduled groups of four or five families, including their hospitalized members, to meet with a therapist for an hour once a week. The therapist did meet with individual families if the need arose. Most of the patients were defined as young schizophrenics.

One of the reasons for beginning MFT was to help patients adapt to their families when they returned home. Many patients, despite some improvement during hospitalization, frequently regressed upon returning home. This regression led to the idea that the families of the patients were part of the problem of the schizophrenic illness. Therapeutic work with the families could help the patients improve more during and after hospitalization. Leichter and Schulman (1974) reported on their Multi-Family Group Therapy practice, which was similar to Laqueur's. They had developed open-ended groups that the families attended for a rather short period of time, but the group itself tended to go on for a long period of time.

MFT was born because there were not enough therapists to go around in the hospitals and has been used in a variety of ways: weekend marathons, groups from three to thirty families, groups of children and divorced mothers, and groups that are open ended and closed. Laqueur looked upon MFT as a "sheltered workshop in family communication" (1970). He also said that he helped families to help themselves. He felt that the therapist must not only train family members to communicate but must make them aware of their true feelings.

Laqueur was influenced about general systems theory by von Bertalanffy, Ruesch and Bateson, Grinker and Spiegel, Gray and MacIver, and Carl Menninger (Chapter 1). Some of his exercises sound very much like those of Virginia Satir, whom he cited (Chapter 4). In one example of this influence, Laqueur had two people with different opinions stand opposite each other with arms outstretched and hands on each other's shoulders. One stated a wish or command and then shouted "yes" while the other shouted "no."

MFT involves four to five patients, hospitalized or not, who are mostly schizophrenics. They and their nearest relatives or family meet with a therapist, cotherapist, and observers. The weekly sessions meet in the evening hours to ensure participation of working family members. MFT is open ended, with a new family's taking the place of an old family that has shown sufficient improvement. The groups are as random as possible in socioeconomic, ethnic, religious, political, and age characteristics. The new family is told that the therapists do not believe in patient versus healthy family members but that they work on disturbed interaction patterns in the entire family to help them all.

Laqueur saw the family as a system and the MFT group as a larger system. On the basis of their experiences, people develop faulty ways of dealing with stress. This leads to bad habits, addictions, poor communications, and, sometimes, serious illness (Laqueur, 1973a).

Laqueur, in describing his basic assumption about the human condition, succinctly stated that

> No matter what culture, social setting, or time period a family finds itself in, there are specific human behavior patterns that can help people grow and live creatively, while there are others that lead to stunted growth, mutual fear, evasive and non-communicative actions and eventually breakdown and sickness in one or several family members. (1973b, p. 197)

Based on this belief, he argued that it is critical for families to uncover their unhealthy patterns. Then, with the help of the MFT group members and the therapist(s), they can develop new ways of relating and communicating, which will be more creative and growth producing.

Laqueur delineated different types of families who appear in MFT groups (1976). The most disturbed are those in which everyone in the family is isolated from everyone else. Discussion of mundane topics is the only interaction in this type of family. Families that divide themselves along generation or sex lines are considered somewhat healthier. Another type of unhealthy family is one in which two members form a tight symbiotic relationship, while all other family members remain disconnected. Closer toward health are families in which one person, most often the mother, controls all communication and relating in the family. Similarly, there are families that adhere to a strict hierarchy. (Generally, Laqueur noted, the person at the top of the hierarchy rarely comes to the group and often must be reached through the other family members.) The healthiest type of family one sees in an MFT group is one in which most members are in contact and communicating with each other, leaving out only one member, the identified patient. Laqueur's "ideal family" was one in which everyone communicates with everyone else, on both cognitive and emotional levels.

Families with a symptomatic member have a sickness-provoking behavioral pattern that the therapist must detect. When the families themselves discover these patterns, they become free to change, become healthier, and lead fuller lives.

Laqueur does not seem to differentiate among families according to their functionality. A new family is told briefly that he does not believe in primary patient versus healthy family members but that he likes to deal with disturbed interaction patterns in the entire family in order to help them all.

In selecting families for MFT, some practitioners (Lansky et al., 1978) feel that (1) it is best to have some homogeneity among the families; (2) it is helpful if no more than two generations of family are allowed in the group; (3) within the range of pathology, patients should at least be enough in touch with reality to participate appropriately; and (4) some communality of problems should exist to ensure more empathy between families. When MFT is used with a broader spectrum of patients, some researchers (Wellish, Mosher, and Scoy, 1978) feel it best to screen families to see which will benefit from one or two conjoint sessions and which need longer

MFT sessions. Some feel that some preparation for MFT sessions will cause less regression of other families in the ongoing sessions. Laqueur felt that MFT groups should be as random as possible. The more one selects families for special factors, the higher the possibility of pseudointellectualism (Laqueur, 1970, 1972a, 1972b, 1973b, 1976).

History Taking or Equivalent

No history taking of the patient is done as such because none is necessary, but, for most hospitalized patients, the history is available and obtainable from standard psychiatric evaluations on admission.

Diagnostic Framework or Equivalent

By the same token, standard psychiatric nomenclature seems to be used to speak about the identified patient and his or her family. The diagnostic framework used by Laqueur implied that the whole family's interaction patterns need to be helped to help the primary patient. Classification of problems by diseases was rejected.

Therapeutic Foci

Influenced by Kurt Lewin's field theory, Laqueur developed the notion of the "delineation of the field of interaction." The therapist notes the interaction between subsystems, such as the family, and the suprasystem, the total environment. The therapists helps the clients to understand their relationships in the total field. Additionally, the therapist has a much greater variety of therapeutic interventions from which to choose in this system than in a dyadic relationship. Due to the large number of individuals in each group, someone is often able to "break the intra-familial code," a difficult-to-understand communication style, when the therapist is unable to do so. From this point, therapy can progress more easily. Competition between families is yet another mechanism that pushes families toward better, healthier relationships. Family can often amplify signals given by the therapist to those in the group who do not receive them. In this way, the therapist is not required to keep pressing the same point.

Families can also "learn by analogy." For example, one family might observe another family with a similar difficulty, but with a more effective way of dealing with the problem. Then, through "trial and error," they begin experimenting with different and, finally, more healthy behaviors in the group. Inasmuch as the group includes a whole spectrum of people—men, women, and children (who are fathers, husbands, children, siblings, etc.) as well as the therapist—it provides an excellent forum in which to learn new behaviors and test them in a not-too-threatening microcosm of the general public. "Learning by identifying with others"—for example, fathers with fathers, sisters with sisters—can also be therapeutic. Similar to learning by analogy is "using models." Rather than learning by comparing solutions to problem situations, people model their behaviors after healthier behaviors exhibited by others in the group. Keeping MFT groups open ended means that there are always families at different stages of treatment. Therefore, there are always people to learn from (Laqueur, 1976).

When a family comes to a Laqueur group, its members are told that the group is designed to help improve family relationships and to teach people how to help each other with their problems. They are told that they may choose how much of their problem they wish to discuss during the group. Families are allowed to increase their participation gradually in the group. This is important when group members all begin the group at different times. Whereas some members have developed a high degree of trust with other members over time, new members are not ready to be as open about deeply personal issues. As mentioned earlier, the therapist(s) acts as an orchestra conductor who must know the score, know where he or she is going with each family, and have long-and-short-term goals (Laqueur, 1973b).

Although the family generally enters therapy wishing to help the identified patient, the therapist's first job is to explain the philosophy of the group. It is explained that the patient is not dealt with as "sick" and needing to be cured; rather, the group tries to help the family see disturbed interactional patterns that keep them all from being happy, fulfilled people. All families serve as co-therapists to help other families ferret out their destructive patterns. Then they may help by offering suggestions based on their own experiences. All the other curative factors mentioned earlier operate simultaneously.

If the talk becomes "chatty" or superficial, the therapist should step in. This kind of nonproductive talk means that the therapist is not being active enough. A good session is considered one in which emotional problems are discussed and all families participate. The therapist(s) can get the discussion started by picking up on commonalities experienced by the group members. This usually leads to conversations among the various families. Role playing between members of different families, psychodrama, and art therapy are all MFT procedures used to increase the families' self-understanding.

Therapeutic Goals

To Laqueur, the ultimate goal of therapy was improved communication in families, leading to improved relationships. The goal in MFT is not to resolve individual pathology; rather, it concentrates on disturbed relationships and intergroup interfaces. The goal of improved communications within families is seen in the therapist's attempt to restore a free flow of information to correct faulty communication. A more specific goal may be to channel information back to the patient and open up a feedback loop of behavior analysis that did not previously exist in the family.

The second major goal is improving understanding of family functioning and dynamics through mutual understanding between patients and families. This can develop increased introspection in the family. Such heightened perception and sensitivity to the environment may be aimed specifically at nonverbal communication or at uncovering conflict that has led to blocked communication.

The third major area of change is the family's functioning. Laqueur felt (1970; Laqueur and LaBurt, 1964) that the family needs to change its behavior pattern. The family needs to be helped to learn to tolerate the open feelings of others, be they loving or critical, and to strengthen its defenses against seduction and apprehension.

A fourth focus is on family and marital roles. Goals are to demonstrate roles not only in areas of family life but also in peer relations, work, and education. Supportive roles are observed in other families. Ambiguous roles are clarified, pecking orders are altered, and the scapegoated member is less isolated. Also, the family stigma of having a "crazy" member is reduced.

Although the therapeutic goals are derived from the problems presented by the families, Laqueur saw all families as having similar problems. The goals of the patient, family, therapist, and institution need to approximate each other for optimal benefit to all.

Luber and Wells (1977) reported on a structured short-term (seven-session) multiple family therapy treatment. They used the techniques of homework assignments, sculpting, exploring multigenerational family patterns, and poetry. This study shows that the composition of a group made up of more than one family does not necessarily mean that the techniques and methods are the same.

Therapeutic Processes

The principal processes used in MFT are

1. *Learning by analogy.* With several families in this group, one father can learn father-type behavior from other fathers in the group, and so on. This observation can be less threatening than in a smaller group in which there is more focus on one person's behavior.
2. *Learning by indirect interpretation.* The therapist can say something that could apply to all children in the room. If the patient thinks that this may apply to him or her, the patient can respond accordingly. If the patient were the only child in the room, he or she might build up defenses against this accusation.
3. *Use of models.* The therapist uses the healthier aspects of one family as a model and a challenge to motivate other families to change their own behavior. This could also mean one family's serving as a co-therapist to the group.
4. *Learning through identification.* Young people can learn from other young people, and one family's experience helps other families to cope with problems.
5. *Learning through trial and error.* Members of the group can try new modes of behavior and reinforce them if they are approved by the group. New insights may be achieved through role playing.
6. *Modeling healthier coping patterns.* The therapist asks families to describe their reaction and behavior to different family situations.
7. *Breaking the intrafamilial code.* Every family with a schizophrenic member

seems to develop a code for internal verbal and nonverbal communications. Often other families are more effective at breaking these codes and are able to help the therapist.

8. *Amplification and modulation of signals.* A sensitive member of the group can pick up on what the therapist says and repeat or amplify a statement and give it to the group. This may be further commented on by someone else. This multiple impact makes a greater impression on the group than if only the therapist said something once to the group.

Therapeutic Stages

Laqueur divided each session into four parts. In the first part the therapist asks the group if it wishes to pursue a previous topic or start a new one. The second phase occurs when the therapist describes the first common denominator beginning to form in the discussion. In the third phase the therapist reviews the common denominator and its discussion by the group. The fourth phase is the end-of-group summing up.

The first stage of MFT treatment is often one of relief. There is an expectation, to some degree unreal, that "something is to be done," which in turn generates a spark of hope. On the other hand, the first stage of treatment also may involve a denial of problems by the families, followed by feelings of being blamed for causing the patient's illness. There may be a division among group members in the initial state according to familial structure or identified patient status. During the first phase, reduction of symptoms often occurs, bringing about a feeling of relief. Seeing other families improve sparks a feeling of hope. When family members actually realize that the problem of the identified patient is a systems problem, however, they become resistant to change. When the family accepts the problem as a family problem, and the family members feel safe enough to try new behaviors, real changes begin to occur. In addition, these families are now able to serve as models for families still at an earlier phase.

Laqueur described the second stage as "resistance to treatment," in which the individual sees that change of attitude and behavior is required from him or her as the one who behaved in such a way that misunderstanding and rejection came about. Behavior of people and families during this stage is often hesitant, reluctant, and argumentative. They may doubt that a person can change or be afraid of losing what little good relationship they do have if they open up and confront the "sleeping dogs" in their lives. During this stage, there is examination of feelings of guilt, failure, and helplessness, increased group interaction, and more direct communication among family members.

The final stage shows individuals' and families' openness and increased self-confidence. In this significant change phase, families come to realize the deeper problems and corresponding ability to deal with them with increased flexibility and number of options. There may be little insight into *individual* problems, but family members have gained a clearer understanding of how dysfunctional communication patterns and interactions have led to difficulty in the family.

Intervention Strategies

Intervention strategies are both verbal and nonverbal:

1. Children divide themselves into two groups, the so-called "good" children, and the "bad" children. Each states his or her problems with the family. This shows problems with good children, too, through learning by analogy.
2. The dyadic relationship is explored with exercises such as yes–if, yes–but, and yes–and and with back-to-back arm locking. Laqueur uses sculpting according to the technique of Papp, Silverstein, and Carter (1973). Videotaping is played back to the group to study body language and contradictions between verbal and nonverbal signals.

Laqueur does not treat the "sick" individual but detects sickness-provoking mutual behavior in families. He lets the families discover such patterns with him so that families may act as co-therapists and teach each other possibilities for change, for coping with problems in a new way.

Role of the Therapist

It is the therapist's task to prevent fruitless discussions of specific behavioral issues. The therapist must provide the MFT group with necessary information for its work on a deeper level. Thus, the therapist provides descriptive information relating to such things as hurt expressions, signs of rejection or rebellion, and intolerance. The therapist attempts to elicit feelings and make those that are covert manifest. Finally, the therapist aims to locate and display for the group the dyadic and triadic alliances and counteralliances that are continually forming and reforming. Group members should become aware of these issues so that they are able later to deal with these problems on their own.

Laqueur felt that therapists should be active in their sessions, as "conductors with their orchestra" (1972b), that is, therapists must know their scores, must know where they are going with these families, and must have short-term and long-term plans for the interactions that they mean to produce. They should not intervene aggressively and close out people who give momentary discomfort. They should respect the "soloist," bring up the shy, and hold back the loud. It is much more comforting to ascribe symptoms to medical or biological causes than to personal attitudes and behaviors that must be modified. "We don't know whether behavior change should precede or follow change in insight. In most instances insight comes later. Better mutual attitudes come first."

Laqueur (1970) saw four qualities as necessary for a multiple family therapist. First, the therapist must be original in handling new situations. Second, the therapist must be able to adjust to cases of unusual group malfunction. Third, the therapist must be able to show initiative in the choice of previously unused approaches to critical situations. Fourth, the therapist must have an excellent sense of timing.

Laqueur's method is circular due to his emphasis on general systems theory. Each open-living system, be it a person or a group, depends on orderly processing of input data, on efficient selection of relevant information, on decision making, and on effective output of actions, the results of which must be fed back for assessment, correction, and adaptive future action. Any friction or malfunction among component parts, including decrease in the discriminatory power of internal and external sensors, leads to a decreased efficiency and survival capability. To survive, a family must be able to perceive and head off external dangers (physical, biological, political, economic) as well as internal frictions (paralyzing quarrels, mutual putdown, and discouragement). If the therapist detects processes that interfere with survival abilities, the therapist must intervene and correct the malfunction before it becomes fatal. If there is a delay at the feedback loop, people may overlook warning signals, while faster perception of such danger could help to avoid collisions. Thinking about the family from a general systems theory viewpoint has helped to see the handling of overloads through bypass techniques and the impairment and restoration of external and internal signal sensitivities. With this circular interaction between therapist and group members, it is possible to produce a "focus of excitation" and interest that can generate insights in many people who otherwise might be left behind. This mechanism Laqueur derived from information theory. According to this theory, those behaviors have the highest information value that have the least probability of occurring and yet do occur. This new pattern or sequence of signals produces an excitation focus in the nervous system and has significant information value (1972a).

Laqueur related the observation of the questioning of a disturbed patient by the eight-year-old son of an older patient. The patient was deliberately holding back expression of his feelings but was disarmed by the innocence and sincerity of the small boy. The staff knew that it could not have asked the question without the patient's having withdrawn still further. The patient responded and expressed his deep and negative feelings for the first time and accepted the support of the group.

The role of the therapist, then, is to (1) detect and recognize features of the affective rather than the cognitive exchanges across interfaces and boundaries; (2) identify with hostility and rage, seductiveness, anxiety and fear, hopelessness, frustration, perplexity, and abandonment; and (3) point this out to individuals and identify constellations among group members, so that what the twenty or so individuals share in feelings and attitudes becomes more important to them than what they "know" or "do not know." Therefore, the therapist must be active, neutral, and circular.

Critique and Evaluation

In summary, Laqueur's multiple family groups have been described as "a sheltered workshop in family communication" (Laqueur, 1972b, p. 405). Laqueur himself described MFT as a program designed to teach families to help themselves (1973b).

Laqueur's theoretical assumptions seem quite logical and reasonable. His theory is based on general systems thinking, the main differences being in the composition of multifamily groups in this therapy. From accounts of his sessions, he seems to have practiced the theory he claimed.

Laqueur (1977) claimed the following improvements in disturbed or unstable family systems: (1) better function and creative operation even within difficult family environments, (2) better mutual liking and respect, (3) better acceptance of shortcomings and capitalization on each other's strengths, (4) better ability to enjoy day-to-day living, (5) greater ability for compassion, mutual love, understanding, support, and cooperation, (6) building of lasting and satisfying relationships with each other, with friends, and environment, (7) better insights and improved judgment, (8) greater openness to new information, and (9) greater wisdom, sense of humor, and willingness to help others.

MFT could be considered high on the list of cost-efficient treatment modalities, as a large number of people is helped at the same time. This means the time of the therapist and the money of the family or hospital goes farther.The average patient and his or her family stay with the open-ended group from six to eighteen months. MFT has been used by many groups as a cost-effective method during times of limited resources for social services. It has been used not only in hospitals but in schools, prisons, drug treatment programs, and guidance centers as well. It has helped the acute and chronically ill deal with their problems (Strelnick, 1977).

Although a number of fairly rigorous outcome studies (Harrow et al., 1967; Shaeffer, 1969) as well as outcome reports (Barcai, 1967; Laqueur and Lebovic, 1968; Leichter and Schulman, 1974) have been published, more rigorous outcome research is critical. One problem is a lack of precise measurement devices (Benningfield, 1978). It is hard to compare length of treatment with that of other therapists' patients, because many of Laqueur's patients were hospitalized and were probably more psychiatrically ill than are those in outpatient clinics or private hospitals. Evaluatively, there is, according to Benningfield (1978), not enough research on the outcome of MFT or, for that matter, on the whole field of family therapy. Benningfield found only three reports based on actual research of MFT and three other reports showing reduced rate of readmission for patients. All other outcome reports are based on clinical impressions or observations of the authors. She reviewed twenty-five authors who reported on MFT. Hospital readmission of patients participating in MFT suggests its effectiveness. Three reports done on empirical research show reduced readmission. The remaining reports of outcomes were based on clinical impressions or observations of the authors. They reported MFT as an effective treatment modality.

Laqueur (various sources) reported on fifteen hundred families in more than twenty-five years. He cited improved communication, reduction in frequency and length of hospitalization, and restructured intrafamilial relationships for greater understanding in families. DeWitt (1978) researched the effectiveness of family therapy. In her study she found Laqueur's treated families with the following results: 15 per cent worse or no change, 18 per cent some improvement, and 67 per cent definite improvement. These results compare with Bowen (Chapter 9) at 33 per cent worse or no change, 42 per cent some improvement, and 8 per cent for definite improvement. Haley (Chapter 6) had 58 per cent in the no-change category and 42 per cent in the improvement category, whereas Minuchin (Chapter 7) scored 71 per cent worse or no change and 29 per cent definite improvement.

According to Laqueur, changes in internal power distribution and behavior occur faster with MFT than with individual family treatment because the external influencing system (the therapists versus the families) is stronger and richer with more varied resources. The family sees how the environment—not just the family—affects an individual and how he or she affects the behavior of those around him or her.

MFT is unique in that it alone allows the suprasystem, the outside world or society, to enter into the therapeutic relationship. In individual therapy the therapist and patient close themselves off from the rest of the world. Information from "out there" only enters through the patient's perception, and the therapist has no direct means of checking the accuracy of this information.

Peer group therapy brings the therapist together with several patients, but, again, the outside information comes through the patient's perception. The patient cannot see his or her interactions with the "significant others" in his or her life, let alone those with society. Conjoint family therapy and social network therapy both focus primarily on the identified patient and only bring in persons directly concerned with the identified patient's problems. Only in MFT is society present in the form of several families other than the patient's family, who are not directly concerned with the patient's or family's fates. The therapist not only directly observes the patient in the context of his family system but also the family system in its relationship with a suprasystem, the MFT group. This makes the MFT group a truly open system for information input.

A large number of important questions are unanswered, and specific areas of research await reliable measuring tools for MFT as well as for family therapy. Questions include

1. For what populations is MFT most appropriate?
2. Would MFT be useful as an adjunct to conjoint or individual therapy, either preceding it to open up the family or following it to help the family assimilate their gains?
3. Is this mode indicated for certain types of families but not for others?
4. Is MFT more effective than conjoint family therapy?
5. What is the "active ingredient" in MFT's success?

When these questions and the many others are answered reliably, MFT can be used most effectively.

In conclusion, MFT is an effective, economic, and fairly reliable method of therapy. It has worked with severely disorganized, socially and psychologically disadvantaged families who were quite unaccustomed to self-examination or self-expression. It has many built-in safety features, which may minimize dangers, and the opportunities for improving performance may be rather substantial. The motto of the entire transaction is to teach families to help each other.

Multiple family therapy links family therapy with more extended network interventions. Laqueur has shown that it is possible to work therapeutically with more than one family at a time. If and when many clinics complain of overload of referrals and waiting lists for clients-patients, one can indicate how Laqueur pointed the way (Raasoch and Laqueur, 1979).

References

American Psychiatric Association. 1977. *Biographical directory of the fellows and members of the American Psychiatric Association.* New York: Jacques Catrell.

Barcai, A. 1967. An adventure in multiple family therapy. *Family Process* 6: 185–192.

Bartlett, D. 1975. The use of multiple family therapy groups with adolescent drug addicts. In *The adolescent in group and family therapy,* ed. M. Sugar, pp. 262–282. New York: Brunner/Mazel.

Benningfield, A. B. 1978. Multiple family therapy systems. *Journal of Marriage and Family Counseling* 4:25–34.

DeWitt, K. 1978. Effectiveness of family therapy. *Archives of General Psychiatry* 35:549–561.

Frager, S. 1978. Multiple family therapy; A literature review. *Family Therapy* 5:105–120.

Harrow, M.; Astrachen, B.; Becker, R.; Detre, T.; and Schwartz, A. 1967. An investigation into the nature of the patient–family therapy group. *American Journal of Orthopsychiatry* 38:888–899.

Lansky, M. R.; Bley, C. R.; McVey, G. G.; and Brotman, B. 1978. Multiple family groups as aftercare. *International Journal of Group Psychotherapy* 28:211–224.

Laqueur, H. P. 1970. Multiple family therapy and general systems theory. In Family therapy in transition, ed. N. W. Ackerman *International Psychiatry Clinics* 7:99–124.

———. 1972a. Mechanisms of change in multiple family therapy. In *Progress in group and family therapy,* eds. C. Sager and H. Kaplan, pp. 400–415. New York: Brunner/Mazel.

———. 1972b. Multiple family therapy. In *The book of family therapy,* eds. A. Ferber, M. Mendelsohn, and A. Napier, pp. 618–636. New York: Science House.

———. 1973a. Multiple family therapy: Questions and answers. In *Techniques of family psychotherapy: A primer,* ed. D. A. Bloch, pp. 75–85. New York: Grune & Stratton.

———. 1973b. Multiple family therapy: Questions and answers. *Seminars in Psychiatry* 5:195–205.

———. 1976. Multiple family therapy. In *Family therapy: Theory and practice,* ed. P. J. Guerin, Jr., pp. 405–416. New York: Gardner Press.

———. 1977. Family therapy (multiple) and general systems theory. In *International encyclopedia of psychiatry, psychology, psychoanalysis and neurology,* ed. B. B. Wolman, pp. 312–324. vol. 4. New York: Aesculapius Publishers.

———, and LaBurt, H. A. 1964. Multiple family therapy. *Mental Hygiene 1964,* 48:544–551.

———; LaBurt, H. A.; and Morong, E. 1964. Multiple family therapy. In *Current psychiatric therapies* ed. J. H. Masserman, pp. 150–154. vol. 4. New York: Grune & Stratton.

———, and Lebovic, R. 1968. Correlation between multiple family therapy: Acute crisis in a therapeutic community, and drug levels. *Diseases of the Nervous System* 29:188–192.

——; Wells, C. F.; and Agresti, M. 1969. Multiple family therapy in a state hospital. *Hospital and Community Psychiatry* 20:13–20.

Leichter E., and Schulman, G. 1968. Emerging phenomena in multi-family group treatment. *International Journal of Group Psychotherapy* 18:59–69.

——, and Schulman, G. 1974. Multi-family group therapy: A multi-dimensional approach. *Family Process* 13:95–110.

Luber, R., and Wells, R. A. 1977. Structural short-term multiple family therapy: An educational approach. *International Journal of Group Psychotherapy* 27:43–57.

Ostby, C. H. 1968. Conjoint group therapy with prisoners and their families. *Family Process* 7:184–201.

Papp, P.; Silverstein, O.; and Carter, E. 1973. Family sculpting in preventive work and with well families. *Family Process* 12:49–57.

Paul, N. L., and Bloom, J. D. 1970. Multiple family therapy: Secrets and scapegoating in family crisis. *International Journal of Group Psychotherapy* 20:37–47.

Raasoch, J., and Laqueur, H. P. 1979. Learning multiple family therapy through simulated workshops. *Family Process* 18:95–98.

Shaeffer, D. S. 1969. Effects of frequent hospitalization on the behavior of psychotic patients in a multiple family therapy program. *Journal of Clinical Psychology* 25:104–105.

Strelnick, A. H. 1977. Multiple family group therapy: A review of the literature. *Family Process* 16:307–325.

Wellish, D. K.; Mosher, M. B.; and Scoy, C. V. 1978. Management of family emotion stress: Family group therapy in a private oncology practice. *International Journal of Group Psychotherapy* 28:225–231.

14

The Multiple Impact Theory of Robert MacGregor and the Youth Development Project

As a technique for working with families, multiple impact therapy (MIT) is the result of an extended study by the family psychotherapy research staff at the University of Texas, Medical Branch, Youth Development Project. The Youth Development Project originated as an outpatient clinic organized in 1952 to study and treat adolescents and their families. The project goal was to utilize the rapid behavioral changes that occur in adolescence in the development of a brief therapy particularly suited to the problems of families with adolescent members (MacGregor et al., 1964).

The preadolescent and adolescent youngsters studied by the project staff were seen as particularly accessible to a brief psychotherapeutic intervention because of the rapid personality integration they were experiencing. The families of these adolescents were also open to change as a result of the crises presented by the respective adolescent youngsters. When the family experienced a strong need for change, effective therapeutic interventions could be kept at a minimum. In light of this belief and the reality that many parents were not able to participate in conventional, weekly treatment programs with their adolescent child because of time, distance, or economic limitations, the project team pursued the notion of developing an intensive, short-term therapy for those families. The project team thought that the obstacles to family group treatment could be eliminated and the family's self-rehabilitative processes motivated if the adolescent, the parents, and other significant family or community members were able to meet for two consecutive days of intensive work with a multidisciplinary psychotherapy team. The therapeutic team would consist of one or more psychiatrists, psychologists, and social workers who would meet with the family in varying group, individual, and multi-therapist situations.

Robert MacGregor was the research director of the demonstration project and

259

the major person to describe the approach. Co-directors were Harold Goolishian and Eugene McDonald, Jr., and the basic team members included Anges Ritchie, Franklin Schuster, and Alberto Serrano. MacGregor left Galveston in the 1970s to become a family therapy consultant for the Illinois Department of Mental Health and is presently the director of training at Henry Horner Children's Center, Chicago-Read Mental Health Center. Dr. MacGregor is the president of the Team Family Methods Association. Multiple impact therapy continues to be used in the University of Texas as well as in other clinical settings.

Three central ideas have guided the therapeutic team's efforts in multiple impact therapy. First, certain patterns of parental interaction are believed to produce and maintain specific forms of developmental arrest in adolescent youngsters. No description of adequate family interaction is provided, only dysfunctional interactions. Specific patterns of adolescent maladjustment have been identified, each of which correlates with a particular mode of parental and familial interaction. In each case, the adolescent's development is stymied by mutually exploitive relationships within the family that limit communication and cause each family member to persist in repetitive roles that are incompatible with growth. The adolescent patient's problem behavior is an expression of development arrested at a level beyond which the family is unable to foster growth.

Second, the therapeutic team's interaction with itself and with the family in crisis is believed to temporarily interrupt the arresting forces in the family by active participation in family discussions as a model of healthy interpersonal interaction. The team demonstrates effective communication by extended example so that the family can witness and participate in the give-and-take process that facilitates the resolution of interpersonal and intrafamilial difficulties. The integrity of the team, when interacting in the presence of the family, is believed to be the prime influence in helping the family become more objective and insightful about its own interactions.

Third, messages of respect from the team to the family regarding the family's ability to make changes in its way of interacting are believed to exert a favorable influence on the family's self-evaluative and self-rehabilitative processes. Respect for the family's predicament in general and each family member in particular is communicated by pointing out that the adolescent's behavior makes sense given the circumstances at home and in the community and by asking each member to explain his or her view of the family crisis. The growth potential of the family, when enhanced by an understanding of its members' recurring difficulties, is expected to improve over time without therapeutic supervision. The team respectfully challenges the family to use the insights gained in the intensive MIT experience to implement new, more meaningful interaction patterns.

The specific therapeutic activities that implement these central ideas include securing life history information, formulating and revising notions about family and individual dynamics, observing and interpreting the reactions of the family to the team and the team to the family, summarizing and reviewing data, defining interpersonal problems, and working on these problems openly until the family becomes aware of ways in which to achieve favorable changes in its patterns of interaction. The team interaction with the family is intended to expose the family to the dynamics of its problems in an atmosphere conducive to change. In general, the MIT approach does not follow a conventional psychoanalytic model. Insights may not appear during the two-day procedure itself but may come after time, once the family has had an opportunity to try the new patterns of interaction experienced with the team.

As with analytical and group analytical therapy, the goal of MIT is to evoke health rather than to suppress undesirable behavior. The therapist's persuasive effort is directed toward demonstrating confidence in the self-rehabilitative potential of the family. The project team disagrees with the notion that roles and illnesses in families can be understood completely through a homeostatic model. The team prefers to view families as potentially open systems. The latter position better accommodates the therapeutic mobilization of self-rehabilitative family processes and the aspects of growth that mediate an individual's emergence from the family nest (MacGregor et. al., 1964).

History Taking and Interview Methods

The first major step following a referral for multiple impact therapy is an intake conference. The conference includes the troubled adolescent, the parents and siblings, and relevant personnel from the referring agency. Prior to the actual conference with the family members, the therapeutic team and the representative from the referring agency meet in a briefing session. Information from the referring source is reviewed, and a tentative plan is made for staffing the individual conferences that follow the initial joint team–family conference. Speculations regarding family interactions are also made based on the background data in preparation for the intake meetings.

The intake conference itself is not a screening session but a planning session with diagnostic and therapeutic functions. The team collects historical data during the initial hour-long team–family conference and during the individual conferences that follow with various family members being seen in single or multiple therapist situations. Family and individual historical data unfold from this very first session onward.

During the opening team–family conference, the individual representing the referring agency introduces the family before attention is directed to the identified patient and the reason for referral. This team–family conference gives the team clues as to family interaction patterns, its strengths and its weaknesses. The team is able to highlight the critical aspects of the presenting problem to mobilize the family members to address their problems and to evoke self-rehabilitative processes. This conference helps to clarify the problem and starts the family thinking about its situation. Tentative formulations of the problem are made, and diagnostic or therapeutic measures are suggested regarding medical or psychological tests or drug therapy.

The initial team–family conference is followed by a series of individual conferences. Parents and/or siblings may also be seen together before being separated for their individual meetings. The individual conferences may help to relieve some of the tension that family members may have experienced in the initial team–family conference. These conferences are followed by a final team–family conference during which time the possibilities of a two-day MIT session, workshoplike therapy, or other therapeutic options are discussed with the family. The therapeutic plan best suited to the family is formulated during this session and is the product of a group decision. If a two-day MIT session is agreed upon, an appointment is made for the family to return to the clinic, and the family members are asked to collect more observations on some basic family issues before the next appointment. The team also openly expresses confidence in the family's ability to study themselves and to cope with the situation at home.

For some families the work of reinforcing the self-rehabilitating forces within the family was sufficiently underway during the intake meeting so that the full-scale two-day procedures were not necessary. The family had begun to pursue new avenues of thinking and observing in just a few therapeutic hours.

The intake session is more than just an information-gathering phase. Family treatment starts with the intake conferences and is continued at home if the self-rehabilitative processes of the family are mobilized or is further facilitated by the full-scale two-day MIT experience.

The interview methods used in the two-day MIT program are really extensions of the kinds of interviews utilized during the intake procedure. Before the family arrives, the team holds a briefing meeting to review the referral and intake data and make speculations regarding family dynamics. The team also studies each other for countertransference attitudes toward family members. Tentative plans are made as to which team members will meet with which family members in individual and overlapping interviews. The day then proceeds through a series of "impact" and "release" situations. Family members experience the impact of team–family conferences followed by the opportunity for release in individual sessions.

The opening team–family conference is followed by separate conferences, with individual family members' seeing one or more therapists at a time. These conferences may become overlapping sessions in which a therapist who has terminated his or her session with a family member joins another session still in progress. After a noon break for the family and a luncheon conference for the team, the team and family reconvene in separate conferences with different therapists. These conferences are followed by a team-parent conference and finally a team–family conference during which the entire group interacts and shares observations.

The second day of MIT follows a pattern of conferences much like that of the first day. There is an opening team–family conference followed by separate conferences with more overlapping sessions and a final team family conference.

The MIT technique uses a combination of group and individual therapy methods. The various conferences and interviews occur in rapid succession to take advantage of their cumulative therapeutic effect.

Diagnostic Framework

The MIT project team found that, in general, traditional diagnoses made at the time of referral for MIT failed to differentiate usefully among the various cases seen.

They noted, however, that each of the nominal patients could be identified as coming from one of four family patterns. Each of the four family patterns is associated with a particular level of developmental arrest that manifests itself in the behavior of the troubled adolescent. The most primitive level of arrest is manifested in schizophrenic reactions that represent an infantile maladjustment in adolescence. The second level of arrest is manifested in autocratic, nearly psychopathic, or nearly psychotic reactions that reflect a childish maladjustment in adolescence and preadolescence. The third level of arrest is manifested in neurotic or intimidated behaviors, which reflect a juvenile maladjustment in adolescence. And, the fourth level of arrest is manifested in personality disorders or rebellious behaviors, which reflect a preadolescent maladjustment in adolescence (MacGregor et. al., 1964; MacGregor, 1962; MacGregor, 1967).

These levels of developmental arrest are derived from the developmental epochs and tasks described by H. S. Sullivan and E. H. Erikson. The symptomatic behavior of these adolescents reflects their attempts to master developmental tasks that surpass their family's ability to be of assistance. It is this familywide arrest in development that MIT techniques address. The early diagnosis of a family into one of the four patterns of family functioning helps to coordinate the team's work. The work done in the intake session is very important here, as each family syndrome suggests different therapeutic goals.

The family provides a setting within which an individual becomes a distinct person, but it is impossible for any family to meet all the needs of its members. Family members need a variety of stimuli from outside the family to develop socially adaptive skills. Family members may be deprived of external stimuli when the family, or specific individuals in the family, become defensive about their inability to meet all the needs of their members. When this occurs, external influences are unwelcome, and the family operates as a relatively closed, reverberating system. Such a system presents a deteriorating environment characterized by emotional scarcity, inflexibility, and the expenditure of internal energy to maintain positions of power or to receive gratification by exploiting other family members. These family systems induce collusion to exclude any new experiences, inquiries, or explorations that might cause constructive contact with the outside and enhance growth. The neurotic equilibrium of these families is broken down when the exploited adolescent's behavior becomes intolerable to the family or to society. At this point a crisis exists that can cause the family to seek help and serves to mobilize existing family self-rehabilitative forces. Change occurs in these families as they depart from a relatively closed system of neurotic checks and balances to a relatively open system of freer communication with the outside world and each other. By interacting with the family and modeling open and honest communication, the team can facilitate family movement from the closed to open position.

An analysis of family communication patterns can help family members to appreciate the ways in which they keep the family system defensively closed. For such an analysis to occur and be accepted by the family, the team must first view with respect the circumstances under which the family presumptions of inferiority in meeting family needs were acquired. Then, the team must weaken the collusion necessary to secure the rewards of repetitive exploitative functioning. In terms of communication, the team models healthy interactions and provides a protective setting within which the family members can dare to change (MacGregor, 1967).

Communication problems among staff members may also be of diagnostic value in understanding the ways in which the family tends to involve others in its patterns of pathological interrelationships. The increased number of team members allows a member of the team to become more deeply involved in the family process than is otherwise possible. The watchful monitoring of colleagues allows a team member to be safely drawn into the family dynamics without sacrificing therapeutic perspective.

A family's emotional functioning can also be represented graphically in terms of its members' immature responses to stress. Such a graph identifies family members as functioning in an aggressive, passive-aggressive, passive-dependent, or emotionally unstable fashion. The relatively healthy counterparts of these immature interaction modes are leadership, criticism, cooperation, and spontaneity. A decrease in extremely immature behavior on the part of a family member or movement from an immature interaction mode to a more healthy mode usually leads to increased freedom and growth for all family members.

Each of the four family syndromes characterized by a particular level of developmental arrest has a typically family constellation that can be graphically represented in terms of the aggressive, passive-aggressive, passive-dependent, and emotionally unstable roles they play within the family. Such a graphic representation of family roles helps the team to plan therapeutic interventions and to plot role changes and movements toward more mature behavior as therapy progresses. These notions of family role constellations as a part of diagnosis are undergoing some refinement. It has been noted that, except for carefully selected middle-class families, the presenting constellation is often not the one that precipitated the mental health problem but is a constructive or maladaptive result (Macgregor, 1967).

Family members are studied with respect to the flexibility they display in terms of role and function in the family. Is the father, for example, able to take leadership when it is called for? Can he relinquish the aggressive position and accept being cared for at appropriate times? Can he express spontaneous playfulness, a form of normal unpredictability or emotional instability? Flexibility patterns can guide team therapeutic efforts. The MIT diagnostic framework also studies patterns of motherhood, fatherhood, and value transmission in addition to the division-of-labor aspects of sibling relationships.

Therapeutic Foci and Goals

Multiple impact therapy is a short-term intensive therapy whose goal is to mobilize the intact family's self-rehabilitative processes through a brief pyschotherapeutic intervention. The method requires devoting the entire time and facilities of an orthopsychiatric team to one family for the two-day session. Personal interaction with the team and the development of a trusting attitude allows the family to be receptive to the team's efforts to encourage self-revisory functioning. The team's acceptance of the exploitative aspects of family life has a calming influence on the family. This, together with the respect the team shows for the family situation and potential for change, enhances the family's trust in the team.

MIT is not really an insight therapy; rather, it is an attempt to free natural growth processes. MIT does strive to encourage insight into some matters and give the family tools to analyze and recognize recurring, unrewarding patterns of behavior. MIT's model for health is based on obtaining and maintaining the conditions necessary for growth rather than on an economical distribution of limited family emotional supplies. MIT believes that change occurs when a family opens up and looks to the future rather than when the family reaches a detailed understanding of the inner conflicts. The goal of MIT is to help a family move from the position of a closed system, which maintains its status quo by collusion and balance-of-power strategies, to an open system, which permits its members to attend to appropriate developmental tasks. Because closed family systems exclude information, the MIT technique makes an effort to challenge these systems with new experiences.

The MIT team members demonstrate and model healthy interaction and communication patterns. They attempt to help the family learn to be aware of and discuss their mistakes openly. The team members teach this communication skill by showing that they can be self-critical and accept corrections from others in the group. The group setting, with its atmosphere of trust and respect, helps the family members to become less afraid of open, honest communication among themselves. In team-family conferences the team models healthy interpersonal communication skills by allowing itself considerable expression of the feelings engendered by attitudes of family members. The team members may also protect family members by openly criticizing other members' premature interpretations. When the family has difficulty expressing personal matters, the team may debate the family or team members face to face. Changes in plans are also openly discussed by the team in the family's presence as are discussions of evaluation or strategy changes. The team may work through to insight a few crucial socio- and psychodynamic issues that have arrested family members in their developmental growth process. All these activities enhance the family's awareness of alternative healthy communication methods.

The emphasis that the team places on communication enables the family members to recognize their own patterns of inadequate and distorted communication. The family's evening together between the day sessions often demonstrates, however painfully, the communication breakdowns discussed during the therapy sessions.

The team members focus careful attention on the nominal patient's ability to recognize his or her recurring patterns of interaction. In an individual interview with the adolescent, the interviewer helps the youth to see his or her behavior as meaningfully related to family patterns. The interviewer may indicate that what appears to be unreasonable behavior may be the result of being taken in or exploited to serve the poorly understood needs of others. The adolescent's influence on present and future family patterns is acknowledged, and the therapist may make an interpretation about the nature of the adolescent's relationship with a parent and how it serves the needs of the parent. Such an open and direct approach helps the adolescent to begin to recognize the patterns of behavior in the family and the role that he or she plays in family processes.

The MIT approach focuses keen attention on the adolescent's parents. On the first day of therapy, the team defers discussions with the parents about their concern for their youngster on the grounds that the family and nominal patient are still being studied diagnostically. Having their teenager thoroughly appraised and tested appeals to the parents and helps them to accept the team's attention to their personal lives. A crisis, precipitated by a child's behavior, can affect parents in such a way that what they are missing in life is acutely reexperienced. This situation further helps parents to put aside their resistance to looking at their own problems and unexpressed needs. The team communicates the belief that the benefits that the parents receive from a consideration of their relationship, namely, the interruption of patterns that interfere with happiness in their lives, will be what is best for their teenager. When parents are emotionally close or are more invested in each other than in the nominal patient, the patient improves. When parents are emotionally divorced, any and all management techniques are unsuccessful (MacGregor, 1962).

The therapeutic foci and goals of MIT are many, and rarely are the goals all met at the end of the two-day session. If the family resources have been mobilized, a primary goal of the MIT approach, the other goals can continue to be addressed by the family in the days and months following the MIT intervention. MIT is not usually a definitive therapy. It is an attempt to help a family reach a position from which return to previously patterned ways is hampered by the new awareness of the old patterns' limited rewards (MacGregor, 1967).

Intervention Strategies and Techniques

Two primary differences between MIT and other forms of family therapy are the utilization of a multidisciplinary team and the concentrated time in which the formal therapeutic work is done. The team typically consists of a social worker, a psychiatrist, and a psychologist or psychology intern, each of whom is accompanied by a student from his or her respective discipline. The team may also include another experienced multiple impact therapist such as a supervisor. Individuals responsible for referrals (i.e., physicians, chaplains, or mental health professionals from other clincs) may be invited to participate in some team–family conferences. During the course of therapy, the team members use each other as consultants in the presence of parents. The team works with one family two to three consecutive days for six to eight hours each day (MacGregor et al., 1964).

A majority of the intervention strategies and techniques employed in MIT can be highlighted in the context of a step-by-step review of the general conference sequences used during therapy. The intake sessions have been reviewed previously but should be kept in mind as an important step in the therapeutic process.

Prior to meeting with the family each day, the team participates in a briefing session. The team speculates on the data at hand, reviews preconceptions, and sets initial objectives for its work. The therapeutic objectives and family interaction constellations are diagrammed on a blackboard so that each therapist has a clear idea of the tactics of each member and the probable course of events. Assignments for individual interviews and the sequences of overlapping interviews are tentatively outlined. A flow chart indicating these interviews and other team–family or team activities is constructed. These team visual aids are reviewed and revised as necessary in the morning briefing sessions or at other team conference periods.

In the initial team-family conference, the team cites the urgency of the family's situation and explores the family's reasons for coming to the clinic. These comments are followed by an "ice breaker" interpretation of family functioning and a team discussion of the interpretation. Discussions and demonstrations of the role of defective communication in family relationships follow, and threats to the adolescent's individuality are discussed. This initial conference allows the team to witness gross patterns of family interaction and established patterns of family communication. The novel interchange that occurs in this conference often causes increased tension in individual family members.

Individual conferences follow the initial team family conference and allow family members an opportunity to ventilate any pressure that has built up. Parents are typically under pressure to have someone appreciate their defensible position in the family and in the team–family conference. The team member gets an idea of what the parent's spouse has been up against in preparation for a later interview with the spouse.

The initial interview with the adolescent is kept brief. The interviewer tries to help the youth see how his or her behavior relates meaningfully to family patterns. Upon terminating this interview, the team member telephones for permission to join the ongoing session with the mother or father.

The resulting overlapping session begins with the parents' therapist summarizing what has been learned about the family situation and recent developments for the entering therapist. The parent has the opportunity to listen to the summary and make comments, clarifications, or criticisms regarding the content of the summary or any interpretations made by the therapist. The overlapping therapist usually indicates that this information makes sense in view of what has been learned from contact with a particular family member. The team members have the opportunity to represent the family members to each other so that the behavior of one family member can be understood as a response to another family member's behavior.

These sessions are followed by a team luncheon conference. The family is free to have lunch on its own. During the noon conference the team becomes aware of each others' attitudes toward different family members. The afternoon strategy is planned.

The afternoon continues with cross-ventilation of individual interviews. Team members who saw one parent in the morning interview the other parent to discover how the parent can be a greater resource for his or her mate and how the mate contributes to the unhealthy family interactions. An interviewer and a parent might join the other interviewer and parent in an overlapping parent-team session. Work with the parents focuses on recurring problems in the marriage and faults in the communication pattern at home. During this time the nominal patient and siblings are having diagnostic psychological evaluations.

A team-family conference ends the day's activities. By this time the family has usually developed a good understanding of the current crisis. Family and individual problem areas have been identified, and unrealized potentials for emotional growth have begun to appear. Family discomfort is high because the barriers to communication maintained by collusion among some family members are losing their effectiveness as the family becomes aware of their divisive qualities.

Conference procedures on the second day follow, with more variability, the pattern of the first day's afternoon. The early team-family conference may be brief or omitted. Typically, the second afternoon begins with each family member's meeting with the therapist he or she saw first in the individual sessions. The therapist reviews the member's work during therapy and makes interpretations about the individual's therapeutic goals and his or her ability to handle future family interactions.

The final team-family conference focuses attention on the family's concern about immediate and anticipated problems back home. Each family and team member is encouraged to formulate and criticize his or her emerging view of the family's status from his or her perspective. The overlapping interviews and recombinations of family and team members were designed to help facilitate psychotherapeutic convergence or the perception of consistent dynamic themes by team-family members. A pattern of follow-up is agreed upon. The team's respect for the family's ability to deal with problems as they arise limits early follow-up appointments. The team recommends that the family not contact the team for assistance with problems until the members have spent twenty-four to forty-eight hours attempting to deal with post-MIT crises on their own.

The processes of discovering family dynamics have been shared, and each family member leaves with a partial understanding of family dynamics, which may increase as the self-rehabilitative process stated in MIT progresses.

Some of the other therapeutic strategies that the team uses in MIT include "doubling" for a less expressive family member, a technique borrowed from psychodrama; a genetic approach to understanding patterns of behavior by deriving an understanding of the presenting problem through a review of early life histories; and keeping separate team conferences at a minimum. Changes in plans are discussed in the family's presence. This procedure improves family understanding of the therapeutic process and limits distrustful feelings spawned by perceived collusion.

Role of the Therapist

The principal therapeutic effects of MIT come from joining the relatively open system of the team with the relatively closed system of the defensively functioning family. It is the team's function to effect movement from a closed family system to an open system consistent with growth. The team aims to effect this change by participating in and with the family system.

For team members to be effectively drawn into the family system, two conditions must be met. The team must have the family respect the troublesome be- havior as the best strategy for the nominal patient under the circumstances and then show the family that something may be wrong with the circumstances. The next step is to have a team member pose some central dynamic theme and other team members show that they will help family members defend themselves against the implications of the proposed dynamic theme. Now, in the presence of col- leagues, a team member may move from the neutral position traditionally assumed when doing therapy and become deeply involved as a participant in family inter- changes. The team member is thus able to experience directly the collusion and crosscurrents of family conflict while a watchful teammate observes, ready to provide perspective if necessary. Through these kinds of experiences and other interactions with the family, the team is able to reflect back to the family the inter- actions among family members, their distortion of reality, and their struggles to control, exploit, or dominate each other (MacGregor, 1964).

As an open system, the team has the ability to openly analyze some of its processes in a way that teaches the family by example how to look at itself. The team–family conferences are like apprenticeship training in self-study. The team models ways in which to deal with problems of individual responsibility, intimacy, and leadership. The team demonstrates differences of opinion without loss of respect. Team members also model role flexibility and interpersonal adaptability.

Each individual team member's identity with his or her own discipline is a sig- nificant factor in the success of MIT. As an individual the therapist provides a model for individual identity to the adolescent whose fear of emancipation from the family is linked to a fear that his or her only significance is as a family member. Excessive group identity is to be avoided by the team.

Individual therapists also provide a protective intervention role. They help a family member to "save face" when that member reveals more of himself or herself than he or she intended. These actions strengthen the family's confidence in the team. Similarly, therapists in overlapping sessions can be frank in relating the sum- mary material to their own session because the family member has a therapist with him or her who can react with candor in behalf of the patient. A family member always has an advocate within the team.

Critique and Evaluation

Multiple impact therapy is a short-term, intensive family therapy for families with disturbed adolescents. It is particularly useful in situations in which conventional therapies have failed to engage the nominal patient and his or her family. It can be the treatment choice for initiating therapy when a family crisis exists. It is also seen as the method of choice for creating a beneficial crisis within a family already in treatment but experiencing an intrafamilial stalemate. The method is particularly suited for adolescents who are resistive to individual psychotherapy. There are no known contraindications to the use of MIT, although it may not be the wisest method for treating minor problems that tend to respond favorably to techniques that use less concentrated clinic time.

One of the weaknesses of the approach is reflected in the time that it requires to formulate family dynamics and therapeutic strategy. Nearly a full day is required to collect the necessary family background data. The team feels, however, that this weakness is inherent in all psychotherapies. Another weakness involves the number of staff needed to conduct the therapy. It is expensive in time for a clinic to use this approach. Most clinics would have difficulty scheduling several staff members to meet for that much time. Certainly, a therapist in private practice would have difficulty drawing together a cadre of colleagues to use MIT. The weakness of a team approach can also be a strength.

The strengths of the MIT approach lie in its utilization of the therapeutic team as a model of healthy group functioning and its utilization of the creative capacities of an interdisciplinary group to develop explanatory theories about behaviors observed within families. The multidisciplinary team approach provides several perspectives on family dynamics and can offer divergent ideas regarding the treatment. With different team members' meeting with each family member, there are possibilities that positive relationships will be established between specific people. A single therapist relies on establishing a relationship with each family member and only his or her own diagnosis and treatment procedures.

In addition to providing direct, concentrated service to families, the MIT approach can help to provide diagnostic studies and treatment recommendations for families handled by other agencies. It can serve as a training medium in family dynamics and provide in-service training in a creative therapeutic approach. The method can be instructive for teachers, psychiatrists, clinical psychologists, marriage counselors, and others who provide interpersonal guidance.

The concept of self-rehabilitative processes in the family is admirable. Early follow-up studies indicated "the method to have treatment results comparable to established intensive methods" (MacGregor, 1962). Follow-up studies were usually done at six and eighteen months and half of them included a home visit. MacGregor reported that in forty-three of fifty families the self-rehabilitative process remained effectively mobilized. In severn of the fifty that remained unchanged or worsened, the mother exploited social relations that thwarted family development. It was reported that many cases continued with self-rehabilitation after minimum procedures. Some families with more severe problems used a series of six two-week sessions for a period of one year. Actually, not much hard data have been presented, and these evaluations are twenty years old. The approach is used and in need of evaluation.

References

MacGregor, R. 1962. Multiple impact psychotherapy with families. *Family Process* 1:15–29.

———. 1967. Progress in multiple impact therapy. In *Expanding theory and practice in family therapy,* eds. N. Ackerman, F. Beatman, and S. Sherman, pp. 47–58. New York: Family Service Association of America.

———; Ritchie, A. M.; Serrano, A. C.; and Schuster, F. P. 1964. *Multiple impact therapy with families.* New York: McGraw-Hill.

15

The Family Network Intervention of Ross Speck, Carolyn Attneave, and Uri Rueveni

Family network therapy emphasizes the importance of family and friendship systems. A team of three or four therapists meets with a family and all other significant relatives, friends, neighbors, and community people for a series of sessions designed to stimulate the social network to resolve a critical family problem. The emphasis is on activating the system to work out solutions rather than on having a professional therapist do it. Family network therapy may involve a group of forty or more people.

When the extended family system is intact but dysfunctional, network therapy is mainly directed toward helping such a system to become less dysfunctional by increasing the communication among the members and other significant people. The increased communication may open up new, as well as, old family issues that have not been resolved within the formal, extended family network. The network therapy may result in a new, more productive pattern of relationships among the family members. Networking the family system may not always produce an immediate resolution of the crisis, however, and further efforts may be made by the ailing member to seek additional relief and help.

When the extended family system is minimal or nonexistent, the network therapy is directed toward developing a substitute family system consisting of nonfamily members including friends, neighbors, and community individuals who could become involved with the family in a crisis as a temporary social support system.

The principal designers of family network therapy have been Ross Speck and Carolyn Attneave, with Uri Rueveni adding significantly to the field. Both Speck and Attneave talk about their life experiences as influencing their ideas about therapy. In early life Ross Speck was involved in a large family and family network in a small town in Ontario, Canada. His parents came from farms but later lived in a small city, where his father worked in a gasoline station. He has alluded to fundamentalist religious experiences and describes large family reunions with four generations' attending and providing the potential interaction consistent with how he now perceives network interventions.

As a youth he was a good student and was encouraged to attend medical school. He claims to have entered psychiatry because of a curiosity about himself and others as well as an interest in helping people. His description of a psychiatric residency reveals the usual experiences but contains an element of dissatisfaction.

He completed a program in a psychoanalytic institute while doing research with families that had a schizophrenic member. He reported greater success with family therapy than with one-to-one therapy. In about 20 per cent of the cases problems arose outside the nuclear family. By 1964 he was using various combinations of significant others as part of family therapy. Elizabeth Bott's *Family and Social Network* (1957) was influential in his working with the social network of schizophrenic families. By 1966 Speck assembled his first schizophrenic family network, which contained forty persons and met for nine months. This long-term intervention provided groundwork learning, and continued experience led to a more specific method of family network intervention.

Carolyn Attneave was born in El Paso, Texas to a mother of Delaware Indian heritage and a Texas father. Her nuclear family was not close to its kin and her parents moved frequently. She describes close relationships with her parents and their friends who served as "aunts" and "uncles."

Her family moved frequently, and she states that two years was the longest she ever lived in a community until after she reached age thirty. The moving around provided her with an opportunity to see many subcultures and to learn about various relationships. She talks about identifying similarities and differences in communities and organizations. Her observation of roles, patterns, and customs helped her to join in.

She continued her observation of social patterns while attending and earning her way through five different colleges. She entered psychology and sociology as it made sense out of her observations. These fields suggested concepts regarding her social development and the recognition that there were other ways of growing up. She also moved through professional jobs: from school counseling to clinical, child, and eventually family therapy.

In addition to her work with various ethnic and cultural groups, Attneave has had experience with many disabled groups. With all people, her goal has been to build coherent relationships between persons who could stimulate each other and provide reciprocal growth. This led to developing treatment teams of local people to help with problem situations. Treatment teams often included the clergy, scout leaders, neighbors, merchants, and relatives as well as family members. Her ideas seemed to contrast to the professional mainstream. Once she met Ross Speck they shared ideas and explored what could be done with the concept of retribalization.

Uri Rueveni began his experience in family network therapy as a team member with Ross Speck. Rueveni received his educational training from the University of Pittsburgh and Michigan State University. Since that time he has been employed professionally in the Philadelphia area, where he has continued to develop and write about family network interventions.

Concept of the Family

Proponents of the social network approach to family therapy are concerned not only with the nuclear family but also with the extended family, which may include friends and neighbors. Rueveni (1979) suggests that a social network consists of a group of people who maintain an important and often ongoing relationship in the family members' lives. These people may include the family, relatives, friends, neighbors, or other individuals in the community with whom they interact. A network may be defined as a pattern or system that interconnects, a linking device, or a communication system or a support device. Boissevain (1974) describes five concentric network zones: one personal, two intimate, one effective, and one nominal. The personal network zone involves close relatives and intimate friends. The first intimate zone involves close relatives and friends with whom the person keeps active contact; the second intimate zone involves friends and relatives who are not maintained in close contact. The effective zone includes people who are not emotionally involved but who have economic and political interactions. The nominal zone includes individuals who have little or no relationship with the person's own self. Boissevain suggests that the individual's network provides a field of friends and relatives that supplies a meaning to life, establishes and maintains norms to regulate one's behavior, and protects individuals from the impersonal world.

Speck and Attneave (1973) used the word "tribe" as a metaphor to describe the social network. The social network includes the nuclear family and all the relatives of each family member. It also includes friends, neighbors, work associates, and significant helpers from all social agencies who are willing and able to risk their involvement with the family. They believe that this network of interrelated people, when organized along lines consistent with its own culture, has within itself resources to provide creative solutions to the human predicament.

Speck and Attneave (1973) state that most behaviors traditionally defined as symptoms of mental illness are derived from the alienation of human beings from social networks and resources. Although traditionally the individual was regarded as the sick member, more recently the family has been identified as a sick unit. They indicate that in some instances the entire social network causes or perpetuates pathology—scapegoating of the individual and possibly the family. The proponents of family network therapy do not specify particular concepts about the family or the causes for dysfunctional behavior. Their focus is on a retribalization through the assembly and creation of a social network for the person and the family in distress.

Therapeutic Foci and Goals

In each family network therapy specific and general goals are defined. The specific goals depend upon the nature of the problem with which the members of the family have been struggling. The therapist will learn about the concerns and issues during the preliminary screening meeting with the family and then develop specific goals that can be modified as events unfold during the network sessions. Rueveni (1979, p. 72) lists five general goals for network intervention:

1. Facilitate rapid connections, familiarity, and readiness to participate, which increases the level of involvement and energy.
2. Develop and encourage sharing of the problems and concerns by members of the immediate family, which allows for increased involvement and exchange of a variety of viewpoints by network members.
3. Facilitate communication between the family and its extended network system, which emphasizes the need for network activists.
4. Provide direct intervention and a deeper exploration of the nature of difficulty during impasse periods, which leads to crisis resolution.
5. Assist in the development and formation of temporary support groups, which serve as resource consultants.

The general goals correspond closely to the six network phases. The therapist and the network team will be involved in a system intervention to mobilize a network for action in crisis resolution by involving the members of the network in achieving these goals.

Speck and Attneave define the overarching goal of all network intervention as stimulating, reflecting, and focusing the potentials within the network to solve one another's problems. They believe that, by strengthening the bonds, loosening the binds, opening new channels, facilitating new perceptions, activating latent strengths, and helping to ventilate or exercise pathology, the social network is able to become a life-sustaining community within the social matrix of each individual. "There is no other single goal—not cure, not treatment, but to enable people to cope and to share their strengths in coping and also in reaping enjoyments and pleasures that restore their potentials and set them up to handle the inevitable next crisis of living" (1973, p. 50).

Obviously the therapeutic focus is on having the members of the network rather than the professional therapist provide the therapy. It is believed that the network members have the potential to resolve the problems and the professionals focus on bringing about that potential. The intention is that the network members will continue to support each other after the intervention sessions.

The focus involves everyone's perception of the problem. The professionals do not diagnose the problem in a labeling sense but help the network members to communicate their various ideas of the problem situation. An understanding and solutions are generated from that approach. The process and techniques to meet the goals focus on activity rather than on insight and interpretation. There is an attempt to get everyone involved, first in the process and later in doing something to help toward resolution.

History Taking and Diagnosis

What criterion does a therapist use to select appropriate cases for network intervention? Therapists are discouraged from using social network intervention with every case. Although all people have network relationships that might benefit from activation of their inherent potentials, this is not the most efficient, economical, or desirable way in which to ease their distress. Family network intervention is only one approach to resolving problems and is probably used rather selectively. Although most cases appropriate for family therapy could use family network intervention, even specialists in network intervention would not apply the technique to every case.

Actually Speck and Attneave indicate that crisis and desperation are primary characteristics of individuals selected for network therapy. It is probably most appropriate with family concerns that have been difficult to modify by other therapeutic interventions. Previous individual or family therapy that has not been successful may leave the family with the feeling that network intervention is a last hope. The network can provide an excellent modality for gathering sufficient energy to overcome the individual and family difficulty. The inclusion of others in solving problems gives each family member appropriate support in finding ways in which to deal with the desperate situation.

Two elements necessary for an appropriate case are that the stress and strain are mediated through relationships with other people and that some social matrix is available. In fact, Rueveni (1979) states that network intervention is often refused when there is not sufficient interest or motivation on the part of family members to get involved in solving the problem as a family unit. Another criterion may be defined as self-selection. Individuals or families may have heard about the activities of a network intervention team and request its use. Such families may have already moved at least part of the way through the resistance to considering having their family and friends participate in solving their problems. However, Speck and Attneave believe the choice should still remain with the professional, and the presence of a social matrix and intensity of distress must be weighed for each request or referral from a general group of cases. The other end of the self-selection continuum involves those families who find it difficult or are unwilling to assemble a network. They would rather deal with a problem individually than share painful feelings and public exposure. Such feelings are understandable, and the decision to assemble the network is left to the family members. A difficulty may occur when some members of the family agree to a network intervention and others do not. The network is not assembled for the benefit of only one person. It is a collaborative effort for the entire family. The therapist and team members can suggest the polling of votes and going along with the majority; however, one individual may still refuse to attend. If the majority is committed to the process, the intervention network may be assembled. Rueveni suggests that often the individual who has threatened to boycott the meeting will not carry out this threat.

The real history taking and understanding of the family that leads to a decision to use network intervention or not usually occurs in a screening session held in the home of the family. The home is the suggested location because it is the natural habitat of the family, which reinforces the idea that the home is the place to which their friends and relatives may be called to convene if necessary. The home is also a more convenient and less stigmatized place in which to convene than is a hospital or clinic.

The home visit permits the therapist and team members to become familiar with the concerns of the family. The session also permits the family members to become familiar with the team members' expectations and to experience a bit of the network process, therefore allowing them to understand their own roles in the process. This session generally lasts two hours and is described as a mininetwork session that usually includes most of the network phases. The first session is usually attended by the members of the nuclear family but not the extended network. If additional relatives or friends are desired in this meeting, a decision is made by the team leader and family.

The process that develops during this session is similar to that of the fully attended network intervention except that the number of individuals present is smaller. The goal of this session is to determine to what extent mobilizing the family network will provide the best intervention modality. During the initial stage of this session, a retribalization process takes place in which family members meet and get to know the team members. Following this the team leader outlines the purpose of the meeting and shares with the family the previously known information that has been gained from the referral source. Family members are told that additional information will be needed so that a decision can be made regarding their therapeutic process. Each member is encouraged to share his or her feelings about the nature and scope of the problem situation. This activity generally leads to a polarization stage in which family members disagree. They maintain their own points of view as to who is at fault, who promotes conflict, who maintains resentment, what sides are taken, and who is being scapegoated. The intervention team may explore these issues to understand the dysfunctional relationships. Family members generally continue in their usual patterns that promote the conflict situation, and the team members must be aware of the goals of the process and remain sensitive to the pertinent frustration that the family members experience in this process.

The session may become temporarily mobilized if the family feels that there is hope for a solution without activating its entire support system. The intervention team needs to explore previous efforts by family members, either individually or collectively, to solve their problems. The team continues to obtain information about the family by exploring family members' feelings of resistance and hopelessness. Generally there is a depression stage in which the family members feel that nothing has worked and maybe nothing will. The team members persist in examining the nature of the relationships among the family members and help to express the underlying reasons for the feelings of hopelessness. Often there is a family secret or other information that is difficult for the family to reveal. The team will encourage the disclosure of such information because that experience can help to bring family members out of the depression phase into a minibreakthrough. This breakthrough is not meant to imply that the crisis is over. Rather, both the family and team members may be better able to decide if assembling their support system is the best course of action. Decisions concerning the desirability of having a network mobilized can usually be agreed upon by the team and the family during this first session.

Sometimes the team and/or family needs additional time to discuss their options, and arrangements can be made to delay the decision. When the team feels that the family crisis does not justify network intervention because the degree of family desperation is not sufficient or because insufficient preparation efforts have been made by the family, the members are encouraged to attempt some other approach for help. Names of individuals or agencies may be offered, and follow-up may be made by team members.

When a network intervention seems to be the most appropriate avenue but family members are hesitant, the team provides the family with the information concerning the steps involved in the process, supplying reading materials and making telephone contacts for future consultation and decision. Families may need time to discuss the implications of calling on their network support system for help.

When a decision has been reached by both the team and family members to use a network intervention, the team helps each family member to develop a list of family and friends. A date for the meeting is determined, and final arrangements are made to assemble and conduct a network intervention.

The family is given help regarding what statements the members may wish to make when inviting their networks to come to their home. A typical call includes a brief statement of the problem and a need for the network members to come and participate in the session to help the family solve its problems. When plans are being made to videotape the session, the invited network members should be told in advance about the possibility of their being recorded and that written permission will be needed to do this. The advanced information should include a statement that the network member is considered an important person for the success of the session and that his or her participation may help in achieving a successful resolution. The invited members must also be made aware of the networking process and be informed by reading materials that will familiarize them with the process. Network individuals may be invited by phone, by letter followed by a phone call, or just by letter.

Phases of Network Intervention

There is a sense of order to the events that transpire, and a pattern seems to exist in network therapy. The awareness of the phases makes it easier to work with the numbers of people involved as well as with the subgroupings. An awareness of the phases makes sense of the highs and lows or the ploys and counterploys behind the seemingly infinite changes that each network brings to the possibilities of human social relationships. Six distinct network phases have been described: retribalization, polarization, mobilization, depression, breakthrough, and exhaustion and elation.

Prior to the beginning of the network intervention, however, there has been a prenetwork interview and the assembly of the network members. The opening session is generally considered one of a series, although it is possible to have a single network meeting. The one-session intervention might be ideal, but it is seldom able to deal with the distress of the individuals in the family in one session. Speck and Attneave (1973) note that many religious groups who rely on the network effect of a conversion experience suggest that, even though this is a potent force, it needs to be renewed periodically to prevent the group from falling back into fragmentation. Therapists working with the network need to be aware of this and, when possible, direct the energy of the network toward some self-recharging cycle of its own.

Usually the network intervention will involve more meetings to reinforce the shared intervention will involve more meetings to reinforce the shared coping experiences that tend to make the network a stabilized social unit that can continue to function without professional coaching. A series of six meetings seems to be appropriate to all concerned and practical, although occasionally three or four meetings may be sufficient.

The strategy for the first session is designed by the team on the basis of the information about the problem gathered in the prenetwork discussions with the family. The leader will need quick feedback from the team members regarding sub-groupings and the moods as the network gathers. The team members arrive early and watch the host families and others in an attempt to sort out alignments and feelings as well as their relationships with others. Few individuals have any real idea about why they are there, and many are apprehensive about the distress of the family that invited them; many may be concerned about the risks they themselves are taking. The leader's skill in relieving the fears and focusing feelings is important at this stage.

Retribalization

After the group has been assembled the leader takes charge by introducing himself or herself, outlining the problem, and describing the method of the network intervention. The team leader may briefly outline the goals of the network and the need for involvement on the part of each member. A short period is spent identifying each network participant and his or her relationship to the immediate family.

The introductory talk lays out a blueprint of all phases of the network intervention. The assembled network is told that its members will focus on specific issues, that the work at times will be difficult and tiring, that active individuals will need to come forward and be willing to carry out unique and innovative tasks, and that others who are tired should replace themselves in the network with individuals who have more energy. The group is told how many times it is likely to need to meet and what the participants can expect during each session, except for unusual or extenuating circumstances. This talk focuses on retribalization of the crises at hand—while the network is in an affective and affiliative mood.

This brief discussion helps the group members to understand what is going to happen and gives them a sense of purpose and direction. The initial phase is designed to encourage rapid connections, familiarity, and readiness to participate and to increase the members' level of involvement. At first, individuals will mill around, attaching themselves to new people, and reconnecting with old members of the family whom they have not seen for a period of time.

Immediately following the introduction, the leader involves the group in encounter-sensitivity techniques to achieve "group high" in which enthusiasm and activism break down the ordinary social barriers and defenses that have isolated the members. Activities are used to permit the expenditure of some physical energy such as jumping up and down, clapping hands, screaming, or forming a circle and singing favorite songs in unison.

At times the distressed person or an immediate family or a network member may not participate. One of the team members, all of whom are scattered about the room, stimulates and initiates by pulling the fringe members into the group. Having everyone participate helps them feel a part of the group and establishes the leader as the person in control of the situation. The nonverbal period may only last three to ten minutes but should help the group to develop a feeling of solidarity and being in contact with one another.

At this point the team leader forms a structure for a discussion and dialogue. The leader places members into positions to form an appropriate grouping. One set of positions that is adaptable to many settings is the use of concentric circles. The physical arrangement usually involves the living room of a home and may open into a dining room or the doorways of other rooms. Therefore, people may be seated on the floor as well as on chairs or sofas. Rueveni recommends that the immediate family members take a place in the center of the room; however, Speck and Attneave suggest that, if the leader is aware of different factions, he or she may place people in different concentric circles, which will stimulate some polarization.

The family members are encouraged to give a brief outline of the nature of the crisis as they view it and state their own expectations and needs from the assembled network. Each member is asked to describe his or her perception of the crisis situation. This provides an opportunity for the members of the network to learn about the problems firsthand as they are seen by all family members. Some of the network participants may have heard about the crisis from one family member's perception. Because each family member's view of the crisis may be different, most of the issues begin to polarize around the different perceptions and feelings expressed by the various family members. Some network members may also take sides with a family member, bringing the network process to its next phase, polarization.

Polarization

During this phase the network members become involved with the members of the family. They contribute their views and feelings about the nature of the crisis. The intervention team may suggest that the network members sit closest to the family members they feel most supportive of or, while expressing their views, identify on what side of the family they feel most supportive. Although some people have difficulty with this, encouraging side taking can help to achieve continued involvement.

By allowing various subgroups to discuss the problems in the presence of the total network, the leader is able to use the differences of opinion to polarize each group, which can then be brought into a synthesis and immediately repolarized so that the entire assembled network is forced to deal with multiple levels of concepts and interpersonal relationships. Speck and Attneave (1973) believe that differences often exist between generations, and they suggest that subgroups are polarized along the generation gap, perhaps seating the younger members of the network together and sometimes placing the older members in an outer group. The purpose of the multiple circles is to produce a more intense interaction in the small subgroups rather than the large assembled network. It is important to elicit competitive polarities with diverse opinions and to resolve some of these. The wide range of topics discussed helps the total network to begin selecting and focusing on major issues to be dealt with in resolving the predicament in the family. Each subgroup is given its turn to interact with the other subgroups and is instructed not to interrupt but to listen. Later, each subgroup is given a chance to criticize what has been said by the other subgroups.

The intervention team's task during this stage is to discourage dependence on its members as professional problem solvers and to encourage a greater participation and sharing different points of view. The sharing of various ideas concerning the crisis allows the intervention team to identify activists. An activist is one who begin begins to initiate collaborative efforts at solving the crisis. Network activists perceive the need for someone to take over temporarily, and they require the support from the team in stepping into that process. When sufficient network activists are available, the network becomes mobilized. The team encourages specificity of action so that a number of small groups can be formed to discuss further the problem at hand.

Mobilization

The energy that was developed by the polarization process begins to become focused. The leader has an opportunity to mobilize and channel that energy in constructive directions. He or she can gently stimulate the activists in the network to look for tasks and suggest major areas that need network attention. Suggestions are elicited from the entire assembled network for additional tasks and how these tasks could be implemented. Generally in a large network group several activists will begin to attempt practical solutions to the problem. The activists serve as leaders of subgroups that begin working on specific tasks to overcome the problem. The leader is aware that confrontation with a difficult task will meet with initial resistance, despair, and possible desperation.

Depression

This movement toward mobilization is usually followed by a temporary lull in activity caused when members feel discouraged about not finding immediate solutions. The depression phase may also result from difficulties and frustrations of individuals in the network who feel that their contributions are not being accepted. Others feel disappointment because their hopes for crisis solution may take longer than they had expected. This period of time is marked by tension, boredom, and frustration.

During this phase the intervention team tries to encourage the members to acknowledge that they feel frustrated and to suggest making additional efforts. It may be necessary for the team to find other techniques to bring about a greater awareness of the family's problems. Although such techniques as sculpting, gestalt encounter, and pyschodrama may be used, the timing and skill of the intervention team is of utmost importance in this phase. Team members must help the activists to mobilize the network to obtain maximum results for breaking the impasse. When activists can attempt an innovative solution or recruit others to join to support them, the despression is replaced by a determined persistence to achieve a breakthrough.

Breakthrough

The breakthrough phase is characterized by increased activity and a display of optimism and encouragement, with feelings that there are workable solutions and that the members' contributions and energies will pay off. The leader transfers the action from the intervention team to the network itself. This phase may begin with the formation of support groups. During this time, the intervention team helps members to identify the support group with which they are willing to serve. The network members form into smaller support groups that meet in various locations of the home.

Each small network group designs a task related to a specific problem area and reports back through a spokesperson during the second network session. Once the small-group process is underway, members of the intervention team can remove themselves.

Exhaustion and Elation

During the later part of the session the members of the network meet together to work on their assigned tasks. Each small group terminates when it feels some satisfaction and accomplishment. This is generally accompanied by feelings of exhaustion and elation. There is a natural recovery period and then work that continues in between the meetings.

The activities and commitments that develop from the formation and the continued efforts of these temporary support groups are important in resolving the crisis among the family members. These groups continue to help each of the members of the family. The support groups continue the events that took place during the first network session. They work toward specific goals and tasks so that each support group member can make a contribution. The support group members then report their progress to the entire network at the next meeting. During the time between sessions, the support group members keep telephone contact with the family members, each other, and when necessary the intervention team. They discuss, plan, and carry out additional alternatives in an effort to resolve the crisis. The members of the support group plan additional meetings that will occur after the conclusion of the network. They continue individually to have contact with the family members and continuously seek to consider options. The activists in the group function as leaders and give their time and invest their efforts in helping the family members to solve their problems. However, it is difficult to maintain a high level of commitment in support groups for long periods of time. Rueveni suggests that most support groups report a decreasing level of involvement as the crisis abates, which usually varies from three weeks to three months.

Cycles

The network intervention process involves the orderly sequence of the six phases that exist in each of the network sessions. If the family network meets three times or six times, the procsss of each session will involve the same six phases. However, the time and energy may be distributed differently among the phases. In the early meetings most time and energy will be spent on the first two phases, retribalization and polarization. Later phases will have a more intense polarization leading to mobilization. In the later sessions there will still be considerable depression, but the network will focus on breakthrough and a realistic retribalization. The sequence of events is typical, and the need for cycling when the network gets stuck in a depressed phase or is resisting requires the team's ability to recognize where the group is and what needs to be accomplished. Often the reactions of anger, scapegoating, and resistance are attempts to get the intervention team to take responsibility for solving the basic problems.

The retribalization, polarization, mobilization, and breakthrough are activity-oriented phases. The depression phase, however, is a mood brought on by the network's inability to resolve the situation and its members feel that they ought to be able to cope, and it manifests itself in a variety of behaviors. Speck and Attneave (1973) note that to some extent depression alternates with hope throughout the sequence of phases. In effect, the depression phase is a regularly recurring mood, a cumulative phenomenon that follows each of the first three phases. As a single dimension in the scheme, it is represented as the fourth phase because that is the time of its greatest depth. This is when it requires the most attention of the network intervention team to encourage the group to resist accepting failure and cope realistically and effectively with the situation.

The term breakthrough is used to indicate the absence of resistance and depression and the activities that accomplish the goals of the network. Small breakthroughs occur in each session, and recycling them is the task of the successful intervention team. It is apparent that the recycling from one session to another is necessary to bring out the additional factors in the situation and establish new tasks that will lead the group toward a realistic retribalization.

Retribalization as Termination

After breakthroughs occur that offer support for all parts of the system and after individuals develop shifts in behavior and life-styles that remove the original crisis, there is a feeling of satisfaction and elation. The people feel good about the network's activities and about themselves. The network has knit itself into a more cohesive system as a result of shared experiences. And this makes retribalization more real. Following this high, there is a natural lull that resembles normal exhaustion and rest. Continued telephoning, meeting in small groups, planning social affairs, and discussing ideas from the network principles will continue more informally. Once the retribalization has begun and is reinforced by successfully shared problem solving, normal occasions for group assemblies can generally keep it alive. Many of the rituals of established cultures seem to have originally evolved to form this function. It is necessary that the healing effect from these assemblies be renewed so that it is not lost. It is hoped that the social network will establish some means of perpetuating the cycle after the intervention team had established a pattern. The network group that becomes the social network therefore becomes its own agent of change.

Role of the Therapist

Speck and Attneave (1973) point out that social network intervention is accomplished by a team rather than by just one therapist. It would be nearly impossible for one person to undertake the entire task of network intervention. A team may be composed of five or six individuals but not fewer than two or three people who know one another well enough to trust each other and are familiar enough with one another's behavior to work well together. The team must have one experienced person who assumes the leadership, develops a plan of action, and maintains a commitment to see the intervention process to completion. Generally, this person acts as the conductor of the network sessions, delegating considerable responsibility to other experienced team members familiar with the techniques. The leader is generally skilled in large-group situations and is able to command the flow of attention and energy of the assembled network. The leader also knows when and how to turn the network group loose to work with itself.

The team members are involved as soon as the case is accepted. Team members are involved in the data gathering that enters into the decision to accept the case. Evaluations of the type and amount of distress in the social interactions among the people can be better evaluated by a team than by a single individual. This sharing during the introductory phase will help the team in its integration and make it easier to ensure the total team's awareness of the history and social and cultural factors that will characterize the assembled network. If the total team cannot be involved during this phase, the cognitive and affective data need to be shared, role assignments implemented, and the entire team united in its conceptualization of the strategy of the intervention during its phases. This will be necessary for the team members to make appropriate responses when network members call between sessions.

Leader

The role of the leader is similar to that of a good discussion leader who provides direction and permits others to carry much of the responsibility for the discussion. The leader needs a sense of timing and empathy, emotional feelings, and a sense of group moods and undercurrents. In addition to the ability to command attention, the network leader needs the confidence that comes with considerable experience in dealing with difficult situations and knowing individuals under stress. It is equally important that the leader be able to delegate responsibility empathically yet pointedly. Throughout the intervention process, the leader must try to diffuse the responsibility to the members of the network rather than collect it for himself or herself.

The network therapist or leader needs experience and skill in group dynamics and process, psychodramatic techniques, and family dynamics. The leader is responsible for selecting the team members, providing leadership during the initial home visit, and coordinating the establishment of an intervention strategy for the team. Once the network session has begun, the leader will use the specific intervention strategies to coincide with the events that occur during the process of the networking. Cues for initiating an intervention are based on the phase in which the network is working, feedback from other team members circulating among the network, and personal clinical experience. For example, when the leader identifies the depression phase in the network, the leader and team plan a specific network technique that could break up the impasse, permitting the members additional areas for exploration and possible crisis resolution. During the actual network session the therapist and the team members function as network convenors, network mobilizers, network choreographers, and network resource consultants (Rueveni, 1979).

Network Convenor. The role of convenor primarily occurs during the home visit or the retribalization phase. Although the responsibility for assembling the network is primarily left to family members, the leader functions as a resource and outlines ways of developing family maps or lists for assembling the extended membership of relatives, friends, and neighbors. In the event that the task of convening the extended system becomes difficult for the family because there are few remaining family members, the leader helps in considering the convening friend networks and friends-of-friends networks. Rueveni gives examples in which the therapist goes so far as to recruit neighbors who are willing to convene and participate in the network process.

Another aspect of the role of convenor can be observed during the beginning phase of the main network session. In the retribalization phase, the leader provides network members with an opportunity to interact and become acquainted with each other. The therapist develops a sequence of activities, both verbal and nonverbal, that will permit the development of the retribalization phase to take place rapidly. This is done by providing the network members with an opportunity to participate in energizing activities such as milling around, stamping their feet, and singing in unison followed by more relaxing activities such as standing in a circle holding hands and closing their eyes. The leader's role is that of a convenor working to increase the network's energy level and state of readiness for further development in the network process. It is possible that during this period and perhaps throughout the network process the therapist is perceived as taking the role of a celebrant, a term developed by Zuk (1975) that connotes a role traditionally given to members of the clergy for initiating a healing ceremony.

Network Mobilizer. Sometimes during the network session the assembled network must become mobilized for action. The leader and team members should be able to stimulate and encourage maximum participation in disclosures, sharing of conflicting points of view, and open dialogue. Throughout this process the leader cannot be passive or uninvolved but may take sides, confront family or subgroup members, and encourage clear communications and disclosures of painful feelings or secrets.

During the mobilization phase, where network activists begin to work, the leader provides further support for additional exploration of the crisis. When the network seems stuck and concerned that its contributions are not being used by the family, a temporary phase of depression begins. During that phase the leader needs to structure additional exercises that will lead to deeper exploration of the crisis situation.

Network Choreographer. Family choreography is a method of actively intervening with the nuclear and extended family by realigning family relationships through physical and movement positioning. Choreography also allows the leader to draw the system with space, time, sight, and movement (Papp, 1976). To help the network move from one phase to another, the leader must be aware of the interactions between the nuclear family system and the extended network system. When members of either system appear to have difficulty during the process, the leader or team members can initiate active techniques that can mobilize the network for further involvement and provide additional opportunity for further exploration of the crisis. Active intervention techniques include direct encounter, family sculpturing, and psychodrama. These techniques can give the network members a setting in which to restructure and realign dysfunctional and self-destructive patterns. The patterns can then be examined within a supportive network atmosphere where trust can be achieved and public sharing of interpersonal concerns can be communicated openly.

Network Resource Consultant. During the network process the therapist and team members encourage the formation of support groups to begin alternative courses of action in dealing with the family problem. Team members generally provide initial leadership in forming such groups, but they are not required to become active members unless they personally choose to do so. These support groups usually form toward the end of the first network session and meet at various times between the sessions and possibly after the termination of the network meetings. The team members are available to the activists and members of the support group as a resource consultant on various issues with which the subgroup may be struggling.

Network Strategists. Various therapist roles require the therapist to be an effective strategist. The background and frame of reference of the therapist will have an effect on the clinical strategies that are used. The therapist who works as a leader of a network intervention team will use various skills to develop various intervention strategies to lead to the resolution of the family crisis. To be an effective strategist in network therapy, the leader needs to be an active participant. His or her energies are directed toward a rapid mobilization of the network system, and to do this the therapist may need to utilize himself or herself and all his or her personal and professionals skills and talents.

Team Members

All team members should have some of the skills necessary for leadership, but they may contribute special skills as well. If the network is going to include a wide range of generations, it is helpful to have a young team member and one grandparent-type member on the team. This helps members of the network to identify and interact with a team member; moreover, when the network divides into subgroups, team members can help by blending in with the generation groups. In other situations, as when the network includes specific subgroups, team members who can identify with a particular subgroup may be useful.

Speck and Attneave (1973) point out that one team member is usually selected as a scapegoat and is telephoned whenever a network or subgroup is angry with the leader or is frustrated with its own lack of confidence. Team members should be aware of this and recognize that it can be an important role in the process.

Network interventions are still uncommon and tend to be used most appropriately in crisis situations. Each team is put together around an experienced leader and one or two team members who have worked with other networks. Teams may include two or three neophytes who are interested in learning network intervention. Although participating in the network intervention process will help individuals become experienced members of a nuclear team, it is clear they are not qualified or ready to act as leader. Rueveni (1979) suggests an outline for training in network.

Members of the team need skills with nonverbal encounter techniques that they can use with the network groups and individuals. Participation in the nonverbal encounter groups as well as in the discussions help members of the network to become involved. The intervention team members are often scattered through the network and can respond to the leader's directions spontaneously and dramatically, working as a catalyst to draw everyone into the process.

Team members also communicate verbal and nonverbal messages to other members of the team throughout the process. The leader may need to know some information regarding what is happening in one subgroup of the network, and the team members will pass along this information. Team members are also used by the leader to verify impressions, check strategies, and switch roles. Because the network sessions last three or four hours and because leadership demands are strenuous, the ability to change the pace and permit team members to contribute more is helpful. In many respects the team itself is a miniaturized social network, and its diverse activities and its belief in the intervention process can be contagious. The teamwork that exists among the innovators is fundamental as a model for the assembled network.

The team may receive phone calls from peripheral members who are timid about the intensity of the intervention process or who want to communicate personal information to the team. Calls may be made for help or advice with their own personal problems. A judgment about bringing these problems back to the network itself or directing the person to additional sources of help is decided by team discussions. Speck and Attneave (1973) indicate that team members can expect ten to fifteen hours of communication work between each session. If a team works continuously together on numerous network interventions, time can be better utilized and a team might be able to work on several network interventions concurrently; however, most professionals manage to participate in only one intervention at a time in addition to their other responsibilities.

Developing Intervention Strategy. The intervention team develops strategy in two phases. The first phase begins during the team meeting following the initial home visit. The leader and the team members must develop an initial strategy to mobilize the network. From the information the team obtained from the referral source and discussion during the home visit, the team's impressions of the dynamics of the dysfunctional relationships in the family will be used to develop the initial intervention strategy. The team members will establish a tentative strategy for the first network session as a result of relating their impressions and offering their ideas regarding a possible approach. During the first planning period the team members are encouraged to explore in which network phase they prefer to take some leadership role. The team leader usually helps members to identify their preferred areas of active involvement. These decisions are tentative, and they can and do change during the network sessions.

The second strategy meeting takes place after the first network intervention session. In this meeting the team exchanges impressions and experiences of the events that took place during the first session. There is an evaluation of the effectiveness of the intervention techniques used and whether each network phase was fully experienced and where difficulties may have occurred. There is an evaluation of the family members involved and the involvement of the extended network. In addition the leader and team members evaluate their own working relationship and team functioning during the session. The second strategy meeting also provides opportunity for feedback from others in the network. The team members may have received telephone calls from network members wanting to share family secrets, other disclosures, or information regarding the first network session.

At the conclusion of this meeting a strategy must be developed that includes each team member's role during the upcoming session, the techniques to be used, and the general goals to be worked toward. When the networking process is terminated, the team needs to meet again to discuss the outcome of the intervention session and plan for the follow-up of the case. Some team members may join a support group as a temporary member or as a consultant.

Activists

Activists are those individuals who spontaneously provide leadership of the subgroups in the network. They are naturals at enhancing the network effect, especially between sessions. These individuals have spontaneous experience with network phenomena; they can communicate the experience both to the network members and to the team in plain language rather than in professional jargon. Activists help to keep the team's actions and thinking specialized to the network itself and to the importance of facilitating its activities rather than taking over as professional persons.

Activists are the individuals in the network who can mobilize action and organize its execution. Activists are a crucial contributor to the power of the network intervention approach. Activists have a deep sense of commitment and are willing to provide alternatives and participate actively in helping one or more family members to seek new solutions toward productive changes in their lives (Rueveni, 1976). Network activists are important in using their own resources within the extended family and neighborhood. Activists open lines of communication, listen attentively, and push for alternative solutions. Network activists can make the difference between the success or the failure of the intervention. It is the activists who continue to maintain their support of one or more of the members by weekly meetings and telephone calls and by being available for further help. Often network activists continue to be involved after the intervention sessions have terminated.

Techniques

The leader and team members use a variety of techniques to help the family network in resolution of the crisis. Many techniques have been borrowed from other therapeutic approaches. Rueveni (1979) describes the use of the techniques during the network intervention sessions to achieve specific goals for the network phase. He groups the techniques into the three phases of retribalization, polarization, and mobilization.

Retribalization Techniques

The techniques used during the retribalization phase are intended to produce an increasing level of participation by all the members in the network. The techniques involve verbal and nonverbal activities that are intended to be fun and help the members to increase their energy levels and feel acquainted with other members in the network. People mill around for a brief period introducing themselves to others and sharing introductory information. Network members may feel childish when encouraged in these activities, and some may object to becoming involved at all. The leader and team members should permit any member not to engage in the activity. Those members may remain uninvolved, though some will join in an activity later. It is important that the leader and team members participate in the activities to serve as models and show that it is appropriate adult behavior.

Network Speech. Network interventions are usually begun by the team leader who introduces himself or herself and the team and then outlines the need to work toward solving the family's critical problems. The leader states that there is a crisis and that the team needs help from the network to work with the family in solving the problem. The leader emphasizes involvement, sharing, openness, and the importance of support from the members of the network. The roles of the team members will be described with emphasis being placed on the active involvement that is necessary from the network members.

Milling. Milling is a technique used to begin the retribalization phase by having individuals make contact with as many people as they possibly can. Often a time period such as three minutes is designated in which individuals are asked to greet each other, exchange information, and move on quickly to someone else. Members may be asked to change their speed of milling to a slower or faster rate. In some cases they may just shake hands, touch others on the back, and move along. In other cases they may talk to others or merely maintain silent milling activities.

Screaming, Whooping, and Clapping. The activities of screaming, whooping, and clapping can help individuals to release the anxiety and energy. Members may be instructed to scream simultaneously, possibly choosing a partner, exchanging first names with that partner, and then screaming each other's first names. Occasionally, network members are asked to simultaneously scream and jump up and down in place; small groups may also use an Indian whooping verbalization followed by hand clapping and foot stamping.

Circle Movements. The network members may form a circle holding hands and move toward the center and away from each other. Sometimes there may be concentric circles with repeating movements. Occasionally, the circle movements may include the sounds of singing, humming, or whooping.

Family Song. The family may be asked to choose a favorite song and the entire network joins in singing. The group may sing the song while clapping hands and swaying. At times a series of songs that has been suggested may be sung.

Network News Time. When the networking process involves more than one session, the support groups and other participants begin later sessions by sharing the events that have occurred since the previous session. The leader and team members share what they have heard through the grapevine and encourage individuals and representatives from the support groups to do the same thing. This technique serves to initiate the communication and information exchange that should be shared by the total membership. It serves as a source of validation and confirmation of events that have occurred between sessions and may serve to correct misinterpreted communication.

Polarization Techniques

Polarization techniques are designed for rapid involvement of members with specific issues and individuals. When the polarization phase does not occur naturally, some of the following techniques may be used.

Inner-Outer Circle. Nuclear family members may be requested to sit in an inner circle and make statements about the problems that exist. An outer circle is formed behind them to listen to the family's statements. After the family members state their positions, the members in the outer circle switch places so that they become the inner circle. Then the network members share their thoughts and feelings about the statements made by the nuclear family.

The Empty Chair. The empty chair technique involves placing a chair in the inner circle so that any member who wishes may take this seat and make a statement to the whole network. When the person finishes his or her statement, he or she leaves the seat, thereby providing a position from which others may speak.

"Whose Side Do You Take?" This technique is designed to help individuals state their support of one member in a problem situation. Individuals may be asked to sit next to the person to whom they feel closest or to sit next to someone they trust or are asked to say "Whose side are you on?" or "Whom do you support?" Members may be asked who is having the problem? Is there more than one problem? Are there secrets in the family? Such statements may stimulate further discussion and encourage a greater level of exploration.

Removing a Member. When the network focuses on one member to the exclusion of others, scapegoating may occur. The leader describes this situation to the entire network and suggests a change in the topic or suggests that other family members be involved in the process. When this does not yield significant changes, the leader may ask the individual that has been the center of attention to step to the back of the room or even leave the room temporarily with a team member. If the scapegoating process becomes severe, members may leave the room without being told. They should not be stopped from leaving, because their absence will shift the focus of attention to a more intensive exploration of events that led to this person's leaving. Usually a member who has left the room will return to the session after a brief cooling-off period because he or she cannot resist involvement in the network.

Communicating with an Absent Member. When a significant member of the family is not present, the leader may encourage two or more family members to communicate their feelings toward that person. This is particularly important if the individual has an important part in the crisis. The family member may speak to the absent member by imaging that the person is sitting in the empty chair. Other individuals can help in this dialogue by carrying on a conversation with the absent member(s). In some situations a network member who is familiar with the family's concerns may take the role of the absent member and continue the dialogue. When possible, the absent member may be called on the telephone to discuss the specific issues of concern.

Mobilization Techniques

These techniques are used during the mobilization and depression phases to promote direct confrontations. Such confrontations often result in strong expressions of emotions that lead to effective and productive network efforts by the full support system.

Promoting Direct Confrontations. Direct confrontations are an important part of the process, and the leader may use a number of techniques to help individuals express their feelings. A member may be asked to stand on a chair and talk to the family member he or she wishes to confront, or a member may stand on a chair while another kneels down and looks up. The member on the chair is instructed to speak loudly or scream at the person he or she wishes to confront, while other family members stand around the chair giving additional support to the confronting member. It is appropriate for the person on the chair and the one being confronted to switch places. Another technique is to have both members stand apart, look into each others eyes, and without speaking walk toward each other expressing nonverbally the feelings they wish to express. It may be necessary for the team leader to become involved in helping a reluctant member to confront another individual. It is important to recognize that these confrontations produce responses of tenderness and affection as well as anger and disappointment.

Stimulating Disengagement from Home. This technique is designed to help individuals experience and acknowledge leaving home, at least temporarily, as a possible resolution to the problem. The technique of breaking into or out of the circle requires the network members to form a tight circle holding each others' arms while one member inside the circle is asked to get to the outside. The reverse of this technique is to have the member break into the circle from outside it. This breaking out of the circle can represent a symbolic disengagement from the home and help to mobilize the entire network for action.

Rope Technique. Another disengagement technique is to tie a rope to the waist of one family member and attach the other end to the waist of another member. The leader then interprets how the two are viewed as being tied together and they are asked their intensions regarding this relationship. This situation may provoke others in the network to comment on the relationship and give suggestions for changing it.

"Death Ceremony." The death ceremony is a powerful technique for dealing with the issue of disengagement or the loss of a family member. One individual is selected to sit in a chair or lie on the floor and imagine that he or she is dead. The person may be covered by a sheet and other members are requested to eulogize the member's death. After this experience, time is made available for individuals to share their feelings and experiences. This technique may stimulate feelings related to the past death or loss in a family.

Sculpting the Family. Sculpting the family is a technique that requires the members to arrange themselves spatially to depict a particular feeling they have toward one another. Each family member may wish to change another member's sculptured position and present his or her own perception of events that occur in the family. Other significant members in the network may also wish to sculpt the family to show how they see the family or themselves in relation to the family.

Role Playing. Members of the network may play specific roles in the crisis situation by choosing a role that he or she may wish to take. After relating a brief story depicting the events that took place in a crisis, the network can contribute a discussion about the experience and comments on the feedback. By having the family members or even other network members play out a crisis situation, the network may get a better feeling for the problem situatin. This may provide them with better insights for solutions.

Role Reversals. Family members may be assigned to the roles of other family members in an attempt to play out their perceptions of the other person. Role reversals are valuable in highlighting the feelings and issues with which other people are struggling. This is an excellent technique for parents and children as it permits them to depict how they see the other behaving.

Critique and Evaluation

Network intervention is considerably different from most other approaches to family therapy. It focuses more on people outside the nuclear family both for perceptions of the problem and also to suggest and implement solutions. It appears that this concept provides a greater possibility for continuing help and support and perhaps a lasting resolution than when only the nuclear family is involved.

There is less insight and interpretation than in many other approaches. It is even more action oriented than approaches in which the therapist gives directives or sets up plans for a solution. The process involves much activity and leaves the resolution to the network members.

Although there is no comparative research, case studies report good success. The success is not expressed as "they lived happily ever after" but rather that realistic coping has been achieved. This approach is used in tough crisis situations when other approaches to therapy have not succeeded. It is not an approach to use with every family; it is a special approach to apply in special situations.

There is no elaborate theoretical base for practice. In fact, the concepts are quite simplistic; it is the process that is complex. Not every therapist could lead a family network intervention. Many therapists are personally oriented to working with small groups and prefer to feel that they are in control. To be successful with this approach a therapist should have some special training followed by experience as a team member. Rueveni (1979) describes a process for training network intervention therapists. At least as important, however, is the therapist's personality in conducting this approach to family therapy.

References

Attneave, C. 1969. Therapy in tribal settings and urban network intervention. *Family Process* 8:192–210.

Boissevain, J. 1974. *Friends of Friends: Networks, Manipulators, and Coalitions,* New York: St. Martin's Press.

Bott, E. 1957. *Family and social network: Roles, norm and external relationships in ordinary urban families.* London; Tavistock Publications (New York: Free Press, 1971).

Erickson, G. 1975. The concept of personal network and clinical practice. *Family Process* 14:487–498.

Papp, P. 1976. Family choreography. In *Family Therapy: Theory and Practice,* ed. P. Guenn, pp. 326–329. New York: Gardner Press.

Rueveni, U. 1977. Family network intervention: Mobilizing support for families in crisis. *International Journal of Family Counseling* 5:77–83.

———. 1979. *Networking families in crisis.* New York: Human Sciences Press.

———, and Speck, R. 1969. Using encounter groups techniques in the treatment of social network of the schizophrenic. *The International Journal of Group Psychotherapy* 19:495–500.

———, and Winer, M. 1976. Network intervention of disturbed families: The key role of network activists. *Psychotherapy: Theory, Research and Practice* 13: 173–176.

Speck, R., and Attneave, C. 1973. *Family networks.* New York: Vintage Books.

Zuk, G. 1975. *Process and practice in family therapy.* Haverford, Pa.: Psychiatry and Behavioral Science Books.

16

Family Therapy: Present Status and Future Conditions

The purpose of this final chapter is to add some finishing touches, namely (1) to review some of the issues facing family therapy, (2) to prognosticate on some of the trends emerging in the evolution of this relatively new field of intervention, (3) to include some family therapists, who, for one reason or another, were not included for full review but who, nonetheless, merit acknowledgment and consideration, (4) to review exemplary applications of family therapy, (5) to make some dire predictions for the future, and (6) to consider the role of theory construction and testing in the future of family therapy.

Present Status

The phenomenal increase of professional interest in the field of family therapy can be assessed by a variety of criteria: an assumed identification and membership and organizational growth, an increase in training programs, and an increase in literature references in specialized journals and journal articles. Specialization in family therapy has taken place thus far in independent institutes and in a few academic settings, mostly in sociology, home economics, or family studies (Nichols, 1979).

Assumed Identification and Membership. It is estimated from a variety of sources that in the United States there are now approximately 40,000 individuals who claim or desire the label of "family therapist." A great many belong to a variety of professional organizations for their own professional specialization: American Psychiatric Association, American Psychological Association, National Association of Social Workers, and so on. Others belong to interdisciplinary organizations, such as the American Personnel and Guidance Association or the American Orthopsychiatric Association. A good 25 per cent of this estimated number belongs to the American Association of Marriage and Family Therapists (AAMFT) or to the National Council for Family Relations. A small but potentially powerful number belong to the recently created American Family Therapy Association.

Training Programs. As recent publications (Nichols, 1979) illustrate, the number of training programs has increased tremendously in the last few years, both inside and outside academic institutions. Psychologists, thus far, have the smallest number of training programs (L'Abate et al., 1979), unless one counts an occasional seminar on family therapy as training (which we do not). By training, we mean a full-fledged curriculum that meets minimal standards of competence, such as those set by the AAMFT. The July 1979 issue of the *Journal of Marital and Family Therapy* (Nichols, 1979) is devoted entirely to educational and training issues and programs in marriage and family therapy. The interested reader may consult this reference for a more detailed discussion of issues covered briefly here.

Literature References. No actual count needs to be made to consider the number of family therapy-related books in the last decade. All the reader needs to do is look up the years of publication for the references following each of the chapters in this book to reach his or her own conclusions. In the past five years, in addition to *Family Process,* which is the oldest of all family therapy journals (1961), we have seen the emergence of the *Journal of Marriage and Family Therapy* (née *Counseling*), the *American Journal of Family Therapy* (née *Journal of Family Counseling*), the *International Journal of Family Therapy,* and the *Family Therapy Journal of San Marin.* At last count, there were at least three yearly series publications: *Progress in Family Psychiatry, Progress in Family Therapy,* and *Advances in Family Therapy.*

How is this growth to be taken? As an index of success? Popularity? Curative or palliative power? Indeed, this growth is producing and will produce even greater problems or problems in greater numbers. By what criteria should an individual claim to be or call himself or herself a "family therapist"? By degree? There are no degrees in family therapy per se, except perhaps the masters degree program at Hahnemann Medical College in Philadelphia. By credentials? What credentials are necessary and who will check and verify the validity and credibility of these credentials? By competence level? What are the criteria that determine such competence, and, furthermore, how will such an assessment be carried out? Nationally, regionally, or by state? Should family therapists be licensed, certified, or allowed to practice by whom, where, and how? Growth, therefore, only means more serious and widespread issues that will need definition, if not solution, in the future if the welfare of consumers is ever considered.

Family Theory

The whole field of family studies and research, albeit independent of family therapy approaches, remains the substantive background that many family therapists do not have and that some of us (L'Abate et al., 1979) feel they should have (Burr et al., 1979). One of the most unfortunate gaps for the field of family therapy is its separation from the field of family theory as found in sociology (Burr et al., 1979). Broderick (1971) summarized five major theoretical frameworks that seem insufficient for further theoretical developments in social psychology: situational, structural, symbolic-interactional, functional, and developmental. A more recent review of these theoretical models (Hodgson and Lewis, 1979) has found that, among the original five frameworks, symbolic interactionism has retained its popularity although its use seems to have "declined markedly in the last few years." The structural–functional framework has declined somewhat also. However, developmental, institutional (ecological?), and systems frameworks (reviewed in this book in the work of Haley, Watzlawick, Minuchin, and the Milan group) have increased in utilization among family theorists.

In addition to the five conceptual frameworks already in family theory and research, Broderick (1978) has reviewed balance theory (Heider); exchange theory (Kelley and Thibaut); and general systems theory (Chapter 1). In addition to Broderick's list, we need to consider further the importance of attribution theory (Kelley, 1979); resource exchange theory (Foa and Foa, 1974); equity theory (Berkowitz and Walster, 1976); and social comparison processes (Suls and Miller, 1977) as additional and promising conceptual frameworks for family theory and practice; and interpersonal attraction (Swensen, 1973), friendship formation (Duck, 1973), liking and disliking (Berkowitz and Walster, 1976). Murstein (1978) and others (Swensen, 1973) have been very active in attempting to link empirical and social psychology with the field of applications in marital and familial therapy (Altman and Taylor, 1973).

Russell (1976) has said that theory building is still slow and that agreement on definitions, indication, selection, evaluation, and training programs lack a unifying conceptual scheme. Intervention and outcome research remain insufficient, and there is a need for broadness, flexibility, and avoidance of dogmatization. Therapists should stress strengths rather than pathology. Russell has made various recommendations to overcome these obstacles.

There are many indications that the field of marriage and family therapy will profit by interfacing with social psychology (Kelley and Thibaut, 1978; Kelley, 1979). Even though this "marriage" may have been slow in the making, its taking place should be to the good of both specialties. American social psychology for a long time has involved itself in topics that may appear tangential, if not irrelevant, to family therapy. It is only recently that social psychologists may have become aware of the relevance of studying marriage and the family. Increasingly, family therapists are using theories, theorists, or concepts from social psychology, such as Heider's (balance theory). Homans (1974), with Kelley and Thibaut (1978), has been influential in what is now called *social exchange theory* (to be differentiated from *resource exchange theory* of Foa and Foa, 1974). Cohen and Corvin (1978) and DeShazer (1979) have applied Heider's balance theory to brief therapy of couples and families; Brown (1975) has applied social exchange theory to family crisis intervention and conjugal conflicts.

Psychoanalysis: Alfred Adler

Among the most influential disciples of Freud, who eventually broke away from him to found what is now known as the school of individual psychology, we cannot and should not forget the contribution of Alfred Adler, whose concepts of family constellation and ordinal position in birth and their effects on behavior patterns and marital selection are still a source of active theorizing and empirical investigation (Toman, 1976). One of the major forms of parental counseling that is still influential in this country is Adlerian (Dinkmeyer, Pew, and Dinkmeyer, Jr., 1979). Whenever the outcome of this type of counseling is compared under controlled conditions (Fischer et al., 1978), the results, unfortunately, leave the reader somewhat skeptical.

Object Relations Theory

Fairbairn (1954), originally an unknown Scottish psychoanalyst, is mainly responsible for object relations theory (ORT). The overall theory was developed by Melanie Klein, M. Balint, G. W. Winnicott, and Fairbairn. ORT concentrates on the individual's strong tendency to seek relationships with other persons, or parts of other persons, on the basis of *introjects* from one's parents. This relational tendency, to seek gratification in and with others, is just as primary and just as important as Freud's pleasure principle. Fairbairn is considered the purist of this theory, since he rejected all nonobject relational concepts. The infant receives primary gratification from the mother and, through this gratification, incorporates her as an object that will determine the child's relationship to other women for years to come. Fairbairn (1954) has emphasized the child's separation anxiety at the mother's absence, either actual or threatened, as a form of punishment and seen by the child as rejection and threat of abandonment. These and parental quarrels are seen by the child as threats to survival and actually increase the dependence and attachments to his or her parents. When attempts to abuse this increasing dependence (derived from the child's increased separation anxiety) are frustrated by the mother, the child becomes angry and may attack her directly or vent his or her anger against substitute targets (siblings, objects, other children). Bowlby (1969, 1973) takes a position similar to Fairbairn's (1972, p. 256).

Framo (1978) has reviewed the context of marriage and the troubles of marriage in the last decade. Dicks (1967) has applied ORT to the marital relationship, sharing of similar internal objects in marital partners, using among others the projective identification in marriage and family.

Berenson (1976) has attempted to link Bowlby's attachment theory, especially in its relevance to the separation anxiety and individuation, to Fairbairn's object relations theory, which makes separation anxiety a primary aspect of personality:

> Infantile dependence is abandoned in favor of a mature dependence based on the differentiation of object from self. The attempt to make the bad object good is an internalization of the bad object with concurrent repression. (p. 188)

> Both object relations theory and attachment theory start with the same premise: the basic human anxiety is separation from the mother. (p. 193)

It is the purpose of the therapist to help family members to learn how to separate with as minimum of anxiety and conflict as possible. Consequently, therapists need to be aware of their own problems in separating (from their families of origin as well as from their spouses and children) before they can help family members separate from each other.

Leonhard (1977) credits family ecology theory (family networks' overlapping with other social networks, i.e., school, church, etc.) and analytic object relations theory (Fairbairn, Winnicott, and Guntrip) as theoretical predecessors and bridges to his theory of object relations systems. The main points of this theory are as follows: (1) emotional conflicts exist in various hierarchical systems and subsystems, both inside and outside individuals; (2) the systems principle of equipotentiality explains why different therapeutic approaches may lead to the same goal, namely, family functionality; (3) both internal (intrapsychic) and external (interpersonal) forces interact fluidly in continuous tension within any individual; (4) different causes may produce the same reaction, and one cause may produce different reactions (equipotentiality and multicausality); (5) most kinds of family networks can be broken down into triangles, both inside and among individuals; (6) therapists should use mutual deviation-amplifying systems, that is, pathology or dysfunctionality is the outcome that results from transactions among intimates, whose introjects or introjected objects (inside individuals) have external manifestations that tend to find and match with individuals with similar introjects (Friedman, 1978).

Helm Stierlin

Stierlin (1974) presents a theory that concentrates on the dynamics of adolescent running away. His approach is dialectical, constantly changing the perspective from parent to adolescent, back to parent again. His theory is cast within the context of the interplay of generational forces extended to a three-generational setting (including the parents' parents). Stierlin is able to show through his case studies how intergenerational conflict between parents and adolescents evolves from unresolved conflict between those parents and their parents. He postulates centripetal and centrifugal pressures within the home situation that either keep a child from running away or cause the child to do it. He develops this dichotomy by positing three basic transactional modes that generally reflect the home situation: the modes of *binding, delegating,* and *expelling.*

The *binding* mode (abortive runaways, nonrunaways, lonely schizoid types) keeps the adolescent locked within the parental orbit and squelches opportunities for autonomous growth and individuation. Although individuation and differentiation were discussed as parameters of healthy adolescent growth, they were not defined. However, Stierlin had considered these concepts fully in previous work (1969).

The *delegating* mode, exemplified by crisis runaways, allows the child to leave the parental orbit, associate with peers and individuate, and so on, but the youth always remains tied to the parents by what Stierlin calls "the long leash of loyalty." Additionally, he posits that running away was intended by the parents (perhaps subconsciously) to fulfill their needs for excitement and the like, which they could experience vicariously through a profligate child.

The *expelling* mode, reflected through casual runaways (sociopathic types), results from strong centrifugal parental pressures for the child to leave. The parents perceive the child as a hindrance to their goals and neglect, reject, and/or actively push the child out of the parental orbit at an early age. All three modes are considered within the framework of Freud's personality structure—id, ego, superego—so that, for example, the binding mode has the subcategories of affective or id binding, cognitive or ego binding, and binding through the exploitation of loyalty or superego binding.

Schizophrenia and waywardness in adolescence can occur or be preserved through these three transactional modes. Mutual liberation is the answer to the separation drama. The process of growing up involves a struggle. We cannot ignore the inevitable intergenerational conflict, especially when middle age is the harbinger of the upswelling of unresolved parental needs as well as the time when the adolescent is stirring to grow, but Stierlin maintains that it must be a "loving fight." If parents and adolescents can (1) differentiate their needs by articulating them (i.e., communicating), (2) be aware of their interdependence and mutual obligations, and (3) from the preceding, develop a feeling that promotes "repair work," then the separation crisis-drama can be alleviated, not avoided. Separation from the parents at some point is necessary and healthy.

Transactional analysis (Berne, 1971) is another offshoot for psychoanalysis with promise for successful application to family therapy.

Some Exemplary Contributions

Some trends indicate that monosymptomatic groups or groups of families, put together because of similar behavior present in the identified patient (whether a victim or a perpetrator, such as in sexual abuse), will make it easier to compare outcome with or without family therapy. Although a detailed analysis of these studies would bring us too far from the mark, we can safely predict that there will be an increase in applications of family therapy with families defined by at least one single dimension, that is, reason for referral. Some of the outstanding studies, in addition to those of Patterson and the Oregon group (Chapter 10), focus on families of (1) sexually abused children, (2) self-starving or anorectic children, (3) handicapped children, (4) addictive or addicted adolescents and adults, and (5) delinquent adolescents and families that are (6) disadvantaged, (7) in crisis, and (8) nonlabeled.

Sexually Molested. One of the outstanding studies in this area is by Kroth (1979). However, in considering his mostly favorable results as to outcome, one must remember that the way in which he uses the term "family therapy" is misleading. Families were not seen together in therapy. On the contrary, they were broken up so that men joined a men's group, women joined a women's group, and children joined various groups, according to age levels. Thus, the model used here is family therapy to the extent that most family members were in therapy in same-sex–same-age groups. There were couples communication groups for parents, but nowhere in this noteworthy report is it indicated whether and how families were treated *together*. Nonetheless, this report remains a milestone in the empirical evaluation of psychotherapy of sexual abuse in groups or otherwise.

Self-Starving Children. Although anorexia nervosa has been the subject of study for at least two of the therapists reviewed here (Minuchin, Chapter 7, and Selvini-Palazzoli, Chapter 8), perhaps in those chapters we did not emphasize enough the importance of this condition for the treatment of the family. Minuchin and his co-workers (Chapter 7) have devoted a great deal of attention to it; Selvini-Palazzoli has used her painstakingly honest appraisal of her results from an individual psychoanalytic approach to develop a family model in the treatment of this and other conditions.

Handicapped Children. The work of Berger and his co-workers (Berger and Wuesher, 1975; Foster and Berger, 1979) with families of handicapped children, using structural, strategic, and behavioral approaches, deserves attention, especially for its eclectic combination of methods based on pragmatic considerations.

Families of Addicted Adolescents and Adults. Stanton (1979) reviewed the literature to illustrate the uses and frequent benefits of a family therapy approach for families of addicted and alcoholic teenagers and adults. Szapocnik, Lasaga, and Scopetta (1977) compared four different models for intervention with Latin multiple substance abusers. Their experiences led them to conclude that family ecological models are most effective in attracting, maintaining, and rehabilitating poorly accultured families; family models are most effective in the treatment of marital dysfunctions and in cases in which symptomatic behavior is found in young family members; and individual models are effective in promoting personal growth and development in the identified patient, but are not very effective in repairing marital dysfunctions. Of course, combined treatment modalities offer an even better chance for improvement.

Delinquent Adolescents. Alexander (Alexander and Barton, 1976; Barton and Alexander, 1977) and his co-workers illustrate well the use of an empirically evaluated behavioral systems approach toward families of acting-out teenagers. His methodology and wide-ranging theorizing and broadening of behavioral concepts to a systems approach is refreshing as well as exemplary. His findings of a *supportive* climate and communications in families of control adolescents versus the *defensive* communications of delinquent adolescents are quite important in illustrating how family therapy can be considered a method of intervention as well as a method of information gathering.

Family Therapy with the Disadvantaged. Because of overwhelming survival priorities, the ghetto family is inclined to look to therapy in solving external problems. Like Mr. James in *The Black Family in Therapy,* "You're supposed to tell us what to do. . . . Get me a job" (Sager, Brayboy, and Waxenberg, 1970, p. 18). Many who have worked with these families feel that more therapy must be conducted in a social service framework. If therapy can first provide the family with something useful, it can reach its members through fulfilling a concrete need, and there is hope that they may return for further therapy: "The reality of living conditions from day to day is the thing which has to be dealt with first.That's right on the surface. That's right where you start. And then, if you can be helpful there, it's very often possible to go into other family problems which might be considered to be more psychiatric in nature" (Sager et al., 1970, p. 177).

The nonintrospective approach of most ghetto dwellers, their linguistically divergent language, and their action-oriented mode of behavior all contribute to difficulties in communication with middle-class therapists. Minuchin et al. (1967) and Chapter 7), in working with families of delinquent boys, used various techniques with success. They used role playing to help families learn to experience their feelings more clearly and to begin to see how they could change their behavioral patterns. These therapists have often used exaggerated physical movements to communicate messages. Often the family is seen first as a unit but then it is broken up into subgroups (i.e., teenagers alone, mother with younger children, etc.). The one-way mirror has also proved effective with some families. (In one case, a mother could see how she contributed to family disorganization by observing her teenage daughters through the mirror. This experience helped the mother in other ways: Her self-esteem was bolstered as the therapist had her assume the role of a co-therapist, and her relationship with the therapist became more positive.) These authors also stress the need to pursue strategic moments actively, to introduce more subtle evaluative concepts.

Most therapists who work with ghetto families seem to agree that active participation on the part of the therapist leads the family to move gradually to more representational and symbolic levels. "In general we have found that interpretations which employ an almost physical language and which are grounded on more primitive cognitive and communicational systems seem to be more in harmony with the way in which our families communicate among themselves and, therefore, more likely to be effective" (Minuchin et al., 1967, p. 248). Minuchin et al. found that families wanted therapists to produce change without upsetting the old familiar ways of interaction. They concluded, therefore, that therapists must learn how to open, formulate, and enlarge narrower concepts within the family into more differentiated realities. Along with role playing, another method used successfully is that of task assignments. One member or subgroup of the family performs interpersonal tasks assigned by the therapist on the basis of knowledge of vital family issues, while the other members observe. From this kind of demonstration, the observer may better internalize, and the processes of reflection and introspection may be fostered.

Chilman (1966) also suggested that the customary passive approach that many therapists use in treating middle-class families does not work with ghetto families. Mere passive listening may be interpreted as hostility by these families and may actually increase hostility. Therapists must demonstrate to families that their behavior is self-defeating and that they must work cooperatively to change some patterns. Chilman has cautioned, however, that this is not to be interpreted that therapists must impose middle-class goals and values. She asserted, along with

Minuchin, that, through role playing and learning by doing, more specific help can be given in family planning and problem solving.

Although opinions differ as to whether or not black therapists can work better with black ghetto families than can white therapists, Sager et al. (1970) has stressed the need for white therapists to know their own feelings about race, to be familiar with the cultural patterns, living conditions, and value systems of the people whom they are trying to help. Although these authors say that a black therapist may establish a better relationship with a black family than a white therapist, they emphasize the fact that the black must equally earn the trust and respect of black patients. They add that the black therapist is often handicapped by the family's thinking that he or she has taken on "whitey's establishment" values.

In conclusion, the hope is that, where a biracial staff exists, friction and misunderstandings may be resolved so that black families will not be the "private property" of black therapists. To quote Ackerman (Sager et al., 1970),

> I think we're still a far distance from being able to extract a set of principles for this therapy. We need a profound reexamination of the whole issue, of the circularity of prejudice—white against black and black against white. We don't know enough about that yet. The job is to open up both whites and blacks. Nothing short of this will do. (p. 129)

Family Life Cycle

The contribution of Levinson et al. (1978) to the importance of family life cycles in family therapy has alerted family therapists to use this concept in their approaches (Hughes, Berger and Wright, 1978; Weeks and Wright, 1979).

Family Crisis Intervention

This section begins with a presentation of the theory of family crisis intervention, focusing on the historical antecedents, theoretical assumptions, and methods used in family crisis therapy.[1] Crisis is defined as "a disruption of adaptation in which the usual problem-solving techniques do not work" (Ewing, 1978, p. 5). This acute upset presents an opportunity for growth when the crisis is mastered. However, in the susceptible family or individual, the crisis may lead to a regression and the onset of acute psychological distress. Crisis occurs when a family or individual has a maladaptive reaction to the emotional hazard created by an event. Most crises last for a range of one to six weeks, and successful intervention by a helping person can have long-range effects on the family's adjustment and future handling of subsequent stressful situations.

Historical Antecedents. The origin of crisis theory is in the early work of Lindemann (1944). His classic study of the grief reactions of 101 persons, who had recently experienced the death of a close relative in the Boston Coconut Grove

[1] We are grateful to David Adkinson for his contribution to this section.

nightclub fire of 1942, laid the foundation for the theory and practice of human crisis care. Lindemann (1944) postulated that crisis is often a normal reaction to a distressing situation.

The work of Caplan (1961, 1964) extended and clarified theories regarding crisis and became a cornerstone of the community mental health movement of the 1960s. Caplan's (1964) theory is grounded in the concept of emotional homeostasis, namely, that people are always confronted with situations that threaten to upset the consistent pattern and balance of their emotional functioning. These threats are ordinarily short lived, and the situation is mastered through habitual problem-solving activities. However, crisis occurs when individuals cannot readily master threatening situations by habitual methods of problem solving. Precipitants for crisis may be either "accidental" or "developmental." According to Caplan, the essential factor determining the occurrence of a crisis is an imbalance between the perceived difficulty and significance of the threatening situation and the resources available immediately for coping with the situation.

One of the most active developers of family crisis intervention has been Langsley. Langsley and Kaplan (1968) began the Family Treatment Unit at Colorado Psychiatric Hospital in 1964 to study the relationship between mental patients and their families. This was the first major attempt to evaluate the effectiveness of family crisis intervention. Langsley and Kaplan developed crisis therapy for families that included a member who would ordinarily have been admitted to a mental hospital.

Theoretical Assumptions.   Crisis in an individual is frequently a result of crisis in the family. Whereas most families are able to master common stresses without serious decompensation, "when the family includes a susceptible individual or when the family has become used to dealing with problems by using psychiatric hospitalization, the stage may be set for the symptoms of mental illness" (Langsley et al., 1968, p. 146). The action of hospitalizing a patient from a family implies that the family cannot help to solve its own problems. However, proponents of family crisis intervention strongly value the individual's family milieu in the therapeutic process.

There are at least four distinct phases through which a family goes in the typical course of a crisis. Crisis is seen as self-limiting and will usually resolve itself for better or worse in one to six weeks. The initial phase of crisis occurs when the individual or family has a threatening situation and responds to feelings of increased tension by calling forth habitual problem-solving measures in an effort to solve the problem and restore emotional equilibrium. If the habitual measures fail, tension increases further. Feelings of ineffectuality are the hallmark of the second phase of crisis. Here the family members become disorganized and resort to trial-and-error attempts at mastery. The mobilization of emergency and novel problem-solving efforts marks the third phase. If the new measures do not solve the problem, tension mounts beyond what Caplan (1964) calls the "breaking point" and major personality disorganization ensues (Ewing, 1978).

Family functioning during crisis is conceptualized as either adaptive or maladaptive. Crisis is a normal experience of all families; therefore, the concept of mental illness is not used to characterize the type of functioning exhibited by families in crisis.

One of the first applications of Caplan's (1964) individually oriented theoretical assumptions regarding crisis to families and social units larger than the individual was by Klein and Lindemann (1961). They claimed that individuals' crises are often symptomatic of crises being experienced by one or more of their reference groups. The basic unit of analysis in the understanding of crisis is not the individual subject but "one or more of the social orbits of which he is a member" (p. 285). Parad and Caplan (1960) have maintained that families may experience crisis just as much as individuals do.

Methods Used in Therapy. The method of family crisis therapy developed by Langsley and Kaplan (1968) consists of an average of three weeks of treatment. It includes five office visits, a home visit, and a few telephone calls. The therapeutic process begins once the patient and family come for help. Although their initial request is usually for hospitalization, the entire family is seen at once by a member of the clinical team. Absent family members are called in from home, school, or work, and significant others in the family are included.

History taking is seen by most family crisis therapists as "a crucial part of the clinical procedure inasmuch as prior knowledge of significant objective data helps the therapist to assume an efficient leading role" (Kaffman, 1963, p. 24). However, due to the nature of crisis situations, more emphasis is placed on gathering meaningful data on salient points than on accumulating a complete and detailed history. The central foci of the initial interview are to gather data regarding (1) treatment history, (2) brief medical history, (3) developmental features, (4) current psychological functioning, (5) precrisis adjustment, and (6) factual data on family interaction (Kaffman, 1963; Ewing, 1978). The next stage of therapy consists of contracting, in which the problem to be dealt with in the intervention is clearly stated and specific goals are articulated. This contract is followed by the actual therapeutic intervention, which may take on a wide array of treatment modalities. Termination and follow-up conclude the stages of therapy.

Many family crisis therapists reject the traditional medical model of psychopathology and avoid diagnostic pigeonholing and classification. Instead, psychological disorders exhibited in crisis are seen not as illnesses to be diagnosed but as learned maladaptive responses to be unlearned. It is possible that diagnosis may have a negative impact upon family crisis intervention by orienting the therapists toward seeing and planning for chronic pathology, thereby binding them to important critical events.

Kinney et al. (1977) have described a program whereby therapists entered the homes of eighty families in crisis. They lived there for extended periods of time to prevent the placement of one or more family members in group homes, foster homes, or institutional care. They used techniques such as crisis intervention, effectiveness, assertion, and fair fighting training as well as behavior modification. Preliminary results of this project indicated success in preventing outside placement in 121 of 134 family members at a saving of more than $2,300 per client compared with projected cost of placement. Follow-up, which covered sixteen months of service delivery, indicated that 97 per cent of those avoiding placement continued to do so. This study in some ways replicates the findings of the classic study by Langsley and Kaplan (1968) in which they were able to prevent hospitalization in 84 per cent of a sample of psychiatric patients by providing outpatient family crisis therapy instead of admission to an inpatient setting. Posttreatment follow-up showed that patients treated without admission were less likely to be hospitalized after treatment. For those who eventually did need hospitalization, length of stay was significantly shorter than for control patients. The cost of keeping these patients out of the hospital was one sixth of what it would have been had they been admitted.

Much of the evidence for the efficacy of family crisis intervention is anecdotal (Argles and McKenzie, 1970; Chandler, 1972). However, the bulk of evidence as to the efficacy comes from uncontrolled outcome studies (Ewing, 1978; Kaffman, 1963; Stratton, 1975). Results of all of these studies support the effectiveness of family crisis therapy. However, each study reports data that are subject to methodological pitfalls, such as absence of control groups and inadequate measures of therapeutic outcome.

"Normal" Families. The work of Riskin (1976; Riskin and McCorkle, 1979) with "nonlabeled" families promises to be another way of getting at what seems to be (Chapter 2) one of the most elusive chimeras of the family therapy field, that is, "normal" families.

Commentary

The work of Olson, Sprenkle, and Russell (1979), more than that of any other theorists, has shown clearly the great amount of overlap among many therapists— who insist on using different terminology but who speak very much about the same behaviors. As already discussed in Chapter 2 and again in this chapter, Olson et al. were able to show the many similarities in their two orthogonal concepts of cohesion and adaptability with those used by many other theorists reviewed in this book. Most of the literature reviewed here converges on the same goal of family therapy, namely, to produce autonomous, productive human beings who can work well both inside and outside their families. The processes and means to achieve this goal may indeed vary, but the commonality in what various processes should produce is also impressive.

The work of Olson et al. is also impressive in showing what research can do in integrating various strands of theories that have little, if any, empirical backup. As will be discussed in the following pages, one of the dire needs of family therapy is for more thorough and encouraging research efforts on the basis of its theorists, who presently ride complacently on the crest of success achieved through the numbers of followers that each of them has generated. Greater and better research efforts will take place whenever family therapy unites forces with other disciplines and ideologies that are more research involved in their tactics, namely, sociology, ecology, and environmental and social psychology. Besides Patterson (Chapter 10) and Minuchin (Chapter 7) and the McMaster group (Chapter 2), the rest of the field is clearly stuck at a *dialectical* stage of development. Whether or not and how fast this field will proceed to a *demonstrative* stage, if ever, remains to be seen. More likely than not, accounting at the federal level will mandate some empirical efforts. This may be an unfortunate but necessary outcome especially demanded by the traditional psychiatric establishment, which may see the spreading of this movement with envy and fear of replacement. Whether voluntary or mandatory, it is expected that no more than 5 per cent of all family therapists will ever be involved in any research effort worthy of consideration.

Future Conditions

In considering emerging trends in treating relationships, Olson and Sprenkle (1976) have reviewed conceptual and programmatic trends, in which there seem to be "fewer and clear distinctions and more synergistic interplay between marriage and family counseling." We disagree with this generalization. We suspect that marriage and family therapy will become increasingly differentiated from each other, as even Olson and Sprenkle admit: "The need for specialization within relationship-oriented treatment is being recognized." Indeed, the future may see different specializations (and training) for marriage and family therapists (L'Abate and McHenry, in preparation).

Olson and Sprenkle have predicted "an increasing application of social learning theory, general systems theory, and Rogerian client-centered variable." We agree with predictions for social learning and general systems theory, but disagree about Rogerian client-centered approaches. The last has failed to demonstrate that the individually derived therapy can be applied to dyadic and multiperson relationships, except as they are found in active, structured skill training programs (L'Abate, 1980), as in the Minnesota Couples Communication Program (Miller, Nunnally, and Wackman, 1975) and relationship enhancement (Guerney, 1977). We agree with Olson and Sprenkle that family approaches are going to become more popular over and above individually oriented therapies and that therapists (such as Minuchin, the Milan group, Haley, and the Palo Alto group) will be emphasizing more directive, shorter-term contracts rather than long, open-ended approaches.

In the area of research we tend to agree with Olson and Sprenkle's conclusions that "clearer and more researchable questions" will be asked, that there will be "an increase in systematic studies of treatment programs, both in outcome and in process," and that "greater rigor in evaluation research" will be practiced, with an increase of multimethod approaches involving both self-report and observational methods. Clearly the field of marriage and family therapy is "no longer in infancy." It may even have reached puberty. We would not go as far as Olson and Sprenkle, who diagnosed it as being in its adolescence.

Another prediction that could be subsumed under the trend of *shorter therapy contracts* is the upsurge of structured social skills training programs for couples and families (assertiveness, communication, effectiveness, enrichment, encounter, fair fighting, problem solving, and sexuality, among others) that will become a definite asset to the field of family therapy (L'Abate, 1980b). Although family therapists tend to look down on these methods, and there is a distinct professional and conceptual cleavage between therapists and skill trainers, eventually both fields could profit by each other's increasing applications in preventive as well as in therapeutic endeavors.

Blend of Theories. It is inevitable that the future will see blending and integration of various theoretical viewpoints. What works (pragmatism) will be blended eclectically from the claims of a variety of theorists, most of whom are reviewed in this book.

As part of an increasing empirical accounting of results, family therapy will show an increased concern with analysis of outcomes, which are still in their infancy (Gurman and Kniskern, 1978; Wells and Dezen, 1978) and empirically testable theories (Foa and Foa, 1974; Olson, Sprenkle, and Russell, 1979).

Of the five trends reviewed by Broderick (1971), we will need to see which ones seem to have been adopted by family therapists. Hence, the blend and integration will not only take place within theoretical viewpoints but also within clinical practices, as is beginning to show in the exemplary work of Alexander (Alexander and Barton, 1976; Barton and Alexander, 1977), combining empirically evaluated systems behavioral work with families of delinquent teenagers; the work of Andolfi (1979), integrating humanistic, structural, and paradoxical approaches; the theorizing of Friedman (1978) and Leonhard (1977), combining object relations theory with a systems framework; Berenson, combining attachment theory with object relations theory; and combinations of structured skills training approaches, such as enrichment with couples and families with paradoxical messages (L'Abate et al., 1976, 1977; Spitz, 1978).

Verification of Family Therapy Theories

Demonstrative versus Dialectical Issues

Most of the substantial issues to be faced by family therapy in the future can be conceptualized as moving along a continuum defined by the polarities of demonstrativeness on one hand and dialectics on the other (Rychlack, 1968). The three major issues that will need to be faced, among others, deal with issues of methods versus techniques, issues of quantification versus qualification, and issues of evaluation versus impression.

Method Versus Technique. An important distinction needs to be made about method (replicable) and technique (nonreplicable). Presently, the field of family therapy is characterized by many techniques and very little method, with the possible exception of Haley, as we have seen.

Quantification Versus Qualification. Essentially, this is an issue of objectification versus subjectification. Most family therapists, as do most clinicians, tend to emphasize and prefer subjectivism to objectivism. In fact, it could be said that objectification is considered undesirable and irrelevant to the process of therapy. Quantification is considered irrelevant or interfering with the process of helping. Hence, the clash of demonstrative versus dialectical modes will be more and more apparent as mandated demands for accountability from federal and state health agencies and funding sources will be met by resistance to the whole process of attempting to account for the process and the outcome of family intervention.

Evaluation Versus Impression. As the field of family therapy progresses toward greater and greater differentiation, the need for greater empirical evaluation and decreased reliance on impressionism will take place. The need to use replicable and testable approaches will increase because of political, economic, and social pressures on the mental health enterprise in general and the family therapy business in particular.

One of the crucial issues of family therapy theories is to distinguish them from models. The difference between a model and a theory has been considered in detail by L'Abate (1976). Models are testable; theories usually are not. Models are derived from a theory and, therefore, are part of a larger whole. The most desirable way in which to test a model is through measures and methods that are derived from the theory and that have high validity and reliability. This is the ideal condition, if one can achieve it. The highest ideal would be to relate theory testing to evaluation and intervention, an ideal that is harder to achieve than it is to wish.

As Olson, Sprenkle, and Russell (1979) have noted,

> The model does *not* specify which therapeutic techniques will be most helpful in delivering these goals. Techniques are for the most part atheoretical and can be used regardless of the therapist's theoretical orientation. The therapist must, therefore, select from the techniques with which she or he is familiar and use those that are likely to be most effective in achieving the treatment goals for the couple or family. (p. 24)

Gurman and Kniskern (1979) have defined eight distinct categories within which various psychotherapeutic modalities can be distinguished: (1) behavior therapy, existential therapy, and so on; (2) recipient of treatment, for example, child therapy, group, network, and so on; (3) temporal aspects of the method, for example, brief, short term, long term, and so on; (4) constellation of clinical problems addressed by the method, for example, sex, divorce, and so on; (5) dominant theoretical model of the method, for example, psychoanalysis, behaviorism; (6) dominant treatment strategies of the method, for example, paradoxical, supportive, and so on; (7) political value positions endorsed by advocates of the method, for example, feminism, radicalism, and so on; and (8) creator of the method (Bowen, Jung, Freud, and so on). None of these characteristics alone can be used to categorize any single form of treatment. Hence, a variety of criteria, possibly all those listed, would be necessary, in addition to the actual process of what "really" happens during the course of treatment.

Following Rychlack's (1968) distinction between demonstrative and dialectical modes of verification (and falsibility), a great deal of family therapy verification (with exceptions, Minuchin Chapter 7) has taken place in the dialectical realm. Some family therapists (Boszormenyi-Nagy and Sparks, 1973; Stierlin, 1969, 1977) have explicitly and decidedly rejected a demonstrative in favor of the dialectic alternative. Both aspects of verification will endure because they are both *equally important.*

The field of family therapy is replete with examples of how theoretical assumptions lead to technique and then to a predictable outcome. Examples of this consistency, represented earlier by psychoanalytic and Rogerian approaches, can be found in the work of Haley (Chapter 6), Minuchin (Chapter 7), Selvini-Palazzoli et al. (Chapter 8), and, of course, Bowen (Chapter 9). Unfortunately, in addition to the issue of whether or not therapists really do what they claim to do, there is the issue of technique. A technique depends a great deal on the personality and impact of the expert, in contrast to method, where replications can occur, regardless of the personality of the therapist. Hence, any of the therapies covered here depends on the work of a "founder." Clearly, there is the matter of "halo" effect and how expectations determine certain results. Whoever follows a viewpoint is sympathetic to it. Consequently, there cannot be a bias-free therapist. Even an eclectic therapist has a bias in favor of not being biased toward one specific school or approach.

Most verification of theories in the family therapy field is still at the clinical, impressionistic level. This is clearly the necessary base before one can proceed to more verifiable and intersubjective criteria of an empirical kind. In this context, *clinical* and *empirical* will not be used as one's being superior to another, depending on one's position and predilection. They are different. Clinical impressions are based on observations *internal* to the observer, that is, the therapist. Empirical observations are based on measures *external* to the observer, that is, the therapist. A third level of verification, the experimental, implies control and manipulation of variables that usually take place in the laboratory. Thus, we can distinguish three separate and *different* levels of verification; the clinical impressionistic, the empirical measurement, and the experimental manipulation. The first two can and do take place in the clinic; the third may take place both in the clinic and in the laboratory. A theory, to progress and be verified, needs *all* three levels of verification, in which agreement and consistency are found between and among clinical, empirical, and experimental approaches.

One, therefore, cannot use a technique to test a theory because a technique leaves too much room for idiosyncratic variability on the part of the individual therapist's personality. It follows, therefore, that techniques cannot be used, because they are not replicable. We cannot have therapists who are carbon-copy replicas of each other. If techniques cannot be used to test theories, what are we left with? The major way in which to test a theory is through *methods* and not techniques, because a method is reproducible and replicable; techniques are not. Techniques are as much a matter of style as methods are a matter of interobjective substance. Methods can be tested; techniques cannot. Hence, we are left with the melancholy conclusion that to the extent that much of family therapy is based on techniques, so to that extent a great many family therapy theorists are and will remain untestable. Only *if and when* a theory or technique is translated into method, to that extent, it will allow testing to take place.

There is no question that the field of family therapy has acquired sufficient clout and popularity to have reached its full potential alongside more established and traditional methods of intervention. It is viable and vital; it is, in some ways, evolutionary and, in other ways, revolutionary. It provides new and far-reaching views on personality development, the etiology of psychopathology, and the organization of social groups and society. It provides a group of interesting theories, "theorettes," and models and has shown sufficient stamina to withstand, in some cases alone, the pressures brought about by threats to the status quo of more established and traditional mental health practices, especially those directed toward individuals rather than toward families. Only the future will tell whether family therapy has reached its peak or has fulfilled its potential.

References

Adams, P. B. 1979. *Construct validity of transactional analysis: Ego states.* Unpublished master's thesis, Georgia State University, Atlanta, Georgia.

Alexander, J. R., and Barton, C. 1976. Behavioral systems therapy with families. In *Treating relationships,* ed. D. H. Olson, pp. 167–187. Lake Mills, Iowa: Graphic Press.

Altman, I., and Taylor, D. A. 1973. *Social penetration: The development of interpersonal relationships.* New York: Holt, Rinehart and Winston.

Andolfi, M. 1979. *Family therapy: An interactional approach.* New York: Plenum Press.

Argles, P., and McKenzie, M. 1970. Crisis intervention with a multiproblem family: A case study. *Journal of Child Psychology and Psychiatry* 11:187–195.

Barton, C., and Alexander, J. F. 1977. Therapists' skills as determinants of effective systems-behavioral family therapy. *International Journal of Family Counseling* 5:11–19.

Beels, C. C., and Ferber, A. 1979. Family therapy: A view. *Family Process* 8: 280–318.

Berenson, G. 1976. Attachment theory, object relations theory and family therapy. *Family Therapy* 3:183–195.

Berger, M., and Wuesher, L. 1975. The family in the substantive environment: An approach to the development of transactional methodology. *Journal of Community Psychology* 3:246–253.

Berkowitz, L., and Walster, E. eds. 1976. *Equity theory: Toward a general theory of social interaction.* New York: Academic Press.

Berne, E. 1971. *What do you say after you say hello?* New York: Grove Press.

Boszormenyi-Nagy, I., and Sparks, G. M. 1973. *Invisible loyalties.* New York: Harper & Row.

Bowlby, J. 1969. *Attachment and loss: Attachment.* vol. 1. New York: Basic Books.

——. 1973. *Attachment and loss: Separation, anxiety and anger.* vol. 2. New York: Basic Books.

Broderick, C. B. 1971. Beyond the five conceptual frameworks: A decade of development in family theory. *Journal of Marriage and the Family* 33:139–159.

Brown, A. H. 1975. A use of social exchange theory in family life crisis intervention. *Journal of Marriage and Family Counseling* 1:259–268.

Burr, W. R.; Hill, R.; Nye, F. I.; and Reiss, I. L. 1979. *Contemporary theories about the family.* vol. 1 and 2. New York: Free Press.

Caplan, G. 1961. *Prevention of mental disorders in children.* New York: Basic Books.

——. 1964. *Principles of preventive psychiatry.* New York: Basic Books.

Chandler, H. M. 1972. Family crisis intervention. *Journal of the National Medical Association* 64:211–216.

Chilman, C. 1966. *Growing up poor.* Washington, D.C.: HEW.

Cohen, C. I., and Corvin, J. 1978. A further application of balance theory. *International Journal of Group Psychotherapy* 28:195–209.

DeShazer, S. 1979. Brief therapy with families. *The American Journal of Family Therapy* 7:83–95.

Dicks, H. V. 1967. *Marital tensions.* New York: Basic Books.

Dinkmeyer, D. C.; Pew, W. L.; and Dinkmeyer, D. C., Jr. 1979. *Adlerian counseling and psychotherapy.* Monterey, Calif.: Brooks/Cole.

Duck, S. W. 1973. *Personal relationships and personal contracts: A study of friendship formation.* New York: Wiley.

Ewing, C. 1978. *Crisis intervention as psychotherapy.* New York: Norton.

Fairbairn, W. R. D. 1954. *Object relations theory of the personality.* New York: Basic Books.

Fairbairn, W. R. D. 1972. *Psychoanalytic Studies of the Personality.* London: Routledge & Kegan Paul, Ltd.

Fischer, J.; Anderson, J. M.; Aveson, E.; and Brown, S. 1978 Adlerian family counseling. An evaluation. *International Journal of Family Counseling* 6:42–44.

Foa, U., and Foa, E. 1974. *Societal structures of the mind.* Springfield, Ill.: C. C. Thomas.

Foster, M. A., and Berger, M. 1979. Structural family therapy: Application in programs for preschool handicapped children. *Journal of the Division of Early Childhood* 1:52–58.

Framo, J. L. 1978. An object relations view of marriage and marital therapy. Audiotape, Society for Family Therapy and Research, Cambridge, Mass.

Friedman, L. J. 1978. Integrating object relations understanding with systems interventions in couples therapy. Audiotape, Society for Family Therapy and Research, Cambridge, Mass.

Guerney, B. G. 1977. *Relationship enhancement.* San Francisco: Jossey-Bass.

Gurman, A. S., and Kniskern, D. P. 1978. Technolatry, methodolatry, and the results of family therapy. *Family Process,* 17:275–282.

——, and Kniskern, D. P. 1979. Marriage therapy and/or family therapy: What's in a name? *AAMFT Newsletter* 10:1, 5–8.

Harper, J. M.; Scoresby, A. L.; and Boyce, W. D. 1977. The logical levels of complementary, symmetrical, and parallel interaction classes in family dyads. *Family Process* 16:211–218.

Harris, T. A. 1967. *I'm OK—you're OK.* New York: Harper & Row.

Hodgson, J. W., and Lewis, R. A. 1979. Pilgrim's progress. 3. A trend analysis of family theory and methodology. *Family Process* 18:163–173.

Homans, G. R. 1974. *Social behavior in its elementary forms.* New York: Harcourt Brace.

Horewitz, J. S. 1979. *Family therapy and transactional analysis.* New York: Jason Aronson.

Hughes, S. F.; Berger, M.; and Wright, L. 1978. The family life cycle and clinical interventions. *Journal of Marriage and Family Counseling* 4:33–40.

Kaffman, M. 1963. Short-term family therapy. *Family Process* 2:18–36.

Kelley, H. H. 1979. *Personal relationships: Structures and processes.* New York: Lawrence Erlbaum Associates.

——, and Thibaut, J. W. 1978. *Interpersonal relations: A theory of interdependence.* New York: Wiley.

Kinney, J. M.; Madsen, B.; Fleming, T.; and Haapala, D. A. 1977. Homebuilders: Keeping families together. *Journal of Consulting and Clinical Psychology* 45: 667–673.

Klein, D. C., and Lindemann, E. 1961. Preventive intervention in individual and family crisis situations. In *Prevention of mental disorders in children,* ed. G. Caplan, pp. 283–306. New York: Basic Books.

Kroth, J. A. 1979. *Child sexual abuse: Analysis of a family therapy approach.* Springfield, Ill.: C. C. Thomas.

L'Abate, L. 1976. *Understanding and helping the individual in the family.* New York: Grune and Stratton.

——. 1981. Skill training programs for couples and families: Clinical and nonclinical applications. In *Handbook of family therapy,* eds. A. S. Gurman and D. Kniskern, New York: Brunner/Mazel.

——. 1980. Toward a theory and technology of skill training programs: Suggestions for curriculum development. *Academic Psychology Bulletin* 2:207–228.

——; O'Callaghan, J.; Piat, J.; Dunne, E. E.; Margolis, R.; Bigge, R.; and Soper, P. 1976. Enlarging the scope of intervention with couples and families: Combination of therapy and enrichment. In *Group therapy 1976: An overview,* eds. L. R Wolberg and M. L. Aronson, pp. 62–73. New York: Stratton Intercontinental Medical Book Corp. Also in L. L'Abate, *Enrichment: Structured approaches with couples, families, and groups.* Washington, D.C.: University Press of America, 1977, pp. 135–153.

——; Berger, M.; Wright, L.; and O'Shea, M. 1979. Training family psychologists: The family studies program at Georgia State University. *Professional Psychology* 10:58–65.

——, and McHenry, S., eds. *Methods of marital intervention* (in preparation.)

Langsley, D. G., and Kaplan, D. M. 1968. *Treatment of families in crisis.* New York: Grune & Stratton.

Leonhard, E. 1977. Toward a new formulation of object relations-systems theory from analysis and family ecology theories. In *New directions in family therapy,* eds. T. J. Buckley, J. J. McCarthy, E. Norman, and M. A. Quaranta, pp. 42–56. Oceanside, N.Y.: Dabor Science Publications.

Levinson, D. J.; Darrow, C. N.; Klein, E. B.; Levinson, M. H.; and McKee, B. 1978. *The seasons of a man's life.* New York: Knopf.

Lindemann, E. 1944. Symptomatology and management of acute grief. *American Journal of Psychiatry* 101:141–148.

Miller, S.; Nunnally, E. W.; and Wackman, D. C. 1975. *Alive and aware: Improving communication in relationships.* Minneapolis: Interpersonal Communications Program.

Minuchin, S.; Montalvo, B.; Guerney, B. G., Jr.; Rosman, B.; and Schumer, F. 1967. *Families of the slums.* New York: Basic Books.

Murstein, B. I., ed. 1978. *Exploring intimate life styles.* New York: Springer.

Nichols, W. C., ed. 1979. Education and training in marital and family therapy. *Journal of Marital and Family Therapy* 5:3–105.

Olson, D. H. L., and Sprenkle, D. H. 1976. Emerging trends in treating relationships. *Journal of Marriage and Family Counseling* 2:317–329.

——; Sprenkle, D. H.; and Russell, C. E. 1979. Circumplex model of marital and family systems. 1. Cohesion and adaptability dimensions, family types, and clinical applications. *Family Process* 18:3–28.

Parad, H. J., and Caplan, G. 1960. A framework for studying families in crisis. *Journal of Social Work* 5:3–15.

Riskin, J. 1976. "Nonlabeled" family interaction: Preliminary results on a prospective study. *Family Process* 15:433–440.

——, and McCorkle, M. E. 1979. "Nontherapy" family research on change in families. *Family Process* 18:161–162.

Russell, A. 1976. Contemporary concerns in family therapy. *Journal of Marriage and Family Counseling* 2:243–250.

Rychlack, J. F. 1968. *Philosophy of science for personality theory.* Boston: Houghton Mifflin.

Sager, C.; Brayboy, T.; and Waxenberg, B. 1970. *Black ghetto family in therapy.* New York: Grove Press.

Sheehy, G. 1974. *Passages: Predictable crises in adult life.* New York: Dutton.

Spitz, H. I. 1978. Structured interpersonal group psychotherapy with couples. *International Journal of Group Psychotherapy* 28:401–414.

Stanton, M. P. 1979. Drugs and the family. *Marriage and Family Review* 2:1–10.

Stierlin, H. 1969. *Conflict and reconciliation.* New York: Doubleday (Anchor)/ Jason Aronson.

——. 1974. *Separating parents and adolescents.* New York: Quadrangle/New York Times Book Co.

——. 1977. *Psychoanalysis and family therapy.* New York: Jason Aronson.

Stratton, J. G. 1975. Effects of crisis intervention counseling on predelinquent and misdemeanor juvenile offenders. *Juvenile Justice* 26:7–18.

Suls, J. M., and Miller, R. L., eds. 1977. *Social comparison processes: Theoretical and empirical perspectives.* New York: Halsted Press.

Swensen, C. H., Jr. 1973. *Introduction to interpersonal relations.* Glenview, Ill.: Scott, Foresman.

Szapocnik, J.; Lasaga, J. I.: and Scopetta, M. A. 1977. Culture specific approaches to the treatment of Latin substance abusers: Family and ecological intervention models. Department of Psychiatry, University of Miami, Miami, Florida, June 13, 1977.

Toman, W. 1976. *Family constellation: Its effects on personality and social behavior.* New York: Springer.

Weeks, G. R., and Wright, L. 1979. Dialectics of the family life cycle. *The American Journal of Family Therapy* 7:85–91.

Wells, R. A., and Dezen, A. F. 1978. The results of family therapy revisited: The nonbehavioral methods. *Family Process* 17:251–274.

Author Index

Sager, C., 256, 301–303, 314
Sartre, J. P., 3, 4, 7, 10, 25
Satir, V., 2, 5, 7, 23, 35, 67, 71, 73–78, 80–81, 83, 103, 115, 123, 246, 254
Schulman, C., 245, 246, 254, 257
Schutz, W. C., 3, 4
Schumer, F., 313
Schur, E. M., 3, 25
Schuster, F. P., 260, 270
Schwartz, A., 256
Scopetta, M. A., 301, 314
Scoresby, A. L., 312
Scoy, C. V., 247, 257
Sears, R. R., 16, 25
Selvini-Palazzoli, M., 5, 99, 145, 146, 147–150, 153–154, 157–159
Serrano, A. C., 260, 270
Shaeffer, D. S., 257
Shannon, C., 21, 25
Shaw, 180
Sheehy, G., 314
Silverstein, O., 245, 252, 257
Skinner, B. F., 4, 18, 25, 204
Sluimer, F., 143
Sluzki, C. E., 113, 129
Soper, P. H., 158, 159, 313
Sorrell, J., 129
Sparks, G. M., 148, 158, 310, 311
Speck, R., 271, 274, 279, 282, 283, 286, 293
Speer, D. C., 140, 143
Spence, K. W., 4
Spiegel, J., 4, 22, 25, 50, 66, 246
Spiegelberg, H., 6, 25
Spitz, H. I., 308
Spitzer, R. S., 69
Sprenkle, D. H., 35, 38, 41, 43, 306–309, 314
Stabenau, J., 113, 129
Stachowiak, J., 68, 80, 83
Stampf, T. A., 4
Stanton, M. P., 301, 314
Stein, G., 117
Stierlin, H., 5, 39, 44, 113, 130, 145, 159, 299, 310, 314
Stratton, J. G., 306, 314
Strelnick, A. H., 257
Stuart, R. B., 5, 19, 25
Sues, J. M., 297, 314
Sullivan, H. S., 2, 4, 102

Swensen, C. H., 297, 314
Syngg, D., 4
Szapocnik, J., 301, 314

Taschman, H. A., 68, 83
Taylor, D. A., 297, 311
Thibaut, J. W., 297
Thomas, F. J., 5
Thorndyke, L., 4
Tillich, P., 7, 25
Todd, T., 143
Toman, W., 169, 298, 314
Tseng, W., 36, 44
Tupin, J., 129

Ullman, L. P., 4, 21, 25

Veltkamp, L. T., 36
Veron, E., 113, 129
Volstead, O. C., 202, 203

Wackman, D. C., 307, 313
Wahler, R. G., 202, 204
Walster, E., 297, 311
Watson, J. B., 4
Watts, A., 5
Watzlawick, P., 2, 5, 22, 25, 85–86, 88–93, 95, 96, 98–100, 102, 113, 115, 124, 130, 147–148, 297
Waxenberg, B., 301, 314
Weakland, J. H., 68, 70, 83, 87, 91, 93, 98, 100, 102, 108
Weaver, W., 21, 25
Weeks, G. R., 23, 24, 158, 159, 203, 303, 314
Weinratt, G. R., 180, 204
Weiss, R. C., 5, 179, 204
Wellish, D. K., 247, 257
Wells, C. F., 245, 250, 257, 308
Wells, R. A., 245, 250, 257, 308, 314
Werner, M., 129
Wertheim, E. S., 44
Whitaker, C. A., 3, 5, 23, 25, 129
Wiener, N., 21, 25
Wilcott, R. C., 199, 204
Winnicott, G. W., 298

Winter, W. D., 112–115, 129
Wittgenstein, L., 85
Wolberg, L. R., 313
Wolman, B. B., 256
Wolpe, J., 4

Wright, L., 313, 314
Wright, M. A., 204, 303
Wuesher, L., 301, 311

Zuk, G., 5, 223–241, 243, 284, 293

Subject Index